HOW TO SOLVE ECONOMIC PROBLEMS

D.F. PAULAHA

Patron Books

ISBN 978-0-9723619-4-1

First published 2008 by
Patron Books

"Education is the acquisition of the art of the utilization of knowledge."

Alfred North Whitehead
The Aims of Education

Introductory Note

This text is based on three critical ideas.

One is that the economy is immediate, personal, and unavoidable. We are all personally affected by how well or how poorly the economy is doing and by policies implemented by governments and central banks. And, like it or not, we cannot avoid the impact the economy and economic policies have on our lives. Therefore, everyone should have a functional understanding of economics, which means that everyone should be able to understand the news.

The second idea comes from Alfred North Whitehead, the British mathematician and philosopher, who, in 1918, wrote, "Education is the acquisition of the art of the utilization of knowledge." That quote, from his book, *The Aims of Education*, was the true inspiration for this text, meaning that the reason I wrote this book is to help the student acquire not only a knowledge of economic principles, but to also acquire the ability to use that knowledge.

The third idea was to use *The Elements of Style* by William Strunk, Jr. and E.B. White as a model. *The Elements of Style* was originally written by Strunk as a handout for students in his writing classes at Cornell. Years later, E.B. White, who had been one of Strunk's students, made some additions and published the handout as a book. Although there are many "style" books on the market that lay out the rules of writing, *The Elements of Style* may be the smallest. But it is not its size that I tried to copy; it is its purpose.

Here are two sentences from the original introduction:

"This book is intended for use in English courses in which the practice of composition is combined with the study of literature. The book covers only a small portion of the field of English style, but the experience of its writer has been that once past the essentials, students profit most by individual instruction based on the problems of their own work, and that each instructor has his own body of theory, which he prefers to that offered by any textbook."

That is what I wanted to "copy." I wanted to create an economics text that would first give the student the "essentials" of economics and that would then direct the student to the practice of using economic, a goal that can be reached only if the student is able to spend sufficient time reading about, thinking about, and writing about real economic issues and policies.

Of course, whether it is English or Economics, not everyone agrees on the rules. In *The Elements of Style*, the rules are the rules according to Strunk. For example, here is Strunk's rule for using commas:

> **2. In a series of three or more terms with a single conjunction, use a comma after each term except the last.**
> Thus write,
> red, white, and blue
> honest, energetic, but headstrong
> He opened the letter, read it, and made a note of its contents.
> This is also the usage of the Government Printing Office and of the Oxford University Press.
> In the names of business firms the last comma is omitted, as
> Brown, Shipley and Company
> The abbreviation *etc.*, even if only a single term comes before it, is always preceded by a comma.

That is Strunk's entire explanation. Other stylebooks, using pages instead of a few lines, say we should avoid the second comma, thereby writing red, white and blue. Who is correct? In my opinion, Strunk's second comma always adds to the ease of reading. Therefore, if we write with the reader's interest in mind, we should use Strunk's second comma.

As such, to paraphrase *The Elements of Style*: "This text is intended for use in Economics courses in which the practice of learning economic principles is combined with the study of economics in the real world."

To do so, I began by asking one simple question: "What do we have to know to understand and explain the economic issues in the news?" The conclusion is that virtually any discussion or issue found in *The Wall Street Journal*, *The New York Times*, a local newspaper, on television, or anywhere else, can be understood by using one of two simple models: a model that explains individual markets (a microeconomic model) or a model that explains the overall economy (a macroeconomic model).

In the end, the intention of this text, as with all serious texts, is to help the student learn *how* to think, not *what* to think.

Contents

PART ONE

1

Economics in the News

1. Why study economics?

The following article, reprinted from the May 26, 2007 *St. Paul Pioneer Press*, should be reason enough for anyone thinking about his or her future.

Men in their 30s lag behind dad's pay

Downturn shown in generational study

BY GREG IP
Wall Street Journal

American men in their 30s today are worse off than their father's generation, a reversal from just a decade ago, when sons generally were better off than their fathers, a new analysis of Census data shows.

The study, the first in a series on economic mobility undertaken by several prominent think tanks. Also says the typical American family's income has lagged far behind productivity growth since 2000, a departure from most of the post World War II period.

The findings suggest "the up escalator that has historically ensured that each generation would do better than the last may not be working very well," says the study, released Friday.

The study was written principally by John Morton of the Pew Charitable Trusts, which is leading the series, called the Economic Mobility Project, and Isabel Sawhill of the Brookings Institution.

In 2004, the median income for a man in his 30s, which is a good predictor of his lifetime earnings, was $35,010, the study says, 12 percent less than for men in their 30s in 1974—their father's generation—

> adjusted for inflation. Just a decade ago, median income for men in their 30s was $32,901, 5 percent higher than 30 years earlier. The median is the midpoint: half of men earn more, half earn less.
>
> Sawhill said she isn't sure why men's wages have stagnated. "It seems there's been some slowdown in economic growth, it's possible that the movement of women into the labor force has affected male earnings, and it's possible that men are not working as hard as they used to."
>
> The study suggests that absolute mobility—the rate at which an entire generation's financial lot improves relative to previous generations—has declined recently.
>
> Of course, the men who run American companies don't have much to complain about. CEO pay increased to 262 times the average worker's pay in 2005 from 35 times in 1978, according to the report's analysis of Congressional Budget Office statistics. The pay gap between executives and the average worker continues to fuel outrage on Capitol Hill and among corporate shareholders nationwide.
>
> The report also found that between 1947 and 1974, productivity, or output per hour, and median family income, adjusted for inflation, both roughly doubled. Between 1974 and 2005, productivity rose 16 percent while median income fell 2 percent, challenging "the notion that a rising tide will lift all boats," the report says.
>
> *This report includes information from the Associated Press.*

2. Questions:

What is happening? What went wrong? It is because of women in the work force? Or immigrants in the work force—legal and illegal? Or the outsourcing of American jobs? Or American corporations moving production to low-wage countries? Or imports? Or the foreign trade deficit? Or the national debt? Or the Federal Reserve's policy of fighting inflation by keeping economic growth low? Or is it something we have not even thought about? And, what about women's wages?

Or is it a false concern? Is it something that will "automatically" correct itself? If we think it will turn around by itself, what do we see that might cause a change in course?

If it is a real concern, why is it happening? Is it natural? Or is it the result of bad policies?

Most important, if the decline is real, can it be reversed? Should we expect the trend to turn around on its own? Or should we do something? If so, what should we do?

Trying to answer these, and other questions raised by just one article, requires an understanding of microeconomic issues, macroeconomic issues, monetary theory and policy, and environmental economics, because real income is affected by market failure, externalities, economy wide events and changes, and monetary policy.

3. The news.

Pick up a copy of *The Wall Street Journal* and look at the front page. Read the short digests of the articles in that day's paper.

Then browse through the paper. Look at the tables and charts; read some of the articles. How much do you think most people truly understand?

Virtually everyone has a surface understanding of what is presented in the nation's main business newspaper, as well as what they read in other papers and hear or see on local and national news programs. Few truly understand all the economic information or knowledge that is available to them, even though such information and knowledge may be the key to making good business and investment decisions and avoiding tragic mistakes.

Here are a few items taken from one (old) issue of *The Wall Street Journal*.

> **The Fed raised** its key interest-rate target by a quarter point to 2.25%, its fifth increase this year. The central bank said the economy is growing at a "moderate pace" despite high energy prices and that inflation remains well-contained, and it reaffirmed its intention to raise rates at a "measured" pace.
>
> **GE's earnings will rise** 13% to 17% next year in a strong and broad-based performance, CEO Jeffrey Immelt said in his most upbeat forecast in two years.
>
> **The U.S. trade gap widened** to a record $55.46 billion in October on a big jump in oil prices and demand for Chinese exports.
>
> **United and its pilots union** reached a tentative agreement on a new contract that would further cut the airline's expenses.
>
> **Sprint and Nextel are expected** to announce a $35 billion merger deal today, but investors focused on potential spoiler Verizon.

> **Deutsche Telekom's T-Mobile** could find it difficult to sustain its growth after a Sprint-Nextel deal.
>
> **A Johnson & Johnson deal** for Guidant could face tough antitrust scrutiny over both existing products and products in the pipeline.
>
> **Merck highlighted** drugs in its pipeline and cost-cutting efforts at its business briefing as it sought to restore investor confidence.
>
> **RIM suffered** a setback as an appeals court ruled against the BlackBerry maker on most claims in a patent-infringement case.
>
> **VW and GM's Opel unit** picked up market share in Western Europe last month at the expense of Toyota, Nissan and Mazda.
>
> **Coke and other beverage firms** won a victory as Europe's top court ordered Germany to change recycling rules that block imports.
>
> **Beijing's decision to levy** duties on clothing exports is prompting small Chinese garment makers to rethink expansion plans.
>
> **Alaska wildlife-refuge drilling** and class-action reform are two previously stalled priorities that appear to have the best chance of passage under a bigger Republican majority in the Senate.
>
> **U.S. fourth-graders made** no math progress in the latest international test. Eighth-graders also showed no math gain in 2003.
>
> **Researchers found** dangerous levels of lead, mercury and arsenic in some herbal remedies imported from India, a study says in the Journal of the American Medical Association.
>
> **Pakistan said** it started negations with India on steps to avert an accidental nuclear conflict, including advance notice of missile tests.

There were more, but the above items are sufficient to make it clear that a functional understanding of economics is required to truly understand what is happening in the world and how what is happening might affect an individual, an individual business, an industry, the nation, or possibly the world.

Here are a few questions from the first item about the Fed:

What is the Fed? How does it work? Who makes Fed decisions? Who talks for the central bank? What is a key interest rate? What is an interest rate target? How does the Fed try to hit its target? What does "the economy is growing at a moderate pace" mean? What role do high-energy prices play in the economy and the Fed's decisions? What does it mean to say that inflation is "well-contained"? What causes inflation? What contains inflation? What does it mean to raise interest rates at a "measured" pace? Although such questions are normally handled in depth in macroeconomic and monetary theory courses, daily decisions—whether for an individual or an individual firm—are obviously impacted by actions taken by the Federal Reserve.

Answering just these questions—there are many more that could be asked about this single, seven-line item—requires the ability to use the knowledge of microeconomics, macroeconomics, and monetary theory and policy.

It would take many pages to list even a portion of the questions raised by the other items listed above.

A few are:

What affects future profits? What is a monopoly? What is monopolistic competition? What is the impact of monopoly on the nation's wealth? What is perfect competition? When does it exist? What is a foreign trade surplus or deficit? What does a trade deficit or surplus mean to the economy as a whole or to individual economic variables, such as interest rates? Do labor unions destroy free markets? What happens to economic efficiency when labor unions bargain with employers? What is the economic impact of corporate mergers? How do corporate mergers affect the nation's wealth? Should monopolies and mergers be more controlled or regulated? Why do corporations worry about investor confidence? What role do patent and copyright laws play in the economy and the nation's wealth? Why would a country act to limit its exports? What role do laws play in foreign commerce? How does the government or the Federal Reserve manage the economy?

Who owns the nation's natural resources? How should the nation's resources be used? What role does the market play in allocating natural resources? What is the state of America's education system? Should efforts be made to improve education in the U.S.? How does economics impact the interaction of nations? How should the U.S. deal with international controversies and the threat of nuclear war? Is terrorism related to economics? How should the U.S. deal with poverty in the world?

Looking at a few of the charts and tables:

What is behind all the stock-market indexes? How do economic expectations affect stock prices? How do mergers or market share affect prices? What are all the different interest rates? Prime rate? Federal Funds Rate? T-bill and bond rates? What causes interest rates to change? How do expectations of changing interest rates affect the investment demand for bonds? Who is the largest holder of government securities? Does it matter that foreigners own large quantities of U.S. stocks and bonds? What do the bond tables mean? What causes changes in bond yields? What is behind changes in foreign exchange rates? How do foreign exchange rates affect investors and business? How does inflation affect interest rates? Foreign exchange rates? Commodity prices? Stock prices? Business and personal investment decisions?

These are just some of the things that affect the outcomes of decisions that must be made each day in a world that is constantly adapting to changes.

2

The Foundation of Economics

1. Economics is the study of decision-making.

Economics is the study of how individuals, firms, and governments make decisions concerning the production, selling, and buying of things, and of how those decisions affect changes in important variables.

Microeconomics uses an understanding of how decisions made by households, firms, and government affect individual markets and the allocation of resources. Its emphasis is on how prices are determined in markets, how prices are affected by market imperfections or government actions and policies, and how resources are allocated among alternative uses. Because of its focus on prices, microeconomics was, for many years, called "price theory."

Macroeconomics uses an understanding of how decisions made by households (individuals), firms, and government determine the values of aggregate variables, such as total production, employment, national income, economic growth, and the overall price level. Because of its emphasis on the interaction of the private market and government, economics was, for many years, called "political economy."

In the study of both microeconomics and macroeconomics, the values of variables are normally assumed to be equilibrium values because it is difficult or impossible to make meaningful statements about a variable in a disequilibrium situation.

The standard economic approach to a problem is to explain or predict the values of variables in equilibrium; to explain how a change affects the initial equilibrium; and to explain or predict the new values of the variables under consideration. When the analysis sticks strictly to explaining and predicting the values of variables and the allocation of resources, it is called **positive economics**. When value judgments or personal opinion are used to judge an equilibrium, it is called **normative economics**. Explaining the results of an agricultural price support policy on the incomes of farmers and taxpayers is positive economics. Saying it is good to help farmers because farmers are nice is normative economics.

One of the most important functions of positive economics is to understand market failure. Examples of market failures that will, without question, reduce the nation's wealth include the misallocation of resources caused by letting the market deal with:

1) negative externalities, such as pollution, 2) positive externalities, such as education, 3) public goods, such as national defense, 4) common property resources, such as a fish population, and 5) monopolies and other factors that eliminate or restrict competition.

Virtually all economic questions and answers relating to individual markets are based on understanding how to use the principles of supply and demand.

Demand is defined as the maximum quantity of something that buyers are willing and able to purchase during a given time period at various prices, all other things held constant.

Supply is defined as the maximum quantity of something that producers are willing and able to sell during a given time period at various prices, all other things held constant.

Supply and demand are concepts that apply to the buying and selling of goods, services, and resources that are traded in a market. The concepts also apply to resources that are not traded in a market. There is a price and quantity of apples in the market for apples, and for oranges in the market for oranges, and for any other item produced and sold in a market. There is also a supply and demand for air quality and water quality, although such things may not be traded in a market.

Why do supply and demand exist? They exist as a result of decisions and actions made by households and firms trying to reach goals, given the existence of constraints and choices.

Economists often divide the economy into three sectors: households, firms, and government. Each sector buys and sells things in the market. Each makes decisions as to what, when, and how much to buy and sell.

2. Making decisions.

Decision-making is always a "constrained maximization" problem. It means having a goal, constraints, and choices. Without a goal, such as maximizing profits, there is no real decision to make, because it does not matter what choice is made; one is as good as another. Without constraints, such as prices or income, there is no decision to make because it is possible to have or do everything. Without choices, such as alternative things to do, there is no decision to worry about because the only possibility is to take or do whatever exists.

A constrained maximization problem means choosing to do something that attempts to maximize a stated goal, given more than one alternative to pick from and given constraints that make it impossible to have or do everything. It is an attempt to maximize something within given limits, where some of the limits or constraints are beyond the individual's or firm's control.

3. Decisions and opportunity cost.

The word decision is from the Latin "from" and "to cut." It means that choosing (deciding) to do one thing requires being cut off from being able to do other things.

In the language of economics, the value of the best option that is cut off is called **opportunity cost**.

Opportunity cost, which has been called the most important contribution of economic thought, is the foundation of most economic principles.

At its core, opportunity cost is nothing more than common sense. It is impossible not to understand that when we choose to do one thing we must give up the benefits we could have received from buying or doing something else. A child at a candy counter, trying to decide how to spend a dollar, understands the concept completely. The dollar buys only so much candy, so the child takes all the time necessary (or allowed) to make sure that what is bought is more "valuable" than what must be left behind. The expected happiness from each item is weighed against the happiness of all the other options before deciding what to buy.

Over the years, economists have attempted to define or explain what economics *is* by relying on the combined ideas of scarcity and human wants.

In the 1950's, the standard definition of economics or **the economic problem** was "the allocation of scarce resources among competing ends." That definition requires both scarce resources and competing ends. If resources are not scarce, then everyone can have all they want at a zero price and there is no economic problem. If there are no competing ends, meaning there is only one thing to do with a resource, then there is no economic problem because there is no choice as to how to use the resource.

By the 1990's, the definition had changed. The economic problem became "the allocation of scarce resources among *unlimited* human wants."

The definition from the 1950's is not very good. It limits the usefulness of economics to situations that are difficult to understand. The definition from the 1990's, using "unlimited wants," is ridiculous. It is a definition of a non-functional discipline based on absurd conditions.

The truth is: Scarcity is always a fact. Scarcity is not something that exists here and there. It is always part of the decision-making process. Even in a world with sufficient resources so that everything is "free," the fact is: nothing is free.

The same economists who use the above definitions also want to make it clear that, "There is no such thing as a free lunch." Why not? Because if someone accepts an invitation to a "free lunch," he or she must give up the opportunity to do something else. He or she could be working, sleeping, going for a walk, meeting with friends, reading a book, or whatever. According to the principle of opportunity cost, the real cost of the free lunch is the value to the person who attends it of what he or she must give up to be there.

Therefore, the best way to understand "the economic problem" is to understand that, because of opportunity cost, nothing is free. *Everything* has a cost, measured by the value of the best alternative. As a result, every decision must consider which option adds the most to the stated goal. The idea of scarce resources and competing ends is nothing more than a curious and useless footnote to the simple statement that every decision involves opportunity cost and that it is necessary to understand such costs in order to make the "best" choices.

In the end, it is the decision-making process of households and firms that leads to the existence of supply and demand functions; and it is supply and demand that determine prices and the allocation of resources in markets, which are sometimes affected by government actions, policies, programs, or laws. As with all decisions, the decision-making process of households and firms is a problem of constrained maximization that involves goals, constraints, and choices.

4. The purpose and objective of economics.

The purpose of economics is to help make the world a better place.

The objective of microeconomics is to explain, predict, and judge what happened, is happening, or is expected to happen in individual markets.

The objective of macroeconomics is to explain, predict, and judge what happened, is happening, or is expected to happen in the economy as a whole.

If what is happening or is expected to happen is not "good," economic analysis offers possible actions to "fix what is wrong."

The analysis is almost always based on the use of "comparative statics." Comparative statics is an analytical approach that compares one equilibrium (one static position) with another equilibrium (another static position). It is normally difficult to say anything meaningful about the impact of a change if the beginning or ending situation is not assumed to be an equilibrium.

Economic explanations and predictions deal with the results of changes that are beyond our control, such as weather; outside our control, such as increases in the price of imported oil; or intentional, such as actions by firms or government that impact a market or the overall economy. Government spends money and collects taxes; firms may act to encourage or limit competition.

A market equilibrium, or existing situation, is sometimes judged according to the concept of "perfect competition," which, among other things, assumes that each producer and consumer is responsible for all costs of producing or consuming goods and services and that each producer and consumer receives all the benefits of its production or consumption. The conditions of perfect competition and "economic efficiency" are often used to explain why a "free" market is good—because it will maximize the wealth of the nation—and why markets sometimes do an unacceptable job of allocating the use of resources, thereby causing a decrease in the nation's wealth.

5. Explaining and predicting.

Economic analysis is somewhat abstract, because economists use arguments and models that ignore large parts of the world in order to make explanations and predictions about variables that affect our lives. Such abstractions are necessary if economics is to be useful. Attempting to use "everything that is known" about the world in order to explain something or to make a prediction is a useless task. It is useless either because it can never be completed or, if it were completed, because the explanation or prediction would depend upon so many variables it could not serve any functional purpose. It would be impossible to use.

The strength of economics is that it can use a small amount of information to make rational and accurate explanations and predictions quickly enough to be useful. Spending more time and money to make what might be more accurate estimates could delay answers until they are no longer needed.

6. Judging.

Although the focus of economic analysis is on explaining and predicting, an underlying concern is with the wellbeing or happiness of society. Unfortunately, no one has yet determined how to actually define or measure wellbeing or happiness. Psychologists or sociologists may try to help the individuals they deal with become "happier." But happiness cannot be defined the same for each individual. And wellbeing cannot be measured simply by money income.

Even in the simplest possible cases, there are differences among individuals. Some people look for the chance to work overtime so they can add to their money incomes. Others look for every possible opportunity to skip out early and head for the beach. To make the problem even more complicated, individual "needs" and interests are constantly changing. This week or this year, someone may want to buy *things*, which means they may be willing to work more or harder. Next week or next year, that same person may prefer more free time to more stuff.

Therefore, how well someone does cannot be measured strictly in dollar terms. If it could, then it might be possible to make everyone "better off" by sacrificing everything else on the altar of greed. Make everyone do whatever is necessary to increase his or her money income. Pull people away from family and friends and move them to better-paying jobs. Make people live in terrible places if that is where the best jobs are. Force people to work 16 to 18 hours a day, seven days a week, to maximize their money incomes. Do not let anyone choose his or her own profession. And so on. Few people would choose such a world because, for most people, happiness or wellbeing is affected by many factors, not just money. Some of those factors are under an individual's control. Others are not.

The problem is: If no one can define exactly what it takes to make an individual happy, how can any discipline be used to help make an entire society as happy as possible?

A quick answer might be to give everyone the greatest number of choices, with the greatest possible freedom to choose. That would not work, of course. Too many children would drop out of school before they understand the long-term importance of education. And some people would add to their happiness by taking things away from others. That is why societies have laws and rules to stop people from hurting either themselves or others.

A second problem facing anyone who hopes to make the world a better place is: How can we judge a change that helps some while hurting others?

If a proposed change is expected to help 1,000 people at the expense of one, is it a good plan? If you happen to be one of the 1,000 winners, chances are it will sound okay. On the other hand, if you are the one being sacrificed for the good of the many, it may not sound as good.

But what if you are neither? What if you are an outside policy maker trying to do your best? How would you judge such a policy? Would you say that the total gains to 1,000 people would obviously be greater than the loss suffered by one? Or would you recognize that if the objective is to maximize society's total happiness or wellbeing that is possible for one person's loss to be greater than the happiness gained by 1,000? If you could actually measure happiness, and if maximizing total happiness were your goal, then you could make a rational decision, even though it would mean having winners and losers. But if you admit that it is impossible to make such a measurement and also that it is possible for one person's loss to outweigh the gains of many, then you are faced with an unanswerable question.

Economists devised two ways to avoid being trapped by that unanswerable question.

One, invented by Vilfredo Pareto in the mid 1800s, is to say that a policy or change is good if it helps at least one person without making anyone else worse off. It is a good idea, in theory, but it has little use in the real world.

An alternative solution is to avoid the question altogether. Instead of making an unsupportable decision or recommendation, the economist explains who the winners and losers will be and leaves it up to someone else to decide what to do. Someone else being society.

Such a solution accepts the reality that once a problem has been analyzed and the potential winners and losers identified, economics may not be able to say any more. If it cannot, then the next step—deciding whether or not to implement the change or policy—is not an economic decision. It is a decision based upon social and personal values.

As individuals, economists have opinions. But when those opinions cannot be supported with economic logic, then it must be made clear that the economist is talking as an individual and not offering an economic solution. It is important to understand the distinction between an economist as an "economist" and an economist as a "person" in order to understand the limits of economic analysis.

It is also important to understand the difference between a pure democracy and a republic in order to understand the limits of social decisions. In a pure democracy, fifty percent plus one of the people can vote to do whatever they want, including taking away the life, liberty, and pursuit of happiness of the other fifty percent minus one of the population. In a republic, the minority has rights that cannot be voted on.

The United States is not a pure democracy. It is a republic. And, like any society that chooses to bestow unalienable rights on its citizens—rights that are not subject to a democratic vote—it must constantly question its actions. Actions aimed at improving the wellbeing of an individual or a group, including the majority, must be weighed against the possible harm to the wellbeing of others.

7. A brief history.

Although economics is a social science, its roots are in philosophy. It was not until the late 1700s that economics became a discipline of its own. By then, philosophers had already developed many of the arguments and much of the logic. From the beginning, those who worked with economic principles dealt with two ideas: "best" and "better." They searched for answers to two great riddles: What is the best overall economic structure or system? How is it possible to improve what exists?

The answer to the first question became an argument for the superiority of a free market economy. The answer to the second became an ongoing attempt to understand how to deal with marginal issues: After "proving" that a free market economy is "best," concentrate on how to make incremental changes that add to the wellbeing of individuals or the nation as a whole.

The argument for the benefits of a free market was first presented in a comprehensive and cohesive form by Adam Smith in his book, *An Inquiry Into the Nature and Causes of the Wealth of Nations*, which was published in England in 1776. In America in 1776, it was declared that the people should have unalienable rights to life, liberty, and the pursuit of happiness. In England, in 1776, Adam Smith had apparently explained how to go about pursuing happiness, at least as it relates to the nation.

Smith's argument was that a nation's wealth would be greater if it relied on a free-market economy as opposed to a feudal system or an economic system organized around monopolized industries or organized labor. His argument was so methodical and so persuasive that it still looks good today. And because Adam Smith was educated as a philosopher, it is not surprising that the core of his ideas and arguments can be found in Plato's *Republic*, which presented a description of market forces that is as accurate as any modern version.

After the publication of *The Wealth of Nations*, most Western economists spent their time working out the details of how a market economy works and correcting the few gaps in logic they found in Smith's writing. Of course, as the world changed, new ideas were constantly being developed. One of those ideas was communism or, in its less dictatorial version, socialism, which was an argument against a totally free-market economy. Although few mainstream economists considered communism or socialism to be a good alternative to a free-market or capitalist economy, many non-economists saw communism or socialism as a way to cure or avoid what they saw as the bad aspects of free markets.

One of the bad aspects of a free market was the prediction of continued poverty. While eighteenth and nineteenth century economists believed that the free actions of the market would lead to an increase in the nation's wealth, they did not expect the wealth to be shared by all. Virtually all early economists believed that the wealth of the nation would increase over time, but that the vast majority of people would continue to live in abject poverty.

There were different explanations for the predictions of continued poverty for the "mass of workers," each of which seemed to be supported by the reality of poverty in the world. The argument made by Thomas R. Malthus in his 1798 book, *An Essay on Population*, was that if wages happened to rise above a subsistence level, people would then have more children. The higher birth rate would mean more workers, and the greater number of workers would cause wages to be bid down again, back to a subsistence level. In the end, poverty was inescapable. Although the poverty theories were not very good, and the predictions of future poverty in industrialized nations did not come true, it was those predictions that led to economics being called "the dismal science," an unfortunate reference because economics is not a science.

Karl Marx had a more extreme view of the causes and results of inequality, a view that led him, in the 1840s, to claim that capitalism could not work; that it would self-destruct in a revolution of exploited workers. His argument was based on "historical evidence" and "the labor theory of value." The labor theory of value had been devised years earlier, by Adam Smith and David Ricardo, not by Karl Marx, at a time when economists were struggling with attempts to assign "value" to things, a struggle that was eventually determined to be useless. But before the quest was abandoned, Marx used the "theory" to create an argument that led to massive disruptions around the world.

Marx's basic argument was simple: The labor theory of value says that the value of a thing is equal to the quantity of labor used to make it; but because the production of things requires capital as well as labor, the owners of capital must also be paid. And that, Marx said, is where the problem with capitalism arises. If the value of something is determined only by the labor used to make it, then it cannot be sold for more than its "labor value." But if things cannot be sold for more than their "labor value," the only way for the owners of capital to earn a return that will keep their capital in the production process is if a portion of wages are taken away from workers. The result, according to Marx, is a nation of workers who, *by necessity*, will be exploited by the capitalist process and who will eventually rise up and overthrow the system.

It was not a very good argument, but it, like other economic arguments that have been used or misused over the years by special interest groups, was appealing enough to lend support to the installation of Communist dictatorships around the world. Despite the detractors, mainstream economists were not swayed from their belief in the power of the free market—until the Great Depression of the 1930s led to a "revolution" in economic thinking. The upheaval seemed necessary, because the previously-held idea that market economies would, at least in the long run, operate at full employment, no longer looked very good.

Until the 1930s, virtually all economists expected full employment to be the norm because of "Say's Law," a theory named after its creator, J. M. Say. Say's Law was based on the simple assumption that markets clear—at least in the long run. As a consequence, the assumption was that unemployment would eventually be eliminated as unemployed workers offered their services at lower and lower wage rates. As a result, it was assumed that is natural for an economy to operate at full employment. The reality of the depression showed that no matter how good the idea looked on paper, it did not necessarily apply to the real world. The Depression exposed the fundamental weakness of the assumption that markets will always clear.

In the middle of the Great Depression, another British economist, John Maynard Keynes, came up with an alternative idea. He turned economic thinking upside down by arguing that the level at which an economy operates—its production, employment, and national income—is determined not by supply, but by demand. Keynes dismissed the "law" that said supply would create its own demand by explaining that a nation's output and employment are functions of total demand (spending) and that it is necessary for the government to play a significant role in managing total spending if depressions are to be avoided. His conclusion was that the market does not always achieve full employment and stable prices without correct or corrective government actions. It was a good argument, for its time, and current macroeconomic theory and policy continue to rely heavily on the ideas Keynes put together.

There were, however, major disagreements with some of Keynes' ideas, mainly from economists belonging to the "Chicago school of economics," known also as the "monetarists." The monetarists argued that there were serious flaws in the Keynesian prescriptions for government policies. The mistakes, they said, were related to poor logic and a misunderstanding of the role and importance of money (which is why they were called *monetarists*). Although the split between Keynesian and Chicago School economists still exists, some of the more important monetarist arguments have been incorporated into current Keynesian theories.

Although there may be disagreements, economists have always attempted to answer questions that are crucial to society's wellbeing. The fact that economics is a social science means that economists have tried to answer those questions by studying social relationships and social organization. The fact that economics is grounded in philosophy means that many of the answers were originally derived from logic and careful arguments, rather than from theories with testable hypotheses or arguments that relied on actual data. The thing that defines economics as a separate discipline is its focus on how the production and consumption of goods and services and the allocation of resources affects the wellbeing of society.

3

How To Solve Economic Problems

1. Rules of action.

In general, economic theory is concerned either with understanding how decisions are made or with understanding how to make decisions that will maximize the welfare or wellbeing of individuals, individual firms, or the nation as a whole.

The following concepts form the foundation of the economic approach to problem solving. They are not definitions. They are not digested versions of textbook discussions. They are *rules of action* that will become second nature by the end of this text, although some might not be totally understood at this point.

1. Solve economic problems by comparing one equilibrium with another.

The typical economic problem is solved by comparing one equilibrium with another. It is a logical procedure called "**comparative statics**." It means to compare one "static" position with another.

There is an initial equilibrium (one static position).

A change is introduced.

The impact of the change is explained.

A new equilibrium is described (a new static position).

The values of the variables in the "old" and "new" equilibrium situations are compared.

2. Solve economic problems one step at a time.

Economic problems are solved by completing a step-by-step explanation of how one thing is affected, then another, and another, until the answer is determined. The analysis begins with a described equilibrium, or with a reason for no existing equilibrium. The equilibrium may be that of an individual, an individual firm, a particular market, or the economy as a whole.

Skipping steps or "jumping to conclusions" about a new equilibrium can lead to unacceptable answers or major errors.

3. The existence of an equilibrium does not mean that the value of any variable is "justified."

Solving economic problems means explaining or predicting the past, present, or future. However, the "answer" is almost never a justification of what happened, is happening, or is expected to happen.

4. Most economic problems are answered by explaining or predicting the direction of change of the values of one or more variables.

Few economic questions are given with enough information, time, or money to allow "exact" estimates of future values.

5. Problems with insufficient information to explain or predict the direction of change of a variable's value are often answered by stating the conditions that would cause the variable's value to increase, decrease, or remain unchanged.

Sometimes there is not enough information to determine even the expected direction of change of a variable's value. It is, however, almost always possible to state the conditions that *would* cause a particular variable's value to change in a given direction.

6. State the assumptions behind answers.

Economic explanations and predictions are conditional; they depend upon the assumptions made while solving the problem.

All explanations and predictions depend upon assumptions made about many things. It is impossible to list the assumptions regarding everything in the world that could affect the answer. Therefore, it is normally stated that all things, other than those discussed while solving the problem, are assumed to remain unchanged. When specific or unusual assumptions are made, they should be clearly stated.

7. Unless there is a reason not to, begin the solution to economic problems by assuming a normal equilibrium with normal functions.

Unless the problem states otherwise, or there is information to the contrary, assume that a market problem begins with normal supply and demand functions and a stable equilibrium; and that macroeconomic problems begin with normal aggregate supply and aggregate demand functions.

8. Use all available information and knowledge to describe the initial equilibrium.

A question or problem may require the description of an initial equilibrium based upon a demand function that is vertical (a product that is an absolute necessity) or horizontal (the demand facing an individual firm in a perfectly competitive market) or a supply function that does not slope upward to the right.

9. Do not assume that "everyone" has the same response to a change.

Economic analysis works on the margin. Changes almost never lead to "all-or-none" effects. An increase in the price of oranges means that consumers, as a whole, are willing and able to buy fewer oranges. More precisely, it means that, as the price inches upward, some consumers will buy fewer oranges.

A higher price does not, however, mean that EVERYONE will buy fewer oranges. Some will buy the same quantity of oranges and less of something else. (Unless their incomes are rising or the prices of other things they buy are also changing.)

10. Hold all things, but one, constant while explaining or predicting the results of a change.

The reason for "holding all other things constant," meaning that nothing else changes unless it is a change caused by whatever set off the problem, is to explain the consequences of a single action.

If the price of apples declines, will consumers buy more apples? The answer is: Yes. No. Maybe. If nothing else changes while the price of apples falls, consumers will buy more apples per time period. It is a simple move along the demand curve for apples.

If the prices of oranges, grapefruit, bananas, all other fruit, and all other food items, decline at the same time the price of apples is falling, fewer apples *may* be bought. As other prices fall, the demand curve for apples changes. If it decreases, fewer apples may be bought at any given price. Therefore, the new equilibrium, determined by the new supply and demand curves for apples, can be at a higher, lower, or unchanged quantity and price of apples.

The more things are changing, the less can be said about what happens in the market for apples. That is why, in all cases, a clear statement can be made only by assuming that nothing else is changing while explaining or predicting the impact of a particular change. If tastes and preferences change, consumers may be willing and able to buy fewer apples even if the price falls. Or more if the price rises. Because a change in tastes and preferences can cause the demand for apples to change. A change in income can also cause a change in the demand for apples, and in the demand for everything else.

It is only by being able to use a logical process that permits analyzing one change while holding everything else constant that the impact of any particular change can be understood.

A second reason for explaining one change at a time is that once the analysis is complete, it is then possible to explain and predict the consequences of changes in all the things that were initially assumed to have been held constant.

11. A problem is "solved" when something can be said about the variable or variables asked about in the question.

In the "real world," any change that occurs leads to changes in an "infinite" number of variables. Therefore, the impact of each and every change can be discussed "forever." To be useful, an answer must be delivered while it still has value. That means knowing when to stop. In every discipline or activity, one of the keys to success is "knowing when to stop." An artist must know when to stop working on a painting or sculpture. A writer must know when to stop writing or editing a book or article. Nothing is ever "finished." It is only brought to a conclusion that is believed to be the best under the circumstances, and given the constraints that exist at the time.

2. A few words about economic style.

> "Whoever heard of the style of an amateur painter, or the style of an amateur poet? Style is always the product of specialist study, the peculiar contribution of specialism to culture."
>
> Alfred North Whitehead
> "The Aims of Education"

Is there an economic style?

Or is "style" a concept that applies only to the arts?

If style is defined as *attributes that are distinguishable or distinguishing*, then the notion of economic style is valid.

Clearly, style is an often indefinable or indescribable quality. But its existence makes it possible to identify individual qualities among many experts in any given field.

Economics, along with other areas of knowledge, consists of both the study of rules and theories and the application or use of those rules and theories.

The definition of how to produce an oil painting can be straightforward: Put paint on a canvas. The rules governing the creation of colors can be straightforward: Mix blue and yellow to make green. Even so, it is easy to distinguish the works of one great artist from another, and the works of professional artists from amateurs.

It might be exciting for an amateur to paint a "photographic" reproduction of nature; to "create" a picture of a tree that looks "exactly" like a particular tree. To others, the value of such a painting is likely to be small. Why? Because it does not make anyone think. It does not offer new insights into the world. The artist may be impressed by the accomplishment; few others are likely to care. Paintings that do nothing more than duplicate nature are done by following simple rules. Some skill is required, but little or no imagination.

Vincent van Gogh broke the rules to create paintings that are now worth millions of dollars (although he sold only one painting during his lifetime).

Economics is similar. There are "rules" that are agreed upon by almost all economists. If the rules could always be applied exactly as stated, all economists would reach the same conclusion about any given economic problem. Like amateur paintings, however, the results would be of little real value because the problems would be of little consequence.

The value of economic analysis is that it yields insights into important issues that are not always easy to understand. If economic issues were simple, there would be little need for trained economists, or for economics as a discipline.

The objective, of course, is not to break the economic rules, but to apply them in the most useful and meaningful way possible. The task is to develop new or more meaningful ideas and arguments that can make the world "better."

If a major goal of economics is to explain and predict, then a "style," or way of applying the rules, is required in order to offer explanations and predictions that are accurate and timely enough to be useful. Style is, consequently, more than a perceived *difference*. Style is related to *quality*. In the study of economics, quality is related to the thought process used to approach and solve problems.

PART TWO: MICROECONOMICS

4

A Microeconomic Model

Many important economic questions involve actions in individual markets. Although there is sometimes a tendency to think first of issues such as unemployment, inflation, and recession, issues such as pollution, automobile safety, food additives, gas prices, union contracts, financial investments, and so on are also crucial to the well-being of individuals and society as a whole.

1. Market supply and demand.

Demand is the relationship between two variables: the price of something and the maximum quantity of that something that buyers are willing and able to purchase during a given time period, all other things constant.

Supply is also the relationship between two variables: the price of something and the maximum quantity of that something that sellers are willing and able to offer for sale during a given time period, all other things constant.

Each statement is an absolute truth, in the sense that such relationships do exist. To be useful, however, a little more must be known. Are the relationships positive or negative? Are they stable?

2. The simple logic of supply and demand.

The "theories" of demand and supply that take up a lot of space in most textbooks may be interesting (to economists), but they do not "prove" anything about the relationship between price and quantity for either supply or demand. The truth is that such theories belong more to an understanding of the history of economic thought than to an understanding of functional economics.

On the other hand, simple logic using the concept of opportunity cost tells us that, in the short run, market demand curves will have negative slopes and market supply curves will normally have positive slopes.

All such statements describing supply and demand must be accompanied by the condition, "all other things constant" because if, when the price of apples increases, incomes are also increasing and the prices of oranges and all other things are changing, there is no way of predicting what will happen to the quantity of apples bought or offered for sale. Even so, it is still possible to isolate the impact of the price of apples on the quantity of apples demanded or supplied.

Demand. As the price of something (such as apples) increases, with everything else held constant, buyers of apples must give up more of other things to purchase the same quantity of apples. Therefore, the higher the price of apples, the greater is the opportunity cost of buying apples. As a result, the higher the price of apples, the fewer apples consumers are willing and able to purchase.

Figure 4.1 shows a market demand curve based on the logic of opportunity cost. It is negatively sloped. At price p_1, consumers are willing and able to buy q_1 units of q during a given time period, all other things constant. At a price higher than p_1, consumers are willing and able to buy less than q_1; at a price lower than p_1, consumers are willing and able to buy more than q_1.

Figure 4.1

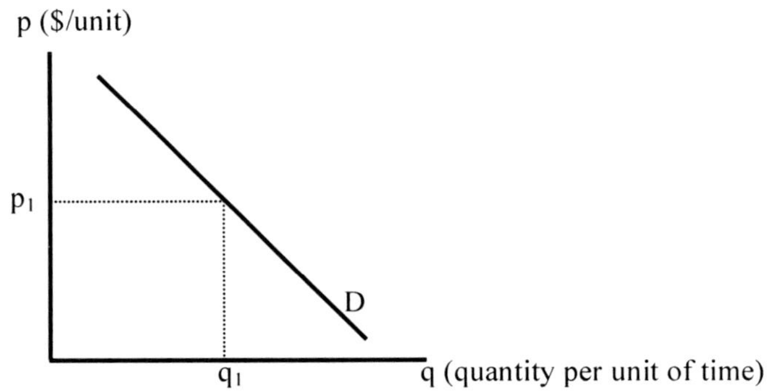

Supply. As the price of something increases, all other things held constant, the opportunity cost to producers of not selling more of that thing and less of other things increases. Therefore, the higher the price of something, the greater the quantity of that thing that will be offered for sale during a given time period.

Figure 4.2 shows a market supply curve based on the logic of opportunity cost. It is positively sloped. At price p_1, sellers are willing and able to sell q_2 units of q during a given time period, all other things constant. At a price higher than p_1, sellers are willing and able to sell more than q_2; at a price lower than p_1, sellers are willing and able to sell less than q_2.

Figure 4.2

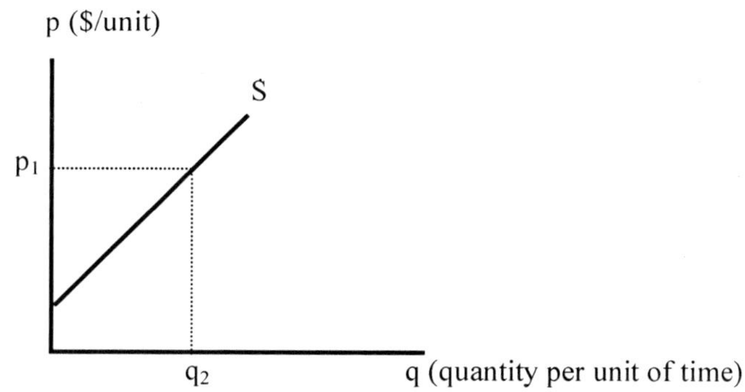

Throughout this text, and in the real world, most market problems are solved by using demand and supply curves that look like those in Figures 4.1 and 4.2.

> The student should be able to construct what is called a demand schedule: a table showing a number of prices and a corresponding quantity demanded for each price.

> The student should be able to construct what economists call a supply schedule: a table showing a number of prices and a corresponding quantity supplied for each price.

3. Other possibilities for supply and demand.

To be complete, the logic of supply and demand should be aware of all legitimate possibilities, even if most market problems are solved using a negatively sloped demand curve and a positively sloped supply curve.

Demand. Figure 4.3 shows a number of possibilities for market demand curves.

Figure 4.3

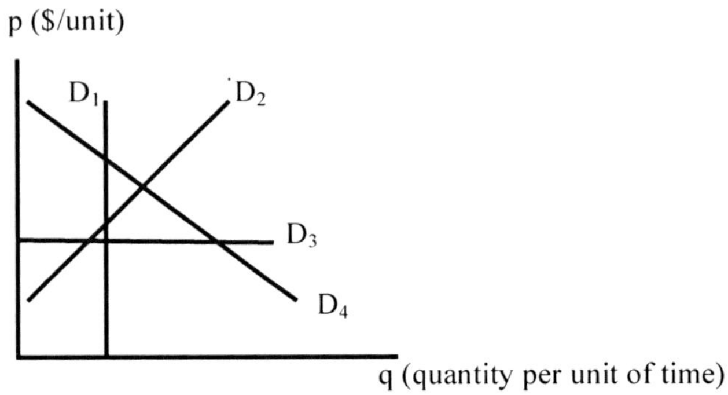

A "life-and-death" product (or possibly an addictive drug) could yield a demand curve that is a vertical line at the quantity "needed," such as D_1 in Figure 4.3. Such a demand curve means that consumers are willing and able to pay any price to obtain the designated quantity.

A single seller of an undifferentiated product (the idea of pure or perfect competition) is assumed to be able to sell as much as he or she can produce at the existing market price; and nothing if the price is set above the market price. Such a demand curve would be a horizontal line at the market price, which is determined by market supply and demand. D_3 in Figure 4.3 is assumed to represent a demand curve faced by a perfectly competitive firm.

Every so often someone tries to uncover an exception to the downward sloping demand curve by finding a good or service where a greater quantity is bought at a higher price, such as D_2 in Figure 4.3. So far, no one has succeeded.

Goods that might be bought in greater quantities at higher prices are often called "Giffen goods," named after the man who spent considerable time trying to find an exception to the rule. Giffen focused on items he thought were purchased as a show of wealth, such as fur coats. His argument was that if the price of fur coats fell, people would not be able to "show off" their wealth by wearing them and would, therefore, buy fewer of them.

Giffen may have been correct in assuming that a decline in the price of a "conspicuous consumption" item would lead some to buy less. But a decrease in "conspicuous consumption" is more than offset by increased purchases by those who could not formerly "afford" the good or service. Therefore:

> *The "law of demand" is that as the price of something declines, consumers are willing and able to buy a greater quantity of that commodity or service during a given time period, all other things held constant; a smaller quantity at a higher price.*

D_4 in Figure 4.3 is the normal short-run demand curve discussed above and described by the "law of demand."

Supply. Figure 4.4 shows a number of possibilities for market supply curves.

Figure 4.4

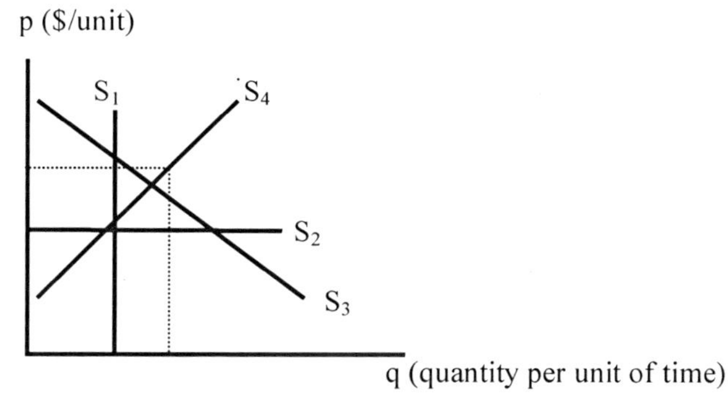

S_1 represents the supply of something that is put on the market and that sellers are willing and able to sell for whatever price they receive. It is a vertical line at the quantity offered for sale. An example is a commercial fisherman's daily catch. If it is not sold on the day it is caught, it will be worth nothing the next day.

S_2 represents the supply curve facing a single consumer. It says that the consumer can purchase as much or as little as he or she wants at the existing market price. If the consumer offers a price that is below the market price, nothing can be purchased. Horizontal supply curves can also represent government imposed price floors (such as rent control) or price ceilings (such as agricultural price supports).

S_3 represents the idea that, in the long run, as the quantity produced increases, economies of scale can lead to falling costs of production. In such cases, as the quantity increases, the price at which sellers are willing and able to sell each quantity declines.

S_4 is the normal short-run supply curve discussed above. It is positively sloped.

4. Reading supply and demand curves.

If you are not used to dealing with such diagrams, they look more complicated than they are. To read a demand curve, choose any point on the vertical price axis, such as p_1 in Figure 4.1. From p_1, draw a straight, horizontal line to the demand curve. When you reach the demand curve, draw a straight, vertical line down to the horizontal quantity axis. The point where the vertical line from the demand curve touches the quantity axis shows the maximum quantity of the item that buyers are willing and able to buy at the price p_1. In Figure 4.1 above, that quantity is q_1.

Using p_1 and q_1 is an abstraction. Some find it easier to see what is happening if numbers are used. For example, instead of p_1, choose a price, such as $4; and instead of q_1, choose a quantity, such as 45 units.

In either case, if you now choose a price higher than p_1 (higher than $4) and draw a horizontal line from that point on the price axis to the demand curve, and then down to the quantity axis, the vertical line from the demand curve will reach the quantity axis at a quantity less than q_1 (less than 45 units).

If you choose a price lower than p_1 (lower than $4) and draw a line from that point on the price axis to the demand curve and then down to the quantity axis, the line from the demand curve will reach the quantity axis at a quantity greater than q_1 (greater than 45 units).

In other words, a negatively sloped demand curve shows that the higher the price of something, the lower the quantity of that thing buyers are willing and able to buy during a given time period, all other things held constant.

Reading a supply curve is the same as reading a demand curve. Choose a point on the vertical price axis, such as p_1 in Figure 4.2. From p_1, draw a straight, horizontal line that reaches the supply curve. When the line reaches the supply curve, draw a straight, vertical line down to the horizontal quantity axis. The point where the vertical line from S touches the quantity axis shows the maximum quantity of the item that sellers are willing and able to sell at the price p_1. In Figure 4.2, it is q_2 units.

If you now choose a price higher than p_1 and draw a line from that point on the price axis to the supply curve, S, and then down to the quantity axis, the line from S will reach the quantity axis at a quantity greater than q_2. If you choose a price lower than p_1 and draw a line from that point on the price axis to S and then down to the quantity axis, the line from S will reach the quantity axis at a quantity less than q_2. Therefore, for a normal, short-run supply curve, the higher the price, the greater the quantity sellers are willing and able to sell during a given time period, all other things held constant.

Therefore, logic concludes that:

1) Figure 4.1 is a picture of what a normal market demand curve looks like.

It is a negative relationship that applies to any market, whether it is a market for goods and services, resources, inputs to production, or investments. It is necessary to be careful when labeling each axis so that each is an accurate representation of what is being studied.

2) Figure 4.2 is a picture of a normal, short run market supply curve.

It is a positive relationship that is expected to exist in markets where the quantity studied varies with its price.

5. A "normal" individual market.

Given the above discussion, Figure 4.5 is a picture of an individual market. In certain situations, however, the demand curve can be either horizontal or vertical; and the supply curve can be horizontal, vertical, or negatively sloped. Therefore, each such possibility for supply and demand should be considered when solving economic problems.

Figure 4.5

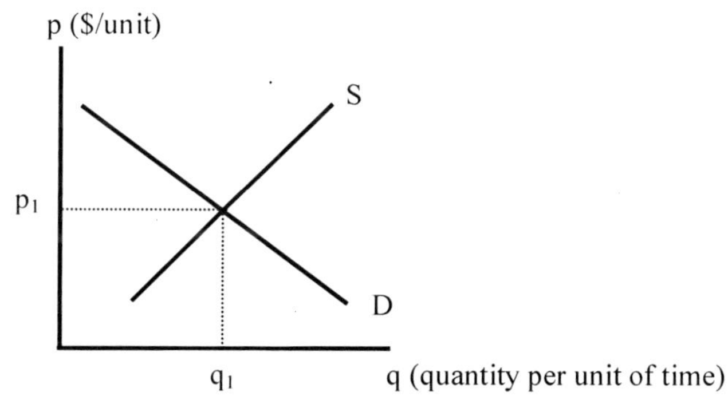

6. A change in supply and demand versus a change in the quantity supplied or the quantity demanded.

The economic meanings of demand and supply are precise. But they are often confused. The term "demand" or "demand curve" refers to a schedule or function representing the maximum quantities of a good or service people are willing and able to buy at different prices during a specific time period. The phrase "quantity demanded" refers to how much will be bought at a particular price during a specific time period. The *quantity demanded* is one point on a given demand curve or schedule. The term "supply" or "supply curve" refers to a schedule or function representing the maximum quantities of a good or service sellers are willing and able to sell at different prices during a specific time period. The phrase "quantity supplied" refers to how much will be offered for sale at a particular price during a given time period. The *quantity supplied* is one point on a given supply curve or schedule.

A change in the "quantity of grapefruit demanded" or the "quantity of grapefruit supplied" occurs when the price of grapefruit changes.

A change in the "demand for grapefruit" occurs when the price of oranges or apples changes, when incomes change, or when medical researchers announce that "grapefruit is good for you."

A change in the "supply of grapefruit" occurs when the weather changes, a freeze affects the crop, or new techniques for growing grapefruit are developed.

To discuss the demand for grapefruit, even as an abstract concept, it is necessary to understand that incomes, personal likes and dislikes, and the prices of other goods and services all affect how much grapefruit people are willing and able to buy at various prices. If incomes increase, consumers are likely to buy more of everything they like (all normal goods). And because everyone loves grapefruit, an increase in incomes means that the demand for grapefruit would increase. At any given price, people would be willing and able to buy more grapefruit than they did before. If the prices of related goods and services change, the impact on the demand for grapefruit is less certain.

A similar understanding of how various things affect the supply of grapefruit is also needed.

7. Most microeconomic problems are solved using market supply and demand.

Most economic problems—*in the real world*—are market problems. The reason textbooks devote so much time and effort to the study of how individuals and individual firms act and react is mainly to explain as much as possible about what is behind the market demand and supply curves they create.

It is normally assumed that each individual firm wants to maximize its profits. Therefore, an analysis of the effects of tighter air pollution standards for automobiles begins with the assumption that the existing supply of automobiles is determined by all manufacturers currently selling automobiles in the U.S. and that each one—GM, Ford, Chrysler, Toyota, VW, etc.—is currently acting to maximize profits.

It is also assumed that each manufacturer will react rationally to the new legislation, meaning that each will continue its attempt to maximize profits, even though there is a new law to deal with.

Of course, profits are normally a long-term objective, not a one-shot goal, for a large corporation. But if each firm is trying to maximize its profits over time, then it is correct to assume that if it is more expensive to produce automobiles that cause less air pollution, manufacturers will be willing to sell fewer automobiles at each price than they were previously willing to sell. On a graph, the supply of automobiles decreases—moves to the left or upward.

As with demand, a change in any variable other than the price of the product under examination can cause a change in supply.

Any change that makes it more expensive to produce automobiles means fewer automobiles offered for sale at each price. Alternatively, it can be said that the minimum price at which each quantity of automobiles is offered increases. Therefore, the supply curve of automobiles moves to the left or upward.

Any change that makes it less costly to produce automobiles—for example, a decrease in the price of steel—means that more automobiles will be offered for sale at each price, or that the minimum price at which each quantity is offered decreases. The result is an increase in supply—the supply curve moves to the right or downward.

A leftward or upward move of a supply curve looks the same on a graph, but it is less confusing to think of a decrease in supply as a leftward move because it can seem odd to show a decrease in supply by an upward move of a supply curve.

A rightward or downward move of a supply curve looks the same on a graph, but it is less confusing to think of an increase in supply as a rightward move because it can seem odd to show an increase in supply by a downward move of a supply curve.

8. Equilibrium.

An equilibrium exists in a market at the price where the quantity buyers are willing and able to buy equals the quantity sellers are willing and able to sell.

On a graph representing a market, equilibrium exists where the demand and supply curves intersect. It is possible to imagine a market where supply slopes upward but is above demand at any given quantity.

In such a market, the equilibrium output is zero; there is no price at which the quantity buyers are willing and able to buy equals the quantity sellers are willing and able to sell. It can be assumed that a market in which things are actually being bought and sold has an equilibrium.

In Figure 4.6, there is an equilibrium at p_1 and q_1. At a price of p_1, the quantity buyers are willing and able to buy is equal to the quantity sellers are willing and able to sell: q_1.

Figure 4.6

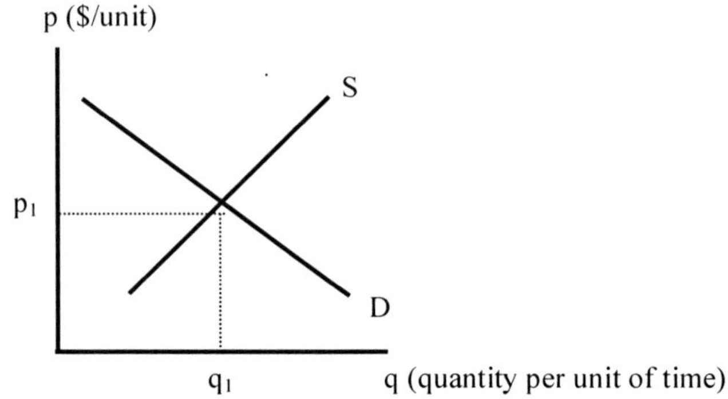

9. Is the equilibrium stable or unstable?

Economists are careful to identify the conditions necessary for a stable equilibrium. The reason for the concern is obvious: An unstable equilibrium, meaning that if something causes a movement away from equilibrium, the market will not return to a position of equilibrium, would be very disruptive.

Fortunately, unstable markets are uncommon in the real world. Even without knowing the specific details of every possible market, an unstable market would be relatively easy to notice.

The conditions necessary for a stable equilibrium are:

1) If the market price is pushed above the equilibrium price, supply *must be* greater than demand. If it is, then the **excess supply**—sellers trying to sell more than buyers are willing and able to buy at the higher price—causes sellers to lower prices and bring the market back to equilibrium.
2) If the market price is pushed below the equilibrium price, demand must be greater than supply. If it is, then the **excess demand**—buyers trying to buy more than sellers are willing to sell at the lower price—causes buyers to bid up the price and bring the market back to equilibrium.

As long as demand slopes downward (buyers are willing and able to buy more at lower prices) and supply slopes upward (sellers are willing and able to sell more only at higher prices), the market has a stable equilibrium at the price and quantity where supply equals demand.

If supply is vertical (suppliers are willing to sell "everything" at whatever price they can receive) the equilibrium is stable.

If supply slopes downward, the market equilibrium will be stable as long as supply intersects demand from above. If supply intersects demand from above, then at any price above the equilibrium price, there will be an excess supply that pushes the price back to equilibrium; at any price below equilibrium, there will be an excess demand that pushes the price back to the equilibrium price.

A vertical supply curve exists when a given quantity of some commodity, normally a perishable resource, is offered for whatever price it can receive.

A horizontal supply curve, describing, for example, a labor union that sets a "take-it-or-leave-it" wage rate, and a downward sloping demand curve is also a stable equilibrium.

In Figure 4.7, the initial equilibrium is at p_1 and q_1.

Figure 4.7

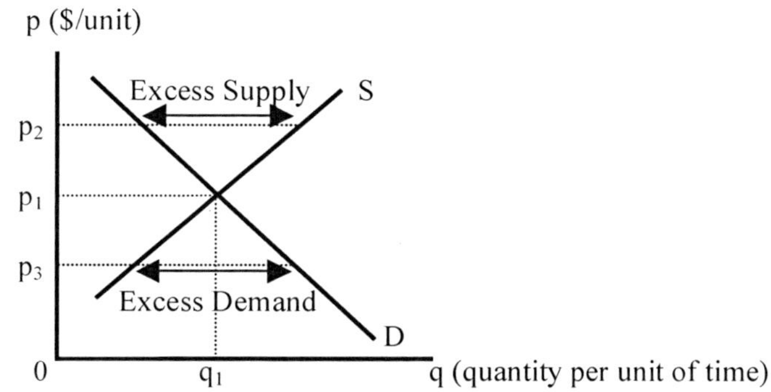

If the price rises above p_1, to p_2, for example, an excess supply is created because, at the price p_2, sellers want to sell more than buyers are willing and able to buy. As a result, the price will fall, and it will continue to decline until the excess supply is eliminated, which is when the price returns to p_1.

If the price falls below p_1, to p_3 for example, an excess demand is created because at the price p_3, buyers want to buy more than sellers are willing and able to sell. The excess demand will cause the price to increase, and it will continue to rise until the excess demand is eliminated, which is when price returns to p_1.

An unstable equilibrium exists if supply slopes downward and intersects demand from below. In such a case, if the price is pushed above the equilibrium level, an excess demand is created that pulls prices higher and higher. If the price is pushed below equilibrium, an excess supply is created that causes prices to fall lower and lower, farther and farther away from equilibrium.

10. How to solve economic problems.

Economic problem solving almost always relies on the logic of "comparative statics," an analytical approach that compares one equilibrium (one static position) with another equilibrium (another static position). It is normally difficult to say anything meaningful about the impact of a change if the beginning and ending markets are not assumed to be in equilibrium. It is also normally difficult to say much that is meaningful about the dynamics of the change—of exactly how the move from one equilibrium to a new equilibrium takes place.

1. Begin with the question.

The analysis always begins with a question. After being given a problem, make certain that you can state the question.

The question is important; it is what sets up the problem. Without a specific question, there is no problem to solve.

What information is being asked for? State exactly what is to be explained or predicted. Is it a change in market price? Or equilibrium quantity? Or profits? Or the well-being of an individual? Be precise. In most cases, it will take only one or two sentences. Be clear about what is being studied. Which variables are being explained or predicted?

It is also necessary to be clear about the change that led to the question? The change may be an outside effect or it may be the desire to achieve a different equilibrium. In either case, the change is likely to affect many things. If the change is increased competition from foreign producers, an announcement from the medical community that some product is good or bad for people's health, or a government program intended to help an identifiable group, you must be clear about what is happening, or happened, or is expected to happen.

2. The three steps of comparative statics.

Given a question, which is often triggered by a change in something that was assumed to be held constant, or a need to explain what happened or is happening, the steps to follow are: (1) describe the initial equilibrium; (2) explain how the change affects supply and/or demand; (3) describe the new equilibrium and compare the old and new equilibrium values.

(1) Describe the initial equilibrium.

Draw a market diagram using supply and demand curves.

The question or problem determines exactly what must be described in the diagram. It may be a situation that existed in the past, that exists in the present, or that can exist in the future. Describe the equilibrium that existed or exists before the change. It is almost always assumed that the beginning position is an equilibrium situation. If not, it may be impossible to say anything about what happened or is expected to happen.

Describe the beginning situation of the firm, market, individual, or overall economy by sketching a simple supply and demand diagram.

In the initial equilibrium, there is an equilibrium price and an equilibrium quantity, both for the market and for individual buyers and sellers.

Label each axis with the "loose" designations p and q. Label the supply and demand functions S_1 and D_1. Label the initial equilibrium values p_1 and q_1.

In most cases, there is no reason to worry about precise values. Simply sketch in the functions. But be careful to label each axis and each curve. When a question asks for an explanation of how a market or the overall economy works, rather than asking for a prediction of how a change will impact particular variables, the analysis is centered on explaining what is behind the functions in the model.

(2) Explain, and show on the diagram, how the change causes an increase or decrease in S and/or D.

Explain how or why the change (and ONLY that change) affects or is expected to affect supply or demand or both in the market or markets being studied. If more than one change is introduced, it is likely that nothing meaningful can be said. It is almost always necessary to isolate individual changes in order to understand the impact of each.

How will the function or functions change? Will they increase or decrease? Will one or both remain constant? For example, increased competition from foreign producers of television sets increases the supply curve of television sets on the market. The change does not, however, affect the demand for television sets.

Show the change on the diagram. An increase in demand or supply means there will be a new curve to the right of the original curve, because buyers are willing and able to buy more at any given price and sellers are willing and able to sell more at any given price. A decrease in D or S means there will be a new curve to the left of the original curve. Sketch in the new supply and/or demand curves and label them S_2 and D_2.

> Note:
> An increase in demand is shown as a new demand curve either to the right of or above the original demand curve.
> An increase in supply is shown as a new supply curve either to the right of or below the original supply curve. Because it is sometimes confusing to think of an increase in supply as a new supply curve below the original supply curve, it is normally easier to show a change in supply by drawing a new curve either to the left or right of the original curve.

(3) Describe the new equilibrium and explain what happens to the equilibrium values of the variables under consideration.

The new equilibrium is determined by the supply and demand functions that exist after the change has worked its way through the system. Label the new equilibrium quantity q_2 and the new equilibrium price p_2.

How do the new price and quantity compare to the original price and quantity? In other words, what happened or will happen to what is being studied?

For example, it might be concluded that: "The equilibrium price increased from p_1 to p_2 and the equilibrium quantity decreased from q_1 to q_2." When describing the new equilibrium, it is normally not necessary to be any more specific than to describe the direction of change of equilibrium price and quantity, and, in some cases, profits. In the case of an increase in the quantity of imported television sets, the equilibrium market price falls, equilibrium quantity increases, profits of domestic producers fall.

Conclusion

Most problems end with a conclusion that describes the new equilibrium and summarizes what happened. It might restate the problem, describe the expected change or changes in supply and/or demand, and state the change in the variable or variables being examined. It should also specify the assumptions that were made to reach the given conclusion. Some questions or problems focus mainly on the initial equilibrium. For example, questions about market failure (such as externalities, common property resources, or public goods) are normally concerned with explaining the reason for the failure and the resulting misallocation of resources, and *then* with finding a solution to the problem: How can the misallocation of society's resources be corrected?

After solving a number of problems, it will be seen that the same logical framework is used over and over again. New problems do not require "new" procedures, new ways of thinking, or new theories.

The world is logical. Knowledgeable individuals know things that can help explain and predict what is happening or is expected to happen as the result of changes.

But all opinions are not of equal value. Individuals with greater knowledge about certain things have opinions about those things that should be more valuable than the opinions of less knowledgeable observers. It is easy to say that an increase in the demand for apples will cause the price of apples to increase. It is better to be able to explain—step by step—why that is the correct answer, even though the answer appears obvious.

It is sometimes possible to determine if a change makes an individual or a nation better or worse off, but not always. Economics is seldom able to *judge* an equilibrium position in a market, other than to point out the possible winners and losers. The exception is when it can be concluded that the change has a positive or negative impact on economic efficiency. Economic efficiency is a term used to describe a situation where resources are used in a way that maximizes the satisfaction of society.

On a larger level, it is often impossible, in a world of scarce resources, to make one person better off without making someone else worse off. And because economics cannot make interpersonal comparisons, economists may be limited to identifying the winners and losers, and not claiming that the change is "good" or "bad."

Appendix to Chapter Four: Judging A Microeconomic Equilibrium

1. Pure and perfect competition.

The concepts of pure competition and perfect competition were created by economists years ago. They are theoretical definitions. They are not descriptions of possibilities that could be expected to exist in the real world.

The conditions of pure competition and perfect competition are used to explain the assumptions under which economic explanations and predictions are made, but it is not assumed that such conditions actually exist in the real world; or that an economy should hope to achieve such conditions.

More important, because the definitions were never assumed to be descriptions of existing economies, they cannot be used to justify the status quo, the conditions in any market, or the equilibrium in any market.

The conditions for **pure competition** to exist are:

(1) No buyer or seller has an effect on price. Individual consumers do not affect the price of anything they buy or sell. Individual firms do not affect the price of anything they buy or sell. Each is a price taker, because each is such a small part of the market that each can buy or sell as much or as little as they want without having an effect on price. This assumption is based partly on another assumption, which is that the products are homogeneous; meaning that the consumer is indifferent as to which seller supplies the product.

(2) There are no restrictions on prices or on the use of resources. The government does not set prices in any market. Monopolies do not exist. Labor unions do not exist.

(3) Goods and services and resources are free to move around the economy. Firms are free to enter or leave industries. Resources can be sold wherever they receive the highest price.

The definition of **perfect competition** adds one more condition.

(4) Individuals and firms have perfect information about prices and opportunities.

There are two common uses for the definitions of pure and perfect competition.

One is to establish a benchmark used for making comparisons. For example, if perfect competition did exist, would the resulting prices and allocation of resources be "better" than those resulting from different economic conditions? That was one of Adam Smith's concerns in 1776. His conclusion was that competition would be better than the known alternatives at maximizing the nation's wealth. He also concluded that competition would create a stable economic system, even though each individual consumer and firm is making decisions based solely upon self-interest.

A second use of the definitions of pure or perfect competition is to establish the assumptions behind explanations and predictions. The argument for using the concept of perfect competition when making explanations and predictions is not that it exists, but that the explanations and predictions that result from making such an assumption are better than the explanations and predictions made using other assumptions, such as that prices are controlled by someone or that consumers are ignorant or uninformed.

Although the benefits of discussing the conditions of pure and perfect competition are real, the distorted discussions of the ideas created two problems.

On an "intellectual" level, the definitions appear to be restrictions on the usefulness of economics. A misunderstanding of what the conditions mean can lead to the belief that economics is useful only if the conditions hold, which is not the case. The assumptions do not have to hold for economics to be useful and accurate in terms of explaining and predicting, or in discussing changes that will improve the well-being or wealth of the nation.

On a political level, a distorted idea of perfect competition has been used by special interests to justify what exists in the world, if it suits their purpose, and to support the view that market solutions are always the best way to allocate resources, if it suits their purpose. Neither claim is supported by the economic ideas of pure or perfect competition or by economic thought.

2. What the market cannot do.

After understanding what markets can do, which is to provide a stable equilibrium and an efficient allocation of resources, it is necessary to understand what markets cannot do. As a general rule, the market cannot allocate resources not traded in markets, such as air quality or water quality in lakes and rivers.

In particular:

The market cannot allocate resources that are not owned and which are used on a first-come-first-served basis, such as fish populations in oceans, lakes, or rivers, because there is no market for fish before they are caught.

The market cannot allocate resources correctly when negative externalities exist that cause the value of a product to consumers to diverge from the true cost to society of providing it, which is the case when the production or consumption of a product causes pollution that affects others, because there is no market for air quality.

The market cannot allocate resources correctly when positive externalities cause the value of a product to consumers to diverge from the cost to society of providing it, which is the case with education, because there is no market for the benefits to others when someone becomes educated.

The market cannot allocate resources correctly with regard to "public goods," things whose benefits cannot be excluded from those who do not pay for them, such as national defense.

The market cannot protect itself from collusion among firms or individuals, such as monopolies and labor unions, which causes a misallocation of society's resources.

The market cannot prevent individuals from making decisions that are not in their own best interest, such as not using seat belts.

The market cannot prevent individuals or firms from hurting others while doing what is in their own best interest, such as stealing from or hurting someone else in order to gain something.

On a national level, a market economy cannot be assumed to provide an optimal level of economic growth, employment, and prices, which are the main concerns of macroeconomics.

Each of these problems results in a market equilibrium where there is a divergence between private costs and social costs or between private benefits and social benefits. In each case, the market equilibrium provides a lower than possible level of well-being or wealth for the nation. The reason is that individuals and firms make decisions based on private costs and benefits, as measured by prices, but the real value and the real costs of actions are measured by social benefits and costs, not private benefits and costs.

Therefore, when private costs diverge from social costs, the prices used by individuals and firms to make decisions yield results that are not in the best interest of society. In other words, economic logic argues that market solutions for items traded in the market can maximize the well-being or wealth of the nation only when the value consumers receive from what they purchase is equal to the true social cost of providing it.

3. Economic efficiency.

The concept of "economic efficiency" is that the wealth of a nation will be maximized if resources are used where they are valued the most. In theory, the conditions of perfect competition yield such a solution, as long as none of the market-failure issues discussed in Section 2 exist.

The Italian economist Vilfredo Pareto (1848-1923), in an attempt to determine how to judge an equilibrium, or to define when an action or change is "justified," argued that: A change is good if it helps at least one person without making anyone else worse off, and an equilibrium is good if it is impossible to make a change that helps at least one person without making someone else worse off. Reaching a "Pareto optimum" equilibrium means that any move away from that equilibrium will reduce the well-being or wealth of society.

Although Pareto's definitions have little use in the real world, the idea of a "Pareto optimum" or "Pareto efficiency" is still taught as a theoretical description of how economists would like to judge an equilibrium or a change.

4. Using the idea of marginal benefits and marginal costs to judge a market equilibrium.

Although the concepts of pure competition, perfect competition, and economic efficiency are not assumed to exist in any real-world market, the "rule" followed when solving problems about individual markets is to assume that:

Market demand curves represent marginal benefits to buyers.

Market supply curves represent marginal costs to sellers.

This assumption, or rule, which is derived from the theoretical arguments behind perfect competition and economic efficiency, makes it possible to judge a theoretical equilibrium and the results of a potential change.

When describing the initial equilibrium, it is assumed that the market demand curve describes marginal benefits to society and the market supply curve describes marginal costs to society. The question that must be addressed in each case is whether or not there is a difference between marginal **private** benefits and costs and marginal **social** benefits and costs. The normal reason for a difference is market failure.

If it is assumed that marginal private benefits and costs are equal to marginal social benefits and costs, then the equilibrium described in a market may be assumed to be economically efficient. If it can be argued that marginal private benefits and costs are *not* equal to marginal social benefits and costs in a particular market, then the equilibrium described in that market is assumed to be *not* economically efficient.

5. A logical method for deciding if a change makes people better or worse off.

Sometimes it is difficult to decide if a change that leads to a new equilibrium, either for an individual or a market, makes the individual or those represented in the market, better or worse off. An easy, and logical, way to reach a conclusion is to determine if the new equilibrium was available before the change. If it was, but it was not chosen, then the new equilibrium can be said to be less preferable than the original equilibrium.

A Microeconomic Model (S & D)--Summary

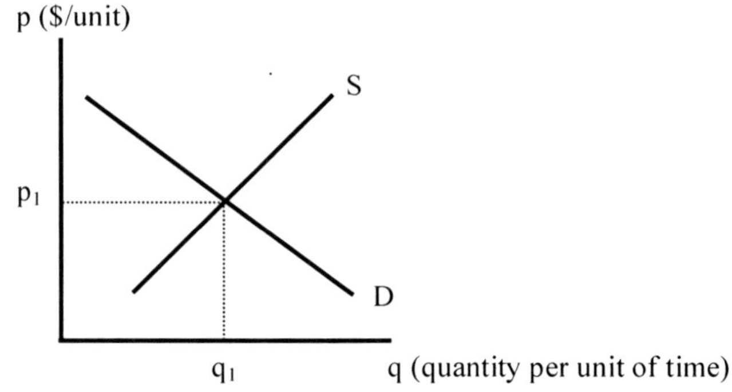

A microeconomic model is used to explain and predict equilibrium values and changes in individual markets. It is used for the automobile market, the apple market, the bond market, the money market, the foreign exchange market, the education market, markets for common property resources, the market for air quality, public goods, and so on. Although "micro" means small, many individual markets are very large, such as the automobile market. It is a mistake to think that microeconomics deals with small issues and macroeconomics focuses on large issues.

Demand: The maximum quantity buyers are willing and able to buy at each price during a given time period, all other things held constant. A normal market demand curve is negatively sloped, meaning that as price decreases, the quantity consumers are willing and able to buy increases.

Supply: The maximum quantity sellers are willing and able to sell at each price during a given time period, all other things held constant. A normal market supply curve is positively sloped, meaning that as price increases, the quantity sellers are willing and able to sell increases.

Equilibrium: The price and quantity where demand and supply are equal.

Stable market: A market is stable if an excess demand causes price to increase and an excess supply causes prices to fall.

What causes a change in demand?
A change in demand is caused by a change in something that was assumed to have been held constant when deriving the original demand curve. It has to be something that would affect how much of the good or service consumers are willing and able to buy at various prices. For example: changes in income, changes in tastes and preferences, changes in the health benefits of a product, changes in the prices of substitute or complementary goods and services, changes in the quality of the product.

What causes a change in supply?
A change in supply is caused by a change in something that was assumed to have been held constant when deriving the original supply curve. It has to be something that would affect how much of the good or service sellers are willing and able to sell at various prices. For example: Changes in costs of production (higher costs of production cause S to decrease), changes in wages (having to pay higher wages causes S to decrease), changes in the cost of inputs (an increase in the cost of any input causes S to decrease), changes in technology, changes in weather.

How to Solve Microeconomic Problems—A Worksheet

(Virtually any market issue can be explained by completing this worksheet.)

The question: *What is being asked for? It is often to explain or predict how a change will affect the value of a particular variable.*

(1) The initial equilibrium: *Describe the initial equilibrium.*

Draw a market diagram using supply and demand curves.

Is there a reason to assume non-normal curves?

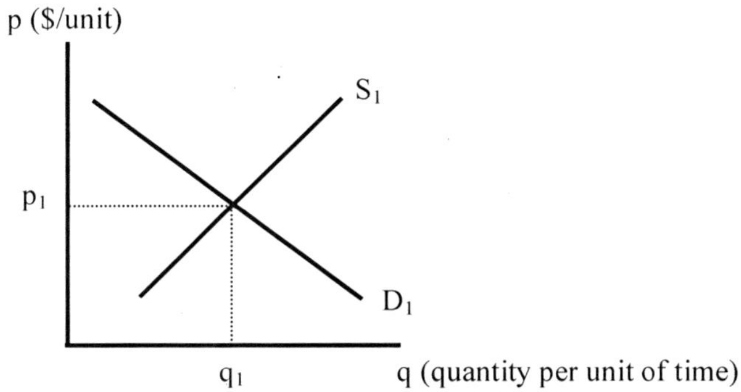

(2) The change: *Explain, and then show on the diagram, how the change causes an increase or decrease in S and/or D.*

(3) The new equilibrium: *Describe the new equilibrium and explain what happens to the equilibrium values of the variables under consideration.*

Summary or conclusion:

5

Supply and Demand

1. A problem with apples.

A simple example of a market, or microeconomic, problem is: What happens to the equilibrium price and quantity of apples in the United States if blight destroys the apple crop in the state of Washington?

The question.

If blight destroys the apple harvest in the state of Washington, what happens to the equilibrium price and quantity of apples in the United States?

(1) The initial equilibrium.

The initial equilibrium is shown by the normal supply and demand curves, S_1 and D_1, in Figure 5.1. No information is given that would lead to the assumption of non-normal supply and demand functions.

The initial equilibrium price is p_1. The initial equilibrium quantity is q_1. There is no market failure to explain.

Figure 5.1

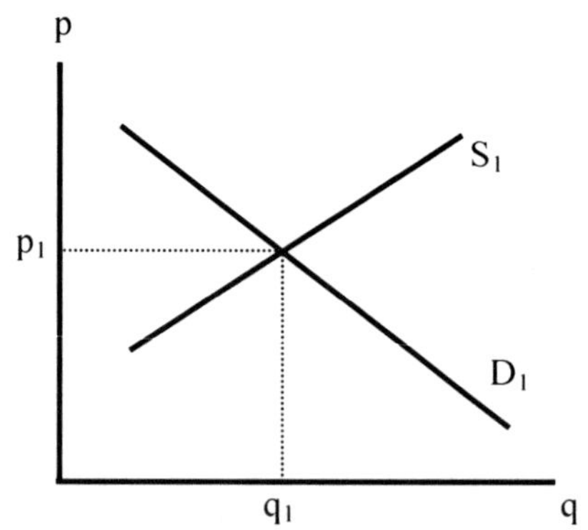

*(2) **The change**.*

In the case of blight, the supply curve will change.

A decrease in supply means there will be a new supply curve to the left of (or above) the original supply curve.

The new supply curve in Figure 5.2 is S_2.

The demand curve remains at D_1.

Figure 5.2

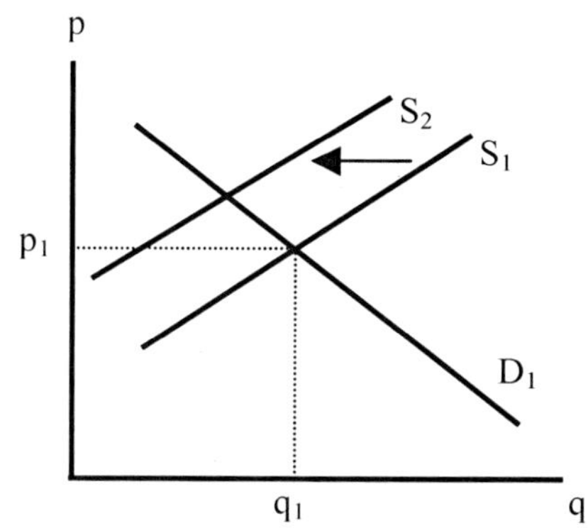

Blight is an example of an "exogenous" change. It is a change in something that was assumed to be held constant when deriving the original supply function—the conditions for growing apples.

There is no reason to assume that something that affects the growing of apples will have any effect on the demand for apples—the maximum quantity of apples that buyers are willing and able to purchase at various prices.

The blight causes the market supply of apples to decrease. At any given price, sellers (nationwide) are now willing and able to offer fewer apples for sale, or, for any given quantity of apples, the minimum price at which that quantity will be offered for sale is higher.

Demand is unchanged.

(3) The new equilibrium.

Assuming there is nothing to prevent the new equilibrium from being achieved in the market, the new equilibrium will occur where the new supply curve and the original demand curve intersect.

The new equilibrium, determined by the new supply curve S_2 and the original demand curve D_1, is at the new equilibrium price, p_2, and the new equilibrium quantity, q_2. It is important to note that the change that initiated the problem did not affect the market demand for apples. It affected the market supply of apples only. The change in supply resulted in a move along the original demand curve—a change in the quantity demanded—not a change in demand.

Figure 5.3

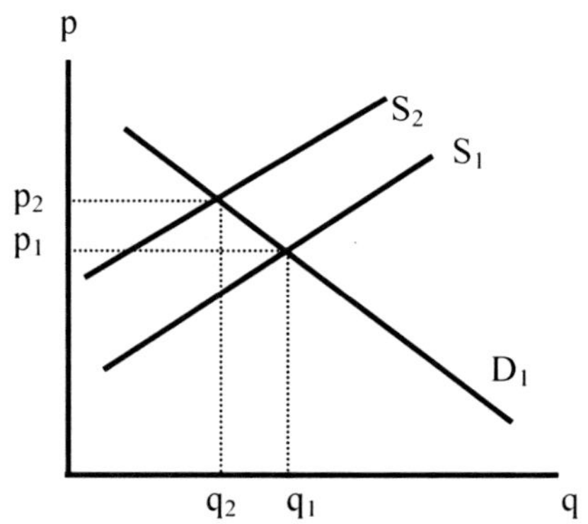

***Conclusion*:**

The conclusion is that something that reduces the apple harvest in the state of Washington results in a decrease in the supply of apples, leading to an increase in the equilibrium price and a decrease in the equilibrium quantity of apples, assuming that all other things remain constant.

Are there winners or losers? In this case, it can be concluded that the profits of apple producers whose crops were not affected by the blight would increase, as long as nothing else changes, because their costs have not changed, but the price at which they can sell apples has increased. Other possible winners and losers, aside from consumers who lose by paying higher prices for fewer apples, are the producers and sellers of substitute and complimentary products.

Suppliers of complimentary products, products used in combination with apples, lose. The demands for complimentary products fall, because, with fewer apples being bought, there is a smaller demand for all such products.

The suppliers of substitute products can either win or lose as the higher price of apples causes consumers to look at substitute products.

The impact on substitute and complimentary products is discussed later.

6

X and Y

Assume that you work for a major supplier of oranges. Your boss hears about a blight that destroyed a large part of the U.S. apple crop and asks you if he should quickly raise the price of oranges. If your answer leads to increased profits, you will get a bonus. If your answer leads to losses, you may lose your job. What do you tell your boss?

If blight destroys part of the apple crop (examined in Chapter 4), businesses involved in the growing, distribution, marketing, and selling of oranges could decide to take advantage of the fact that apples and oranges are substitute products. Knowing that the price of apples will increase, they could decide to quickly increase the price of oranges, in order to get a jump on the increased demand for oranges caused by the lower quantity and higher price of apples.

Investors could also speculate in commodity markets, betting on what they see as a virtually guaranteed increase in the price of oranges.

In most cases, when the demand for a good or service increases, the excess demand for that product pulls its price upward. Sometimes, however, in an attempt to make the greatest possible profit, producers and sellers raise prices before the actual increase in demand takes place. Rather than waiting for prices to be pulled higher, they hope to squeeze as much as they can out of the market. Instead of selling any oranges at the old price, they quickly set what they expect to be the new price, thereby hoping to earn a greater profit on each orange sold.

If they are correct, they will earn a greater profit than if they waited for prices to be pulled higher, little by little.

If they are wrong, they may lose profits and part of their investment.

The question is: Is it always easy, or even possible, to explain or predict how a change in the price of X will affect the equilibrium values of Y? The answer is, no. But it is almost always possible to at least explain the likely pressures generated in one market due to a change in another market.

1. Goods X and Y.

Many economic questions concern the impact of a change in one market on the equilibrium values in another market. What happens to the equilibrium price and quantity of good Y as a result of a change in the price of good X? For example: What happens to the demand for automobile tires or motel rooms if OPEC restricts the supply of oil, thereby causing an increase in oil prices? In order to understand some of the issues behind such problems, we can look first at a simple case of apples and oranges.

2. Apples and oranges.

The impact of blight that reduces the U.S. apple crop was explained in Chapter 4. The conclusion was that the equilibrium market price of apples would increase and the equilibrium quantity would decrease, assuming that all other things remain constant.

The question.

If blight causes the equilibrium price of apples to increase, what happens to the equilibrium price and quantity of oranges?

(1) The initial equilibrium.

The initial equilibrium is shown in Figure 6.1.

The price per unit of oranges is on the vertical axis and the quantity of oranges per unit of time is on the horizontal axis. No information is given that would lead to the assumption of non-normal functions. The initial equilibrium price of oranges is p_1. The initial equilibrium quantity of oranges is q_1.

Figure 6.1

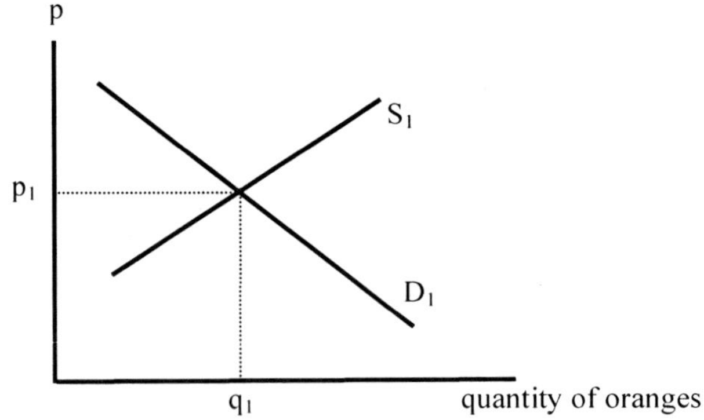

(2) The change.

The increase in the price of apples is an "exogenous" change to the orange market. It is a change in a variable—the price of apples—that was *assumed* to be held constant when deriving the demand for oranges. Therefore, the initial impact on the orange market is a change in the demand for oranges, but not the supply of oranges. The demand for oranges increases from D_1 to D_2 in Figure 6.2. The supply curve remains at S_1 because nothing happened that would cause a change in supply.

Figure 6.2

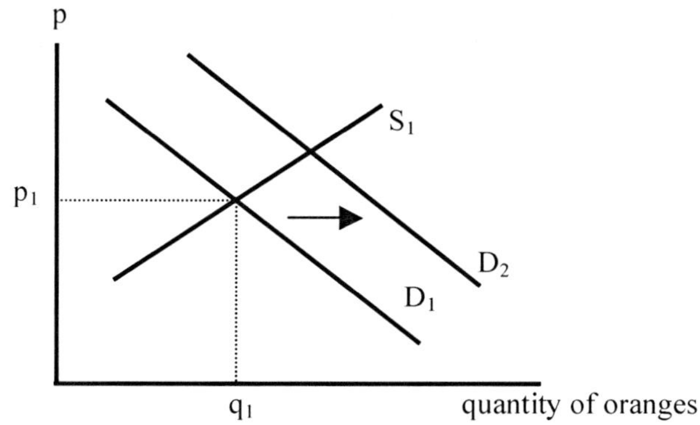

(3) The new equilibrium.

Assuming there is nothing to prevent a new equilibrium from being achieved in the market, the new equilibrium will occur where the new demand curve and the original supply curve intersect. It is important to note that the change that initiated the problem did not affect the market supply for oranges. It affected the market demand for oranges only.

In figure 6.3, the new equilibrium, determined by the new demand curve, D_2, and the original supply curve, S_1, is at the new equilibrium price, p_2, and the new equilibrium quantity, q_2.

The equilibrium price of oranges increased from p_1 to p_2.

The equilibrium quantity of oranges increased from q_1 to q_3.

Consumers pay higher prices for fewer apples and higher prices for more oranges. Apple producers whose crops were not hurt earn higher profits because the price at which they can sell their apples has increased. Orange producers may also earn higher profits by selling more oranges at higher prices.

Figure 6.3

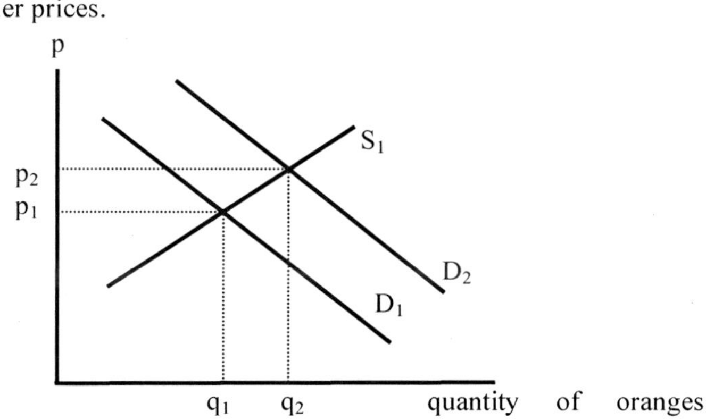

Conclusion.

If you tell your boss, based on the above analysis, to quickly increase prices, will you get a bonus or lose your job? It looks as though you will get a bonus, because it looks as though a blight that reduces the supply of apples and raises the price of apples will lead to an increase in the equilibrium price and equilibrium quantity of oranges, assuming all other things remain constant.

But: Is it really as simple as it seems to understand apples and oranges? Or was something left out? It turns out that quite a lot was left out.

One of the "rules of action" in Chapter 3 was to:

Always state the assumptions behind answers.

In the apples and oranges problem, it was assumed that apples and oranges are substitute products and that a higher price of apples would, therefore, lead to an increase in the demand for oranges.

On the surface, that appears to be a reasonable assumption.

But one of the responsibilities of anyone who is going to make decisions based on explanations and predictions is to look closely at the assumptions behind the answers. In the apples and oranges problem, the assumption that, because apples and oranges are substitute products, an increase in the price of apples would “automatically” lead to an increase in the demand for oranges, is questionable. The truth is: If the price of apples increases, the demand for oranges can increase, decrease, or remain the same.

3. A more complete answer.

It seems obvious that a higher price of apples, leading consumers to purchase fewer apples, should decrease the demand for **complementary products** (such as caramel sauce).

It also seems obvious that a higher price of apples will cause consumers to think about **substituting other products** (such as oranges or grapefruit) for apples, thereby leading to increases in the demands for those products. But will the demand for oranges increase, decrease, or remain the same?

The simplest and clearest way to explain how a price change in one market affects a related market is to begin by looking at the change in total spending in the first market. If the price of something (such as apples) increases, the law of demand says that less of it will be purchased. But, as less of it is purchased, the total spending on that item can increase, decrease, or remain the same, depending upon where the original and ending points are on the demand curve for apples.

As the price of apples increases, there is a move up the demand curve for apples. And at any point on the demand curve, the total spending on apples is equal to price times quantity. In Figure 6.5, with price p_1 and quantity q_1, total spending on apples is p_1 times

q_1, which is the gray rectangle plus the dotted rectangle. If the price of apples increases to p_2, total spending is p_2 times q_2, which is the black rectangle plus the gray rectangle. Therefore, if the price of apples increases from p_1 to p_2, there is an addition to spending equal to the black rectangle and a loss in spending equal to the dotted rectangle. Because it is obvious that the black rectangle is larger than the dotted rectangle in Figure 6.5, an increase in the price of apples from p_1 to p_2 results in an increase in total spending on apples. It should be easy to visualize that if the original price were p_3 and the price increased to p_4, that total spending on apples would decrease.

Figure 6.5

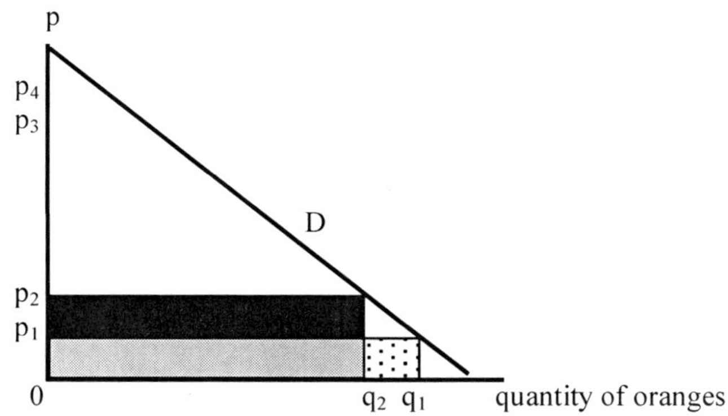

Figure 6.6, on the following page has the demand curve from Figure 6.5 and also a total spending or total revenue curve corresponding to that demand curve. The total spending curve shows total spending at each quantity (and related price) of apples. It is an inverted "U" shaped curve, because as the price increases from zero to higher and higher levels, total spending increases for a while (moving up and to the left along the total spending curve beginning at q*), to higher and higher levels, and then decreases to lower and lower levels, eventually falling back to zero.

If the price is zero, total spending is zero. If price increases to p_1, total spending increases from zero to p_1 times q_1, which is greater than zero. In the total spending diagram, the vertical distance from 0 to TS_1 is equal to the area p_1 times q_1. If price increases to p_2, total spending increases to p_2 times q_2, which is the vertical distance from 0 to TS_2 in the total spending diagram. A price increase from p_3 to p_4 causes total spending to decrease, which is what the total spending curve shows. If the price is so high that no apples are purchased, total spending is back to zero.

The rule is: If the two prices are on the lower half of a straight-line demand curve, the move up the demand curve as price increases means more money will be spent on apples and less will be available for other purchases. If the two prices are on the top half of a straight-line demand curve, less money will be spent on apples as the price of apples increases, meaning that more is available for other purchases. It is also possible that the higher price times the new quantity purchased can be the same as the original price times the original quantity.

Figure 6.6

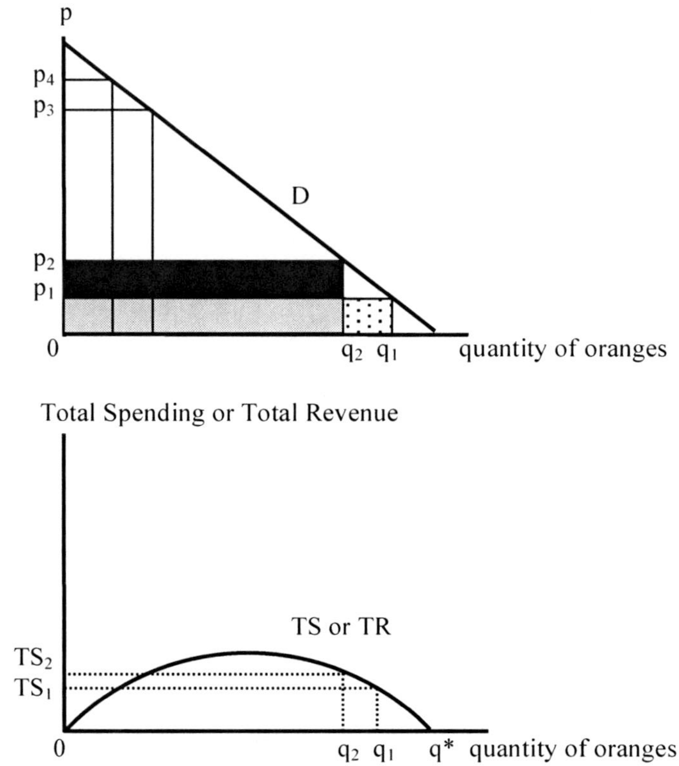

In the top figure, total revenue is shown as an area—a rectangle defined by price and quantity. In the bottom figure, revenue is shown as a distance—from the horizontal axis up to the total spending curve. At q_1 and p_1, the dollar value of the gray rectangle plus the dotted rectangle is the same as the dollar value shown by the distance 0 to TS_1.

Therefore, the actual change in the demand facing the sellers or producers of substitute products is the sum of two effects. The higher price of apples causes buyers to want to substitute oranges for apples, thereby increasing the demand for oranges. But the change in total spending on apples can either reinforce the substitution effect, or counter it. As a result, the demand for oranges can either increase or decrease, depending upon whether the change in the price of apples leads to a decrease or an increase in the money spent on apples.

Meanwhile, all suppliers of complimentary products, products used in combination with apples, lose. The demand for complimentary products falls because with fewer apples being bought, there is a smaller demand for all such products.

Unfortunately, unless specific information on the demand for apples is known, it is impossible to predict the actual change in demand for substitute products.

As a result, those who try to get a jump on the expected increase in the demand for oranges must be cautious.

The question is: Can you explain the real apples and oranges situation to your boss?

> An expanded explanation of the relationship between demand and total revenue, or total spending, is given in Appendix 4—Elasticity.

4. Substitute factors of production.

In the early 1970s, some knowledgeable investors made money investing in soybeans. They invested in soybeans believing that soybean prices were going to rise, which they did. The "trigger" that they believed would set off the price increase was a dramatic decrease in Peru's anchovy catch. Why would a decline in the anchovy harvest of a South American country affect the price of soybeans in the U.S.? The answer to that question sheds some light on the value of economics.

Peru is the world's number one fishing nation, in terms of tons of fish caught. The major catch is anchovies. And the major use of anchovies is, not pizza, but chicken feed. Anchovy meal is the chicken farmer's number one choice for chicken feed. So when the anchovy catch dropped drastically, chicken farmers turned to their second best choice—soybean meal. The result was a large increase in the demand for soybeans, a huge increase in soybean prices, and quick profits for those who understood the two markets and how they interacted.

But, were investments in soybeans really "guaranteed" to earn a profit? In other words, were soybean prices certain to increase? The answer, following the above discussion is, No.

The higher price of anchovy meal caused chicken farmers to switch to the relatively less productive soybean meal. However, the switch to soybean meal did not prevent their costs of production from rising. Before anchovy prices increased, farmers could have chosen the combination of anchovy meal and soybean meal they used after the price of anchovy meal increased, but they did not. Therefore, it can be assumed that the combination used after prices increased led to higher production costs. And higher production costs meant higher prices for chickens, and fewer chickens purchased.

As with apples and oranges, the question is: Will the increased demand for soybeans, due to the substitution effect, be greater than the decrease in demand for soybeans due to fewer chickens being sold? Producers, unlike consumers, are not restricted by income. They can spend more to increase production—and are assumed to do so if the increased production appears profitable. But they cannot dismiss the law of demand that says fewer chickens will be sold at higher prices.

It is easy, using 20/20 hindsight, to see that, in the anchovy-soybean example, the substitution effect, due to a change in relative prices, was greater than the negative effect on the demand for soybeans due to the decrease in the quantity demanded of chickens. It is obvious now, because we know that soybean prices soared. At the time, however, it was not certain how much the demand for soybeans would increase.

Appendix to Chapter 6

An old academic argument, called "indifference curve analysis," is still used to explain the impact on Y due to a change in the price of X, when X and Y are consumer goods. The argument is similar to the above discussion, but it is applicable only to problems with two goods, it is much more complicated, and it is based on two incorrect assumptions.

According to the indifference curve argument:

Two goods can be either substitutes or complements with each other. They are substitutes if one can be used *instead* of the other, such as apples and oranges. They are complements if they are used *together*, such as apples and caramel sauce.

Goods are also classified as either "normal" or "inferior." A normal good is something that consumers buy more of as their incomes increase. Inferior goods are things people buy less of as their incomes increase, such as the least expensive automobiles. The world is filled with both normal and inferior goods.

When the price of apples increases relative to the price of oranges, it is assumed that consumers will want to substitute some oranges for some apples, thereby increasing the demand for oranges. Such a change in the demand for oranges is called the "substitution effect." It is what was used in the "simple" apples and oranges problem above.

Added to the issue of substitute and complementary products is what indifference curve analysis calls the "income effect." The income effect says that if the price of something, such as apples, increases, consumers end up with lower *real* incomes, because if the price of something they buy increases, they cannot buy as much of everything as they did before. The income effect, caused by the higher price of apples, means that consumers will buy less of all "normal goods" and more of all "inferior goods."

Putting all the possibilities together, if the price of one good changes, the change in the demand for another good depends upon whether that good is a substitute or a complement and whether it is a normal or inferior good.

If oranges are a substitute for apples and a normal good, an increase in the price of apples means the substitution effect will cause the demand for oranges to increase while the income effect causes the demand for oranges to decrease. Whether the demand for oranges increases, decreases, or remains the same depends upon the size of the substitution and income effects. If the substitution effect is greater than the income effect, the demand for oranges will increase. If it is less, the demand for oranges will fall. If the substitution effect is exactly equal to the income effect, the demand for oranges will remain unchanged.

If oranges were an inferior good, an increase in the price of apples would definitely lead to an increase in the demand for oranges, because the substitution effect and the income effect would then work in the same direction.

Meanwhile, the demand for complementary products that are normal goods will definitely fall as the price of apples increases. With fewer apples being bought, there is a smaller demand for complementary products and the income effect simply adds to the fall in demand.

The demand for complementary products that are inferior goods is uncertain. If the decrease in demand due to the decline in apple purchases is greater than the increase in demand due to the decline in real income, the demand will decrease. If the income effect is greater, demand will increase. If the effects are equal, demand will stay the same.

One of the incorrect assumptions, which is the result of constructing a theory with only two goods, is that the income effect is always negative. By assuming that an increase in the price of apples reduces the consumer's real income, thereby automatically reducing the demand for all normal goods, the income effect is always working against the substitution effect for substitute products that are normal goods.

More accurately, as shown above, an increase in the price of apples leads to more, less, or the same total spending on apples, which means there is less, more, or the same money available to spend on other goods and services.

The second incorrect assumption is more a matter of logic. Without seeming to be aware of it, indifference curve analysis incorrectly assumes that when the price of one good either increases or decreases, the consumer will begin at the beginning again, deciding how to spend his or her income, given the new prices and the same level of income, rather than taking into account the fact that the consumer is initially spending a given amount of income on each product and that the change in total spending on the good whose price changes is affected by the initial level of consumption, not just by a change in price.

The consumer will definitely be worse off if the price of apples increases, because the consumer initially chose the bundle of goods and services that maximized his or her well-being, given the original prices. If the price of something increases, the consumer will then choose a new bundle of goods and services that will maximize his or her well-being under the new circumstances. But the rule is: If the new bundle could have been purchased under the original prices, but was not, then the new bundle cannot offer as much satisfaction as the original bundle.

However, that is a separate issue from the question of how much money the consumer will have to spend on goods and services, other than apples.

7

Price Floors

You work in a bank, and a farmer comes in to apply for a loan, based on the idea that a new government price support program will increase his profits. Do you give him the loan? Will granting the loan jeopardize your job?

1. A price floor is a minimum price set in a market.

A price "floor" is a price that is set above the market equilibrium price. Its purpose is to raise the price received by producers or sellers. For example, price floors have been used to raise agricultural prices. Price floors are also used to raise wages, such as when a minimum wage sets a lower limit on wages in particular types of employment.

2. Agricultural price supports.

Agricultural price support programs intended to help farmers are examples of price floors. The argument behind such price floors is that farmers cannot earn enough to remain profitable if they have to sell their produce at the going market price. Although it has been argued that it would cost society less to give dollar subsidies to farmers, many believe that farmers do not want to receive "welfare" payments, but prefer to succeed in the marketplace, even if that market has been interfered with by government. Behind such arguments are questions as to whether or not the existing market price is a free-market price or a price that has been artificially lowered because of "unfair" market practices.

Putting such arguments aside, it is clear that a price floor helps some farmers—those able to sell at the higher price. But at a price above the market equilibrium price, buyers are willing and able to buy less while sellers want to sell more than they did at the original equilibrium price. Therefore, the result of the price floor is an excess supply in the market.

The excess supply of farm produce may end up in storage, or it might be plowed under. The only way farmers, in total, can sell as much as they want to sell at the higher price—the price floor—is if the government steps in and purchases whatever cannot be sold to the public. The government can then destroy, store, or sell what it buys, often to foreign markets at low prices, a practice called "dumping."

If the government purchases the surplus, consumers get less produce and pay higher prices, farmers sell more at higher prices (but they sell less to consumers), taxpayers pay for the produce that consumers do not buy (the excess supply the government buys at the higher price) and possibly for storage costs for what the government buys.

3. Using comparative statics to explain the results of a price floor.

The question.

What happens to the equilibrium price and quantity of wheat if the government attempts to help farmers by imposing a minimum price in the market? What happens to the income of farmers? What does such a program cost the government and taxpayers?

(1) The initial equilibrium.

The initial equilibrium is shown by the normal supply and demand curves in Figure 7.1. No information is given that would lead to the assumption of non-normal functions.

The initial equilibrium price is p_1. The initial equilibrium quantity is q_1.

Figure 7.1

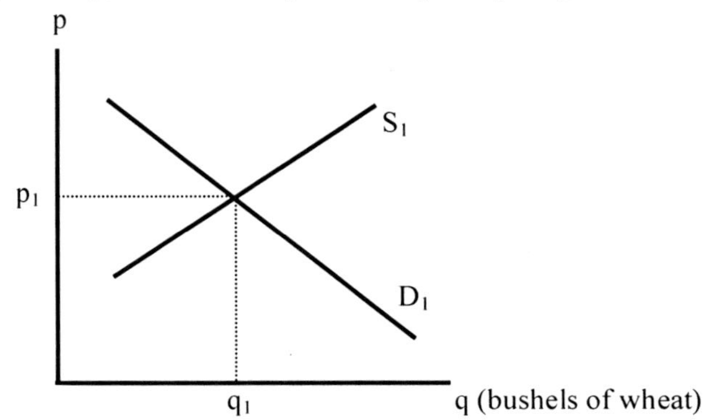

(2) The change.

A "price support" program is an "intentional change introduced by the government. It is a change in something that was assumed to be held constant—the freedom of prices to be determined in the market. The heavy black line in Figure 7.2 shows the government's price floor. It is a horizontal line at p_f, the price-support level.

Figure 7.2

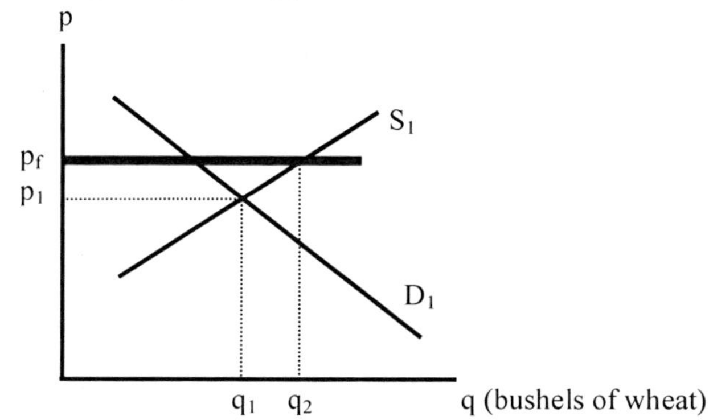

For any quantity less than q_2, the minimum price is now p_f. If the quantity demanded is greater than q_2, the price will be determined by the original supply curve, because it will be above p_f.

There is no reason to believe that setting a minimum price for wheat will have any impact on the demand curve for wheat--the maximum quantity of wheat buyers are willing and able to purchase at various prices. The demand curve is assumed to remain at D_1.

(3) The new equilibrium.

The minimum price set by the government leads to a move up the demand curve, lowering the quantity of wheat demanded from q_1 to q_3. The higher price also leads to an increase in the quantity of wheat supplied, from q_1 to q_2. At a price of p_f, farmers want to produce and sell q_2 bushels of wheat and consumers want to buy q_3 bushels. The result is an excess supply of wheat, equal to q_2 minus q_3 bushels at price p_f.

It is important to note that the change that initiated the problem did not affect the market demand for wheat. It affected the market supply of wheat only. The change in supply resulted in a move along the original demand curve—a change in the quantity demanded—not a change in demand.

Figure 7.3

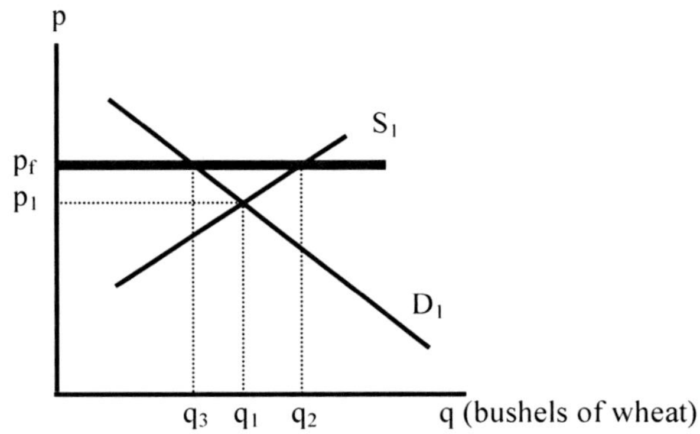

Under normal circumstances, an excess supply causes prices to fall.

However, with a government imposed and enforced price floor, the price cannot fall below p_f, regardless of the fact that producers want to sell more than buyers are willing and able to buy.

Therefore, the excess supply of wheat has no effect on price.

The price set by the government causes farmers to produce q_2 bushels of wheat—the quantity farmers want to sell at a price of p_f. But the government cannot force consumers to buy q_2 bushels of wheat. The result is an overproduction of wheat—meaning that farmers produce wheat that cannot be sold in the market.

If farmers produce q_2 bushels of wheat while selling only q_3 bushels, and the price cannot fall, there will be an excess supply of wheat on the market each year. The price will remain at p_f; the quantity purchased will be q_3; the quantity produced will be q_2.

What happens to the excess supply? Some farmers may pay to store it, hoping to sell it later. Some may dump what they cannot sell. Some might try to sell their wheat illegally, at prices below the price support level, but it is unlikely that much could be sold under such circumstances.

The new market equilibrium is at p_f, q_2, and q_3. It is an equilibrium with an ongoing excess supply of wheat. The new equilibrium quantity demanded, determined by the minimum price set by the government, p_f, and the demand curve D_1, is at the quantity q_3. The new equilibrium quantity supplied, determined by the minimum price set by the government, p_f, and the supply curve S_1, is at the quantity q_2. Farmers are producing q_2 bushels and consumers are buying q_3 bushels. The excess supply, $q_2 - q_3$, is stored or dumped.

In the new equilibrium:

The price paid by consumers increased from p_1 to p_f.

The quantity of wheat bought by consumers decreased from q_1 to q_3.

The price received by some farmers increased from p_1 to p_f.

The quantity of wheat produced increased from q_1 to q_2.

Some farmers are not selling any wheat, even though they are producing more because of the higher price set by the government.

The total revenue to farmers changed from p_1 times q_1 to p_f times q_3. The result could be an increase, decrease, or no change in the revenue collected by farmers, in total (depending upon where p_1 and p_f are on the demand curve).

Conclusion:

The disequilibrium created by the government price support program helped some while hurting others.

Farmers able to sell their wheat at the price support level are better off than they were before. Farmers producing more wheat, because the government raised the price, but who are unable to sell it, are losers. They are worse off than they were before because they are producing wheat and selling nothing. Consumers are worse off because they pay a higher price and receive less wheat.

It is unlikely the government will leave the market in such a state.

However, the government's solution to "correcting" the problem it created with a price support policy imposes additional costs on taxpayers.

One solution is for the government to purchase the excess supply of produce (q_2-q_3) from farmers at the price support level, pf. The produce is then destroyed, stored, or sold to foreign countries at low prices.

If it is destroyed, taxpayers pay the bill for buying the excess supply, which is equal to p_f (q_2-q_3) plus the cost of destruction.

If it is stored, taxpayers pay the bill for buying the excess supply, which is equal to p_f (q_2-q_3) plus the cost of storage.

If it is sold abroad, taxpayers pay the bill for buying the excess supply, which is equal to p_f (q_2-q_3) plus the cost of selling it. In return, the government receives some revenue from its sales.

All told, price supports are a relatively expensive way to increase the incomes of farmers. And if the government does not purchase the surplus, some farmers actually lose.

The question is: Can you, as a banker, explain the price support program to the farmer asking for a loan?

4. Alternatives to price floors.

Rather than using price floors to aid farmers, the government can:

(1) Pay some farmers to not produce.

In Figure 7.4, the government could raise the price of wheat received by farmers to p_f (the price support level) by paying farmers to cut total production from q_1 to q_3. (q_3 is the quantity that will yield a price of p_f.)

Under such a program, which was relatively common in the past, the price received by farmers selling wheat is the same as the price-support level above. Farmers not growing wheat are paid enough so that they freely choose to not produce. Consumers still lose because they receive less wheat and pay a higher price—the same as under the price support program. But there is no surplus to deal with. And the cost to taxpayers is less.

Figure 7.4

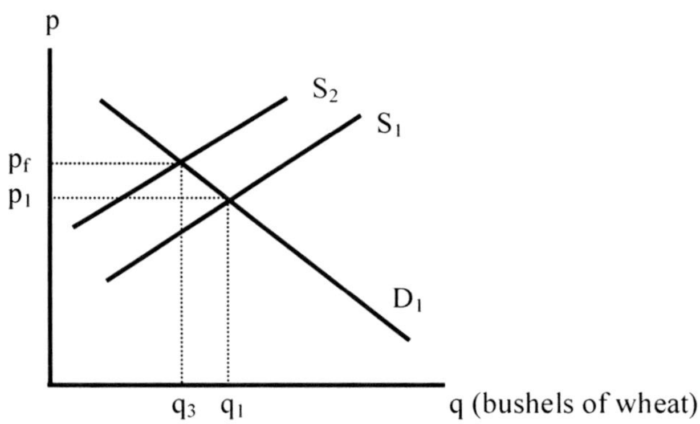

(2) Give farmers an income subsidy.

In Figure 7.5, the government gives farmers an income subsidy. The market is left to reach an equilibrium at p_1, q_1. Then, farmers are given an income subsidy equal to the rectangle $q_1(p_f - p_1)$, which is also the cost to taxpayers.

With an income-subsidy program, consumers are not hurt; they still end up with q_1 bushels at a price of p_1. Farmers produce the equilibrium quantity q_1, but receive a total income based upon a price of p_f per bushel. There is no surplus to store or dump, so the cost to taxpayers is the rectangle $q_1(p_f - p_1)$.

Figure 7.5

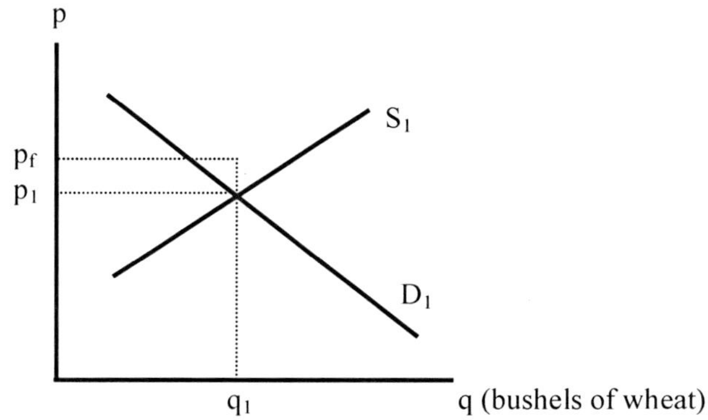

Under most circumstances, a price or income subsidy is a more efficient method of increasing the incomes of farmers than a price support program.

5. *Union wages.*

What happens if an industry is unionized and the union is able to negotiate a contract that establishes a higher wage for union workers?

The question.

What happens to wages and employment of union workers if a contract is negotiated that sets a higher-than-equilibrium wage for union workers.

(1) The initial equilibrium.

The initial equilibrium is shown by the normal supply and demand curves, S_1 and D_1, in Figure 7.6. No information is given that would lead to the assumption of non-normal functions. The initial equilibrium wage is w_1. The initial equilibrium quantity of labor employed is L_1.

Figure 7.6

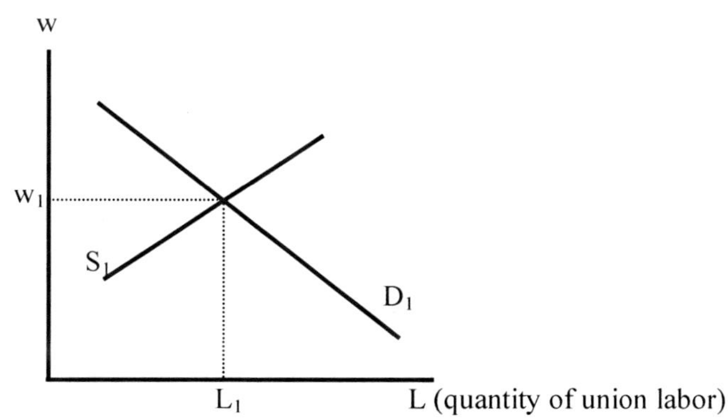

(2) The change.

This is an intentional change made by the union in an attempt to help union workers.

The union contract sets a wage above the equilibrium level. It means that the supply of labor is now the heavy, dashed black line in Figure 7.7 that begins at w_u on the wage axis and is horizontal until it reaches the original supply curve. It then follows the original supply curve, showing that if demand were great enough, the wage rate would be above the negotiated wage.

The demand for labor remains at D_1.

Figure 7.7

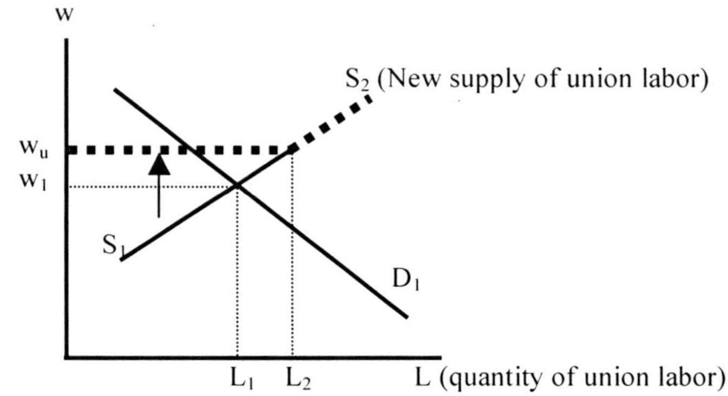

(3) The new equilibrium.

The higher wage negotiated by the union leads to an increase in the quantity of labor supplied, from L_1 to L_2; at wage w_u, there are L_2 units of labor wanting to work. The wage negotiated by the union also leads to a move up the demand curve, lowering the quantity of union labor demanded from L_1 to L_3.

Given the original demand curve, D_1, and the new supply curve, S_2, there is an excess supply of labor equal to L_2 - L_3 at the new union wage, because at w_u, firms are willing and able to hire only L_3 units of labor, while workers now want to sell L_2 units. The result is a disequilibrium, with supply greater than demand.

Figure 7.8

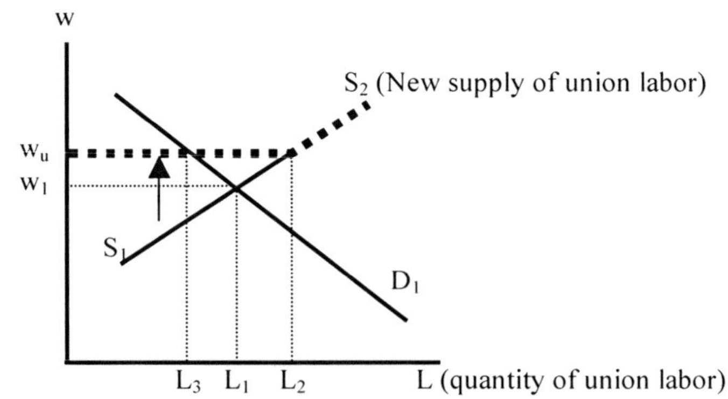

The disequilibrium—the excess supply of labor—puts downward pressure on wages.

Under normal circumstances, an excess supply would cause prices to fall.

However, with a union imposed and enforced minimum wage rate, the wage cannot fall below w_u, regardless of the fact that workers want to provide more labor than firms are willing and able to hire at w_u. Without the labor contract, the excess supply of labor, L_2 minus L_3, would cause wages to fall. With the contract, wages cannot fall, and the equilibrium remains at w_u and L_3.

In the new equilibrium:

The wage received by employed union workers is higher.

The quantity of union labor employed is lower.

The total revenue to union workers changed from L_1 times w_1 to L_3 times w_u. The result could be an increase, decrease, or no change in the total wages paid to all employed union workers. The change in total wages depends upon where the market wage and union wage are on the demand curve. As in previous chapters, if the points are on the bottom half of the demand curve, the total wages paid to union workers will increase. If the points are on the upper half, the total will decline as a result of the union wage.

Conclusion:

The union contract, with a wage set above the equilibrium wage rate, creates an excess supply of labor at the union wage rate and reduces the total employment of union labor.

The union contract helped some while hurting others.

Union workers who are employed win.

The ones that are hurt are those who lose their jobs so that others can gain.

What happens to the excess supply of labor? Some formerly employed union workers may remain unemployed; others may find work elsewhere, but will most likely not be paid as much as the new union wage, possibly not as much as the original equilibrium wage.

If the loss of union jobs is significant, the unemployed union workers looking for work elsewhere, thereby increasing the supply of non-union labor, will lead to a decrease in the wages of non-union workers.

8

Price Ceilings

You are a consultant asked by members of a city government if they should pass a rent-control law.

The purpose of the price "ceiling," is to lower rents by setting maximum rents below the market equilibrium price.

Also important to members of the city council is the political benefit of such a policy. The council members want to know if rent control will help renters and, as a result, help them in the next election.

As such, your answer may affect future consulting jobs.

1. Using comparative statics to explain a price ceiling.

The question.

If government sets and enforces a ceiling on rents: What happens to real rents and the availability of rental units? Will it help renters? Who might lose?

(1) The initial equilibrium.

The initial equilibrium is shown by the normal supply and demand curves in Figure 8.1.

The supply of rental units slopes upward. It is sometimes argued that the supply of rental units should be shown as a vertical line, because there are a fixed number of rental units available at any given time. In most cases, however, the quantity of units offered for rent will vary with the rental price, especially when considering rooms or apartments in private homes.

In Figure 8.1, the initial equilibrium rent is R_1. The initial equilibrium quantity of units rented is H_1.

Figure 8.1

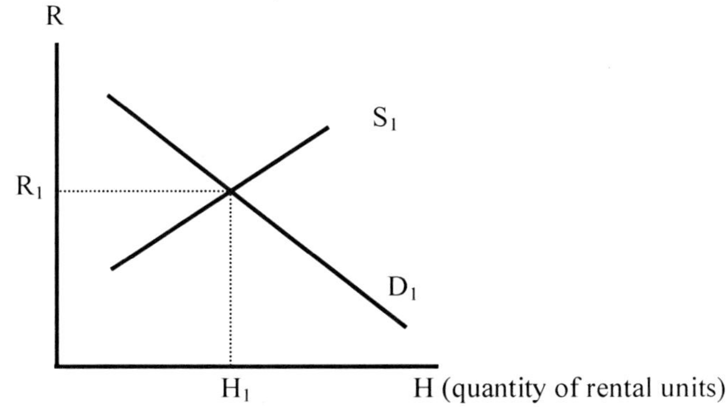

(2) The change.

The rent-control policy sets rents below the equilibrium level, as shown by the horizontal line at R_c in Figure 8.2. The policy means that owners cannot legally charge renters more than R_c. But there is no reason to believe, at least initially, that setting a maximum rental price will have any impact on the supply curve or the demand curve for rental units. The supply of rental units remains at S_1. The demand for rental units remains at D_1, because rent control does not alter what renters are willing and able to pay for rental units, only what they can legally be charged (or pay).

Figure 8.2

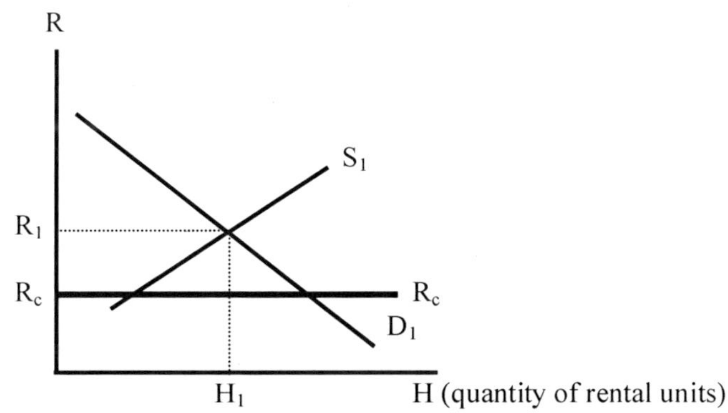

(3) The new equilibrium.

The rent-controlled price, R_c, causes a move down the original supply curve, lowering the quantity of rental units offered for rent from H_1 to H_2. It also causes a move down the demand curve, increasing the quantity of rental units demanded from H_1 to H_3. The result is an excess demand for rental units. At the rent-control price, R_c: The quantity of rental units supplied is H_2. The quantity of rental units demanded is H_3. And the difference, $H_3 - H_2$, is the excess demand for rental units.

The excess demand for rental units puts upward pressure on rents. Without rent control, the excess demand for rental units would lead to an increase in rents and rental units supplied, returning the market to R_1 and H_1. With rent control, rents cannot legally be raised and the market cannot return to its original equilibrium. However, rents will not remain at R_c. With only H_2 units offered for rent, renters are willing and able, according to the demand curve, to pay rents equal to R_2, which is above R_c.

Figure 8.3

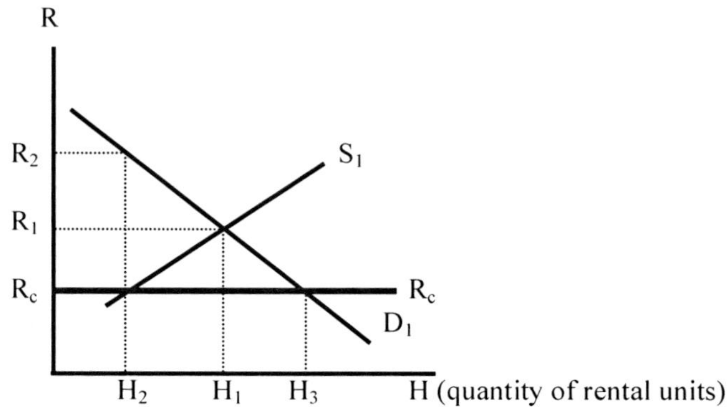

How can it happen that rents will increase to R_2? It happens because the available units (H_2) will be rationed or rented on a "black market." The price that renters can legally pay may be R_c. But the price they actually pay is R_2, the price on the demand curve corresponding to H_2 units offered for rent.

Therefore, in the new equilibrium:

The quantity of rental units offered on the market, and actually rented, fell from H_1 to H_2.

The legal rent collected by owners of rental units fell from R_1 to R_c.

The rent actually paid by renters increased from R_1 to R_2.

The difference—R_2 minus Rc—is what renters pay to obtain rental units, possibly as "bribes" to property managers, or as costs incurred in waiting. Or it may be the costs associated with moving away to find other housing.

A number of renters are without rental space.

Conclusion:

Owners of rental units lose, because they receive lower rents.

In response to lower rents, owners may allow properties to deteriorate rather than spend money on necessary maintenance. If that happens, the supply of rental units will decrease over time; meaning that the supply curve will move to the left. As supply decreases, real rents increase even more.

Renters able to rent units at the rent-controlled price win—if they do not have to bribe someone to obtain their space.

Renters able to rent units at the rent-controlled price—but who end up bribing someone to obtain their space—pay more than they did before rent control.

Renters unable to find rental spaces lose.

Property managers may win if they can collect bribes from renters.

The question is: What do you tell the city council?

Here is what you know: A price ceiling does help some renters—those able to rent at the lower-than-equilibrium price. But setting a price below the equilibrium price leads to an excess demand for rental units. Even more important is the fact that at a price below the market equilibrium price, owners of rental units are willing and able to offer fewer units than they did at the original equilibrium price.

And if it is illegal to raise rents in response to the excess demand, a type of "black market" is created. With a smaller number of units available, compared to the quantity in the original equilibrium, some people are willing and able to pay even more than the original market price. But because rents cannot legally be raised above the price ceiling, the excess demand may lead to payoffs to managers that raise the actual "rent" paid above the old market price.

Other costs that raise the actual cost of renting include the cost of waiting to find a unit and the possibility of moving away to find available space, which then add to the cost of commuting. An additional cost to society is the deterioration of rental units. At a lower than equilibrium price, owners are less likely to pay for needed upkeep.

9

Some Tax Issues

1. Governments impose taxes for various reasons.

The main reason for taxes is to raise revenue to pay for government expenditures. But taxes are also used to discourage "harmful" activities, such as smoking or drinking, or to force individuals or firms to be responsible for the external costs of their actions, which is one reason for imposing taxes on activities that cause pollution. And some taxes are levied to pay for specific projects, such as tolls to pay for bridges or taxes on gasoline used to build or repair roads.

When governments tax people or firms to obtain money to spend, the government is, in effect, taking resources away from the private sector and transferring them to the public sector. Taking money away from people through taxes means people are able to buy less than they could if they had their entire income to spend themselves. As such, instead of letting individuals use resources to satisfy private wants, the government uses some of them to satisfy public wants.

Some common questions are:

What right does the government have to take resources away from private use and putting them into public use?

What is a fair way to tax people?

2. What right does the government have to take resources away from private use and put them into public use?

Some believe that the best government is no government; that whatever the government does can be done better by the private sector. Although it is easy to find examples of government waste and mismanagement, it is not true that the "free market" is best at handling all resource use, or that everything the government does in non-productive. Even those who believe in minimizing government expenditures will almost always agree that the United States must have a strong national defense, which was, until recently, the federal government's major expense.

Whether it is national defense or other *public goods*, many valuable things cannot be provided in sufficient quantity or quality by the free market. Education is one example. Others are roads, bridges, parks, police and fire protection. The list is lengthy. However, the length of such a list does not mean that whatever government does is justified. That is why it is necessary to decide, on rational grounds, whether or not government should take on certain tasks and to determine the size of government programs or projects.

In theory, the use of resources should be handled in a way that attempts to maximize the wealth or wellbeing of the nation. If that is to happen, we will have to take account of the value to the people of public goods as well as private goods, of things not traded in the market, such as common property resources, and of things with no obvious or easily determined dollar value, such as air quality.

3. What is a fair tax?

Deciding what is and is not fair almost always boils down to personal opinion (or personal gain). The reason it is personal is that no absolute standard of fairness exists.

Some think it is fair for those who earn more to be taxed more; not just more in dollar terms, but more as a percentage of income paid in taxes.

Others think it is fair to tax everyone equally, so that everyone who is taxed pays the same percentage of their income in taxes.

Although few think it is fair to tax those more who earn less, such taxes, called regressive taxes, are common.

Even though it is impossible to state what is or is not fair, it is possible to classify taxes according to who pays a larger or smaller percentage of their income to the tax.

Progressive taxes are taxes that take a greater percentage of income as income increases. The federal income tax is considered to be progressive. As income increases, the marginal tax rates on income go up. Therefore, those with higher incomes pay a larger percentage of their incomes to federal income taxes. The same is true for corporate income taxes. State income taxes are also somewhat progressive when they are calculated as a percentage of federal taxes.

Proportional taxes are taxes that take the same percentage of income from all taxpayers. Federal payroll taxes are considered to be proportional taxes.

Regressive taxes are taxes that take a smaller percentage of income as income increases. Federal excise taxes, which are taxes on specific items, and state or local sales taxes, which are taxes on a broad range of spending, are regressive taxes. They take a larger percentage of income from those with lower incomes because those with higher incomes spend a smaller percentage of their income on taxable items.

Taxes that are not as easy to categorize as a percentage of income are property taxes and use taxes.

Property taxes are a significant source of revenue for local governments. But the way property taxes are calculated varies greatly. In California, property taxes are a percentage of the purchase price of a house, which means two people with houses that have the same *current* market value will pay different property taxes if they paid different prices for their houses. In most cases, property taxes are a percentage of *current* market value, although the ways of calculating market value can vary greatly.

Use taxes, which are taxes on those using a particular thing, are normally independent of income. The Newport Bridge in Rhode Island was paid for quickly by collecting tolls. The tolls, which still exist, are paid by those who use the bridge that connects Jamestown to Newport. But should businesses or individuals in Newport also pay for the bridge, even if they do not use it? Many businesses and workers in Newport profit from the increased number of visitors, because the number of visitors is no longer limited to those who were able to take the old ferry from Jamestown. Few situations exist where the actual users are the only ones to benefit. Therefore, it is often difficult to tie taxes to a particular expenditure. For example, how could taxes needed to pay for national defense be levied if such taxes were assessed according to use? How would each person's use or benefit from national defense be calculated?

Value added taxes are taxes placed on each stage of production. A piece of plywood would have taxes paid by a lumbering company, a lumber mill, the producer, and a lumberyard or retailer. The value added tax (VAT) is used in many countries and is often brought into tax discussions in the U.S. It has the advantage of being a relatively efficient tax, in that it does not distort relative prices the way some other taxes do and, because it is a tax on consumption rather than income, it may encourage saving. The disadvantage is that it is, in fact, a sales tax. And like any other sales tax, it is regressive; it takes a greater percentage of income from those with lower incomes than those with higher incomes. Therefore, it is not surprising that the major supporters of a value added tax are normally those with higher incomes who, if it replaced an income tax, would benefit the most.

4. Efficiency.

Although individuals and politicians tend to worry about the size and fairness of taxes, economists worry, as well, about how taxes affect economic efficiency.

Assuming that economic efficiency leads to maximizing the nation's wealth, because economic efficiency means resources are used where they are valued the most, it should be obvious that taxes can negatively impact the efficient use of resources.

One of the arguments behind the "supply side" tax cuts of the Reagan administration was that high marginal tax rates discouraged people from working up to their true potential. It was argued by President Reagan's economic advisors that reducing the highest marginal tax rates would spark an economic surge. Although the highest marginal tax rate was dropped from 50% to 28%, the idea remains an unproven theory.

What is known for certain is that taxes affect relative prices, real returns on various investments, and decisions concerning how to use resources over time. Over the years, economists and others have tried to devise taxes that would cause the least disruption to the use of resources, as determined in the market.

One idea was to tax only land, on the premise that no matter how high the tax is the land cannot be moved. Therefore, a land tax would not alter the use of resources at all. A second part of the argument was that a land tax would be borne mainly by the wealthy—those who own most of the land.

Another idea was to tax only specific items, such as food, where a higher price, due to the tax, would not cause much of a decrease in the quantity bought.

Although such taxes may not cause a major change in resource use, most people do not think they sound fair.

In the end, as is the case with many other economic issues, there is no answer as to what is the "best" or "fairest" or most "efficient" tax. While the discussions and ideas will (and should) continue to flow, the concern facing individuals and decision makers will remain centered on who wins and who loses. Understanding who pays for various taxes allows politicians and voters to make decisions that are in the best interest of society (or their friends).

5. Who pays for taxes?

It seems fairly easy to see who pays for income taxes, estate taxes, and taxes on profits. It is not always as clear to see who pays sales or excise taxes.

An excise tax is set as a percentage of the sale price of an item. The seller of an item that is taxable adds the excise tax to the price of the item. The buyer pays the total bill, including, for example, a 6% tax. A $10 purchase subject to a 6% tax means the buyer pays the seller $10.60. The seller then sends $ .60 to the government.

On the surface, it seems obvious that the buyer pays the excise tax. In reality, the buyer and the seller share the tax because the higher price (the original price plus the excise tax) causes buyers to buy less than they did before the excise tax was imposed. As a result, while the seller and the buyer may believe the tax was passed on to the buyer, the seller cannot always see the difference between how much is sold with and without the tax, and what price is actually received from the buyer.

6. Using comparative statics to explain who pays for an excise tax.

You work for a large retail corporation that is looking for ways to maintain or increase its profits in the midst of a government budget crunch.

At a meeting, you are asked for ideas. You come up with a plan to lobby the state government to increase the state sales tax, instead of increasing taxes that will affect the corporation. Your argument is that a tax levied on sales will not affect corporate profits, because the tax will be passed on to consumers.

At the end of the meeting, you are told to draw up a proposal that can be discussed at the next meeting. Obviously, your proposal is not meant for public release.

If the corporation follows your plan, will you be a hero, or will your job be in jeopardy?

The question.

If an excise or sales tax is imposed on the purchase of certain items, who actually pays the tax? Your boss, based on your recommendation, wants you to explain to the corporate officers how such taxes are passed on to consumers.

(1) The initial equilibrium.

The initial market equilibrium is shown by the normal supply and demand curves, S_1 and D_1, in Figure 9.1. It is assumed that the supply curve slopes upward and the demand curve slopes downward. In Figure 9.1, the initial equilibrium price is p_1. The initial equilibrium quantity is q_1.

Figure 9.1

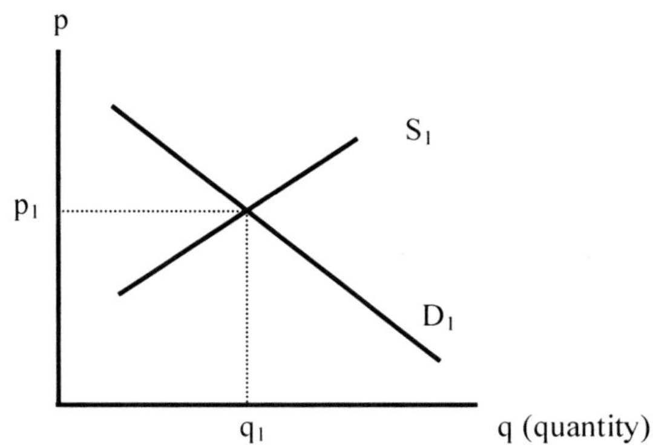

(2) The change.

Imposing a sales or excise tax is an "intentional change" introduced to collect tax revenues, or possibly to discourage certain purchases.

The introduction of an excise tax can be shown as a change in supply. The original supply curve shows the minimum price at which sellers are willing to sell each quantity. If the government requires a tax to be paid on each purchase, it can be assumed that sellers will add the tax to the price. Sellers who were willing to sell quantity q_1 for a price of p_1 are now willing to sell q_1 for p_1 *plus* the tax.

The new supply curve will be above the original supply curve by the amount of the excise tax. In Figure 9.2, the vertical distance between the original supply curve, S_1, and the new supply curve, S_2, is the dollar value of the tax. Demand remains at D_1. The excise tax does not change what buyers are willing and able to pay for each quantity.

Figure 9.2

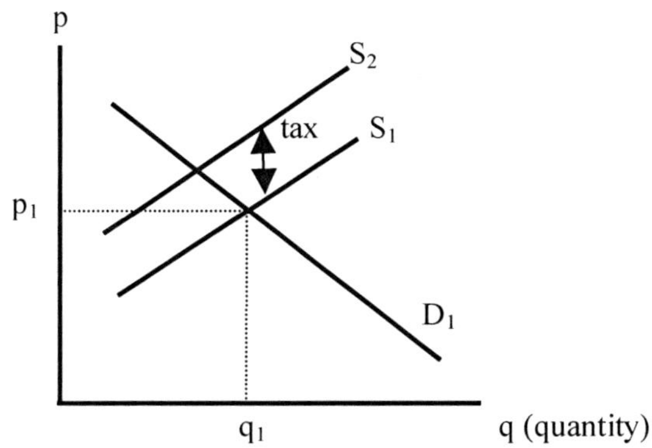

(3) The new equilibrium.

At the original equilibrium quantity, q_1, sellers now want to receive a price of p_2, which is p_1 plus the excise tax. (In this case, the tax is equal to $p_2 - p_1$.) But at price p_2, buyers are willing and able to buy only q_2 units. Therefore, at p_2, there is an excess supply equal to q_1 minus q_2.

Because price is free to move without restraint, the excess supply of the item causes price to fall below p_2. As the price decreases, there is a move down the demand curve. Price continues to fall and the quantity demanded continues to increase from q_2 until a new equilibrium is reached where the original demand curve (D_1) and the new supply curve (S_2) intersect. In Figure 9.3, the new equilibrium is at p_3 and q_3.

Figure 9.3

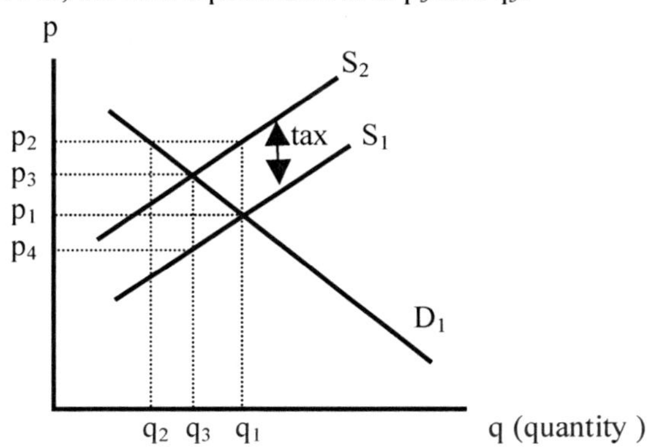

In the new equilibrium:

The new equilibrium quantity is below the original quantity, falling from q_1 to q_3.

The new equilibrium price is above the original price, rising from p_1 to p_3.

The price actually paid by buyers is p_3.

The price actually received by sellers is p_4.

The difference between p_3 and p_4 is the excise tax that goes to the government.

The part of the tax paid by the consumer is p_3 minus p_1.

The part of the tax paid by sellers is p_1 minus p_4.

Conclusion:

Consumers lose because they pay a higher price for a smaller quantity.

Sellers lose because they sell less at a lower price.

Sellers think they passed the entire tax on to consumers because they simply added the tax to their price. The accountant for the seller may also claim that the tax was paid entirely by consumers, because in the new equilibrium, the price paid by consumers is equal to the price received by the seller (p_4) plus the tax (p_3 minus p_4).

But the seller and the accountant are wrong. The buyer and seller share the tax, and each is worse off than before the tax was introduced.

The same logic is used to explain why the buyer and seller share increased costs that many believe are passed on to buyers.

This problem can be also solved by assuming that the excise tax causes a decrease in demand instead of a decrease in supply. The student should be able to show that the answers are identical.

The question is: What do you tell the head of the corporation at the next meeting?

10

Imperfect Competition

You work for the Federal Trade Commission. A manufacturer of medical products is taking actions that will virtually eliminate all competition in the market. The FTC is considering whether or not to allow the actions. A representative from the corporation explains that such a move will be good for society because it will allow the corporation to spend more on research, thereby helping people and the economy. You are ordered to prepare a case for the FTC. Obviously, you have a lot of work to do to explain the repercussions of a move that will monopolize an industry.

1. Some definitions.

Although a large part of economic study is concerned with the idea of perfect competition, a large part of the world consists of markets that do not meet the definition of perfect or pure competition.

Monopoly is one example. A monopoly is normally defined to be a market with a single firm. An example is a local utility company that is the only provider of electricity or natural gas.

Monopolistic competition is another case where the conditions of perfect competition do not exist. Monopolistic competition is defined as an industry made up of a small number of competing firms, where the products are similar but not identical, and where each firm faces a downward sloping demand curve. An example is the soft-drink industry.

Oligopoly is defined as an industry made up of a few dominant firms where the individual firms have the ability to make agreements to restrict industry output in order to raise the market price. The most publicized example of such a market, often called a cartel, is OPEC (the Organization of Petroleum Exporting Countries) that periodically restricts oil production and raises oil prices.

Anti-trust laws, many of which were first implemented under President Theodore Roosevelt (who was known as "the trust buster"), are sometimes enforced to limit the dominance of corporations determined to have too much market power.

On an economic level, the concerns also include: (1) What happens to the equilibrium price and quantity in a market, and to the allocation of resources in general, as a result of imperfect competition? (2) If a lack of perfect competition does cause a misallocation of resources, what can be done to correct the problem?

2. The case of the single-firm monopoly.

***The question*:**

What happens to price, quantity, and resource allocation if a single firm takes over a competitive market?

(1) The initial equilibrium.

Figure 10.1, shows a competitive market with normal demand and supply curves. The equilibrium price is p_1. The equilibrium quantity is q_1. Given the assumptions about perfect competition, it is assumed that the supply curve, which is the horizontal summation of the marginal cost curves of all the individual firms in the industry, represents the marginal cost to society of providing the good or service. It is also assumed that the demand curve represents the marginal benefits to society of obtaining the good or service. Therefore, the free market equilibrium equates the marginal costs of providing the good or service with the marginal benefits form consuming it. As such, the free market equilibrium is considered to be economically efficient, meaning that resources are used where they are valued the most.

Figure 10.1

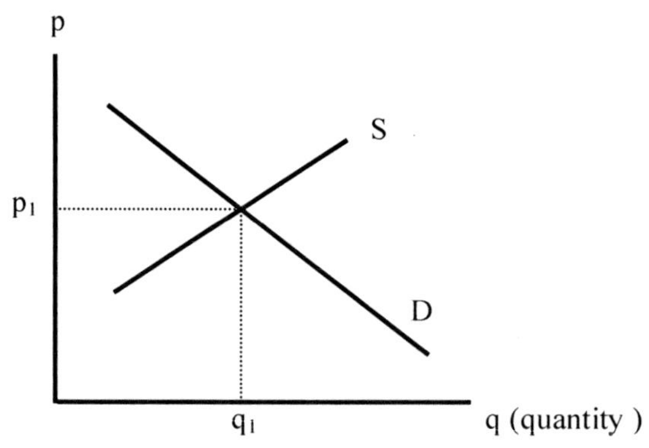

(2) The change.

The change that occurs when a monopolist takes over a competitive industry is straightforward, but not as precise as everyone might like, and it is based on a number of assumptions. The assumptions are:

(1) The competitive industry's supply curve, which is assumed to be equal to the sum of the marginal cost curves of the individual firms in the competitive industry, becomes the monopolist's marginal cost curve.

(2) When a single firm takes over a competitive industry, the market demand curve becomes the demand curve faced by the monopoly.

(3) The condition for maximizing profits is always the same. It is to produce that quantity where marginal revenue is equal to marginal cost.

The reason for making the first two assumptions is not that either is believed to be true, but to allow an easy comparison between the equilibrium of a perfectly competitive market and that of a monopoly. The reason for the third assumption is that it is always assumed that firms, either firms in a competitive industry, a single-firm monopolist, or one of the few firms in an oligopoly, will make decisions intended to maximize profits.

Figure 10.2 shows the first two assumptions listed above:

(1) The curve labeled S = MC was the competitive industry's supply curve and is now the monopolist's marginal cost curve.

(2) The curve labeled D = AR was the competitive industry's demand curve and average revenue curve; it is also the monopolist's demand curve and average revenue curve.

Figure 10.2

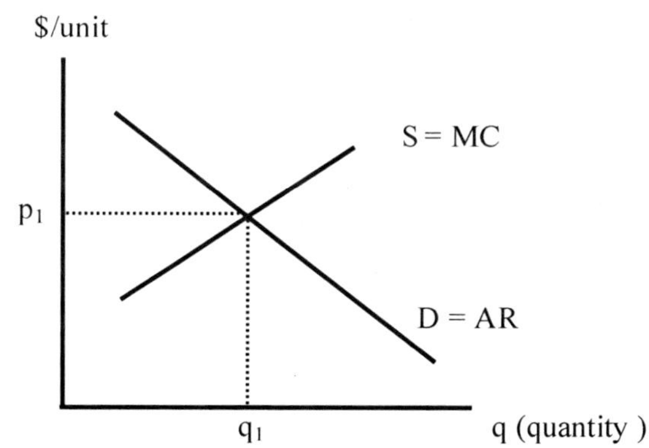

Although the demand curve is unchanged if a monopoly takes over the industry, its relationship to the profit-maximizing rule must be defined more carefully.

In any market where a good or service is sold at a single price, demand is also, by definition, equal to "average revenue." Average revenue is total revenue divided by the quantity sold, which is, in fact, the same as the price if all units are sold at the same price.

The market demand curve is not equal to average revenue if sellers are able to charge different prices to different buyers, such as when a movie theater charges different admissions to different age groups.

(3) The new equilibrium.

After marginal revenue has been determined, the new equilibrium created by the monopolist can be shown.

In Figure 10.3, the equilibrium for a competitive industry, given the demand curve D, and with each profit-maximizing firm choosing to produce an output where MR=MC, is at q_1 with a market price of p_1. It is where supply equals demand.

The profit maximizing output for the monopolist, also producing where MR=MC, is at q_2. And, at an output of q_2, the market price for the monopolist, read off the demand curve, is p_2.

Figure 10.3

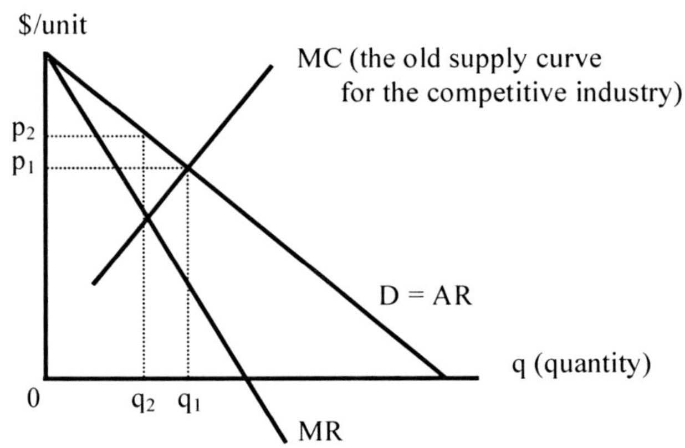

The result of monopoly is that output is restricted and the price increases. The objective of the monopolist is not to restrict output, but simply to maximize profits. Just as a competitive firm has to find the output where MR = MC, so must the monopolist.

It is important to recognize, however, that a monopolist is not guaranteed to earn a profit. A monopolist may earn a positive profit, a zero profit, or a negative profit. The process of determining the profit or loss for a monopolist is to first use the MR=MC rule to determine the profit maximizing output. Given that output, use the demand curve to find the price per unit the monopolist will receive. Then look at the difference between the price (which is also, by definition, average revenue) and the average total cost of producing that quantity (ATC). If price is above ATC, profit will be positive. If price is below ATC, profit will be negative (a loss). If price=ATC, profit will be zero. The average total cost curve is not shown in Figure 10.4. (See the Appendix to this chapter.)

***Conclusion*:**

The competitive market equilibrium is assumed to be "efficient," because it is an equilibrium where the value of the product to society is equal to what it costs society to provide it. The question is: Will a monopolist do something to change the equilibrium, and if so, why? The answer is: Yes, a monopolist will change the equilibrium. The reason is that a monopolist, like a competitive firm, attempts to maximize profit, which is the third assumption listed above.

And, as was also stated above, the rule for maximizing profits is the same for a monopolist as it is for a competitive firm: Produce that quantity where marginal revenue equals marginal cost.

The question is: What action does your report to the FTC recommend?

***Recommendations*:**

The problem with monopolies is not that they earn a monopoly profit. A monopoly may not earn a profit at all, and may, in fact, suffer losses. The "inefficient" thing about monopolies is that by trying to maximize profits, just as any firm does, output is less and price is higher than they would be under perfect competition. As a result, resources are not used in a way that maximizes the satisfaction or wellbeing of society. The conclusion is that a monopoly reduces the wealth of the nation by producing where marginal social benefits are greater than marginal social costs. In other words, forcing a monopolist to expand its output would add more to society's benefits than to society's costs.

Regulating a monopoly is an attempt to remove its negative impact on the allocation of resources.

One form of regulation is to **set a maximum price** the monopolist can charge. If the monopolist has to sell at a set price, then that price becomes the demand, average revenue, and marginal revenue to the monopolist. When the monopolist looks for the profit maximizing quantity to produce, by equating MR and MC, it will choose the output where MC equals the set price (because the set price is MR).

If the price is set at p_1 in Figure 10.3, which is where MC=D, the monopolist will produce the same output and sell it at the same price as if the market were a competitive industry. Depending upon costs, the monopolist may or may not earn a profit at the set price. In terms of society, the regulation increases the nation's wealth because it forces the industry to operate where marginal social benefits equal marginal social costs.

Whether or not the monopolist earns a profit is not the issue, although it may matter if setting a maximum price forces the monopolist to shut down. The issue is to reallocate resources so that the equilibrium price and output are where the value consumers receive from the product (D) equals what it costs to produce it (MC or S).

Taxes are sometimes suggested as a solution to the monopoly problem; either a tax on each unit sold or a lump sum tax that is independent of the quantity sold.

Without showing either solution in a diagram, it is possible to explain what each accomplishes.

A tax on each unit sold can be shown by raising the monopolist's marginal cost (MC) and average total cost (ATC) curves and leaving demand (D) and marginal revenue (MR) unchanged. If MR does not change while MC increases, both the profit maximizing output and profits must fall. MC will equal MR at a lower output and ATC will be higher at all levels. Therefore, while the plan reduces monopoly profits (which may be a politically or socially motivated objective), it causes an even worse allocation of resources. It leads to an even smaller output and an even higher price than would occur without such taxes. It also causes an even larger gap between the value consumers receive and what it costs to produce the product.

The same result can be shown by having the per-unit tax lower the demand curve while leaving the cost curves unchanged. If the monopolist must pay a tax per unit, that tax can be shown either as an increase in costs or a decrease in what is actually received from a sale.

A lump sum tax that is independent of output does not change the monopolist's MC, ATC, D, or MR curves. If MR and MC do not change, the profit maximizing output is also unchanged. The only thing that changes is the monopolist's profit. The tax does not affect output or price. Therefore, while the plan reduces monopoly profits (which, again, may be a politically or socially motivated objective), it does not improve the allocation of resources. And it does not change the gap between the value consumers receive and what it costs to produce the product.

Digression on marginal revenue and the profit-maximizing rule.

The profit-maximizing rule is based on simple logic. If a firm increases output by one unit and that additional unit adds more to total revenue than to total cost, profits increase. Therefore, it makes sense to add that unit to production (or sales). The same is true for each additional increase in output that adds more to revenue than costs. On the other hand, any additional unit of output that adds more to costs than to total revenue will decrease profits. Assuming that marginal cost is increasing, and knowing that marginal revenue is decreasing, the firm will add units to output up to the point where marginal revenue equals marginal cost. Up to that point, each additional unit will have added more to revenue than costs. After that point, each additional unit will add more to costs than to revenue.

Marginal revenue is defined as the change in total revenue due to a one-unit change in output.

When a competitive firm changes its output by one unit, it is assumed that the price it receives stays the same, because it is assumed that a firm in a competitive industry has no impact on price, no matter how much or little it produces. Each firm in a competitive industry is assumed to be a "price taker," meaning that it can sell all it wants at the existing market price and nothing at a higher price. When a competitive firm adds one unit to output, its total revenue increases by the price of the good or service it sells. Therefore, by definition, for a competitive firm, price equals marginal revenue.

When a monopolist changes output, the price of the product does change, because a monopolist faces a downward sloping demand curve. The monopolist can sell a greater quantity only if it lowers the price of all units. If it sells less, the price will rise for all units. As a result, marginal revenue (the change in total revenue from a one unit change in output) is not equal to price, as it is for the competitive firm. If a monopoly sells one more unit, the change in total revenue is equal to the new quantity times the new price per unit minus the original quantity times the original price per unit.

In order to understand how a monopolist decides how much to sell, it is necessary to derive the monopolist's marginal revenue curve.

When a single price is charged for all units of output, there is a relatively simple relationship between a demand curve and its corresponding marginal revenue curve.

The relationship between demand and marginal revenue is shown in the figure below. The geometric description of the relationship between demand and marginal revenue is based on the fact that total revenue can be measured two ways:

Total revenue is equal to price times quantity, which, for quantity E, is the area OCBE. (Price is OC and quantity is OE.) Total revenue is also the sum of all the marginal revenues (the addition to total revenue made by each added unit), which is the area OAHE.

Therefore area OAHE equals area OCBE.

Because area OCGHE is part of both OAHE and OCBE, if it is subtracted from each, the remaining areas, ACG and GBH are equal.

Because angle CGA equals angle BGH, and because triangles ACG and GBH are right triangles, HB equals CA.

Therefore, the marginal revenue curve is the line from A that passes through H.

Determination of Marginal Revenue

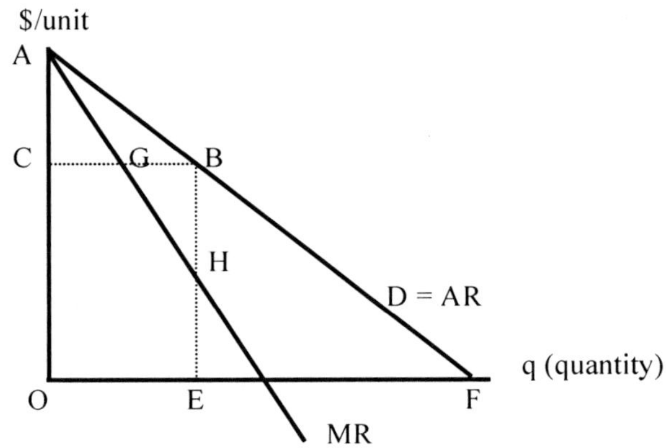

For a straight-line demand curve, such as D in Figure 10.3, because AC equals BH, CG must equal GB.

Therefore, for a straight-line demand curve, the MR curve is drawn from A through a point halfway between the price axis and the demand curve. (The marginal revenue curve bisects the angle OAF.)

3. Monopolistic competition.

Monopolistic competition is different from "normal" competition for two reasons: One is that each firm faces a negatively sloped demand curve. The other is that the firms may earn positive profits. The assumption for perfect competition is that each firm earns no "above normal" profits. If profits are positive in a competitive industry, existing firms will increase output and new firms will enter the market, with each action causing the price of the product to fall and the costs of production to increase. If profits are negative in a competitive industry, existing firms will decrease output and some will leave the market, with each action causing the price of the product to rise and the costs of production to fall.

The assumptions that make monopolistic competition different from perfect competition are that there are some barriers to entry that prohibit new firms from freely entering the market, even if profits in the industry are positive, and there is competition among firms because each is able to create some sort of product differentiation. Examples are toothpaste, soap, clothing, soft drinks, beer, etc.

There are no highly developed logical arguments to explain monopolistic competition. The one thing that can be argued is that competition among monopolistic firms is likely to lead to advertising expenses. Perfectly competitive firms do not have to advertise because it is assumed that each can sell all it wants at the market price and that each sells a product that cannot be differentiated from the others.

As a result, profits for monopolistically competitive firms may be affected by the costs of advertising. An exact explanation is difficult, but it can be argued that the monopolistically competitive firm should deal with advertising the way it deals with other profit-maximizing decisions. It should buy advertising up to the point where its marginal cost is just equal to the marginal revenue it generates.

4. Oligopoly.

Oligopoly is defined as a market with a small enough number of sellers so that the actions of each affect the others. Oligopolistic industries tend to be found where the products are more or less identical, which means that product differentiation is less likely than in monopolistic competition.

The problem with discussing oligopoly is that no matter how important it is in the real world, it has been impossible to develop solid arguments to explain and predict such industries. As a result, the literature is filled with explanations of oligopoly, none of which is seen as a final answer.

One area that can be explained, at least on a surface level, is the cartel. An example of a cartel can be found in the oil producing industry. A cartel is defined as a market arrangement, including some or all of the firms in an industry, intended to regulate or control or limit total production in order to control or raise the market price of the product. Normally, each firm (or country) agrees to a quota covering its output. Then, with each firm (or country) producing less than it would without a cartel agreement, each receives a higher price for its product. OPEC (the Organization of Petroleum Exporting Countries) is the oil cartel that off and on is able to limit the output of oil from its member countries.

If the argument could stop there, it would be a good explanation of at least one type of oligopoly. But it cannot. The problem with cartels is that even if the market price is raised, the profits to any one country or firm may increase, decrease or stay the same, because even though the price is higher, each is selling less than it did before the arrangement.

The result is that each member can gain by cheating. Once the overall quota is established and prices rise, each member can make a greater profit by selling more than its agreed upon part of the quota-- at least that is the case if it is the only cheater. In the end, it is in the interest of the individual firms to form a cartel and it is then in the interest of each to cheat. That is why cartels have, historically, been short-lived enterprises. Assuming that each member makes decisions intended to maximize its own profits, the cartel will disintegrate.

Oligopoly, like monopolistic competition, rests on the assumption that the existing firms in the industry have the power to prevent the entry of new firms. It is an assumption that seldom holds in the real world, partly because every product has a substitute. If not an exact substitute, there is always an alternative place for the consumer to spend money. Oil has substitutes, not the least of which is to consume less as the price increases. From the standpoint of economics, nothing is "necessary," because everything has a substitute.

Appendix to Chapter 10

Figure 10.4 is taken from Figure 10.3. However, the marginal cost curve and the average total cost curve (which was not shown at all in Figure 10.3) are shown as non-linear functions, which is a normal textbook description. The competitive-industry's equilibrium quantity and price are not shown. Only the monopolist's equilibrium price, p_2, and quantity, q_2, are shown. Instead of labeling the MC curve S = MC, it is labeled only MC. The reason is that a monopolist does not have a true supply curve. Every time there is a change in demand, the monopolist looks again for the quantity that will equate marginal revenue and marginal cost. The result is a distinct point for each set of circumstances, not a supply curve that shows the maximum quantity offered for sale at various prices.

Figure 10.4

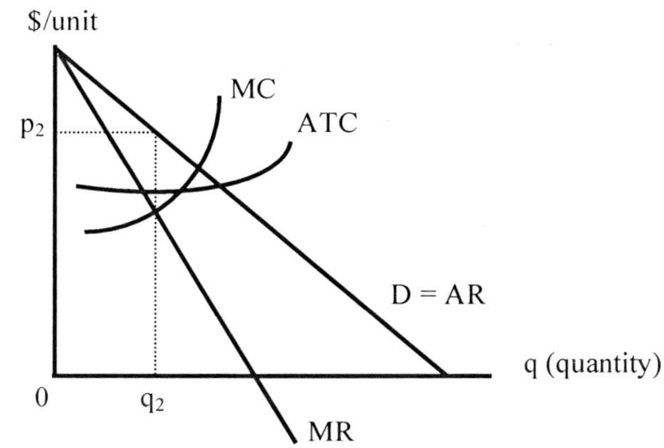

In Figure 10.4, the monopolist is earning a profit because AR (which is p_2) is above ATC at q_2. If the ATC curve were above p_2 at q_2, there would be a loss. If the ATC curve were equal to p_2 at q_2, profits would be zero.

The easiest way to draw a figure representing a monopoly is to first draw a demand curve. Then draw the corresponding marginal revenue curve. Then draw a marginal cost curve that intersects MR and D from below. Then draw a vertical line through the intersection of MC and MR that goes from the quantity axis to the demand curve. (The vertical line's intersection with D gives the price the monopolist will charge.) Then draw a "U" shaped average total cost curve that has its minimum point where it crosses MC; the ATC can be above, below, or equal to the price at the profit maximizing quantity. (It is not possible to draw the curves without knowing ahead of time what you want to show.)

Profits can be found by subtracting ATC from AR (which is the price) and multiplying by the profit maximizing quantity (q_2), or by subtracting total cost (TC = ATC at q_2 times q_2) from total revenue (TR = q_2 times p_2).

> Although the competitive industry's equilibrium price and output are not shown, the student should know that the equilibrium quantity would be determined where MC (which was the competitive industry's supply curve) intersects the demand curve; and that the equilibrium price would be determined by the price corresponding to that point on the demand curve.

11

Legalizing Drugs

You are part of a task force whose directive is to look at ways to reduce the rising drug and crime problems. Someone brings up the idea of legalizing drugs. Other members of the task force point out that it is an idea supported by many economists.

The argument is simple. Legalizing drugs will put pushers out of business. Without pushers, fewer people will be encouraged to take drugs. With fewer addicts, there will be less crime committed to pay for their habits. With less drug-fostered crime, everyone will be safer.

It is an appealing argument—IF the assumptions turn out to be correct. Your job is to put the idea together in a paper.

1. The assumed result of legalizing drugs.

The question.

Will legalizing drugs reduce the drug problem, including concerns with the number of addicts, the cost of crime, and the negative impact on the nation's wealth caused by the misallocation of resources?

(1) The initial equilibrium.

The initial equilibrium can be described using normal supply and demand functions (even though it is an illegal market). In Figure 11.1, the initial equilibrium price for drugs is p_1, the initial equilibrium quantity is q_1.

Figure 11.1

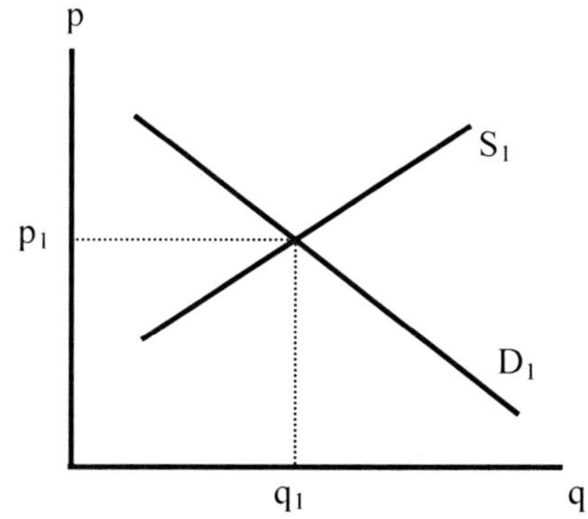

(2) The change.

The common argument for legalizing drugs is that doing so will decrease the demand for drugs. The assumption is that if drugs are legalized, pushers will be put out of business and that pushers are the main reason for creating the demand for drugs. If demand decreases, the new demand curve is D_2 in Figure 11.2.

What about supply? The legalizing-drugs argument often assumes that the supply of drugs will increase—move to the right or down—because the excessive costs of illegal drug production and sales will be replaced with lower-cost legal production. The truth is: It is unclear what will happen to the supply of drugs. It could increase if the above assumption is true. It could decrease (move to the left, or up) if it ends up costing more to provide drugs legally, which could happen if the cost of packaging, retail outlets (which may be more expensive than dealing out of cars), and advertising offset any possible savings. Supply could also remain unchanged if the changes in costs and savings exactly offset each other.

In order to keep the argument simple, it can be assumed, for now, that the supply curve does not change.

Figure 11.2

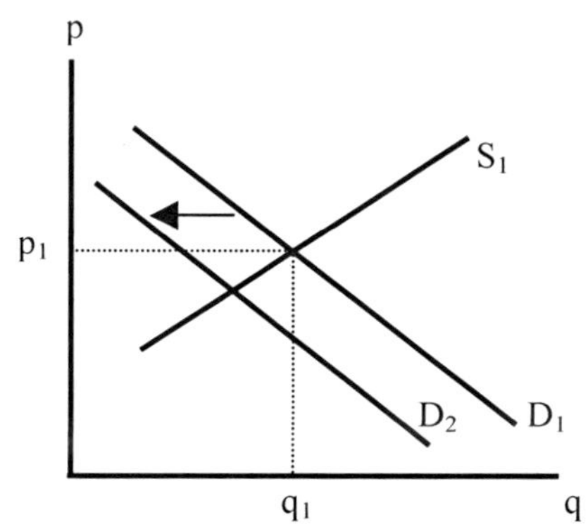

(3) The new equilibrium.

In figure 11.3, the new equilibrium, determined by the new demand curve, D_2, and the original supply curve, S_1, is at the new equilibrium price, p_2, and the new equilibrium quantity, q_2. The equilibrium price of drugs decreased from p_1 to p_2. The equilibrium quantity of drugs decreased from q_1 to q_2.

There are fewer addicts, lower prices for drugs, and, it can be assumed, less drug-related crime. Therefore, legalizing drugs looks like a pretty good idea.

Figure 11.3

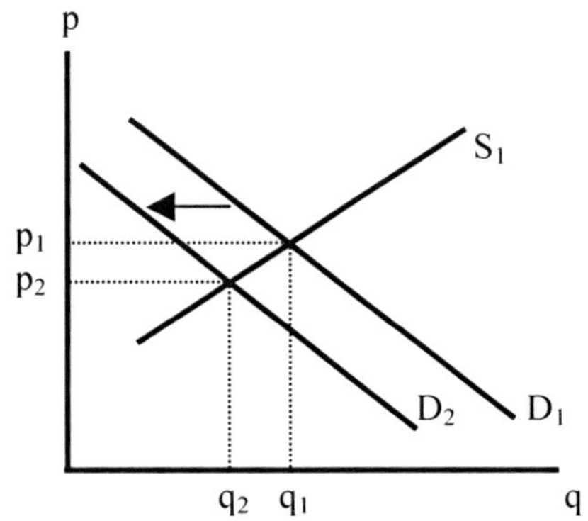

Conclusion.

Before you hand in your paper, there are a few assumptions that should be examined, because if you look a little closer, the assumptions behind the push to legalize drugs are not very good.

The most problematic assumption is that the demand for drugs will decline without pushers. A more likely assumption is that if the legal sellers of drugs are free to advertise their product, the demand for drugs will increase.

Turning drug production and sales over to legal corporations is not likely to lower the costs of drugs. If producers can legally sell drugs for a profit, there will be competition and advertising. As with alcohol and cigarettes, advertising and packaging adds a substantial amount to costs. Then there are the middlemen—wholesalers and retailers—each of whom requires a profit margin and each of whom may have expenses greater than those currently selling drugs out of their cars. Along with adding to costs, advertising, if it is successful, may increase the demand for drugs, as it has done for alcohol and cigarettes. And because drugs, like cigarettes, are addictive, once hooked, the customer is a long-time customer.

The other lesson to be learned from alcohol and cigarettes is that legalizing a "bad" product does not take the "excitement" out of it. As a result, legalizing drugs can increase both the costs of production and the number of users, which will add to, not subtract from, the crime necessary to pay for the goods.

An additional issue, which is seldom raised, is: What would the legal age limit for drugs be? Wherever the age line is drawn, the consequences are virtually certain. The old pushers, driven out of the adult business by legal sales, will turn even more seriously to the child market. In the end, the illegal pushers will still be in business, but they will be focusing on children. And if all the illegal pushers deal only with children, drug use by children could soar.

Legalizing drugs has always relied on simplifying the argument. As such, it is a good example of Saul Wurman's observation that "Simplification has led to the dumbing of America."

Figure 11.4 shows another possible equilibrium, where, because of an increase in demand, both drug use and drug prices increase after drugs are legalized.

Figure 11.4

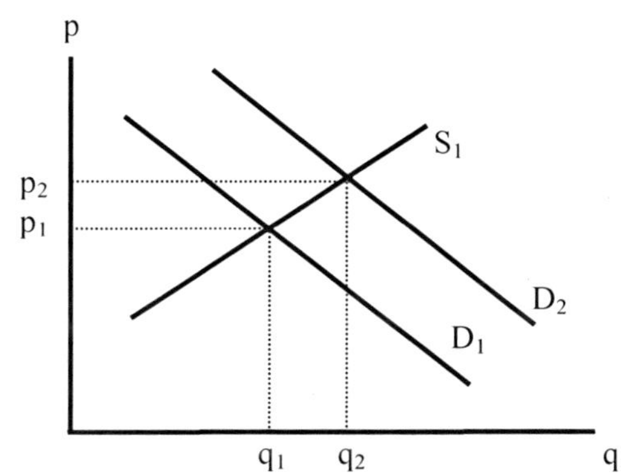

Conclusions are always dependent on the assumptions that were made regarding the changes in demand and supply. In the case of legalizing drugs, if demand increases and supply remains the same, then drug use will increase and crime caused by drug addicts, doing whatever is necessary to raise money to buy drugs, will increase as well.

Therefore, before jumping to the conclusion that legalizing drugs will reduce the drug problem, the following questions must be answered.

(1) Are pushers the true reason for creating a demand for drugs? Or would some people use drugs even without pushers?

(2) Will the demand for drugs decrease if drugs are made legal? Or will legal sellers advertise, thereby increasing the demand for drugs, which was and is the case for alcohol from the time prohibition ended.

(3) Will supply increase, decrease, or remain the same? Will the removal of costly and illegal methods of drug delivery cause supply to move to the right? Or is legal delivery even more expensive?

(4) What about children? Where would the age cutoff be set? And would legalizing drugs cause pushers to focus more on children?

This problem is a good example of how, depending upon the assumptions made, it is possible to reach almost any conclusion or predict any outcome.

If demand increases and supply increases, the quantity of drugs used will increase, and the price will increase, decrease, or remain the same, depending upon the relative sizes of the changes in demand and supply.

If demand decreases and supply increases, the quantity of drugs used will increase, decrease, or remain the same, depending upon the relative sizes of the changes in demand and supply, and the price will definitely decrease.

If demand increases and supply decreases, the quantity of drugs used will increase, decrease, or remain the same, depending upon the relative sizes of the changes in demand and supply, and the price will definitely increase.

If demand decreases and supply decreases, the quantity of drugs used will decrease, and the price can increase, decrease, or remain the same, depending upon the relative sizes of the changes in demand and supply.

Will people be less likely to be victims of crime if the price of drugs falls, because drug addicts would not have to get as much money to pay for their habit? It is not clear. Each addict would need less money to buy drugs at a lower price, but if there are more addicts, total crime may increase. As long as the price is above zero, addicts would still have to find money somewhere to buy drugs. Even if the price were zero, there could be a greater number of addicts who, although they do not have to steal to pay for drugs, may still have to steal to live.

Therefore, what is the expected result of legalizing drugs?

Anyone who claims to know should be asked a lot of questions.

First, of course, is: What is the objective of legalizing drugs? Is it to reduce drug use? To reduce crime? Or to give the profits now made by pushers to legal businessmen? Maybe most important: What is likely to happen to the effort to sell drugs to children?

Then there are the assumptions. Is it true, as is often assumed, that the spread of drugs is due to pushers' attempts to make money? If pushers create the market, then the demand for drugs could decrease if drugs were legalized. On the other hand, if more people decided to use drugs once they were legalized, then the demand might increase. Legalizing alcohol did not eliminate the use and abuse of alcohol.

The legalizing-drugs issue is an excellent example of why all explanations and predictions are conditional. It shows clearly how explanations and predictions are tied to the assumptions that are made when setting up a problem.

NOTE:

The discussion in this chapter assumed that legalizing drugs meant that drugs would be treated like alcohol or tobacco. There are other possible meanings to the idea of legalizing drugs, such as decriminalizing use, but not production and sales. Under that assumption, the above analysis would change. The discussion would then begin by deciding how decriminalizing only the use of drugs would affect the demand and/or supply of drugs.

12

Negative Externalities

You run a large mutual fund, which means that you have to make decisions every day that are dependent upon expectations of the future health of the nation's economy. The federal government is considering a policy that will impose taxes on polluters. The purpose of the policy is to protect people from the harmful effects of chemicals dumped into the air, water, or ground. Many businesses, as well as a number of mutual funds managers, are upset. All see a tradeoff between environmental protection and the economy.

You have to decide if such a policy will harm the economy and reduce the nation's wealth.

The question you have to answer is: Will imposing taxes on polluters hurt the economy and reduce the wealth of the nation assuming that the tax is equal to the damages caused to society by the pollution?

1. The problem of pollution.

No one likes pollution. The problem is: Almost everything we do, including breathing, has some impact on the environment that may negatively affects others, and there is no way of eliminating, or even reducing, such actions or activities without incurring a cost. But the high cost of reducing pollution is only one reason for its existence. Even more important is the fact that if you do not own the air you breath, you cannot legally stop someone from reducing its quality.

Imagine someone who decides that the cheapest way to get rid of his garbage is to throw it on the lot next door. That is not likely to work, because the person whose property is being used as a dump has the legal right to prevent anyone from dumping things on his or her land. If the neighbor then decides to burn his garbage, because he cannot dump it, the smoke from the burning trash can also damage the next-door neighbor, as well as other people in the area. However, if no one owns the air above them or has property rights to air quality, and there are no laws to prevent such actions, then there is no legal way to stop the trash burner.

Why is pollution an economic concern? Because negative externalities cause a misallocation of resources that reduces the wellbeing or wealth of the nation.

Negative externalities exist when a producer or consumer is not responsible for all costs of consumption or production. Pollution is one example. If a firm produces a product and, in the process, pollutes the air, ground, or water, thereby imposing costs on someone else, those costs are not considered by the producer when making the profit-maximizing decision of how much to produce. The costs that producers or consumers consider when making decisions, whether it is to maximize profits or happiness, are private costs—the costs they are actually responsible for paying.

The cost to society, called social cost, is the sum of private costs to the consumer or producer plus all external costs—the costs or damages imposed on others. Anytime there is a divergence between private costs and social costs, there is a misallocation of resources. The primary reason for such a divergence is a lack of property rights

2. A free market produces too much of goods whose production or consumption creates negative externalities, such as pollution.

Negative externalities exist when the production or consumption of something harms someone else.

Firms that pollute the air, water, or land while manufacturing a product, damage others. Driving an automobile causes a decline in air quality that can affect many others. The harmful effects of secondhand smoke make smoking an activity with negative externalities.

Negative externalities exist because of a lack of property rights. Individuals cannot prevent the polluting of the air they breath because they do not own the air or the rights to air quality.

One of the great accomplishments of a free market is that the forces of supply and demand work to allocate resources so that the value buyers place on what they buy is equal to the cost of producing it. The catch is that the market can only allocate resources "efficiently" if there are no external costs or benefits associated with production and consumption.

If the production or consumption of a good creates negative externalities, such as pollution, it means that the producer or consumer is not paying the full cost. If a producer or consumer is not responsible for all costs of consumption or production, then he or she will produce or consume too much of that good. A production or consumption process that pollutes the air, ground, or water, imposes costs or damages on someone else. But if the producer or consumer is not responsible for costs imposed on others, those costs are not considered in the decision-making process, even though they are real costs to society.

The costs considered by producers or consumers, when making decisions about how much to produce or consume, are private costs—the costs they actually pay. Anyone who does not have to pay the full cost of what he or she does will do more of it than they would do if they had to pay the full price. Therefore, whenever producers or consumers are not responsible for all costs of their actions, the result is a reduction in the nation's real wealth.

The reason the free market cannot handle negative externalities correctly is because of a lack of property rights. You cannot legally stop someone from damaging something that affects you if you do not own it. If people had always had the right to stop a polluter who was negatively affecting the air they breathed, pollution would not have developed as it has. There would be less of it, and there would be fewer goods produced and consumed that damage others. There would not be "no" pollution. There would be an "optimal" level of pollution, an economic concept that weighs the cost of reducing pollution against the benefits to society from having a lower level of pollution.

There are ways to correct the misallocation of resources caused by negative externalities, and to increase the wealth of the nation. Some common proposals are: (1) Create property rights for things, such as air quality, so they can be handled by the market or in the courts. (2) Impose a fine or tax on those causing the damage, where the tax is equal to the damages caused to others. (3) Pass laws to make the activity illegal.

(1) Creating property rights.

At the end of the 1980's, President George H. W. Bush initiated a plan to reduce acid rain that, in effect, gave utility companies property rights over air quality. It may seem strange to give property rights to polluters, but from an economic standpoint, it does not matter who gets the property rights. What matters is that property rights are defined.

The plan was an attempt to find the cheapest way to meet sulfur emission standards for electric utilities, which were determined to be the major cause of acid rain. According to the plan, the government would first set standards for total sulfur emissions and then issue "permits to pollute" to each utility plant, so that each plant could emit a given level quantity of sulfur. Utility companies could then buy and sell the permits among themselves.

Instead of forcing each utility to reduce its yearly sulfur emissions by a given amount, the "permit plan" let the market decide who would reduce emissions and who would not. The plan was based on the assumption that utilities that have to spend a lot of money to reduce their emissions would try to buy permits from other utilities so that they could continue to pollute. If they could buy a permit for less than the cost of reducing their own pollution, they would come out ahead.

On the other hand, utilities that could reduce their sulfur emissions relatively cheaply would try to sell their pollution permits. If they could sell their permits for more than it costs them to cut their sulfur emissions, they would come out ahead by eliminating their emissions and getting more than their costs back by selling their permit.

The result was assumed to be the least expensive way to meet the predetermined emission standard.

It was a relatively good plan, with two economic shortcomings.

One is that the standards for total emissions should be tied to the economic costs of the damages; as it is, the standards are determined more by politics than economics.

The other is that the plan does not take account of the damages caused by each plant. It creates the least expensive way to meet an overall reduction in emissions, but it ignores the fact that plants that continue to pollute may be imposing far greater damages on society than the plants that reduced their emissions and sold their permits to pollute.

A better solution, in terms of economics, would take account of the actual damages caused by each plant, because the overall objective is not just to find the cheapest way to eliminate a given quantity of emissions, but to add the most to society's net benefits, which must take account of both the benefits from reduced pollution and the costs of reducing pollution. It may be that the plant with the greatest cost of reducing emissions is also the plant where, if emissions are reduced, the benefits to society from lower emissions are the greatest. Even so, it is a legitimate plan that deals with a problem that, if left entirely to the market, would reduce the nation's wealth even more.

On a general level, if everyone were given property rights to air quality, then each damaged person could take every polluter to court. Litigating all the cases, however, would use so many resources that it could cause an even greater loss to society.

Imagine all the cars driving on a freeway during rush hour, each of which is polluting the air and reducing the air quality for many people. If each driver had to make legal arrangements with each damaged party before driving to work, the cost would be uncontrollable. Therefore, legal solutions to negative externality problems can work only if a small number of people are involved. Otherwise, the solution itself will reduce the nation's wealth.

(2) Taxing actions that negatively affect others.

An "ideal" economic solution to negative externalities is to make everyone responsible for the total costs of what they do. Impose fines or charges or taxes on all acts of producing and consuming that damage others through their impact on the environment. The tax would be equal to the value of the damage caused.

Some think such a solution is worthless because it does not seem to solve anything. Polluters can simply pay the tax and continue to pollute the air, water, or earth.

That could happen. If it does, it is still a solution that is best for society, because whether or not polluters are able to pay the tax and keep on polluting depends on the damages they are causing, as well as on their costs of reducing the pollution.

Once such a tax is imposed, the polluter has three choices:

(1) Pay the tax or fine and go on with business as usual.

(2) Spend the money to change the production process in order to stop or reduce polluting and avoid or reduce the tax.

(3) Go out of business if it is too expensive to either pay the tax or stop the emissions.

If the tax is levied on an individual automobile driver, to take account of the air pollution caused while driving through town, the choices are the same:

(1) Pay the tax and continue driving. (2) Avoid the tax by purchasing a car that does not pollute the air. (3) Drive less, or stop driving altogether if the tax or an alternative vehicle are not affordable.

It is an economic solution, because it is a solution that weighs all the factors that affect society's wellbeing. But the tax must be imposed on "units of pollution." There would not be a tax on owning a car; the tax would be imposed on driving. The tax could be on miles driven or it could be added to the price of gasoline. Ideally, the tax would vary according to where and when the car is driven, because the damage caused is related to where and at what time the car is driven.

Of course, if an electric utility company were forced to pay a tax for each ton of high-sulfur coal burned, part, but not all, of the fine would be passed on to consumers through higher prices, which is exactly what should happen. The consumers of electricity should also be responsible for the environmental damage caused to generate it. After all, if they were not using the electricity, there would be no production and no damages.

If the damage caused by the production of electricity is severe, the utility company would have to charge a high price for its product if it cannot solve the pollution problem.

The higher the price of electricity, the less will be consumed and produced, and the lower the environmental damage will be.

In terms of maximizing the nation's real wealth, if the tax is truly equal to the value of the damage caused to society, then the market will give the solution economics wants.

If the polluter chooses to pay the tax and not restrain his emissions, because that is the cheaper alternative, it means that the cost of fixing the pollution is greater than the damage it is causing. In terms of using resources in the best possible way, that is the solution economics wants.

If the polluter chooses to fix the pollution problem rather than pay the tax, because that is the cheaper alternative, it means that the cost of stopping the emission is less than the damage it is causing. Again, in terms of using resources wisely, that is what economics wants to happen.

In a case where both the tax and the cost of emissions control are so high that the firm is forced to close down, that is also the best solution. It means that the people who are buying that product are not willing and able to pay for the real cost of its production.

In each and every case, once the tax is imposed, whatever solution comes out, it is best for society.

Making automobile drivers responsible for the pollution damages they cause can be relatively easy. A tax on gasoline, based upon damages, makes the decision to drive take account of social, not just private, costs. The problem with automobiles is similar to that of a factory. People drive too much if they are not responsible for total costs, thereby causing a misallocation of resources. Some resources used for driving would add more to the wealth of society if they were shifted to an alternative use.

However, the idea of imposing a tax must also consider the cost of the program. In some cases, it is relatively inexpensive to impose a tax on a polluter, although it may be expensive to calculate the actual damages.

(3) Making an activity illegal.

When someone burns leaves in the fall or spring, the smoke affects others in the community. If there are no laws against burning leaves, the damaged parties cannot stop the burning. If no one owns the right to air quality, because there are no property rights for air or air quality, no one, even if he or she is damaged by the smoke, can legally prevent others from burning leaves.

A person decides to either burn leaves or bag them, depending upon his or her private costs. If the cost of burning, including the value of the burner's time, is less than the cost of bagging and dumping, the leaves will be burned.

The burner makes a decision that is in his or her best interest, which is what should happen in a free-market economy. Unfortunately, when the decision is made without having to consider, or to be responsible for, the smoke damage to others, the nation (or community) may lose. The community will lose, meaning that there will be a reduction in the community's or nation's real wealth, if the "social cost" of burning leaves, which includes the damage to people affected by the smoke, is greater than the private cost of bagging and dumping the leaves.

The "ideal" economic solution to this problem is to make people responsible for the total costs of their actions by imposing a tax on the person doing the burning, equal to the "external" costs of the activity, which is calculated by determining the damage to the community caused by leaf burning. The tax would vary with how many leaves are burned, from zero if there is no burning, to the estimated damages caused by greater and greater levels of burning. The tax does not outlaw burning. Instead, it gives the person with leaves the opportunity to make a choice between burning and bagging, given the fact that he or she is now responsible for all costs of his or her actions.

Whatever decision the person with the leaves makes, whether it is to stop burning leaves or to continue burning, society comes out ahead. In either case, there is an efficient allocation of resources, meaning that resources are used where they are valued the most.

If the tax the burner has to pay to burn leaves is greater than the cost of bagging leaves and bringing them to the dump, the burner will bag the leaves, because that will be his or her cheaper solution. Burning the leaves and paying the tax will cost more than bagging.

If the tax (the damage) is less than the cost of bagging, the burner will continue burning, because burning and paying the tax will cost less than the cost of bagging.

It is a good solution, on the grounds that it is wrong to spend more to fix a problem than it is worth. Although the burner has a choice of burning leaves and paying the tax or not burning and not paying the tax, the only way leaves would continue to be burned is if the "honest" damages to others are less than the cost of fixing the problem—which is the cost of bagging the leaves.

The problem with the ideal economic solution of trying to impose taxes on people for burning leaves is that it is difficult and expensive, maybe even impossible, to implement. It is expensive to calculate the damages and also to impose the tax. As a result, the best solution to the problem of burning leaves may be to ban the activity.

The justification for such a solution is that it will yield the same result as a tax if the tax on burning leaves, calculated by adding up the real damages caused to everyone else, would be so high that no one would be willing to pay for the right to burn leaves.

Therefore, from the standpoint of resource use, it is easier and more efficient to have a law that yields the same "ideal" result: no leaves burned. And because no resources are needed to measure damages and impose taxes, society gains even more.

As a rule, whenever it can be shown that imposing a tax on offenders would lead to a total elimination of the activity, it is cheaper and easier and uses fewer resources to simply make the activity illegal.

3. How do negative externalities affect the wealth or wellbeing of society?

The question.

If a negative externality, such as pollution, is introduced into a market that previously had none, what happens to the equilibrium in the market and to the wellbeing or wealth of society?

(1) The initial equilibrium.

The initial equilibrium is shown by the normal supply and demand curves, S_1 and D_1, in Figure 12.1.

Figure 12.1

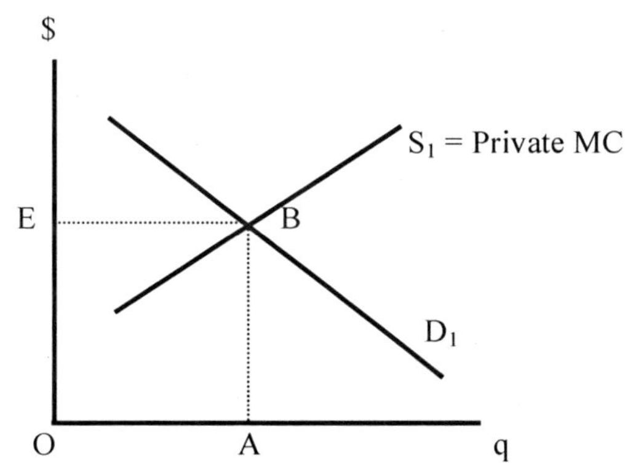

With no external costs, meaning no negative externalities, the market is in equilibrium at quantity A and price B. It is an efficient allocation of resources because it is an equilibrium where the value consumers place on the last unit produced (AB) is equal to the cost of producing the last unit (also AB). When describing the value of the product to consumers and the cost of producing the product, economists take account of opportunity cost—the value the resources could be providing if they were used somewhere else.

(2) The change.

If the industry now begins polluting the air, water, or ground, there will be a change in the true supply curve. The supply curve that represents both private costs and social costs of production is now S_2, which is above S_1 by the value of the damages caused by the pollution.

Figure 12.2

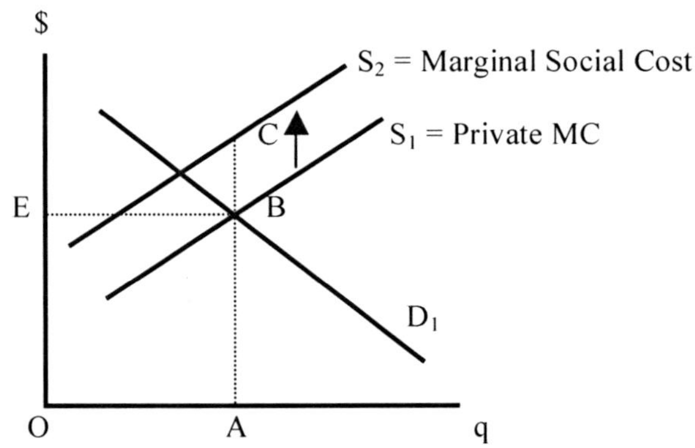

(3) The new equilibrium.

The new equilibrium is the same as the original equilibrium. There is no pressure for change, because there is no excess demand or supply.

Figure 12.3

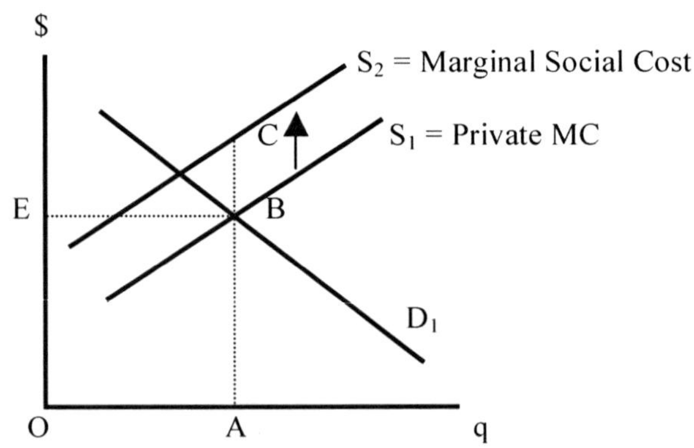

Therefore, producers continue to produce quantity A because that is the profit-maximizing output as long as they do not have to pay any of the damages caused by the production process.

The new equilibrium price and quantity are the same as the original price and quantity. However, in the new equilibrium, there is a difference between private costs and social costs. The marginal private cost of producing A is still AB, but the marginal social cost of producing A is now AC.

Conclusion.

The equilibrium price in the market remains at E.

The equilibrium quantity in the market remains at A.

The private marginal cost of producing A remains at AB.

The marginal social cost of producing A is now AC.

There is no change in the market equilibrium, but there are winners and losers.

Producers win because they continue to produce as before, even though the true costs of their actions have increased. Their profits are higher than they would be if they were required to be responsible for all costs of production.

At output A, the value consumers place on the last unit of the product (AB) is less than the cost to society of producing that last unit (AC). Therefore, if a negative externality is introduced and output remains at A, the wellbeing of society is lower than it could be. There is a misallocation of resources because too much of the polluting product is being produced and too little of other products that could be using the resources are being produced. The result is a decrease in the wealth of the nation.

4. Correcting the misallocation of resources caused by negative externalities.

One of the solutions to negative externality problems is to impose a tax on the polluter equal to the value of the external damages, thereby making the firm or individual responsible for all costs, not just private costs.

The question.

What happens to the equilibrium in the market if a tax is imposed on polluters? Will the tax increase or decrease the wellbeing of society?

(1) The initial equilibrium.

The initial equilibrium is shown by the supply and demand curves, S_1 and D_1, in Figure 12.4. Figure 12.4 is the same as Figure 12.3. The equilibrium is at B, with equilibrium price E and equilibrium quantity A. This is an example of a market failure because the market yields an equilibrium where the value consumers place on the product (AB) is less than the true cost of producing it (AC). In other words, the market fails to achieve an efficient use of resources.

Figure 12.4

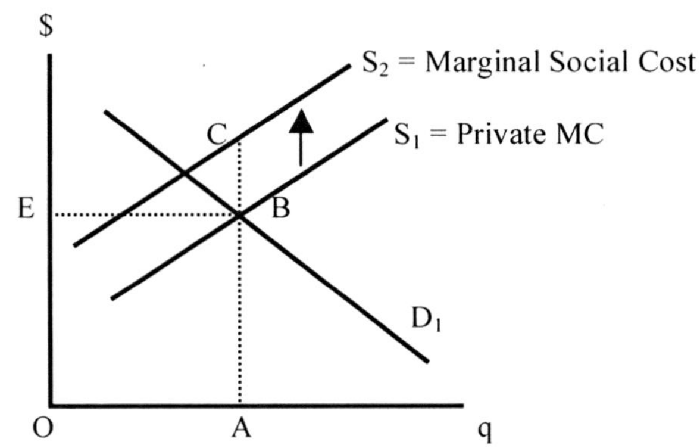

(2) The change.

A tax imposed on polluters, equal to BC—the external damages caused by the activity—changes the producers' costs of production. Producers were previously willing to sell A units at a price of AB per unit. Now producers are willing to sell A units at a price of AB plus BC, the dollar value of the tax. To simplify the discussion, it is assumed that the per-unit tax, BC, is the same for all levels of output. Producers are now willing to sell any level of output at a price equal to the price given by the original supply curve, plus the tax, BC. Adding BC to the original supply curve at every level of output yields a new supply curve, S_2, where the vertical distance between S_1 and S_2 is BC.

Figure 12.5

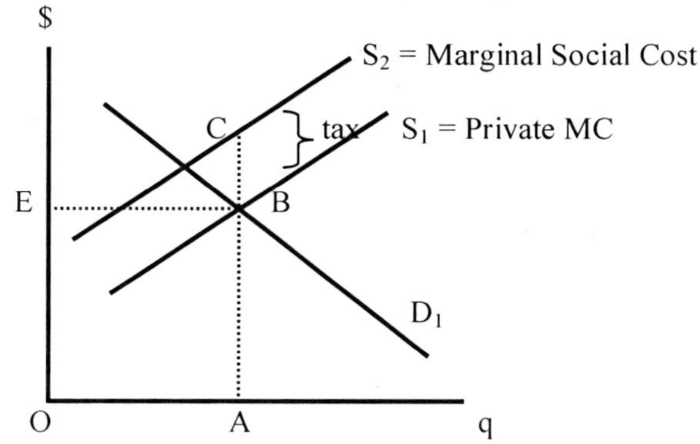

(3) The new equilibrium.

The new equilibrium, determined by the new supply curve, S_2, and the original demand curve, D_1, is at J in Figure 12.6. The new equilibrium price is E; the new equilibrium quantity is G. The tax does not affect market demand. It affects only the market supply curve. The change in supply results in a move along the original demand curve; a change in the quantity demanded, not a change in demand

Figure 12.6

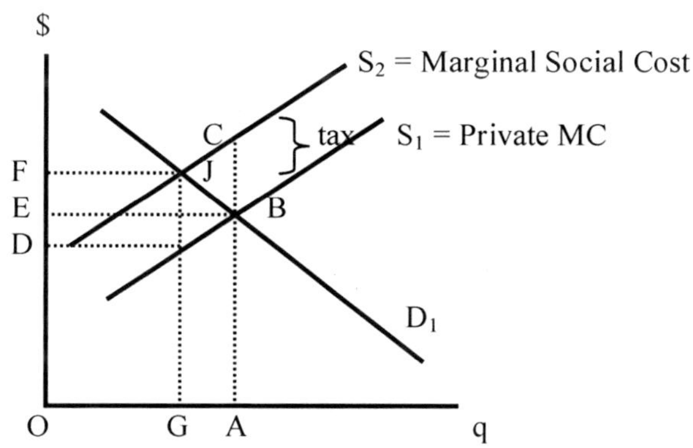

The equilibrium price increases from E to F.

The equilibrium quantity decreases from A to G.

The tax per unit is BC, or DF.

The price paid by consumers increases from E to F.

The price received by producers falls from E to D.

The part of the per-unit tax paid by consumers is EF.

The part of the per-unit tax paid by producers is DE.

Conclusion.

As the equilibrium quantity of the product decreases, starting from output A, each unit taken out of production takes away more from society's costs than from the value received by consumers.

A very small reduction in output at quantity A reduces society's costs by AC while reducing society's value from consuming the product by AB. Therefore, each decline in output adds to the wellbeing or wealth of the nation, until output G is reached. Therefore, G is the output that yields an efficient allocation of resources.

At G, the value consumers place on the product (GJ) is equal to the cost of producing it (also GJ). If output is decreased further, to levels below G, society loses, because every decrease in output below G takes away more from the value the product adds to society than to the true costs of providing it.

> If the damages are very high, it is possible that imposing a tax will cause the supply curve to move up, or to the left, by an amount that results in an equilibrium where production is zero. In such a case, the tax will put the producer out of business, which, from the standpoint of the nation's wealth, is an efficient solution. It means that the value consumers place on the item is not great enough to cover the true costs of providing it.

To summarize: The free market does not yield an efficient equilibrium unless producers and consumers are responsible for all costs—private and external. That is why there is no question that the market cannot handle negative externalities correctly and why the allocation of resources that results in a "free market" with negative externalities will always be wrong, when measured by the wellbeing or wealth of the nation.

Why will the free market equilibrium always be wrong? Because the market cannot allocate resources that are not traded in the market, which is the case when there are negative externalities and a lack of property rights.

When a consumer or producer is not responsible for costs imposed on others, those costs are not considered in the decision-making process. If people damaged by pollution had the right, in the beginning, to stop a polluter who was negatively affecting the air they breathed, pollution would have developed differently. It would not, however, as can be seen in Figure 12.6, be totally eliminated. It would, instead, exist at a level that maximizes the wellbeing of society. In other words, economics argues that society will benefit from having an "optimal level of pollution."

Even if it were technically possible to have zero pollution, economic logic argues that the cost of obtaining such a state would be far beyond the benefits.

Returning to the problem of a mutual fund, it is clear that producers who are causing pollution will be worse off, because they could have chosen the new equilibrium, which is a point on the original demand curve, before the tax was imposed. Therefore, a tax on pollution must decrease the profits of polluters.

However, the question you, as the owner of a mutual fund, must answer is: What happens to the economy as a whole and the nation's wealth?

To answer that question, you must use all you know about the interaction of pollution and the economy.

13

Positive Externalities

Your job, as the CEO of a major corporation, is to make decisions that will help maximize company profits.

It is an election year, and one of the major issues is a government health care program.

The political argument is that millions of people do not have any health insurance.

Your company's profits are related to how well the economy is doing, so you do not want to support something that will hurt the economy. Should you back a government health-care plan?

1. Subsidizing health care.

There are many kinds of health care systems.

In virtually all European countries, government-provided public health care exists along with private health care, similar to how most countries handle private and public education.

Another possibility is to replace private, profit-based health insurance with a government health insurance program.

The question.

Would subsidizing health care add to or take away from the nation's wealth and your company's profits?

(1) The initial equilibrium.

In Figure 13.1, D_1 and S_1 are the private demand for and supply of health care. D_1, represents marginal private benefits. S_1, represents the marginal social cost of providing health care. The equilibrium is at quantity A and price E.

Figure 13.1

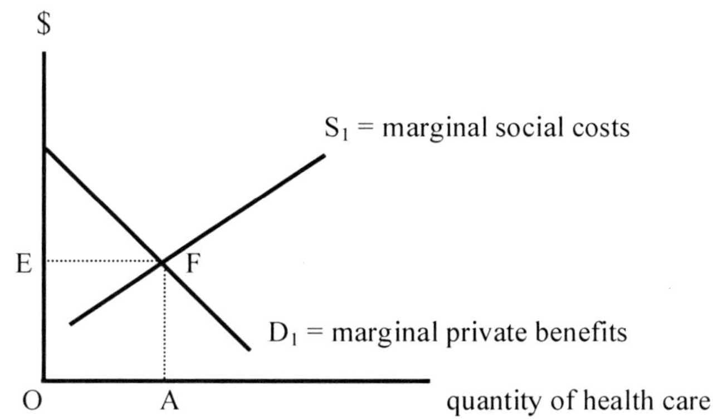

(2) The change.

In Figure 13.2, a second "demand curve," D_2, is shown. D_2 represents the marginal social benefits of health care. It includes what people are willing and able to pay for health care (shown by the demand curve D_1) plus the gains to those who benefit from, but do not pay for, the health care of others (the vertical distance between D_1 and D_2), which is what economists call a "positive externality." Although D_2 is as real as D_1 to economists, it is not a *real* demand curve because the suppliers of health care do not see D_2; they see only D_1.

Figure 13.2

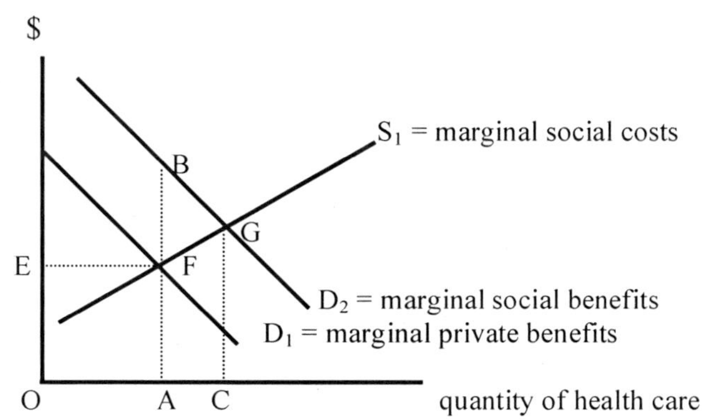

The equilibrium determined by S_1 and D_1 is an example of market failure resulting from a positive externality, because it is an equilibrium where the value society places on health care (AB in Figure 13.2) is greater than the cost to society of providing it (AF). It is also an equilibrium that leaves as many as fifty million people without health insurance. If the nation's wealth is to be maximized, the equilibrium should be at G, because that is the quantity where marginal social benefits (represented by D_2) equal marginal social costs (represented by S_1).

(3) The new equilibrium.

In Figure 13.3, the government moves the market to G by subsidizing health care. The new equilibrium is at quantity C and price H.

Figure 13.3

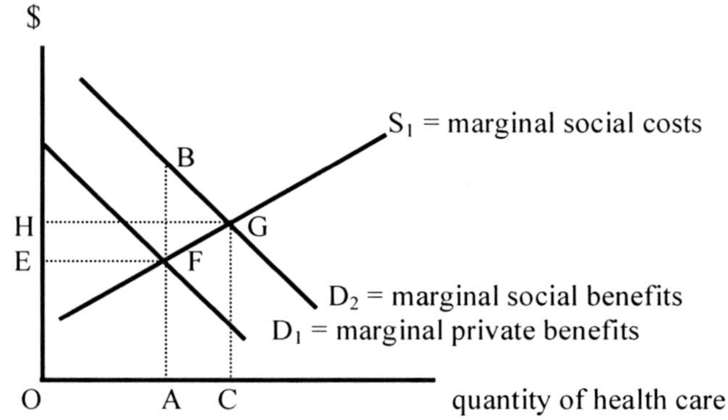

If the government subsidizes health care, it will increase the demand for health care, creating a new demand curve to the right of the original demand curve. In Figure 13.3, the government is so smart, that it creates the new demand curve D_2 that generates an equilibrium where the new demand curve intersects the supply curve S_1 at the level of health care C, because it is at that point that marginal social cost (CG) equals marginal social benefits (also CG). If that is where the market actually ends up, it will be an efficient use of resources, because for every increase in health care, from A to C, each additional unit adds more to society's benefits than to society's costs. If the new demand curve is to the left of D_2, there will still be too little health care. If the new demand curve is to the right of D_2, there will be too much health care, because each additional unit of health care past C adds more to society's costs than to its benefits.

Conclusion.

At the quantity of health care A, marginal private benefits are AF. Marginal social costs are also AF. But marginal social benefits are AB. Therefore, if additional units of health care are added, past A, each additional unit adds more to society's benefits than to society's cost, as long as D_2 is above S_1. But that will not happen in a private market for health care. It will happen only if the government plays a role.

2. Government-provided health care.

Instead of subsidizing health care, the government might try to move the market to the desired equilibrium by increasing supply. It might do so by replacing the private, profit-based health insurance system with a government-run health insurance system that reduces the cost of health insurance. If it works, the change can be shown as an increase in supply from S_1 to S_2 in Figure 13.4.

In Figure 13.3, if the government is very smart, it will create the new supply curve, S_2, that generates an equilibrium where the new supply curve intersects the demand curve D_1 at the level of health care H, because it is at that point that marginal social cost (HI) equals marginal social benefits (also HI). If that is where the market actually ends up, it will be an efficient use of resources, because for every increase in health care, from A to H, each additional unit adds more to society's benefits than to society's costs (D_2 demand is above supply). If the new supply curve is to the left of S_2, there will still be too little health care. If the new supply curve is to the right of S_2, there will be too much health care, because each additional unit of health care past H adds more to society's costs than to its benefits.

Figure 13.4

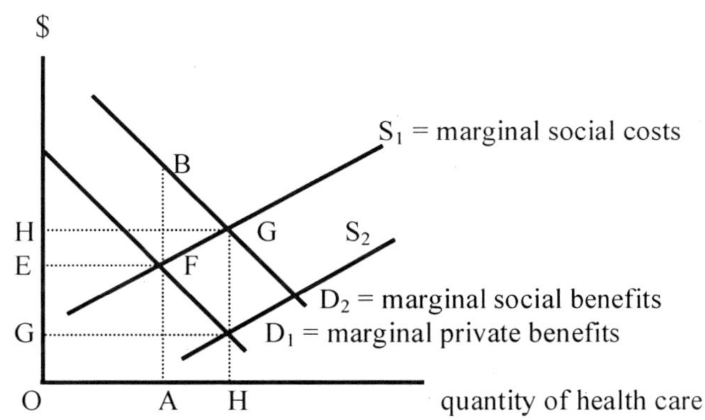

Conclusion.

The objective of the government program is to create an equilibrium where S_1 equals D_2, because that is where marginal social costs equal marginal social benefits. If that happens:

The equilibrium price in the market decreases from E to G.

The equilibrium quantity in the market increases from A to H.

Marginal social costs (HI) equal marginal social benefits (HI).

People are healthier.

Doctors and hospitals are busier.

Medical supply companies benefit.

The nation's wealth increases, because resources are used more efficiently.

How can it happen?

What kind of program could the government introduce that would reduce the cost of health care to people, and that would also increase health care and the nation's wealth?

One possibility is to place the entire population into one giant insurance pool that is managed by the government. The preliminary numbers show that such a program could drastically reduce insurance premiums, without changing the way health care is provided. There are two ways such a government program can reduce health insurance costs. One is by taking the profit out of health insurance. The second is by changing health insurance so that it encourages preventive care.

Another option is to have the government provide health care at a lower cost, thereby increasing the supply of health care, so that S_1 moves to the right, again, ideally, where it intersects D_1 at C.

According to the numbers, more than 73% of health care costs are incurred during the last year of life. Why? The quick answer is that it is the result of an aging population. A more complete answer includes the fact that a system that discourages preventive medicine, mainly because of high deductibles, causes people to get sick and die who might otherwise have been fine with better access to preventive care. Therefore, spending more on preventive care can reduce total spending on health care, which would then lower insurance premiums.

In the original equilibrium in Figure 13.4 insurance premiums are p_1 and the number of people covered by insurance is q_1. According to government statistics, somewhere around 50,000,000 people do not have health insurance.

If the assumptions are correct, a government health insurance program would cause the supply of health insurance to increase from S_1 to S_2 while leaving the demand for health insurance at D_1.

In the new equilibrium:

Insurance premiums fall from p_1 to p_2.

The number of people covered by insurance increases from q_1 to q_2,

And it is the increase in the supply of health insurance that leads to the increase in the supply of health care in Figures 13.2 and 13.3 above.

Figure 13.4

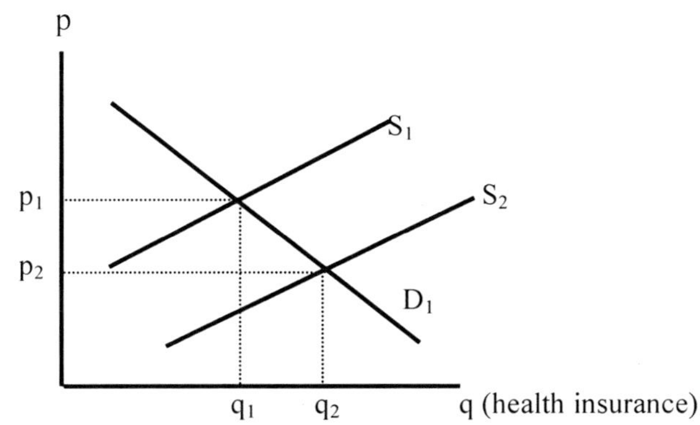

At the same time, business profits increase, because of the decrease in the cost of providing health insurance to employees, and the nation's wealth increases.

The losers are insurance companies that may be cut out of the system.

What would such a program cost taxpayers? Possibly nothing if the program is paid for with taxes that replace current health insurance premiums.

In other words, if the market failure in health care is corrected by a government-run health insurance program, everyone, other than insurance companies, can win.

Therefore, almost everyone should be in favor of government actions that correct the market failure caused by positive externalities, especially big business, because big business will be a major winner if a government health insurance program increases their profits.

3. A totally free market will always produce too little of goods whose production or consumption creates positive externalities.

Positive externalities exist when the production or consumption of a good or service, such as health care, benefits someone other than those who pay for it. Education is another example. Individuals benefit from putting in the time and money it takes to further their education. But others benefit from that education as well. Society as a whole gains as individuals become more educated because educated people tend to be more productive, thereby increasing the wealth of the nation. However, with a totally free-market education system, meaning that each individual pays the full cost of his or her own education, those who gain from the increased education of others do not have to pay.

The quantity of education for which people are willing and able to pay is a function of the private benefits they expect to receive, not the benefits they will bestow on others. That is why a totally free-market system of education will always provide too little education, if the criterion for how much should be produced is education's contribution to the nation's wealth.

The solution is public education. Taxes imposed on society in general are used to provide education for everyone. In the United States, free education is provided through high school, and taxes are used to pay part of the costs for students at public universities. It is not a perfect system, but it is superior to a totally free-market education system where the inequalities would be greater and the quantity and quality of the nation's education would be less.

The GI Bill.

The GI Bill that paid for veterans of World War II to attend whatever colleges or universities they were admitted to is an example of the importance of positive externalities. Although the cost of the GI Bill was significant, the program was actually profitable for the government. The difference between the income taxes paid by those who received the free tuitions and the income taxes they would have paid had they not received a college education, was a multiple of the initial cost of the program. But that was only a small part of the benefits received by society. More important is that the education of that group of people played a major part in the scientific and business advancements that propelled the United States to its leadership role in the world. It is an example of a huge positive externality.

Dealing correctly with positive externalities is important to the wellbeing or wealth of a nation. Cures and inoculations for contagious diseases create positive benefits not only for the treated individual, but also for everyone who is spared from contracting the disease. In order to maximize such benefits, public health programs have been established.

Improvements in technology and new inventions provide profits for the inventor, but also for many others. In a totally free market economy, such innovations are not protected. Others are free to copy and use what was done, thereby eliminating the substantial profits that may encourage such work. In order to promote and encourage innovation, the idea of patent rights was developed. Patents give inventors rights that prevent the copying of their ideas for a specified length of time, allowing the inventor to earn a profit and giving others the incentive to try.

For example, the costs of developing new medical drugs is so high that it would not be in the interest of any company to spend the millions of dollars and years of work necessary to create new products unless there is a possibility of recovering the costs and earning a profit. The only way that can happen is if some sort of patent right protects the discovery. In each case involving a positive externality, if the government does not step in and find a way to increase the consumption or production of such goods, the wealth of the nation is reduced.

4. The wellbeing of society is increased if positive externalities are handled correctly.

The task is to compare the free market equilibrium and the managed equilibrium in markets with positive externalities, such as education.

The efficient equilibrium for education.

The pure "free-market" equilibrium is shown by the private supply and demand curves, S_1 and D_1, in Figure 13.5. If individuals must pay for the entire cost of their education, the demand for education is D_1, which represents marginal private benefits. The supply curve, S_1, represents the marginal social cost of providing education. In a pure private market, the equilibrium quantity of education is A, and the equilibrium price is E. The second demand curve, D_2, represents the marginal social benefits of education; it includes private benefits and the gains to those who benefit from, but do not pay for, the education of others. Although D_2 is as real as D_1, it is not seen by the suppliers of education. In Figure 13.5, the efficient equilibrium is at the level of education B, where marginal social cost equals marginal social benefits. If education is increased past A, each additional unit (up to B) adds more to society's benefits than to its costs.

Figure 13.5

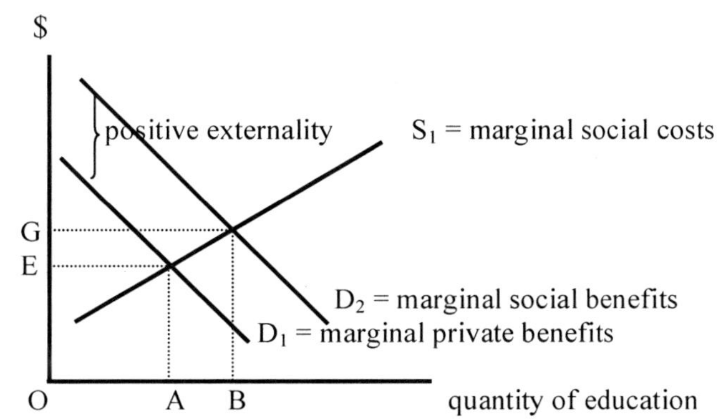

Can the desired equilibrium be reached?

The above analysis is a justification for adding public education to the economy, to coexist with private education.

It should not, however, be assumed that the "ideal" level of education, in terms of both quantity and quality, can easily be reached. Once it is decided that a nation will benefit from public education, there are many specific, and difficult, questions to be asked and answered.

Some are: Should "free" education be provided to everyone? Through what level? And how is quality to be determined and implemented?

In the United States, free public education, paid for with taxes, is offered (even required) through high school. State and federal governments also subsidize public colleges and universities in order to keep higher education costs below the costs of private colleges and universities. Even so, many individuals cannot afford to attend college, partly because of the cost, and partly because they cannot afford to not work.

A question that is seldom asked is: If the GI Bill was a profitable program for the federal government, is it possible that the United States would profit from offering everyone a free education through college?

NOTE:
The argument in this chapter concerning public education as a positive externality is not related to the argument about how vouchers might improve the quality of education by creating competition among schools. Whether or not vouchers improve the quality of education by helping students afford private schools as alternatives to public schools, such vouchers are paid for out of taxes and are, therefore, still a form of public education.

14

Public Goods

You are asked to contribute money to a candidate running for the U.S. Senate. The candidate thinks that you, as a successful businessperson, should be excited about supporting someone whose major platform is: "The best government is no government." The argument is that private, profit-making businesses are productive, while government is wasteful and inefficient.

1. Explaining public goods.

***The question*:**

Will letting the private market handle *everything* guarantee an increase in the nation's wealth? For example, what about national defense?

(1) The initial equilibrium.

In Figure 14.1, D_1 represents the true marginal social benefits of national defense and S_1 represents the true marginal social costs of providing national defense. An efficient equilibrium would exist if the level of national defense were determined by the intersection of D_1 and S_1. At that point, the marginal social cost of obtaining defense equals the marginal social benefits it provides.

Figure 14.1

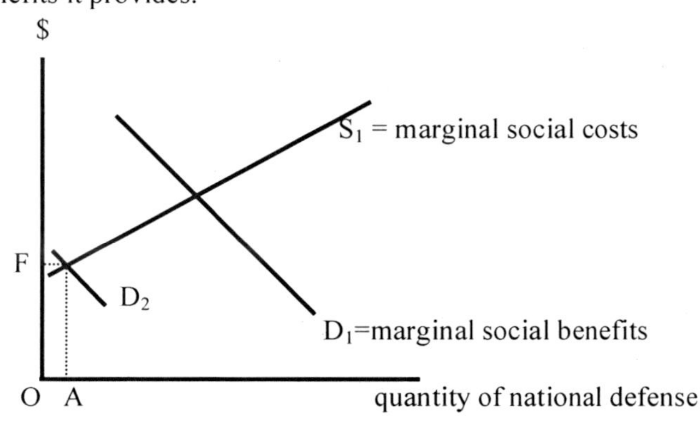

However, D_1 is not a real demand curve, because it does not show what people are willing and able to pay for national defense. It is, instead, an illustration of the benefits people would receive from various levels of national defense if that level of defense existed. D_2 is the real free-market demand for national defense; it illustrates what people are actually willing and able to pay for various levels of national defense. Therefore, the free-market level of national defense is at A, not where $D_1 = S_1$.

According to Figure 14.1, given the cost of national defense and the ability and willingness of individuals to freely pay for it, little or no national defense will exist in a pure free market. In a perfectly private market, where individuals voluntarily pay for the entire cost of national defense, the equilibrium quantity will be at or close to 0, because the real demand is so small. Why is D_2 so much smaller than D_1? Because rational people will not voluntarily contribute much to national defense, even though they know they will benefit from its existence. And if they are not willing and able to pay for it, the free market will not provide enough of it. In other words, national defense cannot be paid for by relying on patriotic donations.

The problem is: If a "fund raiser" for national defense comes to the door asking for a contribution to pay for a six billion dollar tank, the rational response is to give nothing.

There are three reasons for a rational person refusing to contribute to the building of a six billion dollar tank. One is that whether or not someone pays, he or she will receive the benefits of the protection it offers; therefore, why pay? The second is that, given the cost of the project, an individual's contribution is meaningless; it cannot affect the level of national defense for the country. Even if someone ignores the first two reasons and thinks about paying what he or she believes is fair, there is one other reason for not contributing. It is: "If no one else pays, I will have given my money for nothing."

(2) The change.

The solution for correcting the market's failure to provide a sufficient level of national defense is to have government provide it and to pay for it out of general tax revenues. If government provides for national defense, the demand for national defense will increase.

In Figure 14.2, the new demand for national defense is shown by D_1, which, with the government involved, becomes a true demand curve.

Figure 14.2

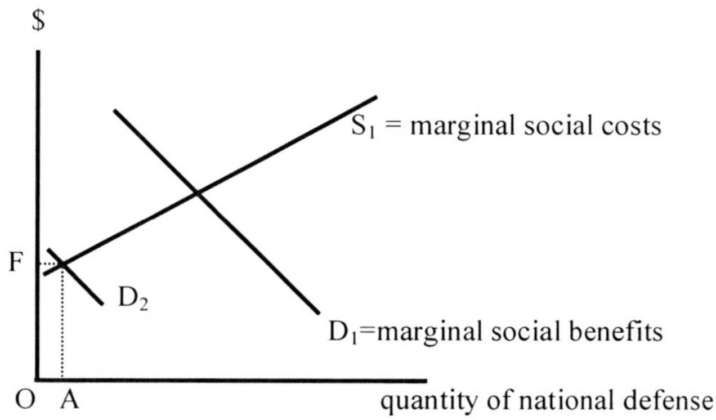

(3) The new equilibrium.

The equilibrium level of national defense, as provided by government, is B in Figure 14.3. The equilibrium price is E.

In Figure 14.3, D_1 corresponds to D_1 in Figure 14.1, meaning that, by being very smart, the government provided the exact quantity of national defense that will maximize the wealth of the nation.

Figure 14.3

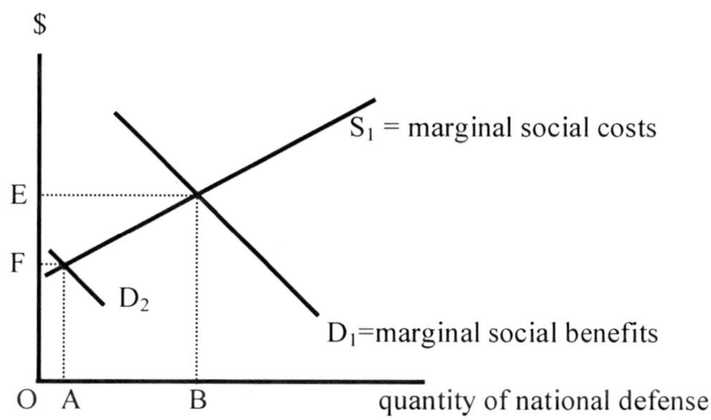

Conclusion:

The level of national defense provided by a pure free market will be too small to maximize the nation's wealth. That is because national defense is a public good, which means it cannot be traded efficiently n the market. The only way to have a sufficient level of national defense is for it to be provided by the government.

Of course, once national defense is under the control of the federal government, there will be an ongoing political argument as to how much defense should be produced because there is no easy answer to the question of what constitutes an "optimal" level of defense. But without government action, that question would never have an opportunity to be debated.

2. A free market will not produce a sufficient quantity of public goods, such as national defense.

Other examples of public goods are lighthouses, parks, freeways, and air-traffic control.

In all cases, if the government fails to accept the responsibility for providing a sufficient quantity of public goods, the nation's wealth is reduced.

Even though the public-goods argument is sound, private individuals, corporations, and foundations do make large contributions to society. Are such contributions contradictions to the idea that individuals will not pay for public goods? Or are they irrational acts? They are neither. Such contributions do not fall under the public-goods argument because they are seldom for anything as large as national defense. Instead, they occur when the contribution can pay for all of, or a substantial part of, a project or building or work of art or park. Therefore, such actions by benefactors are rational and of great benefit to society, because, unlike contributions to large public goods, they guarantee that the thing the money is given for will actually take place. In other words, each such contribution does matter.

Societies, from small towns to nations as a whole, have benefited greatly from the unselfish actions of individuals who choose to bestow gifts that positively affect others.

Public goods are goods whose benefits cannot be excluded from those who do not pay for them and where there is no additional cost associated with providing the benefits to additional people. As such, public goods are a type of positive externality. National defense is an example. The existence of national defense benefits everyone, regardless of his or her political leanings and whether or not he or she pays for it.

3. The wellbeing of society is increased if public goods are handled correctly.

It is relatively easy to compare, at least in theory, a free-market equilibrium and an economically efficient equilibrium for public goods.

The efficient equilibrium.

Figure 14.1

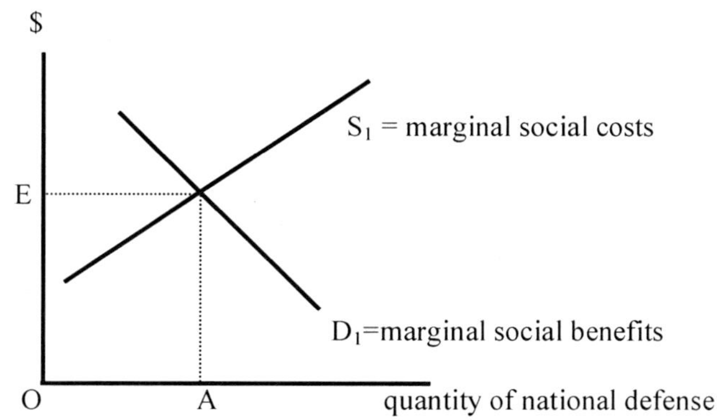

In such a free-market equilibrium, marginal social benefits are greater than marginal social costs. Therefore, each unit of national defense added to the free-market level adds more to society's benefits than to society's costs, as long as D_1 is above S_1.

In Figure 14.2, the efficient equilibrium is at A, where marginal social cost equals marginal social benefits.

If national defense is increased past A, each additional unit adds more to society's costs than to its benefits.

If national defense is decreased below A, each unit taken away subtracts more from society's benefits than from society's costs.

Figure 14.2

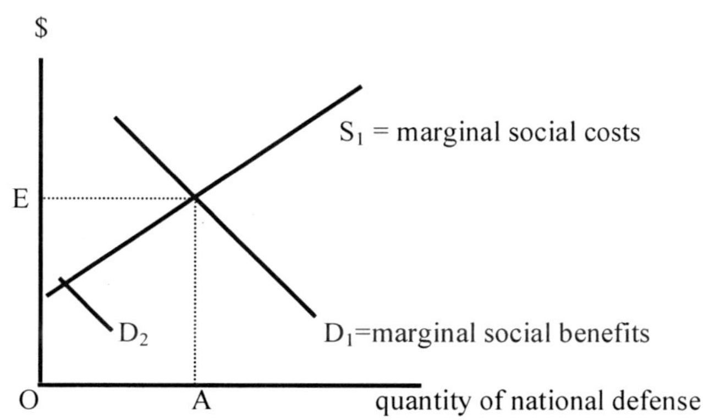

Can the efficient equilibrium be reached?

The above discussion is a theoretical explanation of a real issue.

In the real world, once it is recognized that national defense is a government responsibility, spending on national defense is handed over to politicians and bureaucrats who work closely with military decision-makers. And because it is impossible to accurately derive the true marginal benefits to society from various levels of national defense in total, or of individual projects, taxes and spending related to national defense become political issues, which is one reason many large military projects are spread among as many states as possible. Doing so maximizes the number of senators and congressmen who will be in favor of the expenditure.

The reality of national defense is that not only do expenditures help the nation; they also help those who provide equipment and services to the military. Point A in Figures 14.1, 14.2, and 14.3 is not a "real number" or a real measure of anything; it is an abstract idea. The questions of how and how much to spend on national defense will never have accurate answers. And it is often difficult to limit expenditures when so many individuals and companies and politicians stand to gain.

It is clear that government must be involved with the production of public goods. It is not as clear how it should be done in any particular case. However, as with other issues involving positive externalities, it is often better to error by providing too much than to let the market provide nothing.

15

Common Property Resources

You are a banker. A Cape Cod commercial fisherman comes to you for a loan to purchase a new, high-tech fishing boat. He tells you that the Cape Cod fishing grounds were once the most productive in the world, but that times are tough. There are not as many fish as there were in the past, and he now needs a bigger, more expensive boat. One of his arguments is that the Cape Cod fishermen have prevented government control or regulation of fishing, which means that all he has to do to be successful is to obtain a bigger and better boat, because he can then catch as many fish as he wants. You are a true believer in the power of free markets. But is that enough to justify the loan? Or should you do a little research on the economics of commercial fishing before you hand him the money? If you do a little reading, you should quickly discover the following.

1. A free market will always overuse common property resources, such as fish populations, often to the point of extinction.

Common property resources are resources that no one owns, such as fish in lakes, rivers, and oceans. Without laws, licenses, and quotas, anyone has the legal right to catch all the fish he or she wants.

Under such circumstances, fish are taken on a first-come-first-served basis. Whoever gets there first, can legally take all they want.

The problem is: If one person catches a lot of fish, thereby reducing the size of the fish population, others who want to catch fish have a more difficult time doing so. The fewer fish there are, the more time, effort, and money it takes to catch any given quantity.

Common property resources are a type of negative externality because one person's use of the resource negatively affects others. But there are other, somewhat unique, issues related to common property resources.

One is the fact that a lack of property rights means that non-renewable common property resources, such as oil in the ground, will be used up too quickly, causing a reduction in the nation's wealth. Another is that renewable common property resources, such as fish, are always in danger of being exploited to extinction.

Potential solutions to this type of market failure are: to assign property rights to the resource so that it can be traded in the market; to impose taxes on those who use it so that fishermen, for example, are responsible for the true costs of what they do; or to set physical quotas.

Unfortunately, it is has always been easier to describe theoretical solutions to such problems that to put practical solutions into effect. For example, it has been difficult, or impossible, to assign property rights (ownership rights) to fish in the ocean. It has also been difficult, or impossible, to impose taxes on fishermen. And there is a long-standing debate on the size of an optimal quota for any given fishery. As a result, there are fewer examples of successful intervention than of populations exploited to extinction.

Sport fish in lakes and rivers have been protected for years by requiring fishing licenses and setting daily limits on the number of fish caught.

Ocean species have not been managed as well, although international agreements have led to the comeback of some that were on the verge of extinction, such as certain whales (which are not fish, but still live in the ocean).

> The Alaskan Salmon fishery is an example of a successful program for a commercial fishery. An annual quota was determined that will protect the population from being fished to extinction. The total annual quota is divided into parcels that are assigned or sold to individual fishermen. Each fishing boat is then allowed to freely catch its given quota. The result is a successful and profitable industry that can exist for many years. (On the other side, it is estimated that there are little more than 100 wild salmon left in New England.)

> An example of a bad government program is the disaster that has befallen the Cape Cod fisheries. The Cape Cod fishing industry was based on what were once the most productive fishing grounds in the world. But after years of over fishing, the populations of fish were run down to levels that virtually eliminated any profits for fishermen. Instead of finding a way to regulate the resources for the good of the industry, as well as the good of the nation, an absolutely terrible program was initiated. The program, sponsored by former Senator Magnuson from the State of Washington, financed, at zero down and close to zero interest, the purchase of larger, more efficient fishing boats. The result was predictable. Financing bigger boats to catch fish from dwindling populations simply wiped out what was left. The fisheries that had been in danger were pretty much

eliminated. The loans on the boats could not be paid off. The nation's wealth was reduced. Cape Cod fishermen were thrown out of work. The only winners were the boat builders.

No one wants to be limited in what they do—especially when limits or quotas are seen as attacks on the freedom of individuals and on the free market itself. However, when common property resources are involved, what the individual does and what the market does is not good for the nation or the individual. Individuals who believe they are exercising their free rights to make a living any way they choose may end up having their jobs eliminated along with the resource.

2. What happens to a common property resource that is not managed for the good of the nation?

The question

Assume (even though it is not true) that a fish population in the ocean is owned by people who are able to charge fishermen for the right to catch fish, and that those ownership rights (property rights) are then taken away. What happens to the equilibrium price and quantity of fish?

(1) The initial equilibrium.

The reason for making the untrue assumption that property rights exist is to allow a clear explanation of the problem created by a lack of property rights. If the discussion begins by looking at what currently exists, it is not as easy to compare what exists with what should exist. It is a common method used to explain economic issues.

The initial equilibrium is determined by the normal supply and demand curves, S_1 and D_1, in Figure 15.1.

The existence of property rights (ownership rights) means that each fisherman must pay a fee to the owner of fish in the ocean for the right to catch a given quantity of fish. In order to maximize their profits, the owners of fish calculate the impact of each fisherman's catch on what other fishermen are willing to pay for the right to catch fish, given the fact that the smaller the population of fish, the less each fisherman is willing and able to pay for the right to catch any given quantity of fish. The result is that the supply curve of the industry is determined by the true costs of catching fish, including the fee charged by the owner of fish. The initial equilibrium price is p_1. The initial equilibrium quantity is q_1. There is no market failure.

Figure 15.1

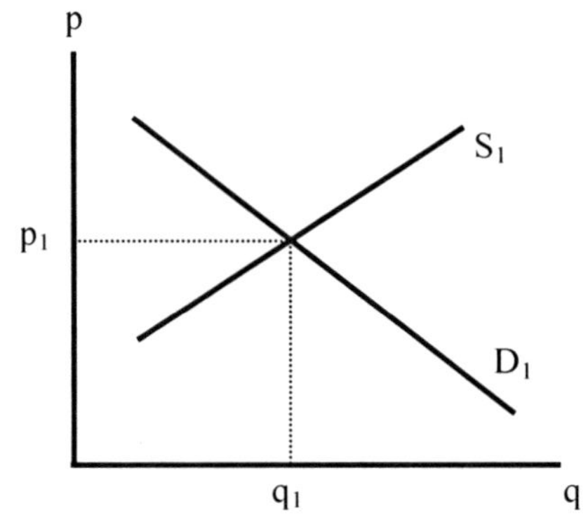

(2) The change.

Taking away the property rights of the imaginary owners of fish in the ocean changes the supply curve for fish, but not the demand curve.

The abandonment of property rights means fishermen can now catch all the fish they want without having to pay a fee. It is a change in something that was assumed to be held constant—access to the resource. Because it is a change in a "constant," the initial impact will be a change in a function, not a move along a function.

The change that affects the cost of catching fish will not alter the demand for fish—the maximum quantity of fish that buyers are willing and able to purchase at various prices. It will cause the market supply of fish to increase: to move to the right or downward. At any given price, sellers are willing and able to offer more fish for sale. The new supply curve is S_2. The demand curve remains at D_1.

Figure 15.2

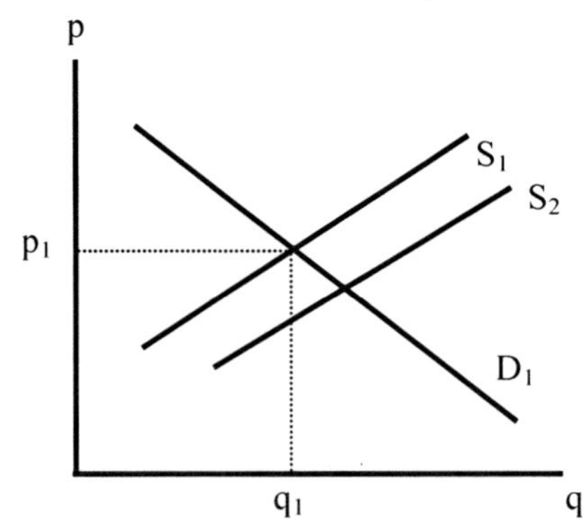

(3) The new equilibrium.

The new equilibrium, determined by the new supply curve, S_2 and the original demand curve, D_1, is at the new equilibrium price, p_2, and the new equilibrium quantity, q_3.

The change in supply resulted in a move along the original demand curve—a change in the quantity demanded—not a change in demand. The equilibrium price of fish decreased from p_1 to p_2. The equilibrium quantity of fish increased from q_1 to q_3.

Figure 15.3

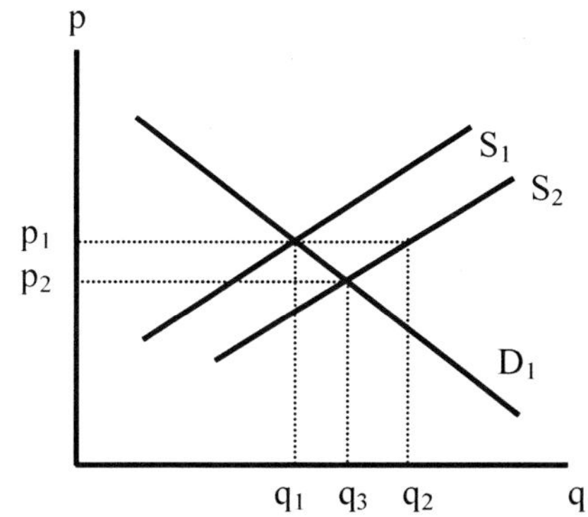

Conclusion.

For many problems, the analysis would now be finished. The changes in equilibrium values caused by the change in the market have been explained.

With common property resources, the analysis is just beginning.

In order to complete the answer, it is necessary to introduce the reality of natural resources, which can be either "renewable" or "nonrenewable." **Renewable resources** are natural resources, such as a fish population, a forest, or wildlife, that can replenish itself over time, or resources, such as agricultural land, that, if managed correctly, can yield productive services indefinitely. **Nonrenewable resources**, such as oil in the ground, are resources that, once used up, are gone (at least in a time frame relevant to human action).

3. Renewable resources.

In the case of the fishery in the above problem, a complete explanation of what happens without property rights can be offered only after understanding the basics of population dynamics (population growth) of a fish stock.

For any fish population, normally measured by weight (biomass), there is an annual growth rate. Studies have concluded that the growth rate is a function of population size, and that there is a maximum biomass that each fish population has the potential of reaching within the environment in which it exists. For any particular fish population, the growth rate will be zero if the population is extinct and the growth rate will be zero if the population reaches its maximum natural size. The study of population dynamics is, therefore, centered on the relationship between population size and its corresponding growth rate.

One of the most common relationships assumed to exist is shown in Figure 15.4. It is an inverted "U" shape. It shows that at biomass B_1, the population grows by g_1 pounds per year. Because the function is U shaped, the growth rate g_1 will also occur if the total biomass is B_2. The growth rate g_2 occurs at biomass B_3 and B_4. If the biomass is at zero or at its maximum level, B_6, the growth rate is zero. (It is zero because if the population does not exist, there is obviously no growth, and if the population is at its maximum size, there is no growth.)

If the fish stock is left alone, with no fishing, it is assumed it will reach its maximum level, B_6. The highest annual growth rate, g_3, is at B_5.

If there is fishing, the biomass is affected. A population that is fished cannot remain at its maximum level. But if the fishing industry harvests the growth rate associated with any level of biomass, then the fish stock can stabilize at that level. For example, an annual catch of g_2 pounds per year can be taken either from population B_3 or B_4 indefinitely. If the annual catch is g_1, the population can stabilize at either B_1 or B_2. From the standpoint of a healthy fish population, it is "safer" to harvest g_2 units from population size B_4 because the population is in less danger of being mistakenly fished to extinction. To biologists, biomass B_5 is important because it represents the "maximum sustained physical yield" that can be taken from the population.

Figure 15.4

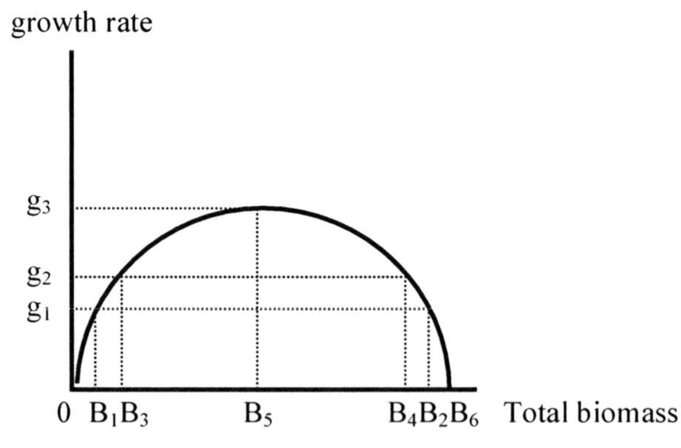

Economists are less concerned with the maximum sustained physical yield, which offers the greatest amount of food each year, than with an economically efficient equilibrium. Each point on the U shaped curve represents a biological equilibrium, because each point indicates the annual catch that can be taken from a stable population level. Each point on the U shaped curve also represents a possible economic equilibrium, because it is impossible to have an economic equilibrium without having a biological equilibrium.

The question is: Where is the economically efficient equilibrium?

The answer, as always, is that the efficient equilibrium is at an output where marginal social costs equal marginal social benefits.

To begin with, economists, along with biologists, prefer an equilibrium on the right-hand side of the U shaped curve. The reason economists want the fishery to be in that range is that it requires fewer resources to take q_2 pounds of fish from population B_4, than to take q_2 pounds of fish from the smaller population B_3. Therefore, there is general agreement that the fish population should not be exploited to the point where it stabilizes at a smaller rather than a larger biomass.

Figure 15.5, which is identical to Figure 15.3, describes the equilibrium for a fishery with no property rights.

Figure 15.5

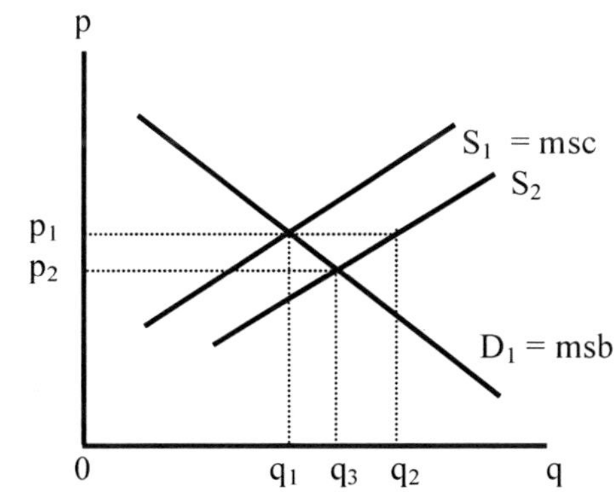

In the original equilibrium (with S_1 and D_1), the imaginary owners of fish charged fishermen a fee that took account of the facts that increased fishing causes the fish population to decrease and that it costs more to catch a given quantity of fish from a smaller population. The impact one fisherman has on another, by affecting the fish population, is a negative externality, and the imaginary owners of fish in the ocean forced each individual fisherman to be responsible for that negative externality. Therefore, S_1 represents the true marginal social cost of catching fish and D_1 represents the marginal social benefits of consuming fish. As such, the equilibrium determined by D_1 and S_1 is economically efficient; it is an equilibrium where marginal social costs equal marginal social benefits.

Without property rights, the initial change was to the equilibrium determined by D_1 and S_2. It is an equilibrium where marginal social costs (measured by S_1) are greater than marginal social benefits (measured by D_1). It is also a situation where greater quantities of fish are caught and the population size is reduced.

The more fish that are caught, the more the population will decrease. As the population declines, the private cost of catching fish increases. As private costs increase, supply decreases; the supply curve moves to the left or upward.

Depending upon the level of "over fishing" that occurs, supply can decrease a little or a lot, with the possibility that the fish population will be exploited to extinction. The new supply curve, which will change year by year as the population adjusts to each new level of fishing, could eventually end up as S_3 or S_4, or it could disappear altogether.

Based upon historical evidence, the final equilibrium quantity, which is also a point on the U shaped curve in Figure 15.5, is likely to be relatively small or, as has happened, zero.

Figure 15.6

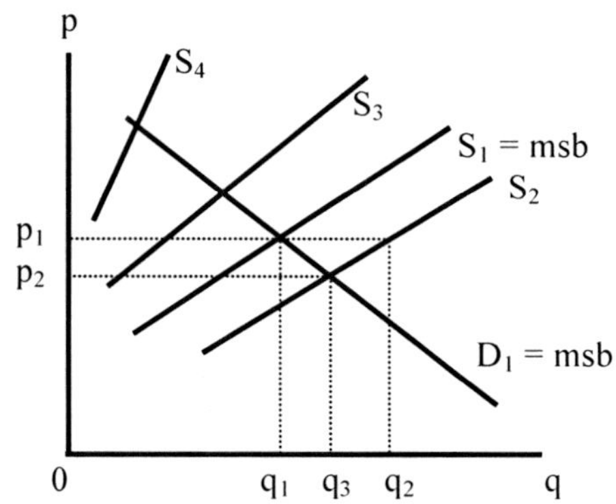

If the fishery were managed according to economic criteria, it would be forced into the equilibrium with D_1 and S_1.

One way to achieve the desired equilibrium is to impose a tax on fish caught equal to the negative externality caused by catching fish. In theory, if everything were done carefully, the fishery would operate at a sustainable and profitable equilibrium that is also economically efficient. Of course, if the management program is introduced after a population has been fished to a very low level, it will be necessary to impose a tax high enough to reduce fishing to a level that allows the population to grow.

One question that is sometimes asked is: Could it be economically efficient to exploit a fish population quickly because of its current market value? It is unlikely, but not impossible, to reach such a conclusion. If it is assumed there will be a future demand for fish, it would be an odd occurrence if the present value of the future stream of benefits would be less than the current net benefit of immediately harvesting the entire population.

4. Nonrenewable resources.

The problem with letting the free market deal with nonrenewable natural resources is that they, like renewable resources, are allocated to users on a first-come-first-served basis. And allocating resources on a first-come-first-served basis does not achieve economic efficiency.

It may be true that nonrenewable resources will eventually be depleted, no matter how they are allocated, but it still matters how they are used over time as well as at a point in time.

With no owners, nonrenewable resources are used without consideration of their value over time. An owner would attempt to maximize profits by looking at present and future revenues from selling the resource and would put a price on the resource intended to maximize profits over time. If the resource owner's profits are maximized, so is the resource's contribution to the nation's wealth.

As with any market, if resources or final products are taken by those who get there first, or who are the strongest, rather than being able to be bought by those who value them the most, economic efficiency is disrupted, along with the nation's wealth.

5. The loan.

Back to the beginning: What do you do about the Cape Cod fisherman's request for a loan to purchase a bigger and better commercial fishing boat?

16

Foreign Exchange Rates

You get a call from someone who says he can help you make big profits speculating in currencies. He says, "Trust me. It's easy." He wants you to send him $5,000 to get started. His argument is pretty good. What do you think?

1. Buying and selling currencies.

Within a country, a nation's currency gains or loses value, as measured by its purchasing power, as prices change. The higher prices are, the less a dollar will buy. The lower prices are, the more a dollar will buy.

That is why people tend to spend money quickly during inflationary times, buying as much as they can before their money loses even more value, and why they want to hold money during recessionary periods, waiting until they can buy even more with their money as prices fall further.

On an international level, a nation's currency gains or loses value against foreign currencies as a result of changes in foreign trade.

Each day hundreds of billions of dollar's worth of currencies are bought and sold in currency markets so that importers of foreign goods can pay for what they buy.

Figure 16.1 is an example of a foreign exchange market.

It depicts the market for Japanese yen, in terms of dollars. The price axis--dollars per yen--represents how many dollars are needed to buy one yen.

The quantity axis represents the quantity of yen bought with dollars during a given time period.

A move up the price axis means that more dollars are required to buy one yen; meaning that the price of yen is increasing.

Figure 16.1

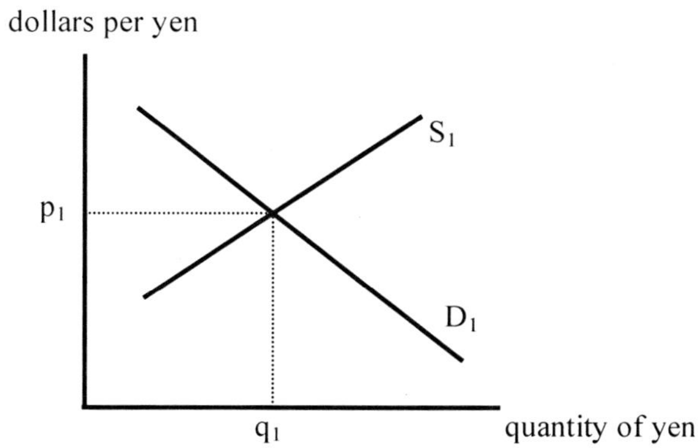

2. The supply of and demand for yen.

The demand for yen in Figure 16.1 comes from Americans who buy Japanese goods and services, or who travel in Japan, or who invest in Japanese assets. Individuals in the United States who buy goods imported from Japan pay for those goods in dollars; but whoever imported those goods had to pay for them in yen. To do so, it was necessary to first buy yen with dollars. Individuals who travel in Japan buy yen with dollars so they can purchase things when they are in Japan. Japanese investments purchased by Americans must also be paid for in yen, which again requires buying yen with dollars.

The demand for yen has a negative slope because as the price of yen in dollars declines, it means that the prices of Japanese goods and services—in dollars—also declines. If the cost of Japanese goods and services declines, Americans will buy more from Japan. And if Americans buy more from Japan, they will need more yen. Therefore, the lower the price of yen in dollars, the greater the quantity of yen Americans are willing and able to buy. If the price of yen increases, the cost—in dollars—of Japanese goods and services increases, and Americans will buy less from Japan, thereby demanding fewer yen.

Currency exchange rates work two ways: whatever the price of yen is in dollars, the price of dollars in yen is the inverse. If the price of one yen is two dollars, one yen can be purchased for two dollars, and one dollar can be purchased for one-half yen. If the price of yen decreases to one dollar per yen, then it will take one dollar to purchase one yen, and it will take one yen to purchase one dollar.

The supply of yen in Figure 16.1 represents yen used to purchase dollars. It comes from Japanese who buy American goods and services, who travel in the United States, or who invest in United States assets. Although it is called a supply curve, it is also a demand for dollars.

The supply of yen has a positive slope because as the price of yen in dollars increases, it means that each yen buys more dollars and the prices—in yen—of American goods and services decrease. If the prices of American goods and services decrease, the Japanese will buy more from the United States. And if the Japanese buy more from the United States, they will need more dollars. Therefore, the higher the price of yen in dollars, the greater the quantity of yen the Japanese are willing and able to sell to obtain dollars.

But what happens if Americans choose to increase their travel in Japan?

3. Tastes and preferences and the value of currencies.

The question.

What happens to the equilibrium price and quantity of yen in dollars if Americans decide to travel more in Japan?

(1) The initial equilibrium.

The initial equilibrium is shown by the normal supply and demand curves, S_1 and D_1, in Figure 16.2, which is the same as Figure 16.1. The initial equilibrium price is p_1. The initial equilibrium quantity is q_1.

Figure 16.2

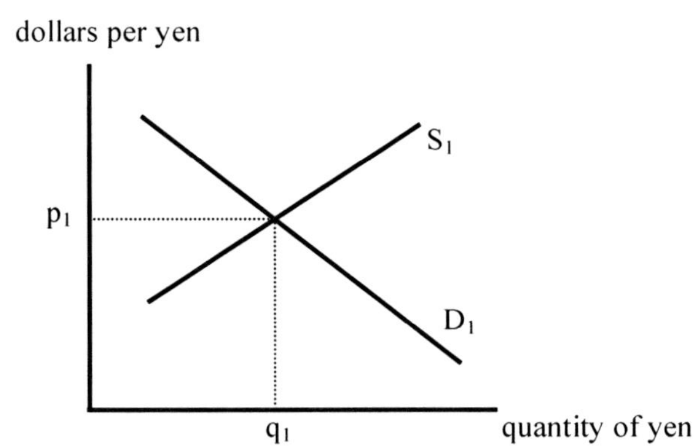

(2) The change.

This is an *exogenous* change. It is a change in a variable that was assumed to be held constant—the desire to travel in Japan. In other words, the change in travel plans is a "change in something that was assumed to be held constant"—tastes in travel. Because it is a change in a "constant," the initial impact is a change in a function. The increase in travel to Japan causes the demand for yen to increase, because Americans now require more yen than previously; the demand curve moves to the right, or upward.

There is no reason to believe that the change in travel will have any impact on the supply of yen. The new demand curve is D_2. The supply curve remains at S_1.

Figure 16.3

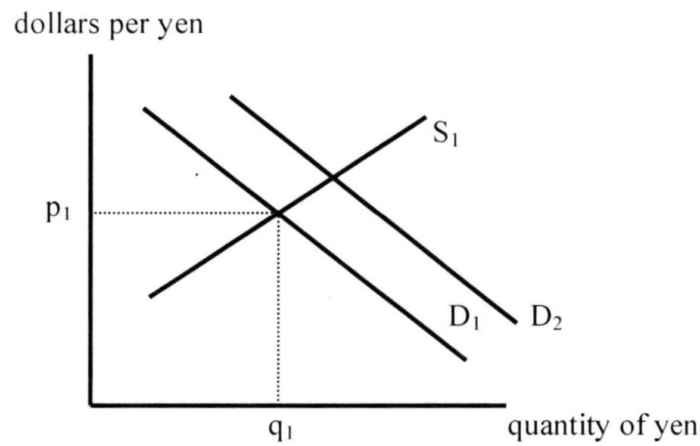

(3) The new equilibrium.

The new equilibrium, determined by the original supply curve, S_1 and the new demand curve, D_2, is at the new equilibrium price of yen, p_2, and the new equilibrium quantity, q_2. The change in demand results in a move along the original supply curve, not a change in supply.

Figure 16.4

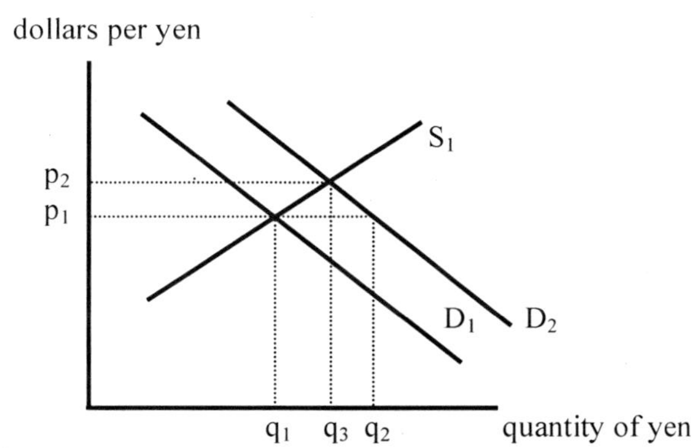

Conclusion.

The equilibrium price of yen increases from p_1 to p_2.

The equilibrium quantity of yen increases from q_1 to q_3.

It can be concluded that increased travel in Japan increases the price of yen in dollars and that the equilibrium quantity of yen traded in the market will increase as well, assuming that all other things remain constant.

It is a change, however, that affects more than international travelers.

If the yen becomes more expensive, increasing in price from p_1 to p_2, Japanese goods become more expensive to Americans and American goods become less expensive to the Japanese. It is a change that may be bad for American consumers but good for American business.

4. It is more than speculation.

Aside from speculating on changing currency values in order to make a personal profit, you may work for a company that is constantly buying and selling currencies, because it is constantly buying or selling goods and services on international markets, which means its profits can also affected by currency values. Being able to explain and predict changing currency values can add to profits, while ignoring such changes can be costly.

17

Final Microeconomic Notes

1. Short cuts.

Throughout this text, issues and problems are examined by following a logical three-step procedure. That procedure leaves out the explanation of *how* a market moves from one equilibrium to another. Explaining such movements requires understanding how changes in supply and/or demand lead to the creation of either excess demand or excess supply, and of how the pressures of excess supply or excess demand push or pull a market from one equilibrium to another. Although those steps should be understood, economists seldom show all such steps when solving problems.

Skipping steps that are truly understood will not necessarily lead to errors. Skipping steps by assuming that changes can be explained by discussing "shifts" in supply and demand curves will yield erroneous results, or results that cannot be explained to someone who questions what is behind the answer. Supply and demand curves do not *shift*. They increase or decrease as the result of a change in a variable or variables assumed to have been held constant. Memorizing tables of "shift factors" is not the way to learn economics. The only way to acquire the ability to use economic knowledge is to understand how changes in variables affect supply and demand, causing one or both to increase or decrease, and how changes in supply and demand create pressures that bring a market to a new equilibrium.

2. An existing-equilibrium problem.

Some questions can best be answered by explaining an initial or existing equilibrium, rather than by explaining how a change impacts a market. For example: How does discrimination lead to lower wages for those discriminated against?

Discrimination means that employers are willing and able to offer lower wages for minority labor, which means the demand for minority labor is less than the demand for non-minority workers. In Figure 17.1, on the following page, D_1 and S_1 are the demand for and supply of labor that is not discriminated against. D_2 and S_2 are the demand for and supply of minority workers. The wage for labor that is not discriminated against is w_1; the wage for minority labor is w_2, which is less than w_1.

Although some studies have concluded that the major factors in explaining lower wages for minorities are differences in education and work skills, not discrimination, such conclusions are questionable. Such studies ignore the fact that discrimination is also responsible for minorities having a lower quality of education and growing up in environments that do not promote an appreciation of job skills.

Figure 17.1

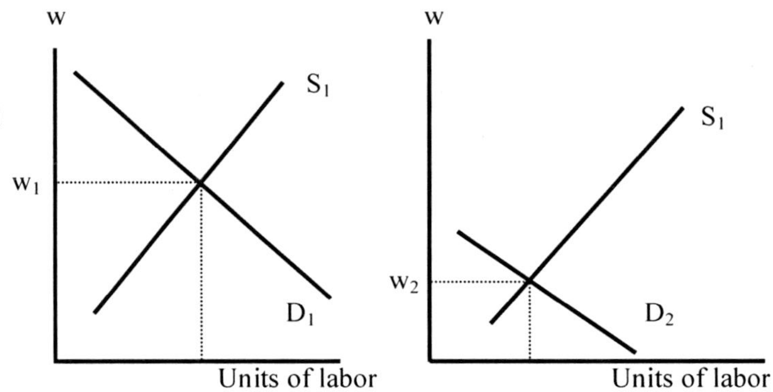

3. A single diagram answer to a simple change.

This text uses a separate diagram for each step in the comparative statics process. Most texts and most economists show everything on a single diagram, which it is assumed you did as you worked through this text. The reason for using three diagrams is to make each step as clear as possible in a book. When you are drawing your own pictures of individual markets, or the economy as a whole, it is obviously easier to put everything on a single diagram.

For example: What happens to the equilibrium price and quantity of grapefruit if medical studies conclude that grapefruit is healthier than was believed?

If people believe grapefruit is better for them than previously thought, the demand for grapefruit should increase.

The increased demand for grapefruit, along with the original supply of grapefruit, yields an increase in the equilibrium price and the equilibrium quantity of grapefruit.

In Figure 17.2, as demand increases from D_1 to D_2, the equilibrium price increases from p_1 to p_2 and the equilibrium quantity increases from q_1 to q_2.

Figure 17.2

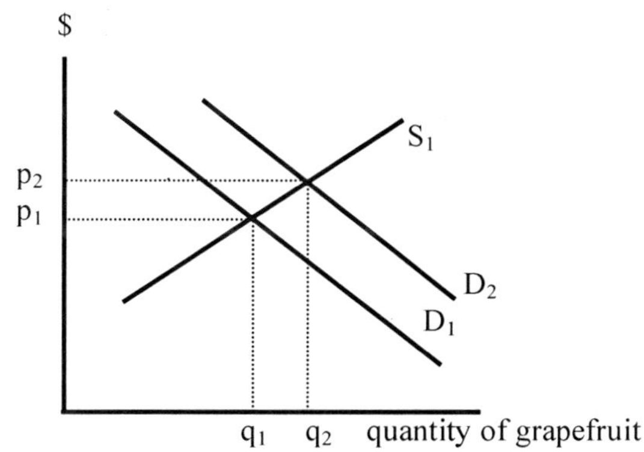

4. A single-diagram answer to a more complex change.

Who benefits, and who loses, from an increase in the minimum wage?

A change in the minimum wage does not affect the demand for labor. It does change the supply of labor. In Figure 17.3, the demand for and supply of labor without a minimum wage are D_1 and S_1. The equilibrium wage is w_1 and the equilibrium level of employment is L_1. If a minimum wage is set at w_2, the supply of labor becomes a horizontal line at w_2 until it reaches S_1, then it follows S_1 upward.

Figure 17.3

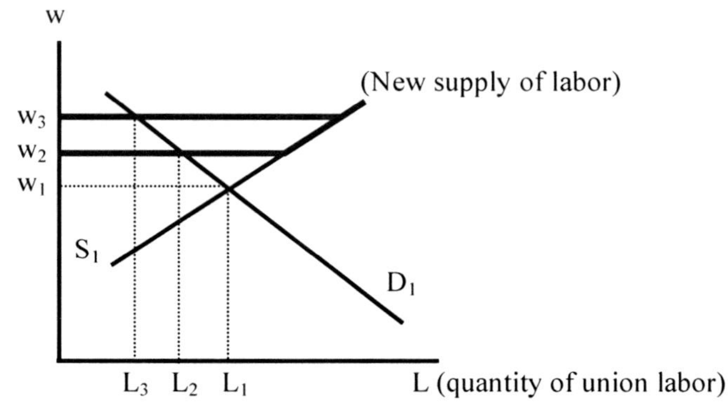

Introducing the initial minimum wage, w_2, raised the wage from w_1, the free-market level, to w_2. It also reduced employment from L_1 to L_2. Those who found jobs at w_2 came out ahead; those who did not (L_1 - L_2 units of labor), lost.

If the minimum wage is then raised again, to w_3, those still employed earn an even higher wage; those who now lose their jobs (L_2 - L_3 units of labor) are worse off.

The conclusion is that those who maintain their jobs when the minimum wage is increased, win; those who do not, lose. A minimum wage, like a union wage, can raise wages for some, but cannot keep employment at the same level. Is a minimum wage a good idea? That is a social question. Economics can explain what will happen. Society must decide if it is a good choice.

5. The microeconomic role of government

Pure democracy versus a republic.

In a pure democracy, the majority can choose to do whatever it wants, no matter what the repercussions are, to the minority.

In a republic, certain things cannot be voted on, such as life, liberty, or the pursuit of happiness.

In a pure democracy, every possible issue could be voted on and the government's role would be to carry out the policies that win a majority vote.

Because the United States is a republic, not a pure democracy, government does not exist simply to carry out the will or wishes of the majority, as determined by democratic votes.

> In a representative republic, such as the United States, government has the goal of making and implementing decisions that involve protecting and maintaining individual rights to life, liberty, and the pursuit of happiness, and of making and implementing decisions intended to maximize the wellbeing or wealth of the nation.
>
> The constraints include the political process (decision-makers must stand for election or appointment), laws, the ability to raise funds, the influence of special interests, information, and knowledge.
>
> Choices include tax and spending policies, and making and enforcing laws that are socially or politically motivated or aimed at economic concerns.

To meet its goals, government is a major employer of labor; it buys and sells many resources; it adds to or subtracts from the available capital; and, on a national level, the federal government, along with the monetary authorities, plays a crucial role in promoting and maintaining full employment and stable prices—issues normally dealt with in macroeconomics.

Government provides a long list of goods and services, such as parks, roads, police and fire protection, national defense, education, health care, etc.

Government also has the responsibility of correcting market imperfections and of protecting the market from abuses of power.

6. The theoretical model of perfect competition.

Economists use the theoretical model of perfect competition as a "benchmark" against which to judge real markets. Although perfectly competitive markets do not exist in the real world, the argument is that if they did, then the actions of individuals doing what is in their own self-interest, with no regard for the common good, would maximize the nation's wealth. Here is how Adam Smith explained it in 1776.

> "Every individual endeavors to employ his capital so that its produce may be of greatest value. He generally neither intends to promote the public interest, nor knows how much he is promoting it. He intends only his own security, only his own gain. And he is in this led by an invisible hand to promote an end which was no part of his intention. By pursuing his own interest, he frequently

promotes that of society more effectually than when he really intends to promote it."[1]

Of course, the "invisible-hand doctrine" applies only when markets are perfectly competitive, because a "free market" cannot allocate resources that are not owned or not traded in the market, markets cannot deal efficiently with externalities, and markets cannot protect themselves from the abuse of monopoly power.

The solution to each market-failure problem is to have a regulatory plan or policy implemented by government, or to have government provide goods and services that cannot be provided at all or in sufficient quantity by the market.

Because the market cannot protect itself from collusion among firms or individuals, it is up to the government to do it. For the same reason, it is sometimes necessary for government to prevent individuals from hurting themselves or others.

One solution to negative-externality problems is a regulatory plan that imposes taxes or charges on polluters equal to the damages they cause to society. The purpose of the tax is to make private costs equal to social costs so that resources are allocated in a way that adds to the wellbeing or wealth of the nation. It means changing the equilibrium from a situation where *too much* of the product is being produced and consumed to an equilibrium where the *correct* quantity of resources is used to produce the product.

If positive externalities exist for a good or service, such as education, it is up to government to make an effort to provide more of it than the market will provide, because a totally free market will produce too little of it.

Public goods are the same. The market will always produce too few public goods—goods or services whose benefits cannot be excluded from those who do not pay for them. Again, it is the responsibility of government to create a sufficient quantity of such goods and services because, for example, a free market will provide a very small level of national defense.

Government must also regulate the use of resources that are not owned if those resources are to be used in the best interest of society.

In all cases where private costs or benefits diverge from social costs or benefits, the prices used by individuals and firms to make decisions yield results that do not maximize

---

[1] *An Inquiry Into The Nature And Causes Of The Wealth Of Nations* by Adam Smith, 1776.

the wealth of the nation. And government is the only body that can correct the resulting misallocation of resources.

Government is the only entity able to pass and enforce laws on crime and individual behavior (such as not being able to quit school until reaching a certain age). It is the only entity able to use tax and spending policies to correct the misallocation of resources caused by negative or positive externalities, common property resources, and public goods. It is also the only entity with the power to protect the market from those who benefit from restricting or elimination competition.

Although government plays a crucial role in a free-market economy, not everything the government does is justified by economics. Governments are made up of politicians and bureaucrats whose decisions are often affected by special interests and by their own ideas as to what should and should not be done. One goal of politicians is to maximize vote getting, which means politicians must pay at least some attention to the people. Unfortunately, the less informed the people are, the more power is handed over to special interests.

Over the years, it has been easy for some to criticize government tax policies, spending policies, regulations, and programs. But no matter how bad government can be made to look, government is a necessary part of a free-market economy. As President John Adams warned, more than 200 years ago, without government and laws, the people will be held hostage to the "tyranny of the market."

Economic study supports President Adam's belief that without government, there can be no free market.

But neither the existence of a problem the market cannot handle correctly nor the recognition that government has the power to correct the problem is sufficient to argue that government should tackle all such problems.

It must always be asked: How much should be spent (resources used) to correct the problem? Because the solution to a problem should not cost more than it is worth.

It should not cost more to fix a problem than the value of what will be saved by fixing it. It is a simple rule that is not always simple to use because it is seldom easy to accurately measure or estimate either the benefits or the costs to society from correcting a problem. A common methodology used to decide what should and should not be done is called benefit-cost analysis.

7. Benefit-cost analysis.

Benefit-cost analysis, as its name implies, compares the benefits of a policy, action, or program with its costs. If the benefits are greater than the costs, it can be argued that it should be done.

The simple benefit-cost equation compares the initial cost of a project (it could be a dam or a plan to regulate pollution) with the present value of its expected future benefits.

To be meaningful, future benefits must be net benefits, which means estimating future benefits minus estimated future costs.

And the future net benefits must be "discounted" to obtain their "present value." Discounting is the reverse of compound interest. \$1 invested at 5% interest will be worth \$1 + \$1(.05) in one year--the initial amount plus the interest earned. For any year (n) in the future, the \$1 investment will be equal to $\$1(1 + .05)^n$, which is a statement of compound interest.

Reversing the logic, \$1 received 10 years from now is not worth \$1 today. It is worth whatever has to be invested at the going rate of interest to grow to \$1 in 10 years.

The formula for computing the present value of a future amount is: $PV = FV/(1+ i)^n$, where PV is the present value, FV is the future value, n is the number of years before the future benefit occurs, and i is the interest rate.

For \$1 received in 10 years with an interest rate of 5%, the $PV = \$1/(1 + .05)^{10}$. The answer to the equation tells how much would have to be invested today, at 5% interest, to grow, with compound interest, to \$1 in 10 years.

The same general equation can be used to make decisions about many government actions. Net benefits can be estimated for each future year. The present value of each future year's net benefit can be calculated, using the appropriate interest rate. Then, the present values of all future benefits can be added together. If the sum is greater than the initial cost, it can be concluded that the project adds more to society's benefits than to its costs.

8. Equity.

Another activity that governments become involved in is the redistribution of income. When a nation, such as the United States, believes in some sort of "equity" for its citizens, however defined, it is government, at national, state, and local levels that is responsible for programs aimed at "equalizing" opportunities, if not incomes.

Progressive taxes, such as the current income tax, tax higher incomes at higher rates. Subsidies for food or housing help those with low incomes. Transfer payments, such as welfare programs and unemployment insurance, give money to those with little or no income. But no combination of taxes and subsidies will, or was ever intended to, make all incomes equal. Few people want a society where all incomes are equal anyway. What most say they want is an opportunity to do as well as possible, which is why free-market societies focus more on reducing discrimination and on making education and training available to everyone than on equalizing incomes.

It should be clear to everyone that a free market does not yield a distribution of income that is "fair." The market will not correct the inequalities of "birth," where some are wealthy by inheritance rather than by their own efforts and accomplishments. The market will not equalize incomes for people with vastly different abilities. And the market will not make up for good or bad luck.

Even so, and given the fact that the distribution of income that occurs does not have to be accepted, it is normally believed that the best way to deal with inequalities is to make certain that each individual has a chance to compete at the highest level. Help those who cannot help themselves, but do not take away the incentive for everyone to work as hard as he or she wants and to reap the gains from that work. The argument normally includes the idea that there is nothing wrong with large inequalities in income, as long as everyone is able to live at an acceptable minimum standard.

9. Conclusion.

The goal of this text is to give each student the knowledge needed to understand economics in the real world. It is hoped that each student will finish with the ability to read newspapers, magazines, and books, watch television, and listen to the radio as a "critic"—someone who can separate truth from fiction and erroneous conclusions from rational thought.

The student should understand:

How to explain or predict the results of changes that affect markets.

Why a free market is "good." How free markets maximize the wealth of the nation by causing an efficient use of resources.

Why a free market cannot allocate resources efficiently in the face of positive externalities, negative externalities, common property resources, public goods, and monopoly power.

Why government is needed to correct the misallocation of resources caused by positive externalities, negative externalities, common property resources, public goods, and monopoly power.

PART THREE: MACROECONOMICS

18

A Macroeconomic Model

Macroeconomic models are used to explain and predict national variables, such as unemployment, inflation, recession, foreign trade, and economic growth. As with microeconomics, if what is happening or is expected to happen is not "acceptable," economic analysis offers possible actions to "make it better."

Prior to the Great Depression of the 1930's, mainstream economists believed that the natural tendency of the economy was to reach an equilibrium with full employment, at least in the long run. Periods of high unemployment were assumed to be short-term aberrations that would eventually be corrected by the economy itself—without government interference. As a result, no one kept track of the economy's performance or economic variables. As surprising as it might sound today, the government did not even keep track of unemployment numbers. After all, if the economy were a self-correcting marvel, there was no reason to spend time and resources tracking variables that no one would try to change.

The Depression showed that to be a false assumption. And when the Depression ended, the arguments of John Maynard Keynes—that that government must be responsible for ensuring full employment and stable prices—led to an explosion in the collection and reporting of economic statistics. If the government were to be responsible for the overall health of the economy, it was necessary to know what the economy was doing.

Today, it is virtually impossible to avoid economic statistics. Every newspaper offers reports on Gross Domestic Product, Consumer Prices, interest rates, unemployment rates, and so on. And, based on such measurements, decisions are made by the government or by the Federal Reserve as to whether or not the economy is doing as well as possible, and, if not, what should be done to correct the problems. If unemployment is unacceptably high, how can it be reduced? If economic growth is inadequate, how can it be improved? If the economy is stuck in a recession or a depression, how can it be brought to an end? If the inflation rate is too high, how can it be lowered?

Along with the revolution in the statistical awareness of economic variables, was a revolution in economic thinking. The Classical models, based on the idea of a self-correcting economy, were replaced by Keynesian models that allowed for an equilibrium with less than full employment. Although the Keynesian argument represented the dominant view of academic and government economists, monetarist (or Chicago school) economists pointed out that such models misunderstood the role of money in the economy.

The simple macroeconomic model used in this text is consistent with both Keynesian and monetarist thinking. It uses two diagrams.

One diagram shows:

1) Aggregate Demand (AD);
2) Aggregate Supply (AS); and
3) an indicator of "full employment" output (Y_{FE}).

A second diagram shows the money market:

1) The supply of money (MS), and
2) the demand for money (MD).

1. The money market

Although interest rates are a general equilibrium variable affected by virtually everything in the economy, most macroeconomic models use the money market to help explain interest rates, which means looking at the supply of and demand for money.

Demand. The demand for money is determined by assuming that money and interest-bearing assets (e.g. bonds) are pure substitutes. The assumption is that people will hold money (as cash and in checking accounts) so they can pay for expected purchases and have funds available to buy bonds (interest-bearing assets) when bonds are attractive investments. Each reason for holding money is negatively related to interest rates. First, the higher interest rates are, the greater is the opportunity cost of holding money instead of having it invested where it earns interest. Second, the higher interest rates are, the more likely it is that rates will fall, thereby leading to the possibility of capital gains on bonds (discussed further in the chapter on the bond market).

Therefore, the higher the rate of interest, the less money people want to hold, meaning the more of their assets they want to transfer into interest-bearing bonds. The lower the rate of interest, the more of their assets people want to hold as money. The demand for money, as a function of interest rates, is shown in Figure 18.1. *The demand for money is not a demand for income; the demand for money is derived from how people choose to hold their assets—as money or bonds.*

If the price level or total output changes, the demand for money will also change, because an increase in prices means people need more money to make the same purchases they made before the price level rose. An increase in total output means there is more stuff to buy, which, again, requires more money.

> **The bond market**
> Macroeconomic models can use either the money market or the bond market, because the money market and the bond market are complimentary markets. The bond market is examined in the following chapter.

Figure 18.1

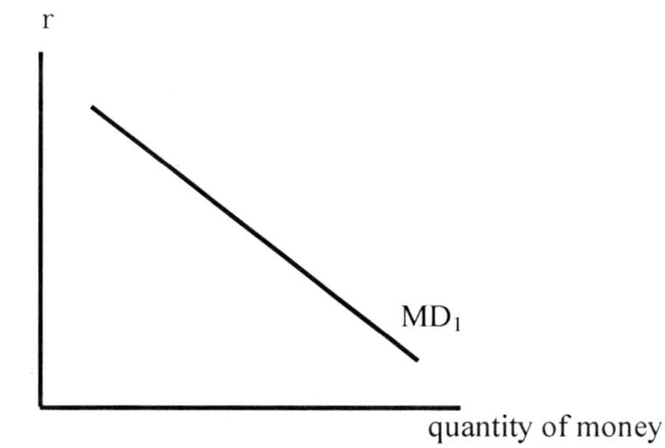

Supply. The supply of money is assumed to be independent of interest rates and the level of economic activity, because, in the real world, the Federal Reserve sets the nominal supply of money at the level it believes is "best" for the economy.

In Figure 18.2, the nominal money supply is shown as the vertical line at MS_1.

Figure 18.2

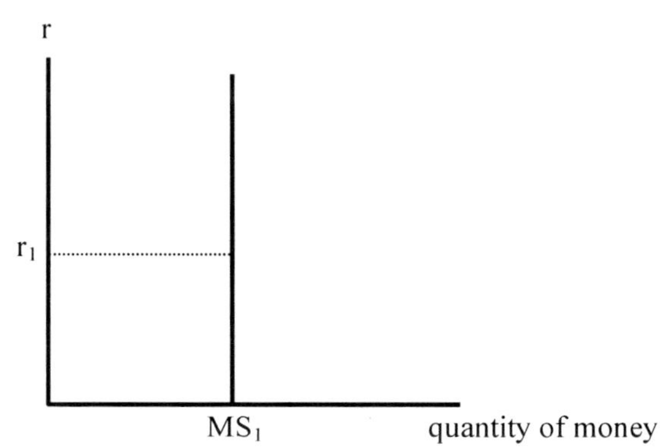

The "nominal" supply of money is the actual quantity of money in the system, unadjusted for inflation or deflation.

The "real" supply of money is the actual quantity of money adjusted for inflation or deflation.

If the total supply of money in the system is ten one-dollar bills, then the nominal money supply is ten dollars. If the price level doubles, the real supply of money is cut in half, to five dollars. Why? Because the ten one-dollar bills will now buy only half of what they could previously buy.

Although the difference between the nominal and real money supply is relatively simple, it is necessary to be clear as to which measure is being used in a model.

> The Federal Reserve does not actually set the quantity of money; it controls the rate of growth of the money supply. Although most models simplify the real world by using the quantity of money, rather than the rate of growth of the money supply, simplifying the concept of money to a quantity rather than a rate of change does not diminish the ability of the models to explain and predict.

Equilibrium. The money market is in equilibrium when the demand for money is equal to the supply of money.

In Figure 18.3, the demand for money MD_1 and the supply of money MS_1 yields the equilibrium interest rate r_1.

Figure 18.3

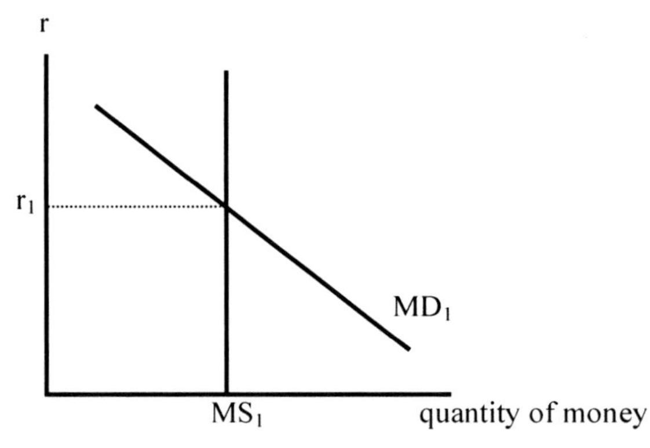

The price level and interest rates.

A question that is crucial to understanding a macroeconomic model is: What happens to interest rates if there is an increase in the general price level?

The importance of this question will become obvious in the following section. For now, we can simply ask: What will an increase in the general price level do to the equilibrium rate of interest?

The initial equilibrium is shown by the demand for money, MD_1, and the supply of money, MS_1, in Figure 18.4. The initial equilibrium interest rate is r_1.

Figure 18.4

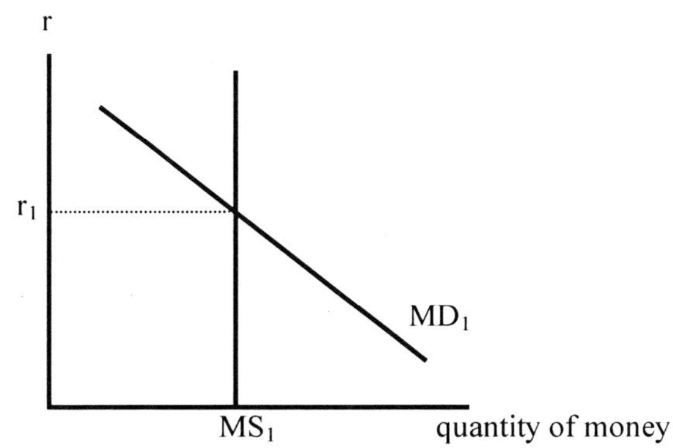

If the price level increases, it will require more money to make the same purchases. The result is an increase in the demand for money.

The new demand for money can be shown as a change from MD_1 to MD_2 in Figure 18.5. The change in the price level does not affect the nominal supply of money. It remains at MS_1.

Figure 18.5

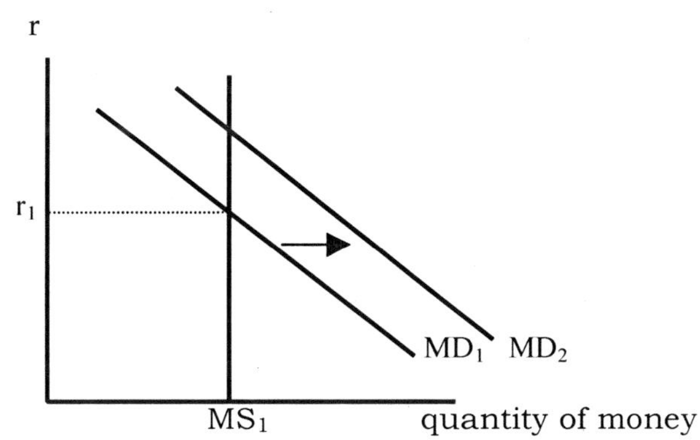

It is assumed that whenever the general price level changes, the demand for money changes, because the quantity of money people want to hold at each interest rate is affected by the prices of goods and services they plan on buying.

If prices increase, people require more money to make the same purchases they made before the price level increased, which means they will trade interest-bearing assets for money.

If prices decrease, people require less money to make the same purchases they made before the price level decreased, which means they will trade money for interest-bearing assets.

In the new equilibrium, shown in Figure 18.6, the new demand for money, MD_2, is equal to the original supply of money, MS_1, at the new equilibrium interest rate r_2.

Figure 18.6

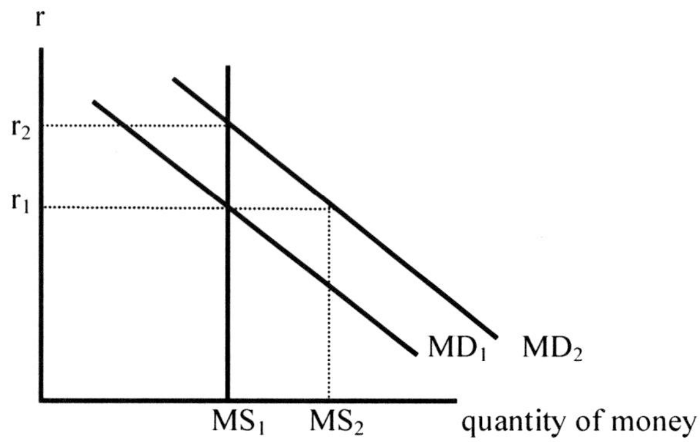

The general price level increases.

The equilibrium interest rate increases from r_1 to r_2.

The nominal quantity of money supplied and held by the public remains at MS_1 (because the nominal supply of money did not change).

Therefore, it can be concluded that an increase in the general price level causes interest rates to rise, assuming that the nominal supply of money and all other things remain constant.

A few definitions:

Nominal money supply is the quantity of money in the economy at a given time. The two most common measures of money are: M1 and M2.

M1 is defined to be paper currency and coins in circulation plus deposits in checking accounts. It is a definition of the most "liquid" form of money, because it represents funds that can be used instantly to make purchases.

M2 is defined to be M1 plus deposits in savings accounts, small time deposits, and non-institutional money-market funds. M2 is not quite as liquid as M1 because it may take time to withdraw funds from such accounts before they can be used to make purchases.

Factors assumed to be constant when deriving the demand for money are the overall price level and Gross Domestic Product. Increases in either lead to an increase in the demand for money, because more money is needed to make purchases if prices rise or if people become wealthier.

NOTE: Some explanations of the money market use the real money supply; some use the nominal money supply. The choice is a matter of preference. Each leads to the same conclusion. The difference is: If you use the real money supply, rather than the nominal money supply, a change in the price level would cause the real value of the money supply to change, while the demand for money would remain constant.

Consumer Price Index (CPI)
The Consumer Price Index calculates the cost of a given "basket" of goods for different time periods.
The measure assigns weights to items based on the percentage of total expenditures they accounted for during a base period.

2. Aggregate Demand (AD)

Aggregate Demand in a macroeconomic model is not the same as a demand curve for a particular good or service, because aggregate demand is not a simple relationship between price and quantity demanded. Neither is it a summation of all market demand curves.

A short-term aggregate demand curve is a series of **equilibrium** points showing the short-run equilibrium level of **Gross Domestic Product** (output) corresponding to each price level. It shows combinations of real output and the price level when both the commodity market and the money market are in equilibrium.

AD is shown on a diagram with the general price level on the vertical axis and real Gross Domestic Product on the horizontal axis.

Gross Domestic Product is used as a measure of economic activity. It is an estimate of the value of production within the country during a given time period, whether by domestic or foreign corporations. Because it is an estimate of current *production*, some things are not included, such as sales of used items, things not intended to be sold in the market (hobbies and things made for personal use), and intermediate goods (only final goods are included). Also important, there is no deduction for the negative value of pollution.
GDP is estimated by adding up the value of goods and services sold in the market during a given time period. Items included when calculating GDP are: Consumer spending on final goods and services (C), private investment (I), government purchases of goods and services (G), and net exports—meaning exports minus imports (NX).

By definition: GDP = C + I + G + NX

Real Gross Domestic Product (Real GDP) is GDP adjusted for inflation or deflation.

***Deriving an aggregate demand curve*:**

Imagine arbitrarily choosing a level of total spending and a corresponding price level, such as Y_1 and P_1 in Figure 18.7. Those values yield point A.

Figure 18.7

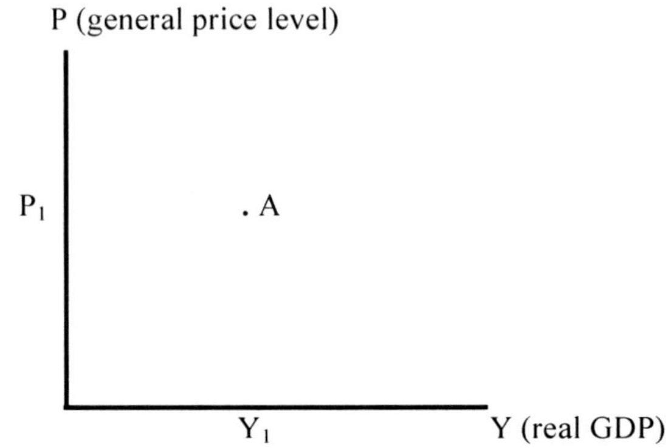

Assume that point A in Figure 18.7 is one point on an aggregate demand curve.

Then determine what happens if the price level increases.

Following the money-market discussion above:

If the general price level increases, while the nominal money supply is held constant, the demand for money will increase, because the demand for money is greater than the supply of money at the original interest rate, thereby causing interest rates to rise.

When interest rates rise, interest-sensitive spending decreases. Higher interest rates cause consumers to buy less, cause business to invest less, and lead to a decrease in net exports. And because virtually all spending—other than government spending—is affected by changes in interest rates, the end result is that at a higher overall price level, total spending will be less than it is at a lower price level.

> An increase in interest rates causes net exports to decrease because as interest rates rise, foreigners will buy more US interest-bearing investments. Doing so increases the demand for US dollars, thereby increasing the value of the dollar relative to other currencies. The result is a decrease in exports (because American goods now cost more to foreigners) and an increase in imports (because foreign goods now cost less to Americans).

The new level of spending that corresponds to the new price level yields another point on the aggregate demand curve—to the left of and above point A—such as point B, shown in Figure 18.8. If many such equilibrium points are plotted on a diagram, they yield an aggregate demand curve (AD) that has a negative slope, such as AD in Figure 18.8.

Figure 18.8

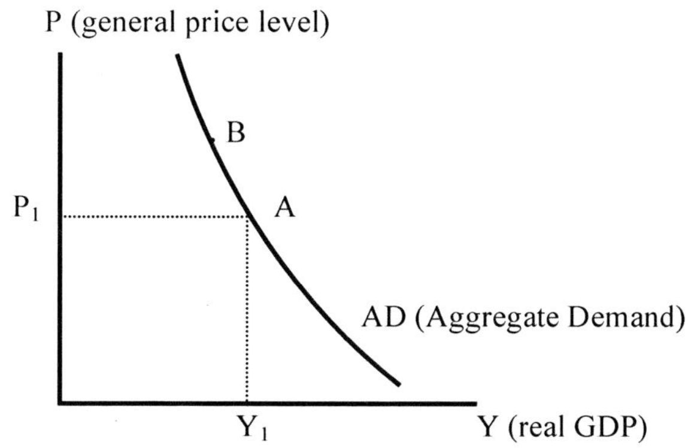

An aggregate demand curve takes account of four separate spending categories: consumer spending, private investment spending, government spending on goods and services, and net exports.

The reason aggregate demand is not the same as a market demand curve is because of the logic used to construct it. A demand curve in an individual market shows the maximum quantity of that product that consumers are willing and able to buy at various prices during a given time period *with all other things held constant.* An aggregate demand curve shows the total spending that takes place at each price level, but it is derived for a fixed nominal supply of money and it *assumes that interest rates will change* as the price level changes.

In other words, a demand curve in an individual market shows what happens to the quantity demanded when the price of that product changes.

An aggregate demand curve shows what happens to the equilibrium level of total spending when the overall price level changes, given the fact that a change in the price level also changes the demand for money, which changes interest rates and, therefore, consumer spending, investment spending, and net exports.

That is why a short-term aggregate demand curve is a series of equilibrium points showing combinations of real output and the price level when both the commodity market and the money market are in equilibrium.

3. Aggregate Supply (AS)

A short-term aggregate supply curve in a macroeconomic model is logically different from the supply curve for an individual market. The supply curve for an individual market shows the maximum quantity that producers are willing and able to sell at each price during a given time period, all other things constant. An aggregate supply curve shows something different: It shows what happens to the general price level as GDP increases or decreases. Rather than assuming that all other things remain constant as we move along an AS curve, it is assumed that all prices will change—except nominal wages. It is normally assumed that nominal wages will remain relatively constant in the short run, even if there is a change in the demand for labor. In the long run (which could be a year or more), an excess demand for labor is assumed to cause wages to increase and an excess supply of labor is assumed to cause wages to decrease.

Deriving an aggregate supply curve:

Aggregate supply is based on the idea that as total output expands, the general price level will increase. There are two reasons for the conclusion that there is a positive relationship between total output (GDP) and the general price level. One is that the increased demand for factors of production (needed to produce more stuff) will cause their prices to rise. The second comes from the concept of "diminishing marginal productivity." Diminishing marginal productivity means that as more and more workers are added to the production process, each additional worker adds less to total output than the previous worker did. That assumption, added to the assumption that nominal wages are constant in the short run, means that each additional unit of output costs more to produce than the previous unit.

Therefore, as GDP increases, the general price level increases.

Imagine choosing an arbitrary level of output and its corresponding price level in equilibrium, such as Y_2 and P_2 in Figure 18.9. Assume that those two values yield one point on an aggregate supply curve (point C in Figure 18.9). Then imagine what happens if output is increased. If output increases, the overall costs of production will increase. Therefore, at a level of output greater than Y_2, the general price level will also be higher. And at a level of output lower than Y_2, the general price level will be lower.

If a number of such equilibrium points are plotted on a diagram, they yield an aggregate supply curve that has a positive slope, such as AS in Figure 18.9.

Figure 18.9

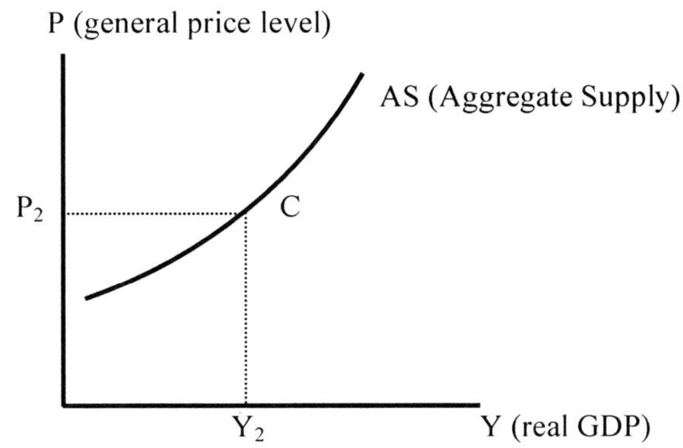

4. Potential output (Y_{FE})

The vertical line in figure 18.10, drawn at Y_{FE}, represents what is called "potential output." It is the level of Gross Domestic Product that would occur if the economy were at its "natural rate of unemployment," which is defined to be "full employment."

Figure 18.10

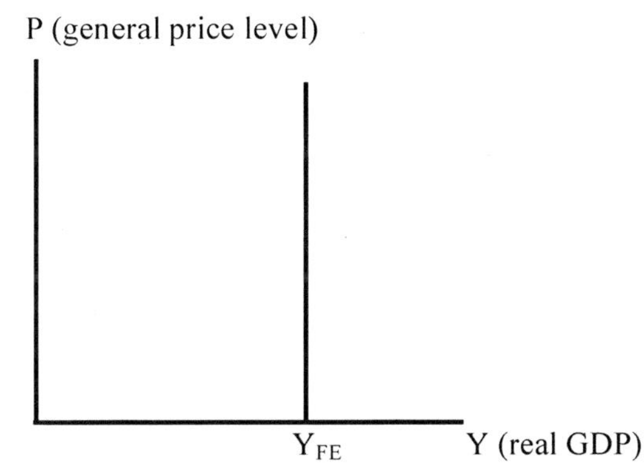

Potential output is a somewhat abstract concept, because the natural rate of unemployment is not a fixed number, because the percentage of unemployed workers that is assumed to represent "full employment" changes over time as economic conditions and expectations change.

One reason for using the concept of "full employment output" is to have a "benchmark," against which to compare economic performance: If the economy is operating at less than Y_{FE}, it means there is "unacceptable" unemployment; if it is operating beyond Y_{FE}, it means there is greater than full employment. A second reason is to show the possible pressure on nominal wages. If there is unemployment, it can be assumed that nominal wages will fall over time. If there is more than full employment, it can be assumed that nominal wages will rise over time.

5. Aggregate Demand, Aggregate Supply, and Potential Output combined

Figure 18.11 is the core of a short-run macroeconomic model that incorporates the money market, consumer spending, private investment spending, government spending, foreign trade, and production.

It is used to explain and predict fiscal policy, monetary policy, foreign trade deficits or surpluses, changes in oil prices, and any other variable that affects either the consumption or production of goods and services. It looks difficult. It is not.

Figure 18.11

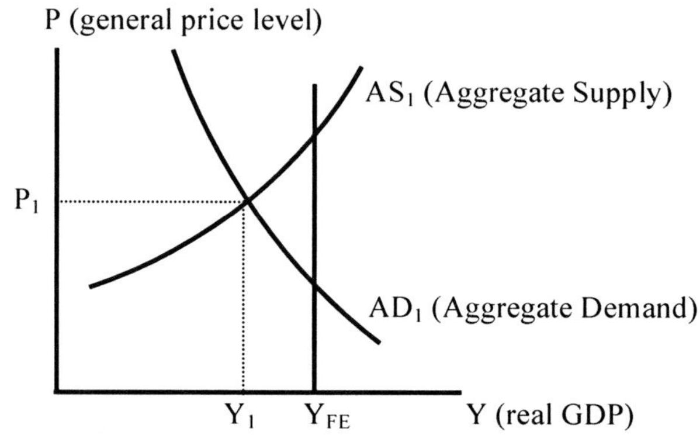

6. Using the short-run model

The model in Figure 18.11 can be used to explain and predict equilibrium values of variables and to explain and predict the consequences of changes. In many cases, changes are introduced to alter an equilibrium that is not acceptable, such as a recession. Intentional changes normally fall into the areas of fiscal policy, which means changing government spending or taxes to alter economic performance, or monetary policy, which means changing the money supply to affect economic performance. It is a relatively straightforward process.

The typical macroeconomic problem, like the typical microeconomic problem, uses the logic of comparative statics, meaning that the analysis explains or predicts an initial equilibrium, a change, and a new equilibrium.

Many macroeconomic problems begin with the observation that there is an unacceptable level of GDP, employment, inflation, or international trade balances. The problem is then to determine how to "fix what we don't like."

In order to use a model to explain and predict, and to offer solutions to unacceptable levels of important variables, it is necessary to understand the forces that create an equilibrium, movements along aggregate demand and aggregate supply curves, and how changes in the world lead to increases or decreases in aggregate demand and/or aggregate supply, or to changes in the full employment level of GDP.

Short-run equilibrium

Given the aggregate demand and aggregate supply functions in Figure 18.12 (which is the same as Figure 18.11), there is an overall equilibrium where aggregate demand is equal to aggregate supply. That equilibrium is where the two curves intersect. If AD and AS intersect to the right of Y_{FE}, it means the economy is operating at more than full employment. If AD and AS intersect to the left of Y_{FE}, it means there is unemployment. If AD and AS intersect exactly at Y_{FE}, it means the economy is in equilibrium with full employment.

Figure 18.12

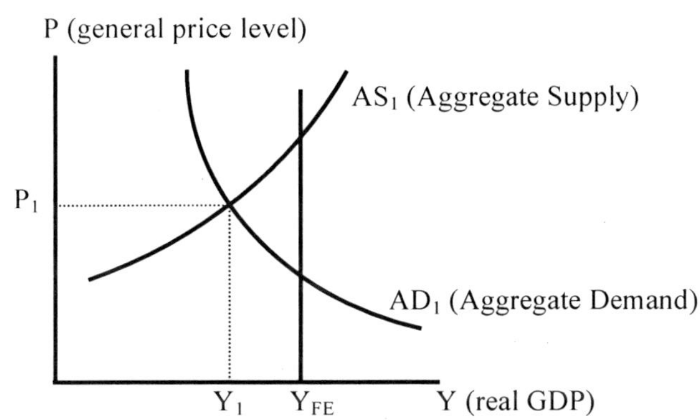

The explanation of equilibrium is straightforward:

1) If the economy is at any point to the right of the AD curve, there is an excess supply of goods and services. More is being produced than purchased at the given price level, causing inventories to build up. In order to maximize profits, firms will decrease production and prices, moving the economy to the left and down—to a point on AD.

2) If the economy is at any point to the left of the AD curve, there is an excess demand for goods and services, meaning that production is too low relative to demand at that price level. The result is an unwanted decline of inventories, which leads firms to increase production and raise prices, moving the economy to the right and upward—until it is at a point on AD.

Therefore, to be in equilibrium, the economy must be at some point on the AD curve.

3) If the economy is at a point to the right of the AS curve, it means that too many workers are being hired and too much is being produced—because the wage rate is above what workers are adding to revenue. As a result, firms will reduce production and

increase prices in order to increase profits, moving the economy up and to the left on the diagram—to some point on AS.

4) If the economy is at a point to the left of the AS curve, it means that too few workers are being hired and too little is being produced—because the wage rate is below what workers are adding to revenue. As a result, producers will decrease prices and increase output until the economy is back on the AS curve. On the diagram, it is a move down and to the right—to some point on AS. In other words, if the economy is at any point to the left of the AS curve, the overall price level is higher than the equilibrium level, meaning that for that level of output, prices must be lower.

Therefore, to be in equilibrium, the economy must also be at some point on the AS curve.

5) Therefore, the economy is in equilibrium only where AD and AS intersect, because that is the only point that lies on both curves.

Movements along an Aggregate Demand curve

Anything that causes the price level to change will result in a move along the AD curve. The process was explained above in *Deriving an aggregate demand curve*.

Movements along an Aggregate Supply curve

A change in the overall price level due to an increase in output causes a move along the AS curve. The process was explained above in *Deriving an aggregate supply curve*.

What causes aggregate demand to increase or decrease?

A change in anything other than the price level that leads to a change in C, I, G, or NX will cause an increase or decrease in the AD curve.

Some important factors, and their impact on aggregate demand, are:

A *decrease in taxes* means that people can spend more at each price level, meaning that aggregate demand will increase, thereby yielding a new AD curve to the right of (or above) the original AD curve.

An *increase in taxes* means that people cannot spend as much at each price level, meaning that aggregate demand will decrease, thereby yielding a new AD curve to the left of (or below) the original curve.

An *increase in government spending* means that total spending is greater at each price level, meaning that aggregate demand will increase, thereby yielding a new AD curve to the right of (or above) the original curve.

A *decrease in government spending* means that total spending is lower at each price level, meaning that aggregate demand will decrease, thereby yielding a new AD curve to the left of (or below) the original curve.

An *increase in investment spending* means that total spending is greater at each price level, meaning that aggregate demand will increase, thereby yielding a new AD curve to the right of (or above) the original curve.

A *decrease in investment spending* means that total spending is lower at each price level, meaning that aggregate demand will decrease, thereby yielding a new AD curve to the left of (or below) the original curve.

An *increase in autonomous consumer spending* means that total spending is greater at each price level, meaning that aggregate demand will increase, thereby yielding a new AD curve to the right of (or above) the original curve.

A *decrease in autonomous consumer spending* means that total spending is lower at each price level, meaning that aggregate demand will decrease, thereby yielding a new AD curve to the left of (or below) the original curve.

An *increase in the money supply* means that interest rates will decline, causing increases in total spending at each price level, meaning that aggregate demand will increase, thereby yielding a new AD curve to the right of (or above) the original curve.

A *decrease in the money supply* means that interest rates will rise, causing decreases in total spending at each price level, meaning that aggregate demand will decrease, thereby yielding a new AD curve to the left of (or below) the original curve.

An *increase in the demand for money* means that interest rates will rise, causing decreases in total spending at each price level, meaning that aggregate demand will decrease, thereby yielding a new AD curve to the left of (or below) the original curve.

A *decrease in the demand for money* means that interest rates will fall, causing increases in total spending at each price level, meaning that aggregate demand will increase, thereby yielding a new AD curve to the right of (or above) the original curve.

> Each of the above changes is relatively straightforward. Each will be examined in greater detail as we look at various issues. They are not presented here as a list to be memorized. Economics based on the memorization of "shift factors" or jargon is not real economics. Economics that is functional and useful is based on understanding the logic of how to make predictions and explanations. Economic functions do not "shift"; they change. They increase or decrease. And the increase or decrease is logical and rational.

What causes aggregate supply to increase or decrease?

A change in anything other than total output that causes prices to change can lead to an increase in aggregate supply. Examples are: changes in technology, changes in oil prices, and changes in the nominal wage rate.

The impact of a change on aggregate supply is logical, as will be seen in the chapters that follow.

For now, it is sufficient to understand that an increase in oil prices, for example, which makes production more expensive, causes a decrease in AS; meaning there is a new AS curve to the left of (or above) the original AS curve. A decrease in oil prices, on the other hand, makes production less expensive and causes AS to increase; meaning there is a new AS curve to the right of (or below) the original AS curve.

In simple terms, if total output is increased, the greater demand for inputs of production causes their prices to rise and leads to a move up the AS curve. But an increase in the price of some item used in the production process raises the cost of production and causes a decrease in the AS curve.

In order to use a macroeconomic model to explain and predict the impact of changes, or to determine ways to correct unacceptable levels of unemployment or prices, it is necessary to understand how outside factors or variables affect AD and/or AS. In most cases, the relationship is simple. An increase in government spending causes AD to increase. An increase in taxes causes AD to decrease. An increase in technology causes AS to increase. A rise in interest rates causes AD to decrease. A fall in interest rates causes AD to increase.

The only somewhat complicated relationship involves interest rates.

Interest rates and Aggregate Demand

We already know that a change in the price level causes a change in the demand for money, which causes a change in interest rates, which causes a change in total spending, which leads to a move along the AD curve.

But what if interest rates change first?

An increase in interest rates (with the general price level unchanged) will cause a decrease in all interest-sensitive spending, whether by consumers or business, thereby causing a decrease in AD.

A decrease in interest rates (with the general price level unchanged) will cause an increase in all interest-sensitive spending, whether by consumers or business, thereby causing an increase in AD.

In other words, if the price level changes first, there will be a change in the demand for money and interest rates that leads to a move along the AD curve; but if interest rates change first, possibly because of a change in the supply of money, then there will be a change in the AD curve.

The difference between these two effects will become clear as the problems in the following chapters are addressed.

7. A complete macroeconomic model, including the money market.

Macroeconomic models incorporate either the money market or the bond market in order to show the interaction between the price level and interest rates, and between interest rates and aggregate demand.

Most textbooks use the money market, because it explicitly shows interest rates.

The only possible confusion from using the money market, rather than the bond market, is that it is necessary to remember that a decrease in the demand for money means an increase in the demand for bonds, and that an increase in the demand for money means a decrease in the demand for bonds.

That is important because:

1) An increase in the demand for bonds, which leads to an increase in the price of bonds, means an automatic decrease in interest rates.

2) A decrease in the demand for bonds, which leads to a decrease in the price of bonds, means an automatic increase in interest rates.

Other than that, it may sometimes be necessary to remember that an excess demand for money is the same as an excess supply of bonds and an excess demand for bonds is the same as an excess supply of money.

Figure 18.13

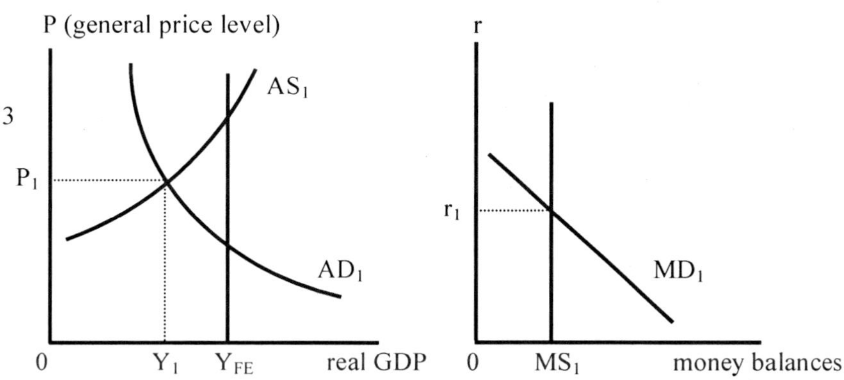

Given the two diagrams in Figure 18.13, it is possible to address the major concerns of macroeconomics: unemployment, inflation, recession, foreign trade, interest rates, and economic growth.

It is also possible to explain and predict the results of changes that directly affect aggregate demand or aggregate supply, or that impact AD or AS through changes in interest rates caused by changes in the supply of money, the demand for money, the supply of bonds, or the demand for bonds.

For some short-run problems, the full-employment level of GDP is not shown. Ignoring full-employment GDP assumes that it does not come into play in the problem being discussed.

8. Judging a macroeconomic equilibrium.

Given that the overall objective of economics is to maximize the well-being or wealth of the nation, the goal of macroeconomics is to use economic knowledge to promote full employment, stable prices, and acceptable economic growth.

The concept of "economic efficiency," which, according to textbooks, can be used to judge a microeconomic equilibrium, is a somewhat abstract concept in the sense that it is not always easy to apply the theory to what is actually happening in real markets.

The goals of macroeconomics are normally easier to see, although they are often overshadowed by politics or self-interest.

Virtually every newspaper in the country offers daily statistics on unemployment, inflation, and reported changes in Gross Domestic Product. When the economy is suffering from recession or inflation, changes in employment or the overall price index become the staple of televised news, as well as moving to the front page of most newspapers.

The question is: What do the numbers mean?

There is an old story about a company that was trying to hire a new accountant. There were three applicants to interview.

When the first came in, he was asked, "How much is two plus two?"

"Three," he answered.

"Not too good," the interviewer thought, "although he might be good at preparing our tax returns."

When the second candidate was asked the same question, he answered, "Five."

"Not too good," the interviewer thought, "But he might be good at preparing our annual shareholders' reports."

When the third candidate was asked the same question, he answered, "Who wants to know?" He got the job.

The third candidate understood one of the basic facts of life: There can be many answers to the same question, and different people *want* different answers. As a result, even the simplest questions are sometimes difficult to answer.

The accounting story is relevant to economics, because the standard method for measuring our nation's economic performance is a statistical procedure called "national income accounting." And if you ask: "How is the US economy doing?" you should be prepared for many different answers, depending on who you ask, what they think you want to hear, and whether or not they make mistakes with their calculations.

To begin with, there are at least six different ways of legitimately answering such a question. How are we doing:

(1) relative to the recent past;

(2) relative to the more distant past;

(3) relative to what other countries are doing;

(4) relative to current expectations;

(5) relative to past expectations;

(6) relative to our potential.

You can probably think of more, but answering these six would give us a good idea of how the US economy is doing today. Unfortunately, it is not quite that easy. The problem is that we cannot begin to make comparisons until we know what we want to compare.

Do we want to focus on total production? Total wealth? Total income? Per capita income? The unemployment rate? The inflation rate? Productivity increases? The growth rate of production, wealth, total income, or per capita income? Military strength? The crime rate? Poverty? Drug abuse? Health? Life expectancy? Literacy? Infant mortality?

The list is endless, because everyone has his or her ideas about what is most important at any given time. Why are there so many different ideas about what matters most? Because each item on such a list is something that can affect our happiness or well-being. In other words, we are back to the same old problem: If we knew how to define and measure happiness, that is exactly what we would do. But because we do not know how to do it, the best we can do is to track things we can measure and that we believe are connected to our happiness. Of course, that means making some big assumptions about the effects of something we can measure on something we cannot. It also means that we must be aware of the fact that gains in one area are almost always going to come by giving up something else that matters.

For example, an increase in defense spending may mean less stuff available for consumers; and a cleaner environment will mean higher production costs for many goods and services. If the quality of our environment had absolutely no impact on our happiness, then it would not matter if production and consumption costs were kept as low as possible by sacrificing the environment. But the environment does matter. In fact, so many things matter and so many things are interconnected that the problem of measuring our progress can seem almost insurmountable.

So what can we do?

We can do what economists normally do: We can begin by recognizing that no matter how long our list of concerns is, virtually everything on the list is related to acceptable economic growth, an adequate the level of employment, and stable prices. If a nation is wealthy enough and if economic growth, which is normally defined as the real rate of increase in total annual production, is great enough, then it will be possible to tackle at least some of the issues on the list.

9. Measuring real economic growth.

In order to track year-to-year changes in total production, statisticians add up everything that is produced in one year and then compare it to the sum of everything produced in previous years and future years. The problem is: How do you add 100,000 Fords to 4,000,000 bushels of wheat, 50,000 new homes, the services of lawyers, plumbers, electricians, and accountants, and so on? You can't, because you cannot add "apples and oranges."

The solution is to keep track of total spending, in dollars, which avoids the problem of trying to add up all sorts of physical products and diverse services. Also, the data is more accessible.

But does it make sense to estimate production by measuring spending? It does if you assume that whatever was bought had to be produced of made available in the market.

Of course, some of what is purchased this year was produced last year, and some of what is produced this year will not be sold this year. So the total spending number has to be adjusted to account for additions and subtractions to inventories.

Also, some of what is purchased in the US was manufactured in other countries, and some of what in produced in the US is sold abroad. Therefore, it is necessary to add in the value of exports and subtract the value of imports.

Finally, after adding up the dollar value of all spending, it is also necessary to adjust everything for inflation or deflation. If prices are increasing, then the dollar value of total spending can increase even if no more is actually produced or bought. If prices are decreasing, it can look as though production has declined when it has not.

Economists calculate "nominal" economic growth using actual market prices. Then they calculate "real" economic growth by adjusting the numbers to take account of rising or falling prices. Doing so makes it possible to measure the economy's rate of growth by tracking the increases or decreases in the real value of total spending (adjusted for changes in inventories and net exports).

In order to make certain that everyone is talking about the same thing and that the calculations will be the same year after year, all these ideas were organized into a simple definition: Total consumption was defined to be equal to total spending by consumers, plus total spending by business on investment (including net changes in inventories), plus total spending by government, plus the total value of exports minus imports. The total spending number is called Gross Domestic Product (GDP) because it is an estimate of total production in the US, whether by US or foreign corporations, and it excludes production by US firms in foreign countries.

$$GDP = C + I = G + NX$$

The result is that the standard way to judge a macroeconomic equilibrium is by keeping track of Gross Domestic Product (GDP), employment, and the general price level, each of which is shown clearly in the model presented above.

10. How to solve macroeconomic problems.

Solving macroeconomic problems follows the same logic of "comparative statics" used to solve microeconomic problems, which means comparing one equilibrium (one static position) with another equilibrium (another static position).

As with microeconomic problems, it is normally difficult to say anything meaningful about the impact of a change without assuming that we begin in one equilibrium and end in another equilibrium.

And, as with individual market issues, it is normally difficult to say much that is meaningful about the dynamics of the change—of exactly how the move from an initial equilibrium to a new equilibrium takes place.

1. Begin with the question.

The analysis always begins with a question. After being given a problem, make certain that you can state the question.

The question is important; it is what sets up the problem. Without a specific question, there is no problem to solve.

What information is being asked for? State exactly what is to be explained or predicted. Is it a change in market price? Or equilibrium quantity? Or profits? Or the well-being of an individual? Be precise. In most cases, it will take only one or two sentences. Be clear about what is being studied. Which variables are being explained or predicted?

It is also necessary to be clear about the change that led to the question? The change may be an outside effect or it may be the desire to achieve a different equilibrium. In either case, the change is likely to affect many things. If the change is a new concern with unemployment, inflation, or economic growth, or a change in tax collections, you must be clear about what is happening, or happened, or is expected to happen.

2. The three steps of comparative statics.

Given a question, which, in macroeconomics, is often triggered by a concern with the current or expected state of the economy, the problem moves to looking at something that was assumed to have been held constant, or a need to explain what happened or is happening. In any case, the steps to follow are: (1) describe the initial equilibrium; (2) explain how the change affects aggregate supply and/or aggregate demand; (3) describe the new equilibrium and compare the old and new equilibrium values.

(1) Describe the initial equilibrium.

Draw two diagrams. One showing aggregate supply and aggregate demand. The other showing the supply of and demand for money.

The question or problem determines exactly what must be described in the diagrams. It may be a situation that existed in the past, that exists in the present, or that can exist in the future.

Show the initial equilibrium by sketching aggregate supply and aggregate demand curves, and designating the full-employment level of real GDP (a vertical line). Show the initial equilibrium in the money market by sketching the supply and demand for money. (The supply of money is a vertical line.) Label each axis: P and real GDP in the aggregate supply and aggregate demand diagram; money balances and r in the money market diagram. Label the aggregate supply and aggregate demand functions AS_1 and AD_1. Label the full employment level of GDP Y_{FE}. Label the initial equilibrium values P_1 and

Y_1. Label the initial supply of money MS_1 and the demand for money MD_1. Label the initial interest rate r_1.

In most cases, there is no reason to worry about numbers. Simply sketch in the functions; but be careful to label each axis and each curve.

(2) Explain, and show on the diagrams, how the change causes a change in AS and/or AD and a change in the demand or supply of money.

Explain how or why the change (and ONLY that change) affects or is expected to affect aggregate supply or aggregate demand and the supply of or demand for money. If more than one change is introduced, it is likely that nothing meaningful can be said. It is almost always necessary to isolate individual changes in order to understand the impact of each.

How will AS and/or AD change? Will one or both remain constant? For example, increased oil prices affects aggregate supply, but not aggregate demand. Remember: It is assumed that a change in the general price level always affects the demand for money and, therefore, interest rates.

Show the change(s) on the diagrams by sketching in the new aggregate supply and/or aggregate demand curves and labeling them AS_2 and AD_2, and the new supply of and/or demand for money and labeling them MS_2 and MD_2.

(3) Describe the new equilibrium and explain what happens to the equilibrium values of the variables under consideration.

The new equilibrium is determined by the aggregate supply and aggregate demand functions that exist after the change has worked its way through the system. Label the new equilibrium price level P_2 and the new equilibrium real Gross Domestic Product GDP_2. Label the new equilibrium interest rate r_2.

How do the new price level and real GDP compare to the original price level and GDP? How does the new interest rate compare to the original interest rate? In other words, what happened or will happen to what is being studied?

For example, it might be concluded that: "The equilibrium price level increased from P_1 to P_2 and equilibrium GDP decreased from GDP_1 to GDP_2. And interest rates increased from, r_1 to r_2."

When describing the new equilibrium, it is normally not necessary to be any more specific than to describe the direction of change of the price level and real Gross Domestic Product and interest rates.

Conclusion

Most problems end with a conclusion that describes the new equilibrium and summarizes what happened. The conclusion might restate the problem, describe the expected change or changes in aggregate supply and/or aggregate demand, and state the change in the variable or variables being examined, such as the level of employment and interest rates. It should also specify the assumptions that were made to reach the given conclusion.

NOTE:

After solving a number of problems, it will be seen that the same logical framework is used over and over again. New problems do not require "new" procedures, "new" ways of thinking, or "new" theories.

The world is logical. Knowledgeable individuals know things that can help explain and predict what is happening or is expected to happen as the result of changes, which is why all opinions are not of equal value. Individuals with greater knowledge about certain things have opinions about those things that should be more valuable than the opinions of less knowledgeable observers. It is easy to say that an increase in the money supply will decrease interest rates and increase real Gross Domestic. It requires more knowledge to explain why, and to explain why that conclusion assumes that the initial equilibrium is at less than full employment. In most cases, it is better to be able to explain—step by step—why that is the correct answer, even though the answer appears obvious.

A Macroeconomic Model (AD, AS, Y_{FE}, MD and MS)—Summary

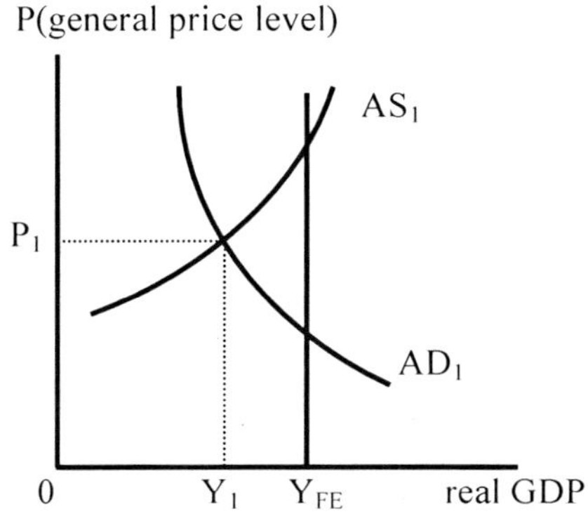

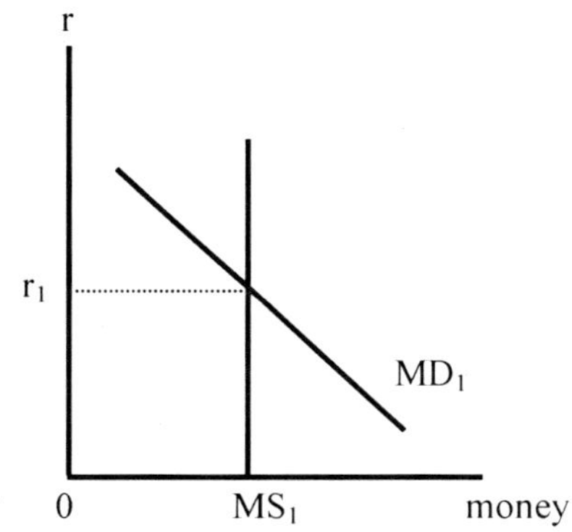

A macroeconomic model is used to explain and predict equilibrium values and changes in national variables, such as the level of employment, total output, the general price level, interest rates, and the impact of foreign trade. Major concerns are: unemployment, inflation, recession, and economic growth.

Money Market: Interest rates, which are affected by virtually everything, are shown in either the money market or bond market. The nominal supply of money is controlled by the Federal Reserve. The downward sloping demand for money is derived from people's desire to hold funds either as money or as interest-bearing assets (bonds). As interest rates decrease, people want to hold more money and fewer bonds. If the price level increases, the demand for money increases; if the price level decreases, it decreases.

Aggregate Demand (short run): A series of equilibrium points where the commodity market and the money market are simultaneously in equilibrium. It is determined as follows: Choose an arbitrary level of total spending (GDP) and a corresponding price. Those two values yield one point on an AD curve. If the price level increases, the demand for money increases, causing interest rates to rise. If interest rates rise, interest-sensitive spending decreases. Therefore, at a higher price level, total spending is less than it is at a lower general price level. If a number of such equilibrium points are plotted on a diagram, they yield an aggregate demand curve (AD) with a negative slope. **Gross Domestic Product** is made up of four separate spending categories: consumer spending (C), domestic private investment spending (I), government spending on goods and services (G), and net exports (NX).

Aggregate Supply (short run): Aggregate supply is the quantity of total output (GDP) firms are willing to produce at various price levels. It is not a horizontal summation of the supply curves of all individual firms. It is based on changes in the overall price level, not changes in individual prices. Aggregate supply is determined as follows: Choose an arbitrary level of output and a corresponding price level. Those two values yield one point on an aggregate supply curve. If output increases, while nominal wages are assumed to remain constant, the costs of production will increase due to diminishing marginal productivity and increases in the prices of inputs. Therefore, at a higher level of output, the general price level must also be higher. If a number of such equilibrium points are plotted on a diagram, they yield an aggregate supply curve (AS) that has a positive slope.

Full employment equilibrium: Shown as Y_{FE}. It is the level of GDP corresponding to "full employment" or the "natural rate of unemployment." It is assumed that an equilibrium at a GDP greater than Q_{FE} will cause wages to increase over time and AS to decrease—move to the left (or up).

What causes Aggregate Demand to change? A change in anything, other than the general price level, that affects consumer spending (taxes, interest rates, tastes), or investment spending (interest rates, expectations), or government spending (could be anything), or net exports (trade policies, interest rates, costs of production) causes AD to change. A decrease in taxes causes AD to increase. A decrease in government spending causes AD to decrease. An increase in the nominal money supply that lowers interest rates causes AD to increase.

What causes Aggregate Supply to change? In the short run, an increase in production costs (not due to an increase in output) causes AS to decrease (move to the left); a decrease in production costs (not due to a decrease in output) causes AS to increase (move to the right). Examples are: changes in weather that affects production (bad weather causes AS to decrease), changes in technology (new technology causes AS to increase), changes in wage rates (an increase in wages causes AS to decrease). In the long run, it is assumed that unemployment will cause wages to fall and AS to increase.

How to Solve Macroeconomic Problems—A Worksheet

(Virtually any macroeconomic issue can be explained by completing this page.)

What is the question?

(1) The initial equilibrium*: Describe the initial equilibrium.*

Draw two diagrams: one with Aggregate Supply, Aggregate Demand and Y_{FE} (full employment GDP) curves; the other showing the supply and demand for money. Label everything. If the problem begins with unemployment, have the initial equilibrium be to the left of Y_{FE}.

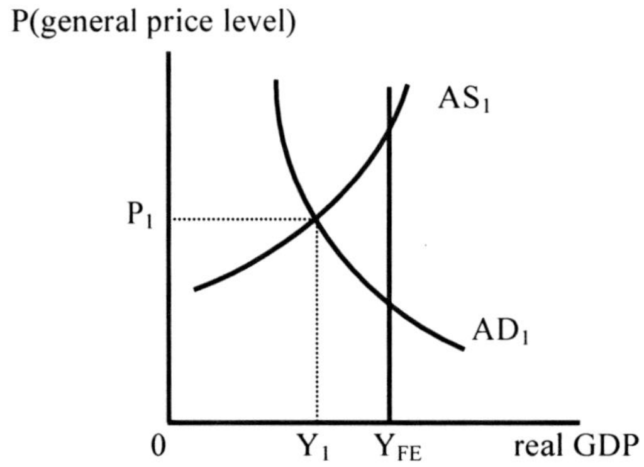

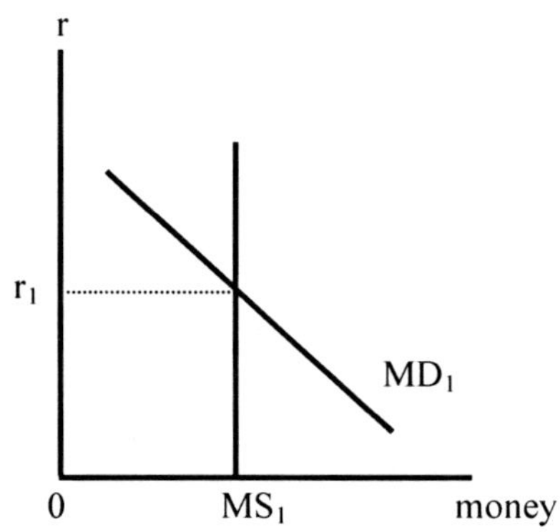

(2) The change*: Explain, and then show on the diagram, how the change causes an increase or decrease in AS or AD, or in MS or MD.*

Does aggregate demand increase or decrease?

Does aggregate supply increase or decrease?

Does the demand for money increase or decrease?

Does the supply of money increase or decrease?

Remember: A change in the price level that causes a change in the demand for money causes interest rates to change, which causes a move along AD.

But: A change in the supply of or demand for money that causes interest rates to increase or decrease causes AD to decrease or increase.

(3) The new equilibrium*: Describe the new equilibrium and explain what happens to the equilibrium values of the variables under consideration.*

Summary or conclusion**:**

19

The Bond Market

Your broker calls and tells you it is a great time to invest in long-term government bonds. She says it is a unique opportunity, because interest rates are so high. You are not so sure. You do not want to get locked into an interest-bearing investment that will tie up your money for twenty years. She says that won't happen. You ask her to call back tomorrow.

1. Bonds and money.

The bond market is the "flip side" of the money market, and it is a key market for both macroeconomic and microeconomic issues. It is included in the macroeconomic section of this text, because of its importance in understanding how changes in the money supply affect macroeconomic variables. It could just as easily have been included in the microeconomic section, because of its importance in the decision-making process of investors and firms.

On a microeconomic level, bonds are important investment vehicles for individuals and institutions, and changes in interest rates affect virtually everything consumers do, from making purchases on credit cards to making decisions about home mortgages. Business, too, is directly affected by changes in interest rates. But, unlike consumers, businesses do not only invest in bonds, they can also issue bonds to raise funds.

On a macroeconomic level, the bond market is where the Federal Reserve conducts open market operations that change the money supply and interest rates in order to affect the overall level of economic activity.

2. What are bonds?

Bonds are "debt instruments." They are interest-bearing IOU's issued (sold) by entities that want to borrow money.

Corporations can raise funds by selling stock or by borrowing money. Although selling stock is common, there are times when a corporation does not want to sell additional shares of its stock, because doing so spreads out the ownership of a company.

If a corporation sells bonds to raise funds, it is incurring a debt to be repaid out of future earnings, but it is not spreading out ownership.

Government, at all levels, sells bonds to pay for spending not covered by current tax revenues. The Treasury Department, federal agencies, individual states, counties, and local governments all sell bonds.

3. A few facts that make it easier to understand the bond market.

Fact 1. When a bond is originally issued, it has a fixed maturity date, a fixed maturity value, and a fixed dollar dividend—not a fixed percentage dividend—that is paid to the owner of the bond. (Some bonds do not pay an annual dividend. Instead, they are sold at a "discount" from their maturity value. The difference between what is paid for the bond and what is received at maturity is the interest earned on the bond. Such bonds are called "zero-coupon" bonds, because they do not have "coupons" used to redeem annual interest payments.) The maturity date is the date on which the owner of a bond receives the maturity value. It is common for bonds to have a maturity value of $1,000. The maturity date can be anywhere from 90 days to 30 years from the date of issue. Bonds with original maturities of less than one year are normally called "Bills." Bonds with original maturities of from one to five years are often called "Notes." Bonds with original maturities greater than five years are called "Bonds."

Fact 2. After a bond is issued, the original purchaser can sell it to someone else, who can sell it to someone else, and so on. Bonds, like stocks, are a marketable asset that can be held for many years, or that can be bought and sold in minutes.

Fact 3. The bond market, which has a total value far beyond the stock market, is made up mainly of "old" bonds, bonds that were issued in the past. A 30-year, $1,000 Treasury bond that was issued twenty years ago can be bought today by an investor or speculator who will then receive the dollar dividend that was set when the bond was issued and, if he or she holds it to maturity, will receive $1,000 in ten years. New bonds are issued daily and old bonds are maturing daily, but the vast majority of the bond market's value is made up of bonds issued in the past that have not yet matured.

Fact 4. Although the maturity date, maturity value, and annual *dollar* dividend are fixed, the market price of a bond fluctuates daily as interest rates change. If a bond with a maturity value of $1,000 and an annual dividend of $100 originally sold for $1,000, the original purchaser would earn a ten percent return on a $1,000 investment. If that bond is later sold in the market for $1,200, the new owner will still receive $100 a year and $1,000 at maturity, which is less than a ten percent return on a $1,200 investment. If the bond is resold again, this time for $800, the new owner will still receive $100 per year and $1,000 at maturity, which is more than a ten percent return on an $800 investment.

Why would a bond be resold for more or less than it sold for originally? *Because the market price of a bond must adjust to current interest rates.* If a $1,000 bond pays an annual dividend of $100, it means that market interest rates must have been ten percent at the time the bond was issued. If market interest rates decrease after the bond is issued and the owner wants to sell the bond, it can be sold for more than $1,000. A new $1,000 bond issued when market interest rates are less than ten percent will pay less than $100 per year in dividends, so a bond that pays $100 a year is worth more than $1,000. If market interest rates increase after the bond is issued and the owner wants to sell the bond, it can only be sold for less than $1,000. A new $1,000 bond issued when market interest rates are greater than ten percent will pay more than $100 per year in dividends, so a bond that pays $100 a year is worth less than $1,000.

Fact 5. Because of *Fact 4*, there is an inverse, and automatic, relationship between the price of a bond and its actual yield. As bond prices increase, the actual return falls. As bond prices decline, the yield or return (the rate of interest actually received) increases.

Fact 6. No matter what happens to market interest rates and the price of a bond after it is issued, the owner does not have to sell it. The owner always has the choice of holding the bond to maturity, when it will be redeemed for $1,000.

4. The bond market and the money supply.

When the Federal Reserve wants to change the money supply, it does so by buying or selling government bonds in the open market. Therefore, it is necessary to understand what happens to the equilibrium price and quantity of bonds, and to market interest rates, if The Federal Reserve decides to increase the money supply by purchasing bonds in the open market?

(1) The initial equilibrium.

The initial equilibrium is shown by the normal supply and demand curves, S_1 and D_1, in Figure 19.1. No information is given that would lead to the assumption of non-normal functions. The initial equilibrium price of bonds is p_1. The initial equilibrium quantity of bonds bought and sold is q_1. There is no market failure to explain.

The reason demand slopes down and supply slopes up is because of *Fact 5* above—the inverse relationship between the price of bonds and interest rates.

Demand has a negative slope because as the price of bonds falls, the return they offer increases, meaning that the lower the price of bonds, the greater the quantity of bonds investors are willing and able to buy. Also, the further bond prices fall, the greater is the chance that interest rates will increase rather than decrease, meaning that the lower the price of bonds, the greater is the possibility of buying bonds that can later be sold for a capital gain.

Supply has a positive slope because as the price of bonds increases, the rate of interest that sellers (borrowers) have to pay buyers (lenders) decreases, meaning that the higher the price of bonds, the cheaper it is to finance projects and the greater the quantity of bonds sellers want to sell. Also, the higher bond prices go, the more opportunity there is for those who bought bonds in the past to sell those bonds for a capital gain.

Figure 19.1

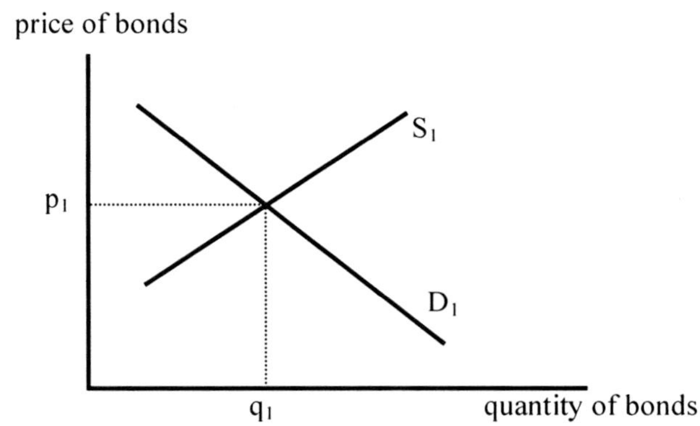

(2) The change.

The increased purchase of bonds by the Federal Reserve is a "change in something that was assumed to be held constant"—the Federal Reserve's purchases and sales of bonds. Because it is a change in a constant, the initial impact is a change in a function, not a move along a function. Therefore, it can be assumed that the change can be shown as an increase in the market demand for bonds: the new demand curve is to the right of (or above) the original demand curve. The new demand curve is D_2. The supply curve remains at S_1.

Figure 19.2

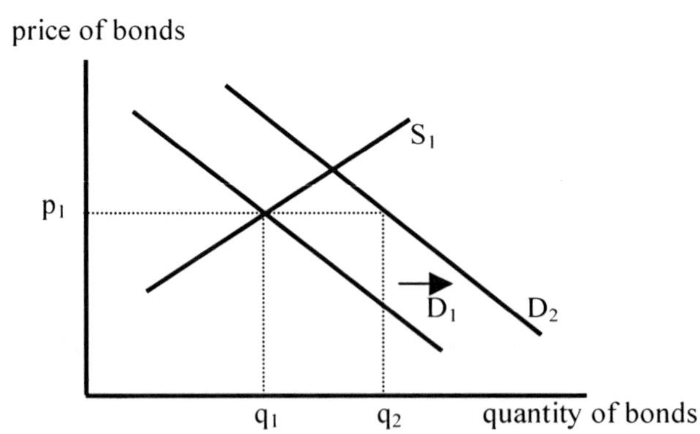

There is no reason to believe that a change in bond purchases will have an impact on the supply of bonds--the maximum quantity of bonds sellers want to sell at various prices. At any given price, buyers (including the Fed) are willing and able to purchase more bonds. (Or, for any given quantity of bonds, the minimum price at which they will be purchased is higher.)

(3) The new equilibrium.

The new equilibrium, determined by the original supply curve, S_1 and the new demand curve, D_2, is at the new equilibrium price, p_2, and the new equilibrium quantity, q_3.

The equilibrium price of bonds increases from p_1 to p_2.

The equilibrium quantity of bonds bought and sold increases from q_1 to q_2.

The equilibrium interest rate decreases because the yield, or market interest rate, is inversely related to the price of bonds. A move up the price axis means that bond prices are increasing and that interest rates are decreasing. A move down the price axis means that bond price are decreasing and interest rates are increasing.

Figure 19.3

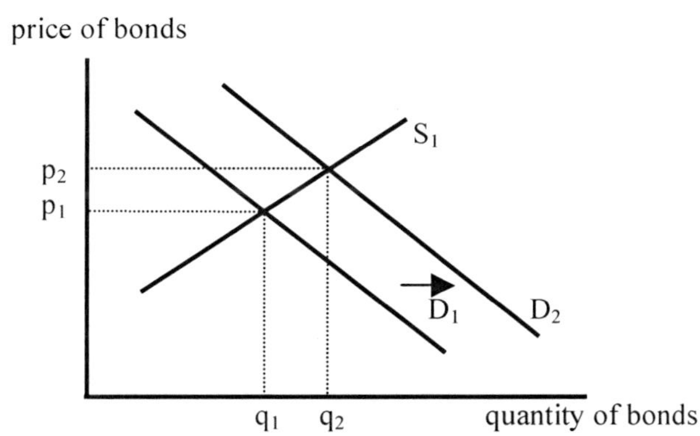

The initial increase in the money supply is the horizontal distance between D_1 and D_2.

There is no government imposed and enforced price ceiling. Therefore, the price is free to move in response to the excess demand for bonds. It is important to note that the change that initiated the problem did not affect the market supply of bonds. It affects the market demand for bonds only (and the money supply). The change in demand results in a move along the original supply curve—a change in the quantity supplied (from q_1 to q_3)—not a change in supply.

Conclusion.

The increased bond purchases by the Federal Reserve cause bond prices to increase and interest rates to decrease.

Investors purchasing new bonds will earn a lower rate of interest. But investors holding old bonds can now sell those bonds for a capital gain. Of course, if such bonds are held to maturity, they will still be worth $1,000.

Businesses and government agencies that want to sell new bonds to raise cash can now pay lower interest rates, which will increase profits for business and may make it easier to justify some government projects.

5. Your broker calls back.

So, when your broker calls back, what do you say?

Do you take her advice? Or do you have some questions, such as, why does she believe interest rates have peaked? You know that the answer is not simple, so she should be able to back up her belief with economic knowledge and facts, and possible with information you do not have.

20

A Change in Technology

When your broker tried to get you to invest in long-term government bonds, you decided to wait. A few weeks later, you read an article that says the U.S. is experiencing a major increase in technology. Do you now call your broker and tell her to buy bonds for your account? Or is there no connection between technology and interest rates?

1. What happens to the general price level, gross domestic product, and employment as a result of an increase in technology?

The question.

How does an increase in technology affect the general price level, gross domestic product, employment, and interest rates in the short run?

(1) The initial equilibrium.

The initial equilibrium is shown by normal aggregate supply and aggregate demand curves, AS_1 and AD_1, and the normal money demand and supply curves in Figure 20.1. The initial equilibrium price level is P_1. The initial equilibrium level of real GDP is Y_1. The initial equilibrium interest rate is r_1. The equilibrium level of GDP is at less than the full-employment level of GDP.

Figure 20.1

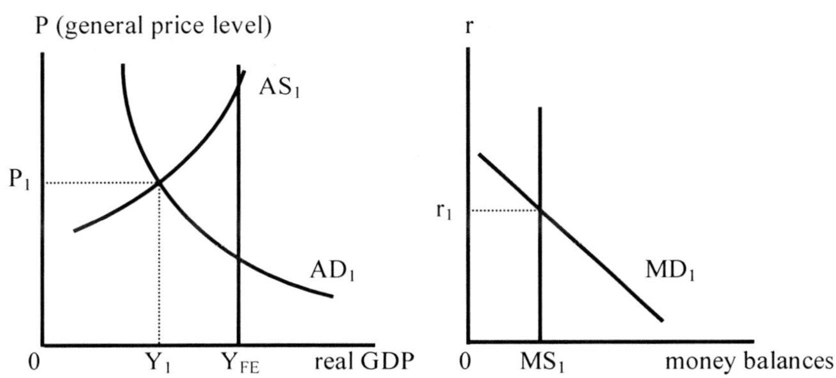

No information is given that would lead to the assumption of non-normal functions.

> It is not necessary to always show the money market. But whether it is shown or not, it plays a part in every answer. Whether it is shown or not, it is necessary to understand and remember the back and forth chain of events whereby a change in AD or AS that leads to a change in the general price level leads to a change in the demand for money that causes a change in interest rates that then causes movements along AD.

(2) The change.

The aggregate supply curve will change. If advances in technology occur, it means that something that was assumed to have been held constant when deriving the initial aggregate supply—technology—has changed.

Each level of total output now costs less to produce than it did. Therefore, aggregate supply will increase.

An increase in aggregate supply means there will be a new AS curve to the right of the original AS curve.

The new aggregate supply is AS_2.

Aggregate demand remains at AD_1.

The nominal supply of money is still MS_1.

And the demand for nominal money balances is still MD_1.

Figure 20.2

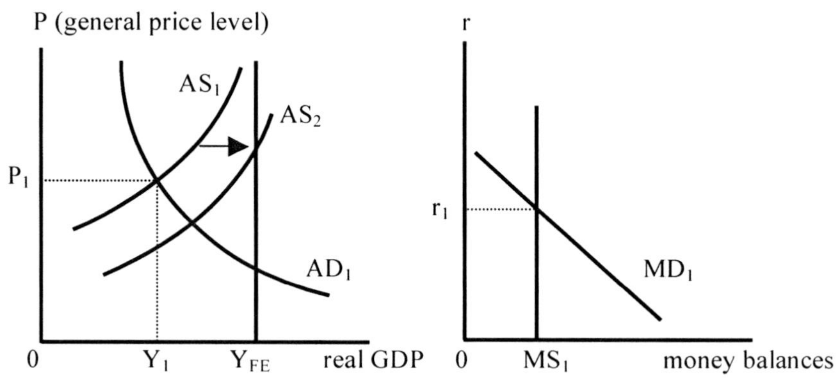

(3) The new equilibrium.

The new equilibrium, determined by the new aggregate supply curve, AS_2, and the original aggregate demand curve, AD_1, is at P_2 (a higher price level) and Y_2, (a higher equilibrium GDP), as shown in Figure 20.3. In the money market, the lower price level causes the demand for money to decrease. The lower demand for money, MD_2, with the original supply of money, MS_1, causes interest rates to fall to r_2.

Figure 20.3

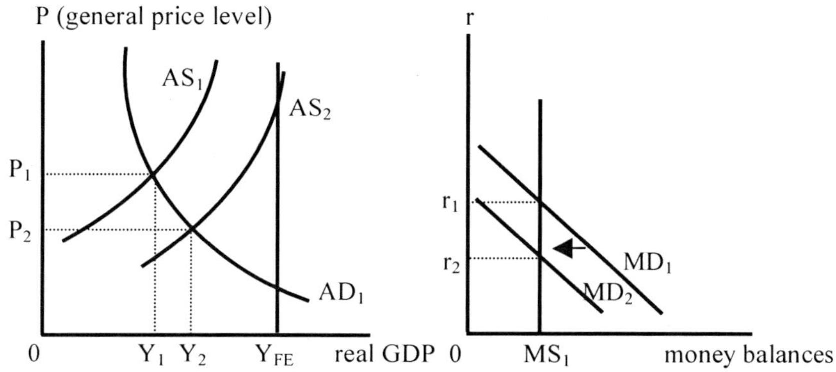

The move from the original equilibrium to the new equilibrium is interesting. At the original price level, P_1, firms want to produce an output greater than Y_1, because the increase in technology lowers the cost of production. But at price level P_1, aggregate demand is still only Y_1. The result is a disequilibrium with consumption less than production, which means the economy is at a point to the left of AS_2.

If consumption is less than production, it means that prices will fall.

As the general price level falls below P_1, the demand for money decreases, shown as a change from MD_1 to MD_2 in Figure 20.3. According to the previous money market discussion, the decrease in the demand for money causes interest rates to fall. As interest rates decline, there are increases in consumer spending (C), private investment spending (I), and net exports (NX). As interest-sensitive spending increases, the economy moves down the AD_1 curve to higher and higher levels of GDP. The price level continues to fall and consumption continues to increase until a new equilibrium is reached at P_2, Y_2 in Figure 20.3, where the new aggregate supply curve, AS_2, equals the original aggregate demand curve, AD_1.

Although firms initially want to increase output past Y_2 (to the level of GDP where a horizontal line at P_1 intersects AS_2), due to the increase in technology, the economy does not actually move past Y_2. Output does increase, but not as much as firms originally intended at the original price level, P_1.

The equilibrium price level falls from P_1 to P_2.

The equilibrium level of GDP increases from Y_1 to Y_2.

The equilibrium interest rate falls from r_1 to r_2.

The equilibrium level of employment increases.

The real wage increases, because the price level falls.

Conclusion.

The increase in technology affects the general price level, gross domestic product, employment, the real wage, and interest rates. Assuming that the full-employment level of GDP is not an issue, and that the nominal supply of money and money wages does not change: AS increases, AD remains the same, the price level is lower; interest rates are lower; total spending is greater than it was; real Gross Domestic Product is higher; employment is higher; and real wages are higher.

2. What about the issue of full employment output?

What if the new equilibrium occurs at a level of GDP that is greater than the full employment level?

For example, what if the increase in technology leads to a new equilibrium for AD_1 and AS_2 that is greater than Y_{FE}?

It is normally assumed that the economy cannot remain at a more-than-full-employment level of GDP in the long run. The argument is that the more-than-full-employment situation will cause money wages to increase. And because aggregate supply is derived assuming that money wages are constant, an increase in money wages results in a decrease in aggregate supply.

In the diagram, aggregate supply would move to the left, or up.

If, for example, an improvement in technology causes the short-run equilibrium to increase from Y_1 to Y_2 in Figure 20.4, money wages would increase in the long run and the aggregate supply curve would move back to the left.

Aggregate supply would continue moving to the left until it reaches AS_3.

When aggregate supply reaches AS_3, the economy will be in long-run equilibrium, meaning that AD is equal to AS at the full employment level of GDP.

It is sometimes assumed that in the long run the economy will always reach equilibrium at the full employment level of GDP, because changes in real wages will bring it there. If, for example, the initial equilibrium is at Y_1, which means there is unemployment, it can be argued that wages will be bid down. And as real wages decrease, AS increases—moves to the right—until the economy reaches equilibrium at Y_{FE}.

That is the conclusion reached by J. M. Say, back in the 1800s, which is why those who still believe it to be true are referred to as "Neo-Classical" economists, meaning that their conclusions are similar to those of "Classical" economists, even though their models are more sophisticated.

Figure 20.4

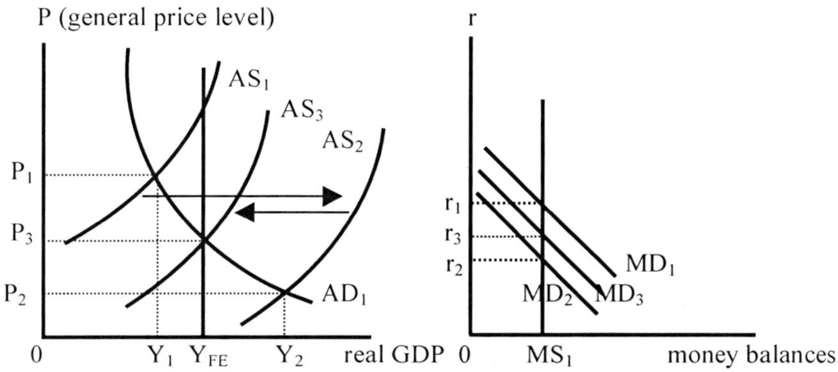

> **Interest rates and aggregate demand**:
> When AS increases from AS_1 to AS_2, the price level falls. As a result, the demand for money decreases from MD_1 to MD_2 and interest rates decrease from r_1 to r_2. Then, when AS decreases from AS_2 to AS_3, there is an increase in the general price level and the demand for money, from MD_2 to MD_3, leading to an increase in interest rates from r_2 to r_3.
> It is important to note that the changes in interest rates are caused by a change in the general price level that affects the demand for money. Therefore, the changes in interest rates do not cause AD to change. They simply lead to movements along AD_1, first down AD_1 to where it intersects AS_2, and then back up AD_1 to where it intersects AS_3.

3. Your broker calls again.

Now that you know how the increase in technology is likely to affect important economic variables, including interest rates, what do you tell your broker?

21

Cutting Taxes to Stimulate the Economy

Your company is suffering, along with many other companies, because of a slow economy. The President of the United States wants to cut taxes to stimulate the weak economy. Although you will not get much of a tax cut, your company would certainly benefit from a healthier economy. Do you support the policy?

1. Do tax cuts stimulate the economy?

If the government cuts your taxes, as part of an economic stimulus plan, you will probably be happy. If the government cuts someone else's taxes and you have to wait for the benefits to trickle down to you, don't hold your breath.

The economic-stimulus argument is simple: Those who get a tax break win, and when they spend part of their additional after-tax income, others win and the economy receives a boost.

The problem with the argument is that it is *too* simple. It ignores the deficit created by the tax cut and the fact that in order to cover that deficit, the government will almost certainly sell bonds in the bond market. The additional bond sales will cause interest rates to rise. And higher interest rates lead to a reduction in spending. In the end, the increase in spending resulting from the tax cut is offset by the decrease in spending due to higher interest rates.

In the meantime, if you were not one of the lucky ones who received a reduction in taxes, you lose, because you have to pay higher interest rates. Even if you did receive a tax break, you now have to pay higher interest rates.

Does the government have to sell bonds, thereby causing interest rates to rise?

No. There are actually three ways the federal government can finance a deficit.

(1) It can raise taxes, which it does not want to do if it just cut taxes to stimulate the economy, because if other taxes are raised, they will negate the expected expansion.

(2) It can reduce spending, which it does not want to do, because doing so will also negate the expected benefits of the tax cut.

(3) It can borrow the money it needs to cover the deficit, which is what it does when it sells bonds.

To hold to the belief that it is doing something to improve the economy, the government has no choice but to go with option three—selling bonds to the public (borrowing money).

The Kennedy tax cut is often used as an example of a successful economic stimulus package. However, the reason it appeared to be successful is that when the government sold bonds to finance the deficit created by the tax cut, the Federal Reserve stepped in and bought enough bonds in the open market to keep interest rates from rising. In effect, the Federal Reserve created money (which is what happens when the Federal Reserve buys bonds in the open market) to finance the deficit. In an important debate that took place years later, between Walter Heller, who, along with James Tobin, was responsible for initiating the tax cut, and Milton Friedman, the most recognizable member of the "Monetarist" school of economic thought, Heller argued that the tax cut had worked and Friedman argued that the tax cut worked only because the money supply had been increased to finance the deficit it created. Friedman further argued that the positive impact on the economy would have occurred if taxes had remained as they were while the money supply was increased. Friedman was correct.

The Reagan tax cut was not covered by Federal Reserve money creation and its impact on interest rates dragged the economy down. It was not until deficit-reduction policies, including tax increases, were implemented years later that the economy picked up and the claims of success began to be heard.

In 2005, some claimed that the Bush tax cut was responsible for the beginning of a recovery from the recession of 2001. What they ignored was the fact that the tax cut, by itself, would have raised interest rates. But interest rates did not increase. Instead, interest rates fell. They fell partly because the Federal Reserve acted to counter the effects of the tax cut, and partly because large quantities of U.S. government bonds were purchased by foreigners. In an attempt to pull the economy out of its slump, the Fed had to act to fight against the upward pressure on interest rates from the deficits caused by tax cuts.

If cutting taxes does not increase production, employment, incomes, and profits, why has the idea been around for so long, and why is it still used?

One answer is that the federal government does not have many tools it can use to pull an economy out of a recession. The only apparent choices are cutting taxes or increasing spending (which also generates deficits). So, whether cutting taxes works or not, as long as it is an idea that is commonly believed to work, politicians will give it a try.

A second answer is that selective tax cuts allow politicians to help their friends and pay back their supporters.

A third answer is that some tax cuts are not intended to help the economy at all; they are implemented with the intention of creating a government deficit that can then be used to "justify" reductions in government spending and regulations.

2. A simple tax cut argument that contains a major error

A federal government tax cut is implemented with the announced intention of increasing the level of economic activity and employment.

The question.

If the economy is in a recession, will a decrease in taxes increase gross domestic product and employment?

(1) The initial equilibrium.

The initial equilibrium is shown in figure 21.1. The full employment level of GDP is Y_{FF}. The equilibrium level of real GDP is Y_1. The equilibrium price level is P_1.

Figure 21.1 is drawn to show an initial equilibrium with an unacceptable level of unemployment, which is why Y_1 is less than Y_{FE}.

The money market is drawn with normal supply and demand curves.

Figure 21.1

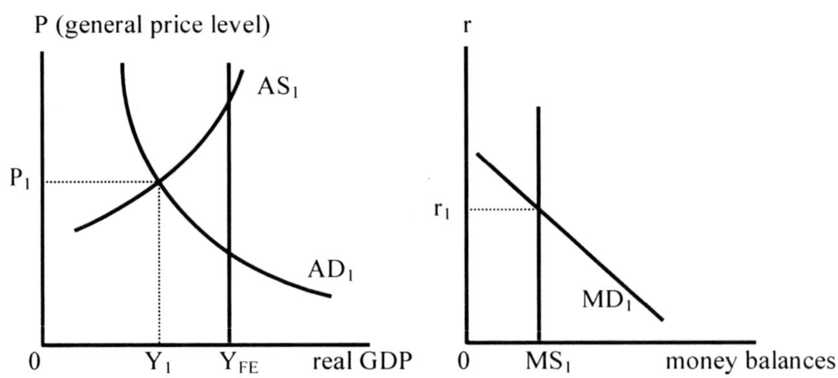

(2) The change.

A decrease in taxes means that something that was assumed to be constant when deriving the initial aggregate demand—taxes—has changed.

Aggregate demand is made up of consumer spending, investment spending by business, government spending, and net exports. Therefore, if taxes are reduced, total spending is greater at each price level, because consumers and businesses have higher after-tax incomes.

The result is an increase in aggregate demand.

In Figure 21.2, the new aggregate demand, AD_2, is to the right of (or above) the initial aggregate demand, AD_1.

Aggregate supply does not change.

Figure 21.2

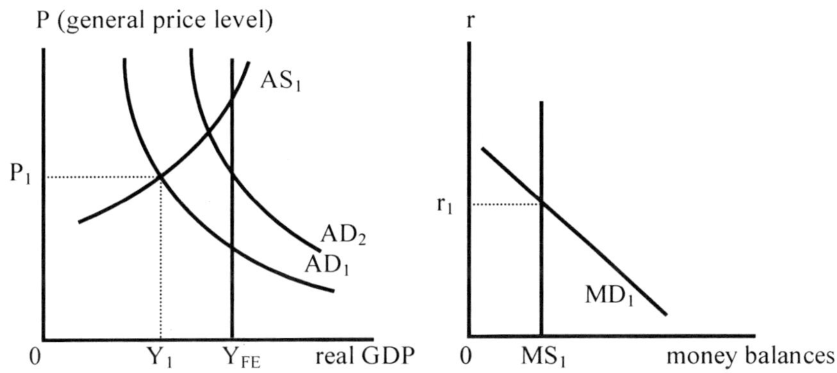

Aggregate supply does not change, because it is assumed that the tax cut is on incomes, not on something that affects the cost of production. The proposals for "supply side" tax cuts are based on the idea that cutting taxes that affect the cost of production will increase aggregate supply. It is not a very good argument, although, as with all tax cuts, the beneficiaries like it.

(3) The new equilibrium.

In Figure 21.3, the economy reaches a new equilibrium at output Y_2 and price level P_2, which is where the new aggregate demand (AD_2) is equal to the original aggregate supply (AS_1). In the new equilibrium, real Gross Domestic Product is higher, employment is higher, and the price level is higher. In Figure 21.3, the economy is still in equilibrium at less than full employment. In order to achieve a full employment level of Gross Domestic Product, taxes would have to be reduced enough to cause aggregate demand to increase to where it intersects AS_1 at Y_{FE}.

Meanwhile, the rising general price level causes the demand for money to increase from MD_1 to MD_2, and interest rates to increase from r_1 to r_2. If interest rates did not increase, we could imagine the tax cut leading to consumption on AD_2 where a horizontal line at P_1 intersects AD_2. Instead, increasing interest rates reduce interest-sensitive spending and move the economy up the new aggregate demand curve to where it intersects AS_1 at Y_2.

Figure 21.3

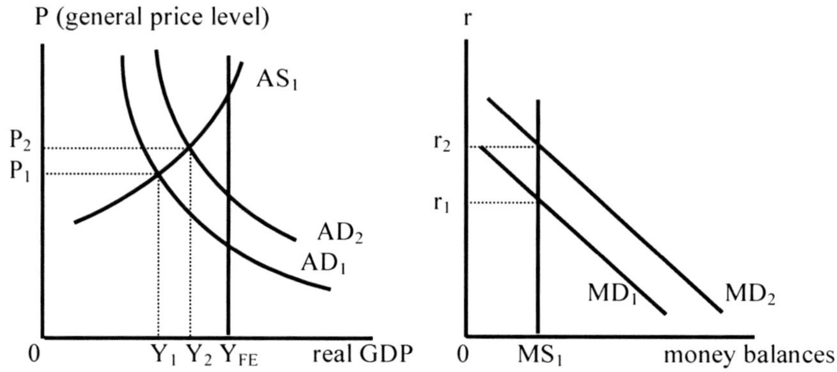

Conclusion.

The increase in aggregate demand, due to the decrease in taxes, is the horizontal distance between the original aggregate demand and the new aggregate demand. It is not the same as the decrease in taxes. The increase in aggregate demand is normally assumed to be a multiple of the decrease in taxes. The argument is that when people's after-tax incomes increase, so does their spending. That additional spending becomes additional income to others, who then increase their spending. And so on. The result is a multiplied impact on aggregate demand.

The increase in equilibrium GDP is the difference between the original GDP, determined by the intersection of the original aggregate demand and aggregate supply, and the new equilibrium GDP, determined by the intersection of the *new* aggregate demand and the original aggregate supply.

Total spending is higher than it was before the decrease in taxes, but not by as much as the increase in aggregate demand, because the increase in spending due to the tax cut is offset somewhat by the decline in consumer and business spending due to higher prices.

Even so, it appears that the decrease in taxes, which is a fiscal policy action, does lead to an increase in GDP and employment.

3. The error in the simple argument.

The error in the above argument is simple: The argument ignores the fact that a tax cut has to be paid for. The only way a tax cut can take place without creating a deficit is if it is implemented when there is a government surplus. If there is no surplus, then the tax cut will create a government deficit. And, one way or another, the deficit must be covered.

There are only three ways the government can cover a deficit:

1) Raise taxes.

2) Cut spending.

3) Borrow.

To fully understand the results of a tax cut, it is necessary to explain what happens in each case.

1) If the government raises other taxes to cover the deficit, it will counter the hoped-for benefit of the original tax cut, because an increase in taxes causes aggregate demand to decrease, moving it back to AD_1 in Figure 21.3. Whether or not the decrease in aggregate demand exactly offsets the original increase in aggregate demand, the two changes can be considered to be a "wash."

2) If the government cuts spending to cover the deficit, it also works against the hoped-for benefit of the original tax cut. In simple Keynesian models, the increase in GDP caused by a tax cut is assumed to be less than the decrease in GDP caused by an equal decrease in government spending. Regardless of that argument, we know that a decrease in government spending causes aggregate demand to decrease, moving aggregate demand back toward AD_1 in Figure 21.3. As a result, any positive impact on GDP cannot be expected to be as great as shown.

3) If the government chooses the third option, it will borrow money to pay for the tax cut.

How does the government borrow money? It sells bonds.

The question.

What happens to the equilibrium in the bond market if the government sells bonds to finance the deficit caused by a tax cut?

(1) The initial equilibrium.

The initial equilibrium in the bond market is shown in Figure 21.4.

The initial equilibrium price of bonds is p_1. The initial equilibrium quantity of bonds bought and sold is q_1.

Figure 21.4

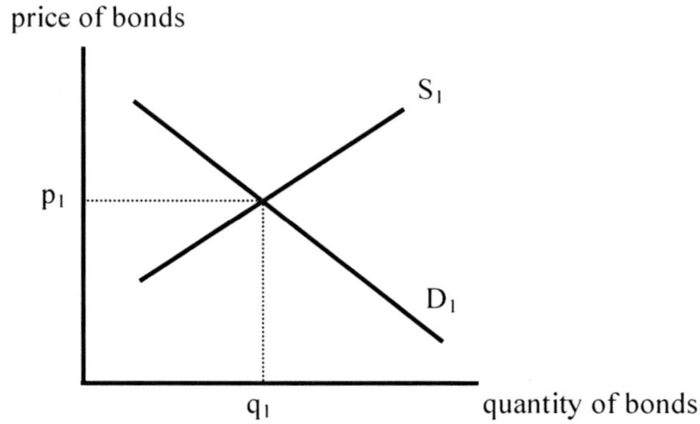

(2) The change.

The increased sale of bonds by the federal government is a "change in something that was assumed to be held constant"—the supply of government bonds. Therefore, the initial impact is a change in a function, not a move along a function.

It can be assumed that the only change caused by the increase in bond sales is an increase in the market supply of bonds: the new supply curve is to the right of the original supply curve. In Figure 21.5, the new supply curve is S_2. The demand curve remains at D_1.

Figure 21.5

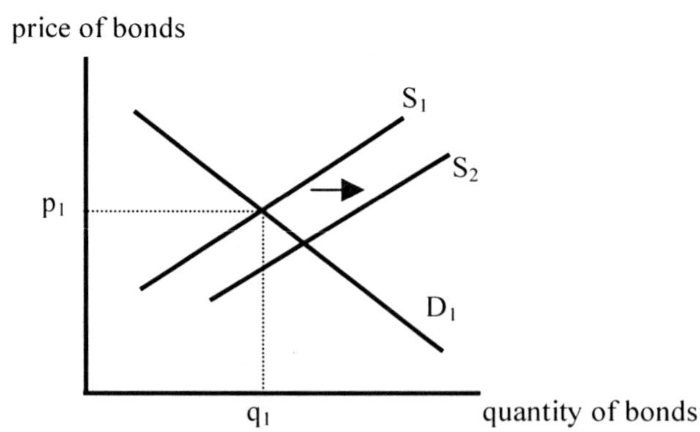

There is no reason to believe that a change in government bond sales will have an impact on the demand for bonds—the maximum quantity of bonds buyers are willing and able to purchase at various prices.

(3) The new equilibrium.

Given the original demand curve, D_1, and the new supply curve, S_2, there is an excess supply of bonds *at the initial equilibrium price p_1*. At p_1, investors want to buy fewer bonds than sellers want to sell. The result is an excess supply of bonds that creates a downward pressure on price. The excess supply of bonds and the downward pressure on price continue until a new equilibrium is reached where the new supply and the original demand are equal.

The new equilibrium, determined by the new supply curve, S_2, and the original demand curve, D_1, is at the new equilibrium price, p_2, and the new equilibrium quantity, q_3, in Figure 21.6.

Figure 21.6

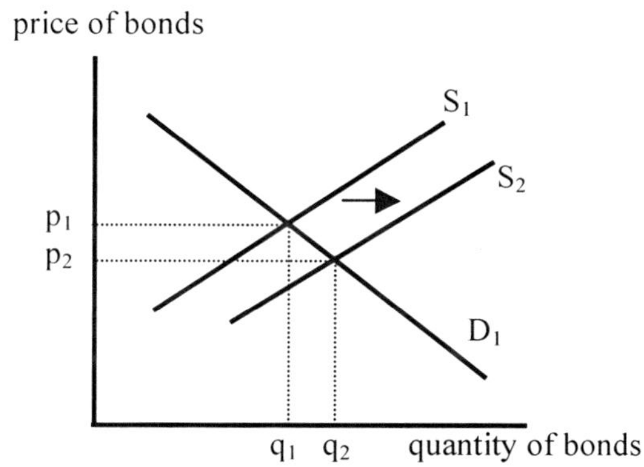

Conclusion.

It is important to note that the increased sale of bonds does not affect the market demand for bonds. It affects only the market supply of bonds. The change in supply results in a move along the original demand curve—a change in the quantity demanded (from q_1 to q_2)—not a change in demand.

The equilibrium quantity of bonds bought and sold increases from q_1 to q_2.

The equilibrium price of bonds decreases from p_1 to p_2.

The equilibrium interest rate increases, because the yield is inversely related to the price of bonds. A move up the price axis means that bond prices are increasing and interest rates are decreasing. A move down the price axis means that bond price are decreasing and interest rates are increasing.

Therefore, increased bond sales by the government, used to finance the government deficit, cause bond prices to decrease and interest rates to increase.

Investors purchasing new bonds will earn a higher rate of interest. But investors holding old bonds can now sell those bonds only if they are willing to accept lower prices. Of course, if such bonds are held to maturity, they will still be worth $1,000.

Businesses and government agencies that want to sell new bonds to raise cash now have to pay higher interest rates, which will reduce profits for business and may make it difficult or impossible to justify some government projects.

What about equilibrium GDP?

If the deficit caused by a tax cut is financed by selling bonds to the public, the increase in bond sales causes interest rates to rise. Rising interest rates cause a reduction in consumer and business spending—two components of aggregate demand. As a result, aggregate demand decreases. In Figure 21.7, which is the same as Figure 21.3, aggregate demand moves to the left, from AD_2 back towards AD_1 and the original equilibrium.

And, as the general price level falls, the demand for money decreases, moving back toward MD_1, and interest rates return to r_1.

Figure 21.7

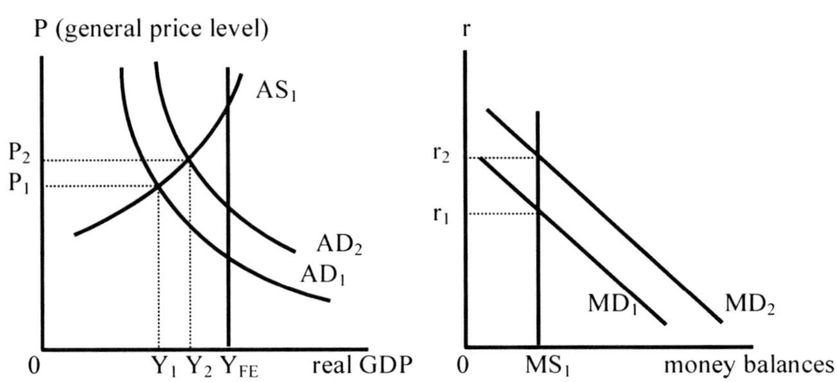

Whether or not the new equilibrium is exactly the same as the original equilibrium, the decrease in taxes has little, if any, impact on real GDP and employment.

4. Using the money market to explain the tax-cut error.

The tax-cut argument that yields a positive impact on real GDP and employment shows aggregate demand increasing from AD_1 to AD_2, while the demand for money and interest rates also increase. But, it ignores the fact that the increased sale of government bonds causes an automatic decrease in the money supply. When people buy bonds, they pay for them with money, which means they are then holding less money and more bonds. And bonds are not money. Therefore, in Figure 21.8, a reduction in the money supply due to increased government bond sales causes the supply of money to decrease from MS_1 to MS_2. With a money supply of M_2, interest rates rise from r_2 to r_3. And as interest rates increase, aggregate demand decreases; it moves to the left, from AD_2 back towards AD_1 and the original equilibrium.

Whether the bond market or the money market is used to explain the consequences of financing a deficit by selling bonds to the public, the result is the same: Interest rates increase, causing aggregate demand to return to (or close to) its original level. Of course, as AD declines, so do the price level and the demand for money. In the end, the demand for money will be between MD_1 and MD_2, and interest rates will be above r_1.

Figure 21.8

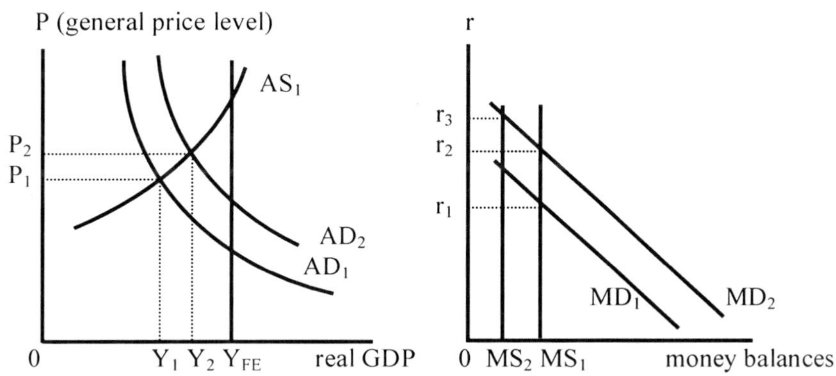

5. Is there any way a tax cut can improve the economy?

There is one way for a tax cut to appear to have a positive impact on the economy: If the Federal Reserve increases the money supply to offset the reduction in the money supply caused by government bond sales, real GDP and employment can increase.

What the Fed does is purchase bonds in the open market. And when the Fed purchases bonds in the open market, it pays for them with Federal Reserve checks. Federal Reserve checks, which are defined to be money, replace bonds, which are not money, in the economy. In Figure 21.8, the Fed's purchase of bonds, which increases the money supply, results in the money supply increasing from M_2 back to M_1. And if interest rates remain at r_1 (or thereabouts), aggregate demand can increase to AD_2.

The question is: Should such increases in real GDP and employment be credited to the tax cut or to the increase in the money supply? The logical answer is that the economic benefits should be credited to the increased money supply. The reason is simple: An increase in real GDP and employment can occur with an increase in the money supply and no tax cut, but not with a tax cut and no increase in the money supply.

22

An Increase in Government Spending

The economy is not doing very well. There is pressure on the government to do something to increase production and employment. A tax cut is proposed, but it is shot down using the argument in the previous chapter. An increase in government spending is suggested. The argument is that increased government spending, such as a war, is good for the economy. No one is recommending a war to help the economy, but there is a lot of support for a spending program, especially from those who hope to be the beneficiaries of the increased spending. If the policy is implemented, should your company expect to benefit from a healthier economy?

1. A simple explanation of an increase in government spending.

The question.

Will an increase in government spending stimulate an economy with an unacceptable level of unemployment?

(1) The initial equilibrium.

The initial equilibrium is shown in figure 22.1. The equilibrium level of real GDP is Y_1 and the equilibrium price level is P_1.

Figure 22.1

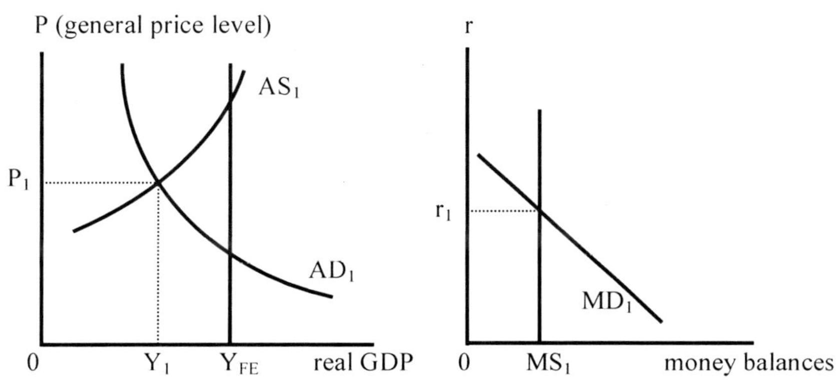

Figure 22.1 was drawn with Y_1 less than Y_{FE} in order to show an initial equilibrium with an unacceptable level of unemployment. The money market has normal supply and demand curves.

(2) The change.

Aggregate demand represents total spending by government, consumers, and business—including net exports—at each general price level.

Therefore, an increase in spending by government means that something that was assumed to be constant when deriving the initial aggregate demand—government spending—has changed. At each price level, total spending is now greater. The result is an increase in aggregate demand. In the diagram, the new aggregate demand is to the right of (or above) the initial aggregate demand.

In Figure 22.2, the new aggregate demand, AD_2, is to the right of (or above) the initial aggregate demand, AD_1.

Aggregate supply does not change, because it is assumed that the spending increase does not affect the cost of production.

Figure 22.2

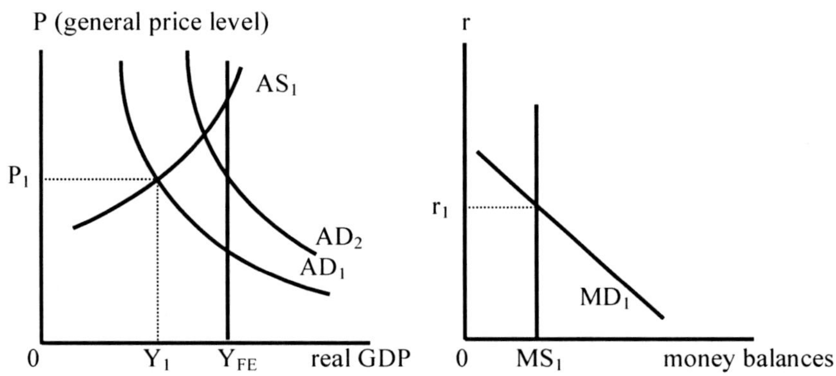

(3) The new equilibrium.

In Figure 22.3, the economy reaches a new equilibrium at output Y_2 and price level P_2, which is where the new aggregate demand, AD_2, is equal to the original aggregate supply, AS_1. In the new equilibrium: real Gross Domestic Product is higher; employment is higher; and the price level is higher.

In Figure 22.3, however, the economy is still in equilibrium at less than full employment. In order to achieve a full employment level of Gross Domestic Product, spending has to increase enough so that aggregate demand intersects AS_1 at Y_{FE}.

Meanwhile, the rising general price level causes the demand for money to increase from MD_1 to MD_2 and interest rates to increase from r_1 to r_2. If interest rates do not increase, the tax cut would supposedly lead to the level of GDP determined by the intersection of AD_2 and a horizontal line at P_1. But, the increase in interest rates reduces interest sensitive spending and the economy moves up the new aggregate demand curve to where it intersects AS_1 at Y_2.

Figure 22.3

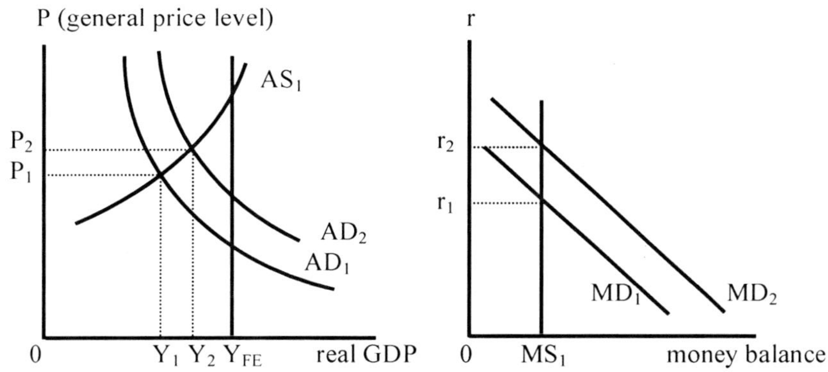

The increase in aggregate demand, at the initial price level, is normally assumed to be some multiple of the increase in government spending, because the additional money spent by the government becomes additional income to many people, and when incomes increase, so does spending. That additional spending becomes additional income to others, who also increase their spending. And so on. The result is a multiplied impact on aggregate demand.

However, the increase in the equilibrium value of GDP is less than the increase in aggregate demand—because of the negative impact of rising prices on spending.

The increase in aggregate demand, due to the increase in government spending, is the horizontal distance between the original aggregate demand and the new aggregate demand, at the original price level.

The increase in equilibrium GDP is the difference between the original GDP, determined by the intersection of original aggregate demand and aggregate supply, and the new equilibrium GDP, determined by the intersection of the *new* aggregate demand and the original aggregate supply.

The change in GDP is less than the change in aggregate demand because, as total spending increases, the rising price level causes some decreases in consumer and business spending.

Total spending is higher than it was before the increase in government spending, but the increase in government spending is offset somewhat by the decline in consumer and business spending. Even so, it appears that the increase in government spending, which is defined as a fiscal policy action, leads to an increase in GDP and employment.

2. A more complete answer:

The "simple" answer above ignores the fact that if government spending increases, the government deficit also increases. If the increased deficit is financed by selling bonds to the public—the most likely choice—then the increase in bond sales causes interest rates to rise, and rising interest rates cause a reduction in consumer and business spending—two other components of aggregate demand. And the new aggregate demand in the "simple" answer decreases. In the diagram, aggregate demand moves back down or to the left, towards the original equilibrium.

Whether or not the "true" new equilibrium is exactly the same as the original equilibrium is less important than recognizing that the increase in government spending will not have much, if any, impact on GDP and employment.

3. An early Keynesian answer:

The "early" Keynesian models predicted that the change in equilibrium GDP, as a result of a change in government spending, would be equal to the actual change in aggregate demand, which was equal to a multiple of the change in government spending.

There are two reasons for that conclusion.

One is that the early models ignored the fact that increased government spending creates deficits that are financed by selling bonds to the public, thereby raising interest rates and reducing all interest sensitive spending.

The second is that the early models also assumed that as long as the economy is operating below its full employment level, increases in GDP would not cause the price level to increase. The assumption about prices can shown by having an aggregate supply curve that is horizontal until it reaches the full employment level of GDP, then increasing afer the full employment level of GDP is reached.

As with a tax cut, the issue of "full employment output" was not handled very well.

In the diagram above, if equilibrium occurs at a level of GDP higher than the full employment level, it is normally assumed that prices will rise even faster. In the diagram, this assumption is shown by having aggregate supply turn up steeply after it reaches the full employment level of GDP.

It is also normal to assume that the economy cannot remain at a more-than-full-employment level of GDP. If the economy is operating at "more-than-full-employment," wages will increase. And, because aggregate supply is derived assuming wages are held constant, an increase in wages causes a change in aggregate supply. Aggregate supply decreases. In the diagram, aggregate supply moves up, or to the left. The new equilibrium is then where the new aggregate supply curve intersects aggregate demand. It is an equilibrium at the full employment level of GDP and with a higher price level.

4. The error in the above argument is the same as the error in the tax-cut argument.

The simple argument above ignores the fact that the increase in government spending has to be paid for. And, as with a tax cut, there are only three ways to cover a deficit:

1) Raise taxes.

2) Cut spending.

3) Borrow.

Again:

1) If the government raises taxes to cover the deficit, it will counter the expected benefit of the increased spending, because an increase in taxes reduces aggregate demand, moving it back toward AD_1 in Figure 22.3. In simple Keynesian models, the increase in GDP caused by a government spending increase is assumed to be greater than the decrease in GDP caused by an equal increase in taxes. Regardless of that argument, an increase in taxes causes aggregate demand to decrease, moving aggregate demand back toward AD_1 in Figure 22.3. As a result, the positive impact on GDP cannot be expected to be as great as shown. Whether or not the decrease in aggregate demand exactly offsets the original increase in aggregate demand, the combined change, which, in simple Keynesian models, is referred to as the "balanced budget multiplier," is questionable.

2) If the government cuts other spending to cover the deficit, it also negates the hoped-for benefit of the increased spending.

3) If the government borrows money to pay for the increased spending, it does so by selling bonds.

The following is repeated from the previous tax-cut chapter.

The question.

What happens to the equilibrium in the bond market if the government sells bonds to finance the deficit caused by a spending increase?

(1) The initial equilibrium.

The initial equilibrium in the bond market is shown in Figure 22.4. The initial equilibrium price of bonds is p_1. The initial equilibrium quantity of bonds bought and sold is q_1.

Figure 22.4

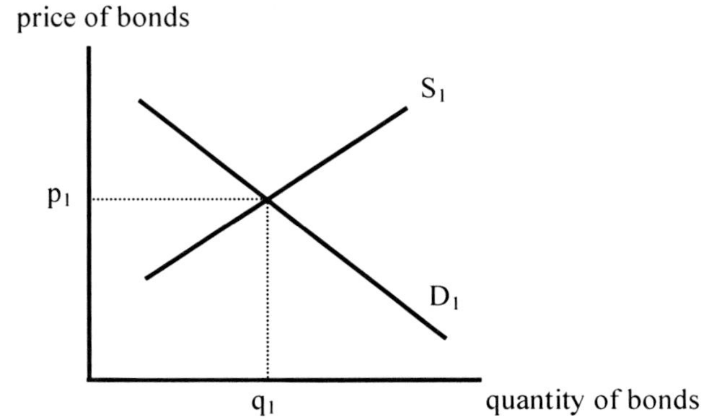

(2) The change.

The increased sale of bonds by the federal government is a "change in something that was assumed to be held constant." Therefore, the initial impact is a change in a function, not a move along a function.

It can be assumed that the only change caused by the increase in bond sales is an increase in the market supply of bonds: the new supply curve is to the right of the original supply curve. In Figure 22.5, the new supply curve is S_2. The demand curve remains at D_1.

Figure 22.5

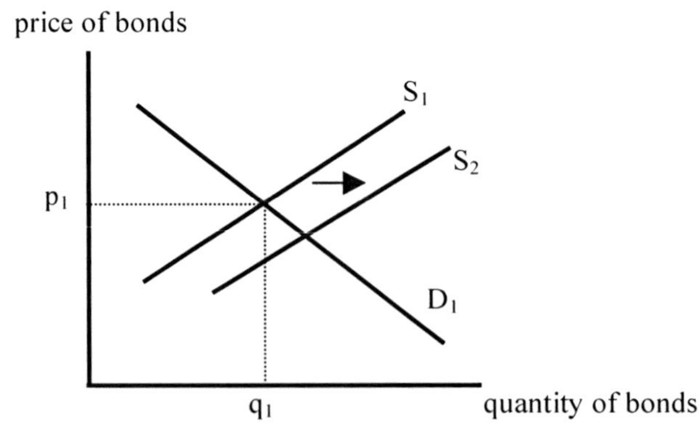

There is no reason to believe that a change in government bond sales will have an impact on the demand for bonds—the maximum quantity of bonds buyers are willing and able to purchase at various prices.

3) The new equilibrium.

Given the original demand curve, D_1, and the new supply curve, S_2, there is an excess supply of bonds *at the initial equilibrium price p_1*. At p_1, investors want to buy fewer bonds than sellers want to sell. The result is an excess supply of bonds that creates a downward pressure on price. The excess supply of bonds and the downward pressure on price continue until a new equilibrium is reached where the new supply and the original demand are equal.

The new equilibrium, determined by the new supply curve, S_2, and the original demand curve, D_1, is at the new equilibrium price, p_2, and the new equilibrium quantity, q_3, in Figure 22.6.

Figure 22.6

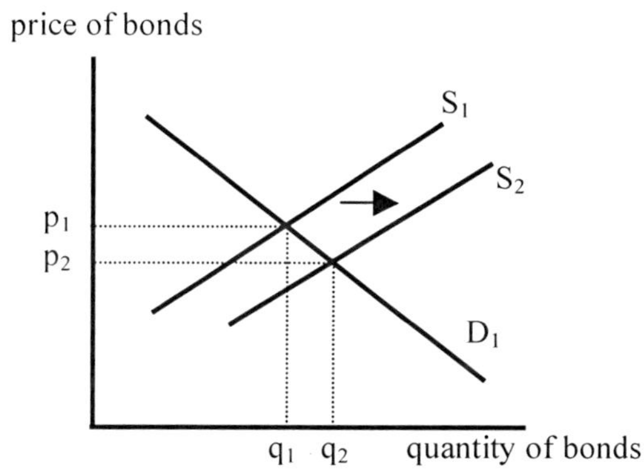

Conclusion.

The increased sale of bonds does not affect the market demand for bonds. It affects only the market supply of bonds. The change in supply results in a move along the original demand curve—a change in the quantity demanded (from q_1 to q_2)—not a change in demand.

The equilibrium quantity of bonds bought and sold increases from q_1 to q_2.

The equilibrium price of bonds decreases from p_1 to p_2.

The equilibrium interest rate increases because the yield is inversely related to the price of bonds. A move up the price axis means that bond prices are increasing and interest rates are decreasing. A move down the price axis means that bond price are decreasing and interest rates are increasing.

Therefore, increased bond sales by the government, used to finance the government deficit, causes bond prices to decrease and interest rates to increase.

Investors purchasing new bonds will earn a higher rate of interest. But investors holding old bonds can now sell those bonds only if they are willing to accept lower prices. Of course, if such bonds are held to maturity, they will still be worth $1,000.

Businesses and government agencies that want to sell new bonds to raise cash now have to pay higher interest rates, which will reduce profits for business and may make it difficult or impossible to justify some government projects.

5. What about equilibrium GDP?

If the deficit caused by a tax cut is financed by selling bonds to the public, the increase in bond sales causes interest rates to rise. Rising interest rates cause a reduction in consumer and business spending—two components of aggregate demand. As a result, aggregate demand decreases. In Figure 22.7, which is the same as Figure 22.7, aggregate demand moves to the left, from AD_2 back towards AD_1 and the original equilibrium.

And, as the general price level falls, the demand for money decreases, moving back toward MD_1, and interest rates return to r_1.

Figure 22.7

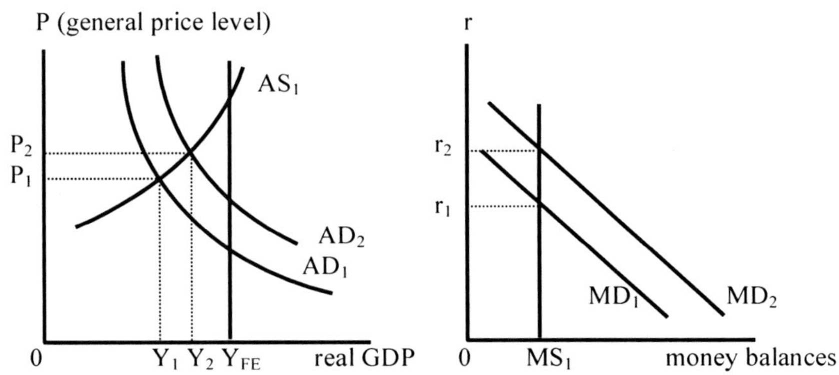

Whether or not the new equilibrium is exactly the same as the original equilibrium, the decrease in taxes has little, if any, impact on real GDP and employment.

6. Using the money market to explain the increased spending error.

The increased spending argument that yields a positive impact on real GDP and employment shows aggregate demand increasing from AD_1 to AD_2, while the demand for money and interest rates also increase. But, it ignores the fact that the increased sale of government bonds causes an automatic decrease in the money supply. When people buy bonds, they pay for them with money, which means they are then holding less money and more bonds. And bonds are not money. Therefore, in Figure 22.8, a reduction in the money supply due to increased government bond sales causes the supply of money to decrease from MS_1 to MS_2. With a money supply of M_2, interest rates rise from r_2 to r_3. And, as interest rates increase, aggregate demand decreases; it moves to the left, from AD_2 back towards AD_1 and the original equilibrium.

Whether the bond market or the money market is used to explain the consequences of financing a deficit by selling bonds to the public, the result is the same: Interest rates increase, causing aggregate demand to return to (or close to) its original level. Of course, as AD declines, so do the price level and the demand for money. In the end, the demand for money will be between MD_1 and MD_2, and interest rates will be above r_1.

Figure 22.8

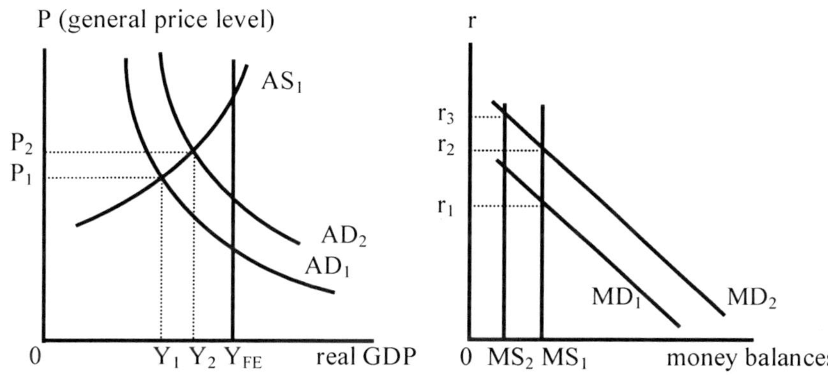

7. Is there any way a spending increase can improve the economy?

There is one way for a spending increase to appear to have a positive impact on the economy: If the Federal Reserve increases the money supply to offset the reduction in the money supply caused by government bond sales, real GDP and employment can increase.

What the Fed does is purchase bonds in the open market. And when the Fed purchases bonds in the open market, it pays for them with Federal Reserve checks. Federal Reserve checks, which are defined to be money, replace bonds, which are not money, in the economy. In Figure 22.8, the Fed's purchase of bonds, which increases the money supply, results in the money supply increasing from M_2 back to M_1. And if interest rates remain at r_1 (or thereabouts), aggregate demand can increase to AD_2.

The question is: Should such increases in real GDP and employment be credited to the spending increase or to the increase in the money supply? The economic benefits should be credited to the increased money supply, because an increase in real GDP and employment can occur with an increase in the money supply and no increase in spending, but not with a spending increase and no increase in the money supply.

23

Fiscal Policy

1. Fiscal policy is straightforward, but limited in its usefulness.

Government has many ways to affect individuals and individual markets. Local, state, and federal governments use laws, rules, regulations, taxes, and spending to regulate, promote, provide for, or discourage various activities. From driver's licenses to laws against stealing or killing to providing education to environmental laws to tax codes at all levels, governments keep track of individuals and activities, redistribute income, provide roads, parks, police and fire protection, and national defense. The list of government activities is long; and many of the things governments do will continue to be debated by those with different social or political views.

When it comes to fiscal policy, however, the main tools available to the federal government—changing taxes and spending—do not work very well.

The purpose of fiscal policy is not to affect individuals and individual markets by imposing taxes on dangerous products, such as cigarettes, or to provide help to individuals, through welfare programs or price support policies. The purpose of fiscal policy is to manage the overall economy so that the nation can have full employment, stable prices, and solid economic growth. Therefore, to be classified as fiscal-policy tools, tax and spending changes must be aimed, not at individual markets, but at overall production, employment, prices, and growth.

According to the logic of the simple Keynesian models—the logic that continues to be used for political-economic decisions in Washington—it is possible to increase national production and employment either by cutting taxes or by increasing government spending. Although Republicans like to blame excessive government spending and on-going deficits on Democrats, who they claim are using outmoded Keynesian ideas from the 1930's, it was Richard Nixon who declared, "We are all Keynesians now." And both Ronald Reagan and George W. Bush used Keynesian arguments to justify tax cuts as a way of improving the economy, regardless of the fact that Milton Friedman, an economist with truly Conservative political ideals, has said, for more than half a century, that tax cuts do not work.

Chapter 21 explained the flaw in assuming that a tax cut will stimulate the economy: When the government cuts taxes, hoping to generate greater spending, that spending is offset by a decrease in other spending due to higher interest rates caused by the government's need to sell bonds to finance the resulting deficit.

Chapter 22 explained the flaw in assuming that a government spending increase will stimulate the economy: When the government increases spending, hoping to generate greater GDP and employment, that spending is offset by a decrease in other spending due to higher interest rates caused by the need to sell bonds to finance the resulting deficit.

Richard Nixon may have been partially correct in implying that both Democrats and Republicans like to use tax cuts to help their friends, even if they know doing so will not stimulate the economy. But it is not entirely accurate to blame the idea on Keynes. Keynes made the argument, in the middle of the Great Depression, that government should not try to balance its budget during steep economic downturns, because as tax revenues shrink, the government will then have to reduce its spending; and if the government reduces its spending, employment and tax revenues fall even further. Then, in a futile attempt to keep the budget balanced, spending will have to be cut again. And so on; with the downturn becoming deeper and deeper with each round of spending cuts.

What Keynes recommended was that government spend its way out of a recession, even if the spending creates a deficit. Then, after the economy recovers, the deficit can be paid off out of the higher tax revenues of a healthy economy. Keynes did not focus on tax cuts, because he was not arguing that a deficit, by itself, was good. He focused on deficit spending, because government spending during a recession can be a direct benefit to those in need.

Keynes, and the Keynesian economists that followed, may have ignored the negative impact of the deficit on interest rates and spending, but the deficit-spending argument has one advantage over tax-cuts. Tax cuts directly help individuals and businesses already employed or earning profits. And because there is no trickle-down reality, those who need help the most, do not get it. Spending, if aimed at unemployed workers and suffering businesses, can directly help those in need.

In the end, the tools of fiscal policy—cutting taxes or increasing government spending—are of limited value, unless they are coupled with a supportive management of the money supply. But, if tax cuts or deficit spending boost the economy only when they are financed with money creation, then it is money creation that is the key to a recovery.

24

Monetary Policy and the Federal Reserve

1. Monetary policy, conducted by the Federal Reserve, is the primary tool for managing today's economy.

Although the supply of money (or changes in the rate of growth of the money supply) has a dramatic impact on the economy, it was not until 1980 that the money supply in the United States was truly brought under control.

Whether money consisted of metal coins struck from precious or non-precious metals, paper currency with or without precious metal backing, or checking account money, history is filled with examples of abuse: fake coins, counterfeit paper currency, banks freely printing their own soon-to-be-worthless paper money, greenbacks and Confederate currency, fraud by banks, the failure of two U.S. central banks, each of which was shut down after throwing its weight behind the wrong presidential candidate, and dramatic cases of Federal Reserve stupidity.

The purpose of monetary policy is to manage the money supply in a way that promotes full employment, stable prices, and beneficial economic growth.

In the United States, as in other developed nations, management of the money supply is handled by a central bank. The central bank in the U.S. is the Federal Reserve System that was created by Congress in 1913 after a lengthy and heated debate. It was clear that the money supply had to be managed, because history had proved that banks could not be trusted to regulate themselves. But because of the abuses of power by two former central banks—the First and Second Banks of the United States—and the inability of the Treasury Department to control the money supply, it was not easy to decide who should be given the responsibility. In the end, the Federal Reserve System was created; rather than having a single central bank, twelve Federal Reserve Banks were established throughout the country. The idea was to spread the power around instead of having it concentrated in one place. It may have sounded like a good idea in 1913, but today it is clear that a few individuals (maybe a single individual) have enormous influence over the economy by being able to control the money supply.

2. The Federal Reserve System

The Federal Reserve System is not a government agency. It is a central bank with, not one, but twelve separate Federal Reserve Banks, each of which is owned, through stock purchases, by the commercial banks it is supposed to regulate and supervise. The New York Federal Reserve Bank receives most of the attention because it handles the day-to-day operations of the Fed.

When it was first established, in 1913, the Federal Reserve's primary function was to be "a lender of last resort," meaning it would loan funds to banks that could not meet depositor's demands, which meant it was also looking after the money supply. It was a crucial need, proven by history's many bank panics, including the 1907 disaster that forced Congress to take the action that created the Federal Reserve.

Although the Federal Reserve did an adequate job while the economy was relatively stable, it did a terrible job of protecting banks, deposits, and the money supply during the Great Depression. Even so, its power and influence grew to the point where it is now the main manager of the U.S. economy. Its current functions go far beyond its original purpose, which was simply to support banks and offer some protection to depositors.

The Federal Reserve's current goals are to achieve acceptable economic growth, low unemployment, and steady prices—goals that are sometimes in conflict with each other. The tools it has at its disposal are its control of the money supply and the authority to set certain interest rates.

The Fed sets reserve requirements for banks, which, in theory, have an impact on the money supply, but which, in reality, are seldom changed.

The Fed sets the discount rate, which is the interest rate banks pay to borrow from the Fed, something that is done mainly to meet legal reserve requirements.

Textbooks devote a lot of time to showing how a fractional reserve system allows banks to create money in a way that leads to multiple expansions and contractions of the money supply when funds are added to or taken out of from the banking system. But that does not actually happen.

A fractional reserve system means that when someone makes a deposit in a bank, the bank is required to keep only a small percentage of the deposit available for possible withdrawals; the rest can be loaned out, which is what banks do to earn profits. However, when all factors are considered, there is virtually no multiple expansion or contraction of money within the banking system when new funds are added or subtracted.

Although the discount rate gets a lot of publicity, the Fed's true method for increasing or decreasing the money supply is its "Open Market Operations." To increase the money supply, the Fed buys government securities in the open market; doing so replaces something that is not money (bonds) with something that is money (Federal Reserve checks that are deposited in banks by the sellers of bonds). To decrease the money supply, the Fed sells government securities in the open market, thereby taking money out of the system and replacing it with bonds.

And because there is no real multiple expansion or contraction of the money supply, the increase or decrease in the money supply is essentially equal to the Fed's purchase or sale of bonds.

As simple as the process is, it is the most powerful tool available for managing modern economies.

Who decides when the money supply, or the rate of growth of the money supply, is to be increased or decreased? Technically, the Federal Open Market Committee makes the decision.

The Federal Open Market Committee is made up of the seven members of the Federal Reserve Board of Governors and five of the twelve Federal Reserve Bank presidents. Four of the five are selected on a rotating basis; the president of the Federal Reserve Bank of New York is always on the committee, because the Fed's open market operations are conducted through the New York Bank.

The President of the United States appoints the seven members of the Board of Governors. Members are appointed to staggered 14-year terms (ending in January of every even numbered year) so that a president cannot easily take over the Board with his own appointees. The president also appoints the Chairman of the Board of Governors to a four-year term. But the Chairman's term is staggered with the president's, so that when a president takes office, it is with an existing Chairman.

The presidents of the twelve Federal Reserve Banks are appointed by each bank's nine directors, six of whom are chosen by the member banks in the district.

This elaborate system of checks and balances was developed by Congress in order to prevent a concentration of power in one place, which had happened in the past.

The reality, however, is that power is not only centered in one place, it is centered with one person—the Chairman of the Federal Reserve Board of Governors.

3. A change in the nominal supply of money.

In order to understand the Federal Reserve and the money market better, we can see what happens to interest rates if the Federal Reserve increases the nominal money supply.

The initial equilibrium is shown by the demand curve D_1 and the supply curve M_1 in Figure 24.1.

The initial supply of money is M_1.

The initial equilibrium interest rate is r_1.

The supply of money is a vertical line at M_1, because it is assumed that the supply of money is fixed at the level set by the Federal Reserve, and is independent of interest rates.

Figure 24.1

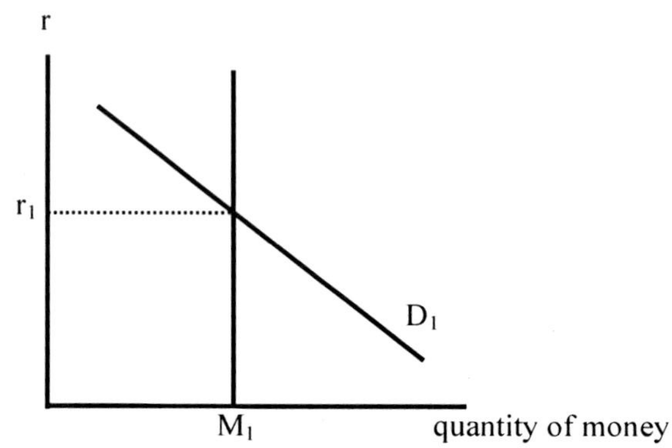

An increase in the nominal money supply can be shown as a change from M_1 to M_2 in Figure 24.2. The change in the money supply does not affect the demand for money; it remains at D_1.

Figure 24.2

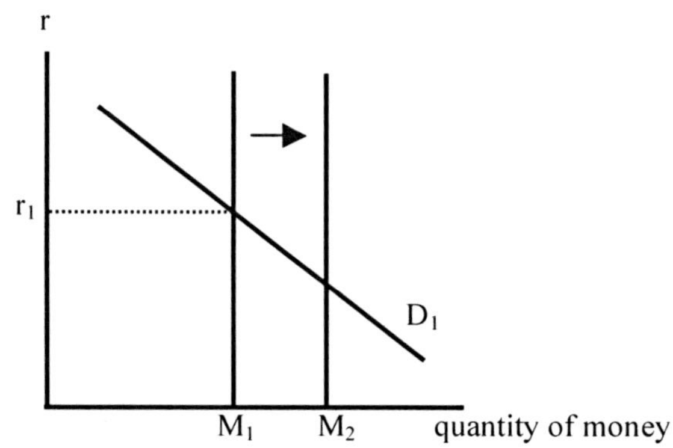

Given the original demand curve, D_1, and the new supply of money, M_2, there is an excess supply of money in the economy at the initial equilibrium interest rate. The excess supply is equal to $M_2 - M_1$. In other words, at r_1, people still want to hold only M_1 dollars, but there are M_2 dollars in the economy.

The excess supply of money, meaning that people want to hold less money than is in the system, means that people want to "get rid of money." They don't want to throw their money away; they want to switch more of it into interest-bearing assets (such as bonds).

The excess supply of money, which is equal to the horizontal difference between the quantity demanded, M_1, and the new supply of money, M_2, at the original interest rate, r_1, means people are holding more money than they want to hold, relative to interest bearing assets at the current interest rate. In order to bring their portfolio balance in line with their desires, people increase their purchases of interest-bearing assets (bonds). The increased demand for bonds leads to an increase in the price of bonds. And as the price of bonds increases, there is an automatic decrease in interest rates.

> Bonds are issued with a *fixed dollar* dividend that may be paid in installments or in total when the bond reaches maturity. Because the *dollar* value of the dividend is fixed, and does not change, an increase in the price of bonds automatically lowers interest rates, because it automatically lowers the *percentage* return on the investment. A decrease in bond prices automatically raises interest rates.

As interest rates fall, there is a move down the demand curve for money, meaning that people want to hold more money and fewer bonds.

As long as the supply of money is greater than the quantity demanded at a given interest rate, there is downward pressure on interest rates. The excess supply of money and the downward pressure on interest rates continue until a new equilibrium is reached where people are willing to hold the new quantity of money in the system.

Figure 24.3

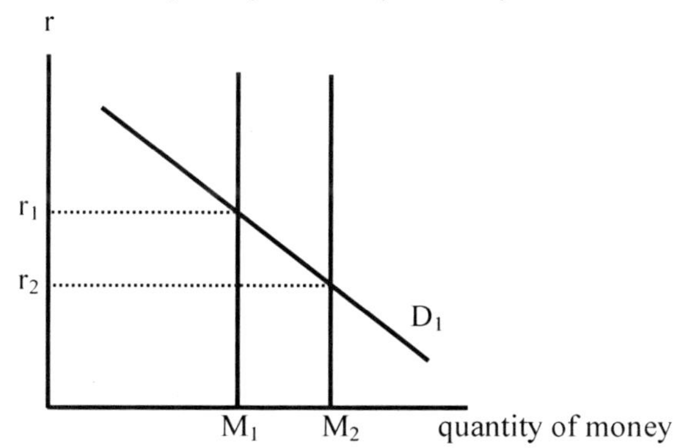

The nominal supply of money increases from M_1 to M_2.

The equilibrium interest rate falls from r_1 to r_2.

The quantity of money held by the public increases from M_1 to M_2.

In the new equilibrium, the new supply of money, M_2, is equal to the original demand for money, D_1, at the new equilibrium interest rate r_2.

The conclusion is what most would expect: An increase in the money supply causes interest rates to fall, assuming all other things remain constant.

But it is one thing to *believe* that an increase in the money supply causes interest rates to fall; it is another to know *why*.

The conclusion is the same if the supply of money were positively related to interest rates.

4. How does a decrease in the money supply affect prices, employment, and gross domestic product?

Without using diagrams, if the nominal supply of money is decreased, it means that something that was assumed to be held constant when deriving the initial aggregate demand and aggregate supply--the nominal money supply--has changed.

It is normally assumed that changes in the money supply do not directly affect aggregate supply.

However, aggregate demand is changed, because the decrease in the money supply causes interest rates to increase. And if interest rates increase, interest sensitive spending is lower at each price level. The result is a decrease in aggregate demand. In a diagram, the new aggregate demand is to the left of the initial aggregate demand.

Given the new aggregate demand and the original aggregate supply, there is an excess supply of goods and services at the original price level, because at the original price level, buyers are not willing and able to buy as much as they did when interest rates were lower, but sellers still want to sell the same quantity.

The excess supply, which is equal to the horizontal difference between the new aggregate demand and the original aggregate supply *at the original price level*, causes prices to fall. As prices fall, the economy moves down the new aggregate demand curve. There is a new equilibrium where new aggregate demand is equal to original aggregate supply.

In the new equilibrium: The price level is lower; total spending is less than it was; real Gross Domestic Product is lower; and employment is lower.

A few definitions:

Nominal money supply is the quantity of money in the economy at a given time. The two most common measures of money are: M1 and M2.

M1 is defined to be paper currency and coins in circulation plus deposits in checking accounts. It is a definition of the most "liquid" form of money, because it represents funds that can be used instantly to make purchases.

M2 is defined to be M1 plus deposits in savings accounts, small time deposits, and non-institutional money-market funds. M2 is not quite as liquid as M1 because it may take time to withdraw funds from such accounts before they can be used to make purchases.

Factors assumed to be constant when deriving the demand for money are the overall price level and Gross Domestic Product. Increases in either lead to an increase in the demand for money, because more money is needed to make purchases if prices rise or if people become wealthier.

25

Oil Prices and Inflation

International problems are causing large increases in oil prices. Your company is concerned about the impact of rising oil prices on sales. Some experts claim that there is nothing to worry about; they say high oil prices cause inflation, and that during inflationary periods consumers spend more than normal. Other experts argue that there is a problem; they say that high oil prices are recessionary, not inflationary, and that in recessions, people spend less. Those arguing for inflation point to the Consumer Price Index, claiming that a rising Consumer Price Index is proof that rising oil prices are inflationary, not recessionary. They also point out that the Federal Reserve is raising interest rates to choke off the inflation being caused by soaring oil prices. You have to make a decision about production levels. Do you expect sales to be helped or hurt by rising oil prices?

1. An increase in oil prices does not cause inflation; it causes a recession.

The belief that rising oil prices cause inflation comes from a misunderstanding of economic logic and facts. It is a belief grounded in a mistaken view of how the world works. As oil prices increase, causing other prices to rise, the Consumer Price Index (CPI) also increases. The CPI must increase, because the CPI is nothing more than an index number devised to track the cost of a given bundle of goods over time.

The error is to assume that any increase in the Consumer Price Index is a signal or measure of current or impending inflation. It is not.

Rising oil prices make many things more expensive. The Law of Demand (the one irrefutable law of economics) says that as the price of anything increases, other things unchanged, less of that thing will be purchased.

Therefore, as rising oil prices cause many prices to increase, less of many things are bought, and the economy is pushed downward. Adding to the downward pressure on the economy is the fact that a large part of the money spent on oil goes out of the country, thereby taking away a portion of America's purchasing power.

Rational policies come from knowing that it is necessary to understand *why* the CPI is increasing, not just that it *is* increasing. If the increase is due to rising resource costs, particularly resources that are imported, the boost in the CPI is an indicator of building recessionary pressures.

Non-rational policies are the result of ignoring the reasons behind a rising CPI.

Therefore, if, in response to the rising CPI, the federal government or the Federal Reserve decides to introduce policies to fight inflation, rather than policies that guard against recession, the economy is dealt a double blow—the negative force of the anti-inflationary policies is added to the negative impact of higher oil prices. The fact is, every time the supply of oil is disrupted, causing prices to rise, the United States economy is pushed into a downturn. It happened in the early 1970s, the early 1980s, at the beginning of the 1990's, and again at the beginning of the twenty-first century.

If something happens that causes constant increases in aggregate demand, the result is inflation. Each increase in aggregate demand yields a greater than full employment equilibrium that leads to more and more wage increases. Each increase in wages causes aggregate supply to decrease—move up or to the left. And each step results in a new equilibrium at the full employment level of GDP, but with higher and higher prices.

The only thing that can cause such constant increases in aggregate demand, thereby causing inflation, is a constantly increasing money supply.

Constantly rising oil prices will raise prices, but will also cause greater and greater decreases in GDP and employment, leading to what has been called "stagflation." It is not a good term, because it implies a combination of inflation and a stagnant economy. In truth, it is a recession with higher prices—but not inflation.

Constant decreases in taxes or increases in government spending do not cause continual increases in aggregate demand because financing deficits created by such actions causes interest rates to rise, which reduces consumer and business spending. If such fiscal policy actions cannot successfully stimulate the economy, they also cannot cause inflation. The only time fiscal policy actions can appear to lead to inflation is when they are financed, not by selling bonds to the public but by creating new money to pay for them. That means the reason for inflation is, again, increases in the money supply.

2. What happens to the general price level, gross domestic product, and employment as a result of an increase in oil prices?

The question.

How does an increase in oil prices affect the general price level, gross domestic product, employment, and interest rates in the short run?

(1) The initial equilibrium.

The initial equilibrium is shown by normal aggregate supply and aggregate demand curves, AS_1 and AD_1, and the normal money demand and supply curves in Figure 25.1. No information is given that would lead to the assumption of non-normal functions. The initial equilibrium price level is P_1. The initial equilibrium level of real GDP is assumed to be Y_{FE}, which is the full-employment level of GDP. The initial demand for money is MD_1. The initial supply of money is MS_1. The initial interest rate is r_1.

Figure 25.1

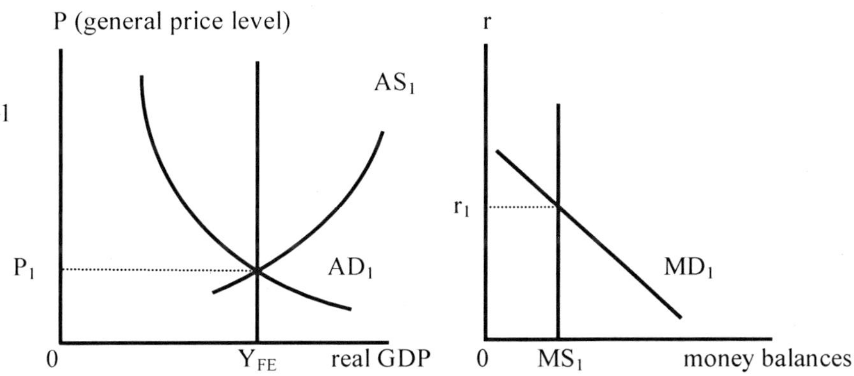

As with many other questions, it is not necessary to show the money market. But whether it is shown or not, it plays a part in the answer. Whether it is shown or not, it is necessary to understand and remember the back and forth chain of events whereby a change in AD or AS that leads to a change in the general price level leads to a change in the demand for money that causes a change in interest rates that then causes movements along AD.

(2) The change.

The aggregate supply curve changes. If oil prices increase, it means that something that was assumed to have been held constant when deriving the initial aggregate supply—the prices of inputs to production—has changed.

Each level of total output now costs more to produce than it did before. Therefore, aggregate supply decreases.

A decrease in aggregate supply means there is a new AS curve to the left of (or above) the original AS curve.

The new aggregate supply is AS_2.

Aggregate demand remains at AD_1.

The nominal supply of money is still MS_1.

The demand for nominal money balances is still MD_1.

Figure 25.2

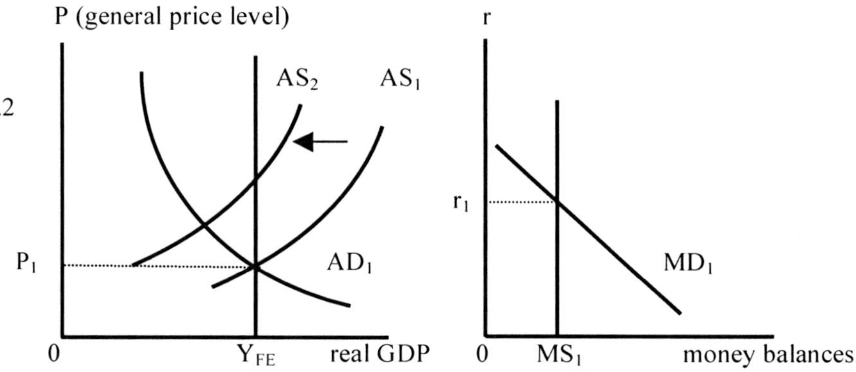

(3) The new equilibrium.

The new equilibrium, P_2,Y_2, is determined by the new aggregate supply curve, AS_2, and the original aggregate demand curve, AD_1.

Figure 25.3

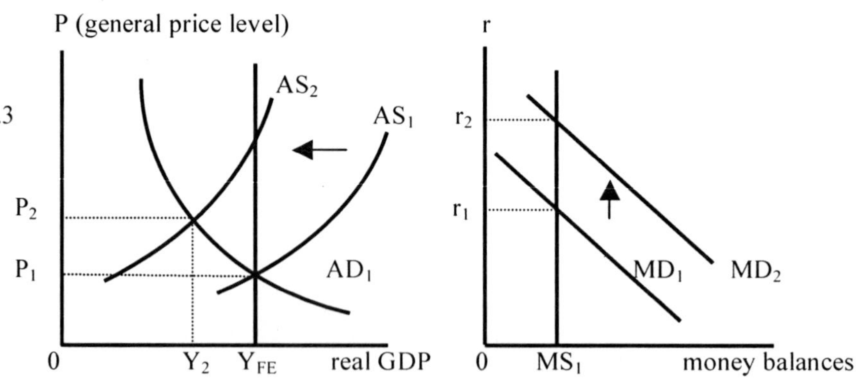

In Figure 25.3, the equilibrium is at P_2 (a higher price level) and Y_2, (a lower level of GDP).

In the money market, the higher price level causes the demand for money to increase. The higher demand for money, MD_2, with the original supply of money, MS_1, causes interest rates to increase to r_2.

The move from the original equilibrium to the new equilibrium is as follows. At the original price level, P_1, firms want to produce an output less than Y_{FE}, because the increase in oil prices increases the cost of production. But, at price level P_1, aggregate demand is still Y_{FE}. The result is a disequilibrium with production less than demand.

If demand is greater than production, consumers will bid up prices.

As the general price level rises above P_1, the demand for money increases, shown as a change from MD_1 to MD_2 in Figure 25.3, causing interest rates to rise. As interest rates rise, there is a decrease in consumer spending (C), private investment spending (I), and net exports (NX). As interest-sensitive spending decreases, the economy moves up the AD_1 curve to lower and lower levels of GDP. The price level continues to increase and consumption continues to fall until a new equilibrium is reached at P_2, Y_1 in Figure 25.3.

Although firms initially wanted to decrease output below Y_1 (to the level of GDP where AS_2 intersects the horizontal line at P_1), because of the increase in oil prices, the economy actually ends up at Y_1. Output decreases, but not as much as firms originally intended at the original price level, P_1. The reason is that rising prices offset some of the negative impact of higher production costs.

The equilibrium price level increases from P_1 to P_2.

The equilibrium level of GDP decreases from Y_{FE} to Y_1.

The equilibrium interest rate increases from r_1 to r_2.

The equilibrium level of employment decreases.

Real wages fall, because the price level increases.

Conclusion.

The increase in oil prices affects the general price level, gross domestic product, employment, the real wage, and interest rates. Assuming that the economy began at full-employment (an unnecessary assumption), and that the nominal supply of money and money wages did not change: AS decreases, AD remains the same, the price level is higher; interest rates are higher; total spending is less than it was; real Gross Domestic Product is lower; employment is lower; and real wages are lower.

3. What about the inflation issue?

The rising price level shows up as an increase in the Consumer Price Index (CPI), which is used as a measure of inflation. Therefore, by focusing simply on the CPI, with no regard for the reason behind its increase, it can be assumed that rising oil prices cause inflation. What rising oil prices really cause, however, is lower output, lower employment, lower wages, and lower profits. That is not inflation. It is, if anything, what is sometimes called "stagflation," a term used to describe a stagnant economy with rising prices (unemployment and inflation at the same time). Technically, inflation is defined as rising prices over time. So, if oil prices are to cause "inflation," they have to keep rising.

More important is the reaction to the assumed inflation. If it is assumed that the rise in the CPI is a signal of increasing inflation, then the Federal Reserve may act to fight inflation rather than the recession or unemployment that is the real problem.

If the Fed decides that it must fight the good fight against the oil-driven inflation, it will reduce the money supply in order to raise interest rates and reduce spending. The assumption is that by reducing total spending, the upward pressure on prices will be reversed. It is, of course, a not very smart idea. In the first place, the rise in prices was not caused by increases in demand or spending; it was caused by increases in resource costs—oil prices. Secondly, by decreasing the money supply, the Fed will reduce GDP, employment, profits, and wages even more.

That is why it is important to not assume that every increase in the CPI means inflation. But, would the Fed ever be so stupid? The answer is, yes. That is exactly what the Fed has done in response to every dramatic increase in oil prices.

In terms of Figure 25.3, if the Fed decreases the money supply, it will cause interest rates to rise above r_2, which will cause aggregate demand to decrease—move to the left of AD_1. The result of such Fed actions, which the student should be able to show, is a new equilibrium with GDP less than Y_1 and a general price level less than P_2, which means lower employment, lower wages, and lower profits. If the Fed's goal is lower prices, it succeeds. If its goal is full employment and a healthy economy, it fails.

4. What about the long run?

The above argument is a short run argument, representing what happens in a short period of time.

The new equilibrium, however, (with or without the Fed's bad policies) is one with unemployment.

And, over time, high levels of unemployment lead to reductions in wages as workers compete for jobs.

As wages decline, the cost of production falls. As production costs fall, aggregate supply increases—moves to the right.

In Figure 25.4, AS_2 moves to something like AS_3, causing an increase in GDP, and employment. In theory, wages would continue to decline until aggregate supply moves back to AS_1.

And as aggregate supply increases due to falling wages, the price level falls, causing a decrease in the demand for money (not shown), which lowers interest rates, which increases spending, moving the economy back down AD_1.

Figure 25.4

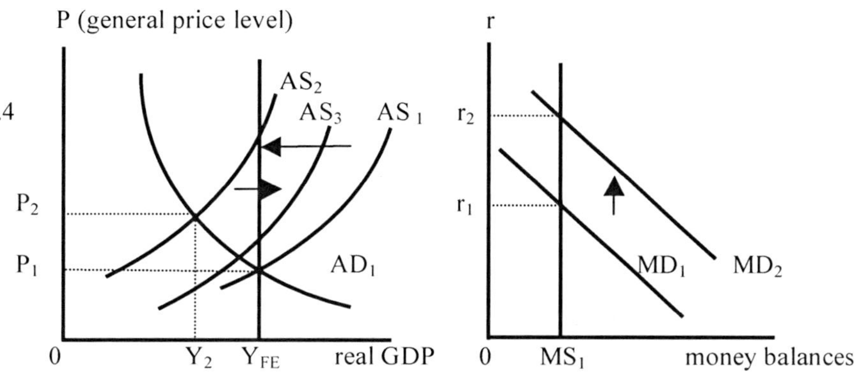

5. So, do rising oil prices cause inflation?

No. Rising oil prices lower GDP, employment, wages, and profits.

Therefore, the response to rising oil prices should be policies aimed at improving GDP, employment, wages, and profits, not policies that cause even more damage in the name of fighting inflation.

26

Economic Growth and Inflation

1. What causes economic growth?

One of the most important questions in all of economics is: What causes economic growth? The question, which is of crucial importance to both developed and developing nations, is also the least understood in all of economics.

Academic journals and textbooks are filled with all sorts of explanations and theories of economic growth, each of which is of little or no value in the real world.

Does that mean economists do not know anything about economic growth? Especially how to encourage positive growth? The answer is, no. The truth is economists have known for more than two thousand years what the key to economic growth is. But, to be useful, that knowledge must be separated into two somewhat distinct categories—economic growth in undeveloped (or developing) countries and economic growth in developed countries. The reason for the distinction is that there are important differences between developing and developed countries.

2. What causes economic growth in developing nations?

There is a clear list of factors that leads to economic growth in undeveloped countries.

1) The first factor, which was explained brilliantly by Plato in 360 BCE, is specialization. So far, no one has done a better job than Plato of explaining the incredible benefits of specialization in a pre-industrialized economy. As people move from being self-sufficient individuals or families—meaning that they are producing everything they need by themselves—to specialized producers, such as wheat growers, shoe makers, candle makers, or pin makers, a whole market economy develops. Specialization in production lets people produce far more of a single product than they can use themselves, thereby giving them the opportunity to sell what they make and buy what they need and want. The result is that people and families end up with much more than they could ever produce by themselves. Out of this specialization, markets develop where things are bought and sold—using money, not barter. Then come retailers, wholesalers, and foreign

trade. It is all described in *The Republic*. And it is the single most important reason for massive increases in economic growth and the wealth of the nation.

2) The second factor, which was described by Adam Smith in 1776, is specialization in factories. Smith took Plato's description of specialization in a pre-industrialized economy and brought it into an industrialized economy. In Smith's pin factory, workers specialize in making one part of a pin. Instead of Plato's pin makers, who, by specializing in making pins, might make 20 pins a day, Smith's pin makers, working in factories, make the equivalent of 200 pins a day. (In Smith's example, ten workers in a pin factory turn out 2,000 pins a day, versus the 20 he assumed each can make on his own.) It is described wonderfully in Smith's *An Inquiry Into The nature And Causes Of The Wealth of Nations*. And it is the single most important reason for the massive increases in economic growth and the wealth of nations that Smith predicted.

3) The third factor is the need for capital to fund the factories that allow the specialization described by Adam Smith. In many developing countries, such capital is difficult, or impossible to find. In developed countries, investment in capital goods occurs when some current production is directed toward the creation of productive facilities and infrastructure. In poor nations, there may not be enough current production to meet basic needs—such as food and shelter—which means that it is virtually impossible to free up production to build for the future. In such cases, the needed capital must come from somewhere else. However, it is difficult for benevolent nations to provide capital goods to improve future conditions when millions of people may be starving today.

4) The fourth factor is property rights, because in order for factors one through three to be implemented, it is necessary for people to have property rights to protect what they have. Without property rights, neither Plato's nor Adam Smith's specialization can take place, because without property rights, everything can be taken away from anyone who prospers. And, in both developing and developed countries, if contracts are not enforced and protected, virtually everything is handed over to those with the brute force to take what they want from everyone who is weaker.

5) A fifth factor is stability—a stable government and a stable economy—because without stability, investment cannot take place in either Plato's or Adam Smith's world. Again, in many poor nations, there is no stability. There is, instead, chaos and civil war.

3. What causes economic growth in developed nations?

The first four factors listed above are present in all developed nations, which is why a reasonable rate of economic growth is the norm.

The fifth factor is also present, but it can vary. Although most developed nations have stable governments, there are times when that is not the case. And although most developed countries have relatively stable economies, that is also not always the case.

Even the most developed countries suffer bouts of inflation and recession, each of which is a detriment to economic growth.

And even the most developed countries experience periods of low saving rates, outside economic disruptions, and government policies that hurt economic growth, each of which disrupts the normal and expected economic growth in industrialized economies.

On the other hand, there are also periods of beneficial change, such as times of significant increases in technology that push economic growth above its expected level.

Therefore, the most important factors for encouraging economic growth in developed countries are economic stability and wise policies by governments and central banks.

4. Showing economic growth caused by Plato's specialization.

The question.

How can our model be used to show economic growth due to Plato's specialization?

(1) The initial, self-sufficiency equilibrium.

The initial, self-sufficiency equilibrium is shown by the normal aggregate supply and aggregate demand curves, AS_1 and AD_1, and the normal money demand and supply curves in Figure 26.1.

The initial equilibrium price level is P_1.

The initial equilibrium level of real GDP is Y_{FE}.

The initial equilibrium interest rate is r_1. The equilibrium level of GDP is at less than the full-employment level of GDP.

It is assumed throughout this analysis that the economy is at full employment.

Figure 26.1

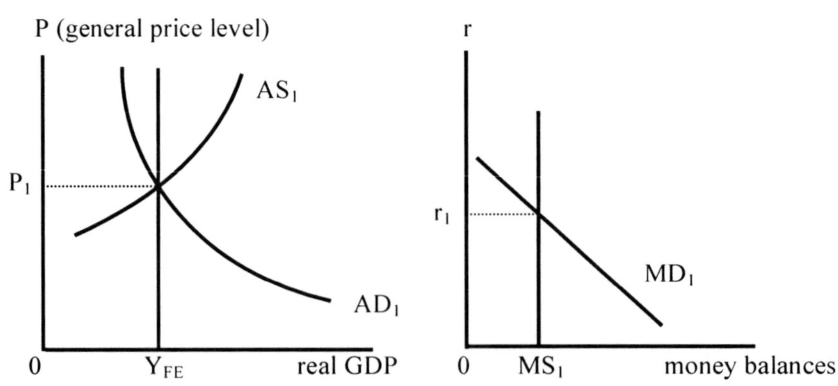

(2) Plato's change.

If specialization is introduced into an economy made up primarily of self-sufficient individuals and families, three things change, as shown in Figure 26.2.

Aggregate supply increases from AS_1 to AS_2, because each level of total output now costs less to produce than it did.

Aggregate demand increases from AD_1 to AD_2, because of the increase in spendable income resulting from specialization.

And Y_{FE} increases, because individuals working at specialized trades combine to create a larger GDP for every price level.

Figure 26.2

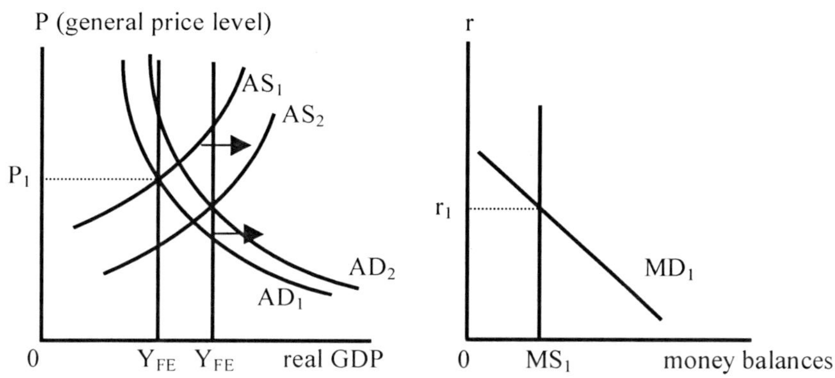

(3) Plato's new equilibrium.

The new equilibrium, determined by the new aggregate supply and the new aggregate demand is shown to be at the new, and higher, full employment level of GDP. (It does not have to be at full employment.)

In the new equilibrium, the price level falls from P_1 to P_2, and the lower price level causes the demand for money to decease from MD_1 to MD_2. The lower demand for money leads to lower interest rates, which cause an increase in interest sensitive spending, thereby moving the economy down the new AD_2 function.

The standard measure of economic growth is the period-to-period change in real GDP.

Therefore, in terms of economic growth, Plato's specialization is a positive factor.

Figure 26.3

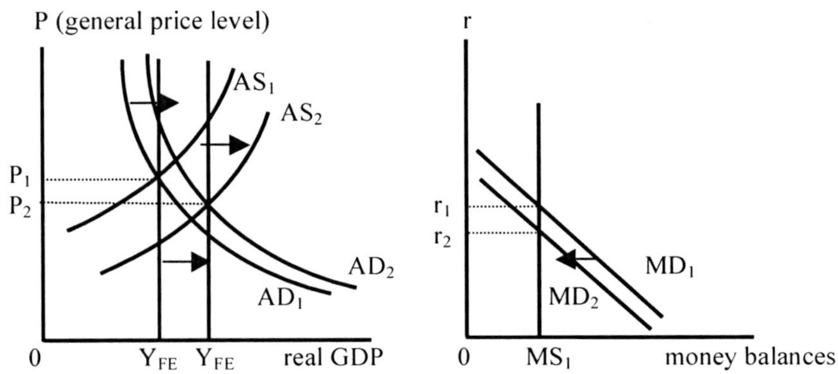

It should be clear that the fall in the price level is the result of arbitrarily drawing new aggregate supply and aggregate demand curves that happen to intersect at a price level that is below the original price level. There is no reason to assume that will actually happen. Therefore, the analysis should not be interpreted to mean that specialization or economic growth causes prices to fall. It is just as easy to draw new aggregate supply and aggregate demand curves that intersect at a higher price level, or at the original price level. In any case, the change in the money market is determined by the change in the price level.

5. Showing the result of Adam Smith's specialization.

The question.

How does the model show economic growth due to Adam Smith's industrial specialization? We can explain what happens without showing it.

(1) The new initial equilibrium.

Figure 26.3 is the new initial equilibrium; it is the equilibrium resulting from Plato's idea of specialization.

(2) Adam Smith's change.

If industrial specialization is introduced into an economy made up primarily of specialized crafts or occupations, the same three things change.

Aggregate supply increases from AS_2 to something to something greater than AS_2.

Aggregate demand increases from AD_2 to something to something greater than AD_2.

The full employment level of real GDP increases again.

(3) Adam Smith's equilibrium.

The new equilibrium, determined by even greater aggregate supply and aggregate demand, is at a higher level of real GDP. (We are again assuming it is at the new full employment level of real GDP.)

In the new equilibrium, the price level can be higher, lower, or the same.

If the price level increases, so will the demand for money and interest rates.

If the price level decreases, so will the demand for money and interest rates.

If the price level stays the same, so will the demand for money and interest rates.

In terms of economic growth, Smith's specialization is also positive factor, because it leads to another increase in real GDP.

6. More questions.

How can the model show the impact on economic growth of access to capital, the protection of property rights, and government and economic stability?

The same as above.

Each factor that adds to economic growth increases aggregate supply or aggregate demand or both, as well as increasing the full employment level of real GDP, which, again, is how economic growth is measured.

Of course, if the full employment level of real GDP is increasing, but the economy is mired down in unemployment, then the change in measured GDP, which is the equilibrium GDP, may not result in any real growth at all.

7. Does fast economic growth cause inflation?

There are no historical examples of fast economic growth causing inflation. There are no acceptable economic theories showing that fast economic growth causes inflation.

> "The whole purpose of the economy is production of goods or services for consumption now or in the future. I think the burden of proof should always be on those who would produce less rather than more, on those who would leave idle people or machines or land that could be used. It is amazing how many reasons can be found to justify such waste: fear of inflation, balance of payments deficits, unbalanced budgets, excessive national debt, loss of confidence in the dollar."
>
> James Tobin—*National Economic Policy*.

Tobin, a Nobel winning economist, is correct.

If the federal government or the Federal Reserve wants to enact policies to intentionally slow economic growth, there should be good arguments for doing so, because such actions hurt people and business. Holding economic growth below its potential reduces the wealth of the nation and may cause a recession.

In an ideal world, economic growth would measure changes in the well-being of the nation. Unfortunately, "well-being" is a concept that cannot actually be measured because it includes too many intangibles--things that cannot easily be calculated in dollar terms, such as health, peace, environmental quality, and so on.

The standard definition of economic growth, using something that can be measured, is: a change in Gross Domestic Product over time.

The idea that substantial increases in production can cause inflation comes, in large part, from questionable statistical studies done years ago in Britain; studies that concluded there was a negative relationship between inflation and unemployment, meaning that lower levels of unemployment seemed to go along with higher rates of inflation. Although those studies have been dismissed over the years, many economists and policymakers continue to argue that a country must choose between a low rate of inflation and a low level of unemployment.

However, none of the economic models used to explain how the economy works show that increases in production cause prices to rise. In all such models, there are two explanations for rising price levels. One is overzealous and erroneous tax, spending, or monetary policies intended to stimulate the economy, but which end up creating a total demand for goods and services that outstrips what is produced. The second is an increase in resource costs that pushes up the costs of production.

In the first case, the nation experiences low levels of unemployment and rising prices, but the reason is not fast economic growth, it is policy mistakes.

In the second case, the result is a rising price level coupled with declining production and employment; again fast economic growth is not an issue. In fact, the outcome is not fast economic growth at all, but slow economic growth. An example of the second case is an increase in oil prices that causes a recession.

8. What factors reduce economic growth?

Anything that causes decreases in the equilibrium values of real GDP will cause a decrease in real economic growth.

Sharp increases in oil prices can do it.

Federal Reserve policies that raise interest rates can do it.

Large government deficits that raise interest rates can do it.

Large foreign trade deficits can do it.

Unemployment can do it.

A lack of capital investment can do it.

27

The One and Only Cause of Inflation

1. The one and only cause of inflation is an excessive increase in the money supply, which normally occurs when the money supply is increased to finance deficit spending by the federal government.

There are two important facts about inflation.

One is that every increase in the Consumer Price Index (CPI) is not an indication or measure of inflation. (See Chapters 25 and 26)

The second is that it is still true that inflation is caused by "too much money chasing too few goods." The only change is where the money comes from.

The Spanish Empire was brought to an end partly by the inflation it suffered as a result of the vast quantities of gold and silver brought back to Spain. Gold and silver taken from the New World added to the money supply and the wealth of those who had it, but it did not add anything to production. As a result, the increased spending on the not-increased supply of goods and services led to soaring prices. It was a classic case of too much money chasing too few goods.

Later, when paper currency became the entrenched "medium of exchange, store of value, and unit of account," horrific inflations occurred when governments printed currency to finance massive spending. In Germany, after World War I, the inflation rate soared as the government printed paper money to pay for rebuilding the country. It quickly reached 1,000 percent per month, and continued to climb. From 1921 to 1923 the price level increased more than 34 billion times. In Hungary, after World War II, the government again printed unbelievable quantities of money to pay for reconstruction, with the unavoidable result of unimaginable inflation. In just a few years, prices rose 1,000,000,000,000,000,000,000,000,000,000 times.

In the United States, from 1775 to 1780, as a result of the Continental Congress printing currency to pay for the Revolutionary War, prices quadrupled, slashing the value of the currency. During the Civil War, the governments of both the North and South printed currency (Greenbacks in the North, Confederate Currency in the South) to finance their war efforts. Neither of those currencies survived.

Today, governments in developed countries do not print currency to finance spending, because the citizens of developed nations are no longer willing to let their governments print all the paper money they want in order to pay for spending, regardless of the circumstances. But the money is still created. It is created, or destroyed, through the actions of central banks.

Now, when governments create deficits, because their spending is greater than their tax revenues, their deficits are financed by selling bonds, not by printing money. Regardless of the size of the deficit, selling bonds to finance it is not going to cause inflation, because the deficit spending is offset by lower business and consumer spending due, in part, to higher interest rates resulting from the bond sales.

However, if the central bank (the Federal Reserve in the United States) wants to prevent the deficit and resulting bond sales from raising interest rates, it does so by purchasing bonds in the open market. By adding its purchases to the public's demand for bonds, the central bank keeps interest rates down, thereby preventing government bond sales from causing a decline in business and consumer spending. Of course, when a central bank purchases bonds in the open market, it is actually creating new money. And if the bond purchases continue, meaning that the money supply continues to increase, the result can be—-but does not have to be--inflationary.

If the Federal Reserve expands the money supply by purchasing bonds in the open market during an economic slowdown, the result can be a beneficial economic stimulus.

However, if the Federal Reserve expands the money supply by purchasing bonds during a time of relatively full employment, the result is likely to be inflation. Why would the government run a deficit in a strong economy? It might do so if it wanted to make large expenditures on something citizens may not want to pay for. An unpopular war is one example.

In the end, citizens pay for the unpopular expenditure anyway, whether they know it or not. They pay either with higher taxes or with inflation that reduces the real value of their earnings and accumulated wealth.

Therefore, in a "fiat money" world, meaning a world where money is no longer backed by precious metal holdings of governments or central banks, it is only when a central bank creates money, which it does when it purchases bonds in the open market to finance a government deficit during times of relatively full employment, that inflation can occur.

The 1970s is an example of modern-day inflation. In the 1960s the United States government was fighting an unpopular war abroad and a not completely popular War on

Poverty at home. Massive spending on two fronts led to federal budget deficits that politicians, for political reasons, did not want to finance by raising taxes. So, bonds were sold to cover the government deficit. And the Federal Reserve bought enough bonds to keep interest rates from rising—for a while.

As the 1960s turned into the 1970s, continuing increases in the money supply meant that excessive government spending was not being offset by reduced private spending, which would have been the case if taxes had been raised to pay for the two "wars." Eventually, the money creation led to inflationary price increases. As the inflation rate increased, so did the upward pressure on interest rate. No one wants to loan money to someone else and receive back money that is worth less, in purchasing power, than what they loaned out. That is why interest rates carry an "inflation premium," meaning that the rate of inflation is added to the "normal" rate.

As interest rates pushed upward, because of the inflation premium, the Federal Reserve tried to keep rates low by increasing the money supply even more. But each increase in the money supply led to higher rates of inflation, and each increase in the rate of inflation added to interest rates. The Federal Reserve's response, year after year, was to keep increasing the money supply in an attempt to prevent high interest rates from bringing the economy down. Unfortunately, the result was a soaring inflation that did exactly what the Fed was trying to avoid—damage the American economy.

It was not until 1981 that Paul Volcker, then Chairman of the Federal Reserve Board, decided to keep money growth in a narrow range and let interest rates be determined in the market, that inflation was brought under control.

The temporary, and expected, result of the Fed's new "tight" policy was the huge increase in interest rates that helped Ronald Reagan defeat the incumbent Jimmy Carter, who bore the blame for both the sliding economy and the high interest rates. Then, as expected, interest rates fell, along with the declining inflation rate.

What about the argument that rising costs of production, caused by something such as labor-union contracts, leads to inflation? The argument cannot be supported by logic or facts, because such actions do not cause inflation. Higher union wages cause prices to rise in unionized sectors of the economy. And higher prices in unionized sectors lead to lower sales, production, and employment, which is why unions cannot demand higher wages and an unchanged level of employment. Unemployed workers in unionized sectors look for jobs in other sectors, thereby lowering wages in those sectors.

That is why the only thing that can cause inflation is something that can constantly increase aggregate demand over time. And the only thing that can do that is an increasing money supply.

Constantly rising oil prices will raise prices, but will also result in greater and greater decreases in GDP and employment, leading to what has been called "stagflation." It is not a good term, because it implies a combination of inflation and a stagnant economy. In truth, it is a recession with higher prices—but not inflation.

Constant decreases in taxes or increases in government spending do not cause continual increases in aggregate demand either, because financing the deficits created by such actions causes interest rates to rise, which reduces consumer and business spending. Just as such fiscal policy actions cannot successfully stimulate the economy, they also cannot cause inflation. The only time fiscal policy actions can lead to inflation is when they are financed not by selling bonds to the public but by paying for them by creating new money. That means the reason for inflation is, again, increases in the money supply.

2. Increasing the money supply to reduce interest rates during an inflation.

The question.

What happens to the price level if the Federal Reserve increases the money supply in order to prevent a government deficit from raising interest rates during an inflation?

(1) The initial equilibrium.

The initial equilibrium is shown by the aggregate supply and aggregate demand curves, AS_1 and AD_1, and the money demand and supply curves, MS_1 and MD_1, in Figure 27.1. The initial equilibrium price level is P_1. The initial equilibrium level of real GDP is assumed to be the full employment level Y_{FE}. The initial demand for money is MD_1. The initial supply of money is MS_1. The initial interest rate, which the Fed wants to lower, is r_1.

Figure 27.1

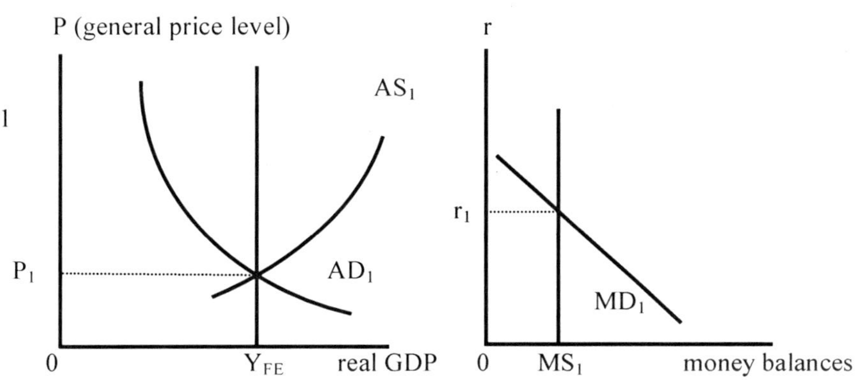

(2) The change.

The change is an increase in the money supply intended to lower interest rates. It is assumed that the economy is at full employment.

In Figure 27.2, the money supply increases from MS_1 to MS_2.

Figure 27.2

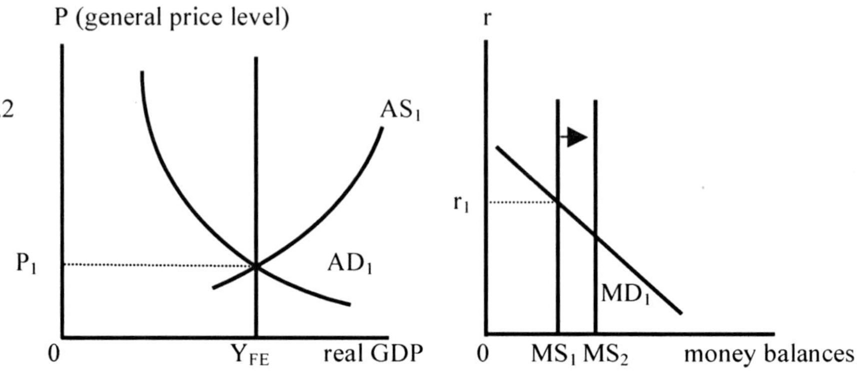

(3) The new equilibrium.

The increase in the money supply lowers interest rates and leads to increases in interest sensitive spending, causing aggregate demand to increase from AD_1 to AD_2.

The intersection of the new aggregate demand, AD_2, and the original aggregate supply, AS_1, is at a more-than-full-employment level of GDP. Therefore, wages increase and aggregate supply decreases from AS_1 to AS_2.

The new equilibrium of AD_2 and AS_2 is still at GDP_{FE}, but at a higher price level.

And the higher price level, P_2, leads to an increase in the demand for money, from MD_1 to MD_2.

The new supply of money and the new demand for money yield an equilibrium interest rate back at r_1 (or somewhere around r_1).

Figure 27.3

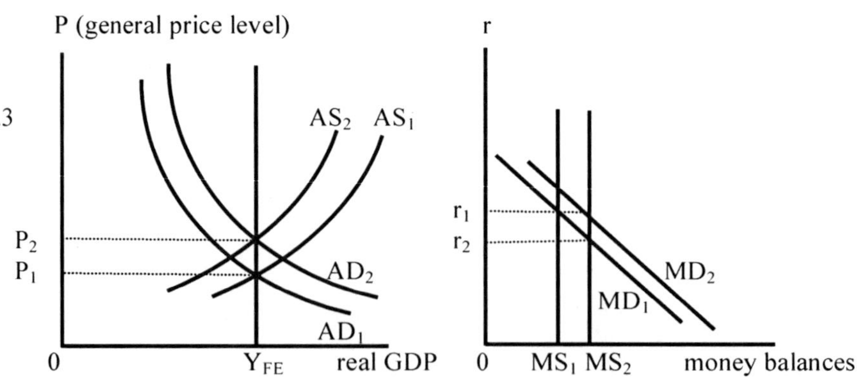

Conclusion.

The increase in the money supply, aimed at lowering interest rates, raises wages and the general price level, but does not reduce interest rates.

The equilibrium price level increases from P_1 to P_2.

The equilibrium level of GDP remains at Y_{FE}.

The equilibrium level of employment remains the same.

Money wages increase.

Real wages stay the same, because the price level increases.

And the equilibrium interest rate remains at (or about) r_1.

3. If at first you don't succeed, try again.

If, after failing to lower interest rates, the Fed tries again, the above steps are repeated. The student should be able to show the following:

The Federal Reserve increases the supply from MS_2 to MS_3.

Interest rates fall to r_2.

Aggregate demand increases from AD_2 to AD_3.

Wages increase and aggregate supply decreases from AS_2 to AS_3.

The price level increases from P_2 to P_3.

The demand for money increases from MD_2 to MD_3.

And the equilibrium interest rate goes back to r_1. (Or close to r_1.)

Once again, the increase in the money supply raises the general price level, but does not lower interest rates.

4. And again.

If, after failing to lower interest rates a second time, the Fed decides to keep trying again and again, the above steps are repeated again and again.

The result is constantly rising prices over time.

And that is the definition of inflation.

Would the Federal Reserve actually follow such a policy? That is exactly what it did in the 1970s, based on the belief that the way to stabilize the economy is to stabilize interest rates.

5. How can inflation be stopped?

Given the above argument, as soon as the Fed stops increasing the money supply, prices stop rising.

6. What happens when, once inflation is underway, the Fed restricts the money supply?

Look at Figure 27.3 and imagine (or draw) a greater and greater supply of money and a higher and higher demand for money.

Then, look at what happens when the money supply is cut back to the original MS_1.

Given the inflation induced high demand for money, a sharp decrease in the supply of money will cause interest rates to increase dramatically.

That increase in interest rates leads to a decrease in aggregate demand; and the new aggregate demand will intersect the existing aggregate supply at a less than full employment level of GDP. The resulting unemployment causes wages to fall and aggregate supply to increase. And prices fall. As prices fall, so does the demand for money. Which then causes interest rates to decline.

That is what happened during the beginning of the Reagan presidency when Paul Volcker had the Fed reduce the rate of growth of the money supply.

7. What about the unions-cause-inflation argument?

The question.

What happens to the price level if unions raise wages?

(1) The initial equilibrium.

The initial equilibrium is shown by aggregate supply and aggregate demand curves, AS_1 and AD_1, and money demand and supply curves, MS_1 and MD_1, in Figure 27.4. The initial equilibrium price level is P_1. The initial equilibrium level of real GDP is assumed to be the full employment level Y_{FE}. The initial demand for money is MD_1. The initial supply of money is MS_1. The initial interest rate is r_1.

Figure 27.4

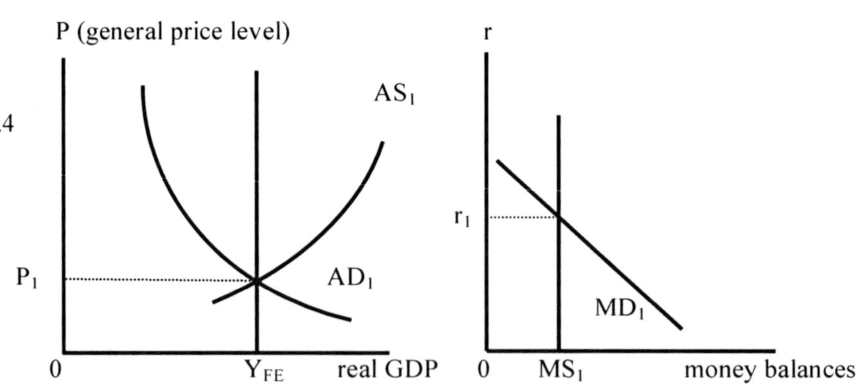

(2) The change.

The change is an increase in union wages.

In Figure 27.5, the increase in wages causes aggregate supply to decrease from AS_1 to AS_2, because it now costs more to produce any given level of GDP.

Figure 27.5

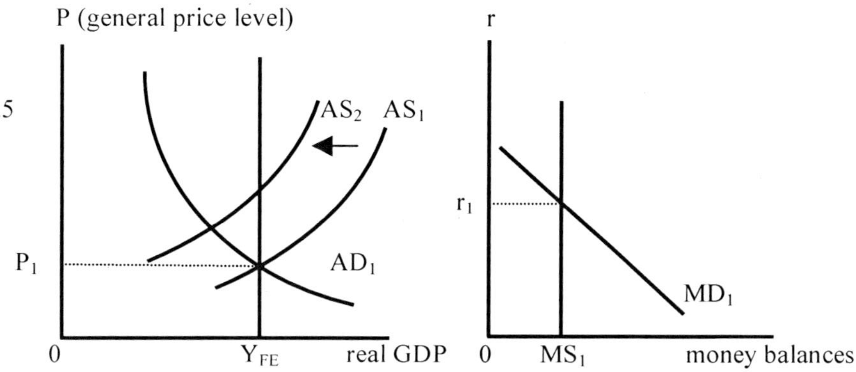

(3) The new equilibrium.

The new aggregate supply, AS_2, and the original aggregate demand, AD_1, yield an equilibrium with a higher general price level, P_2. The higher price level leads to an increase in the demand for money from MD_1 to MD_2, which raises interest rates from r_1 to r_2 and results in a move up the aggregate demand curve, AD_1 to where it intersects AS_2. But, there is now unemployment. And unemployment causes wages to fall and aggregate supply to increase, in theory back to AS_1.

Do union wages fall? Not for those with union contracts who still have their jobs. But wages for other workers fall as unemployed union workers enter the broader work force.

Figure 27.6

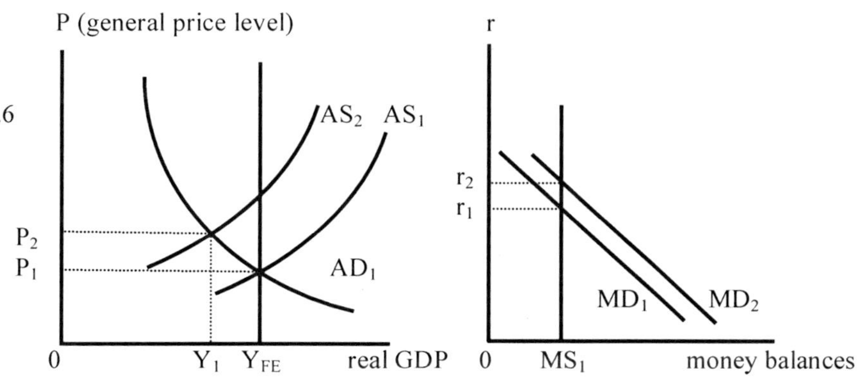

28

Some Tax Issues

1. Taxes and fiscal policy.

Chapter 9 presents a discussion of taxes that applies to both microeconomic and macroeconomic issues.

If you have not read Chapter 9, you should do so now.

If you have read it, you may want to reread it.

There is, however, one use of taxes that was not discussed in Chapter 9. It is the idea of using taxes (or changes in taxes) to stimulate or slow economic activity.

Using changes in taxes to affect the economy is, along with using changes in government spending to affect the economy, referred to as "fiscal policy."

For a discussion of taxes and fiscal policy, refer to Chapters 21 and 23.

For a discussion of government spending and fiscal policy, refer to Chapters 22 and 23.

29

Recession

1. Recessions, which we will define as periods of unacceptable levels of unemployment, are triggered by excessive speculation, mismanagement of the money supply, outside factors, such as rising oil prices, and bad luck; as such, a recession can occur with either increasing or decreasing prices.

Production, employment, and the general price level are determined by the interaction of aggregate supply and aggregate demand.

At times, the interaction yields solid economic growth with full employment and stable prices.

At other times, aggregate demand may outstrip aggregate supply, pulling prices upward—a classic inflation caused by excessive growth of the money supply used to finance government deficits.

A decline in aggregate demand, on the other hand, causes production, employment, and prices to fall—a classic recession. Throughout history, the most common reason for such declines has been market crashes following extreme speculation, such as the 1929 and 2000 stock-market crashes that wiped out large chunks of people's wealth.

Aggregate supply can be adversely affected by things such as bad weather or rising oil prices that lead to higher costs of production. The outcome is lower output and employment, along with higher prices. Referring to such situations as "stagflation" is not always accurate, because it is not really a combination of inflation and a stagnant economy. It is, more accurately, a recession caused by higher costs of production, which is not inflation even though the CPI is rising.

Aggregate supply can be positively, as well as negatively, affected by outside factors. Increases in productivity, good weather, or discoveries of new resources lead to falling costs of production. The result is an increase in production and employment combined with falling prices. An example is the technology boom in the United States in the 1990s. Unfortunately, the 1990s were also a time of excessive speculation in the stock market.

Although there is no cycle that repeats itself in a predictable manner, a careful analysis of history can identify the trigger responsible for every downturn or recession. It is relatively easy to explain and predict the consequences of changes that affect aggregate supply or demand, so it is easy to know which way the economy is being pushed.

The Arab oil embargo of 1973, which led to a four-fold increase in the price of oil, was responsible for a 50 percent drop in stock prices, and set off the recession of 1974 – 1975.

When President Carter imposed an oil embargo against Iran, after the Iranian takeover of the U.S. embassy in 1979, oil prices tripled, stock prices lost about 25 percent of their value, and the United States was pushed into the recession of 1981–1982.

But it was more than high oil prices that were responsible for the dramatic downturn of 1981–1982.

At the same time that rising oil prices were beginning to have a negative impact on the economy, the Federal Reserve was deciding to restrict the growth of the money supply.

The Federal Reserve, with its eye on the Consumer Price Index, chose to ignore the recessionary impact of oil prices and to focus instead on ending the inflation it had fueled with its excessive expansion of the money supply.

It was not stupid for the Fed to do what was required to end the lengthy inflation. But it was a mistake to underestimate the downward forces of high oil prices coupled with its own monetary restraint. The inflation was stopped, but the United States tumbled into one of its worst recessions.

In 1990, oil prices doubled again after Iraq invaded Kuwait, leading to the recession of 1990–1991.

The economic downturns beginning in 1929 and 2001 can be traced to large losses on speculative investments.

And the major stock market "correction" of 1987 was the result of the Federal Reserve deciding to raise interest rates to fight another imaginary recession.

In other words, recessions can be explained. They are not the result of supernatural forces or a "natural cycle" that has yet to be uncovered.

More importantly, when the bad policies or disruptive outside factors come to an end, advanced economies tend to recover.

2. How an increase in production costs can cause a recession with rising prices.

The question.

How does an increase in production costs affect the economy?

(1) The initial equilibrium.

The initial equilibrium is shown by normal aggregate supply and aggregate demand curves, AS_1 and AD_1, and the normal money demand and supply curves in Figure 29.1. No information is given that would lead to the assumption of non-normal functions. The initial equilibrium price level is P_1. The initial equilibrium level of real GDP is assumed to be Y_{FE}, the full-employment level of GDP. The initial demand for money is MD_1. The initial supply of money is MS_1. The initial interest rate is r_1.

Figure 29.1

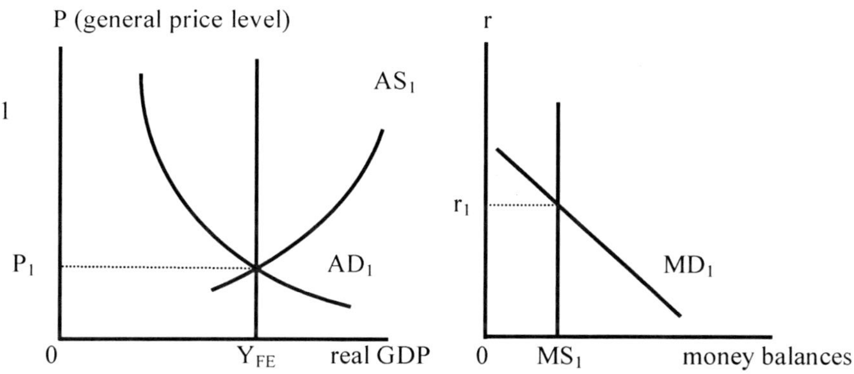

(2) The change.

Some outside factor, such as an increase in oil prices, increases production costs. The result is a decrease in aggregate supply, because something that was assumed to have been held constant when deriving the initial aggregate supply—the prices of inputs to production—has changed.

Each level of total output now costs more to produce than it did before. Therefore, aggregate supply will decrease.

In Figure 29.2, a decrease in aggregate supply means there is a new AS curve to the left of (or above) the original AS curve.

The new aggregate supply is AS_2.

Aggregate demand remains at AD_1.

The nominal supply of money is still MS_1.

The demand for nominal money balances is still MD_1.

Figure 29.2

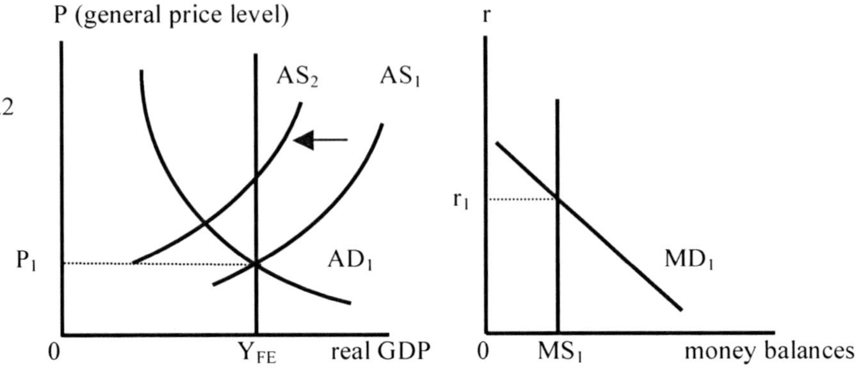

(3) The new equilibrium.

The new equilibrium, determined by the new aggregate supply curve, AS_2, and the original aggregate demand curve, AD_1, is at P_2 (a higher price level) and Y_2 (a lower equilibrium GDP), in Figure 29.3. In the money market, the higher price level causes the demand for money to increase. Given the higher demand for money, MD_2, and the original supply of money, MS_1, interest rates increase to r_2.

Figure 29.3

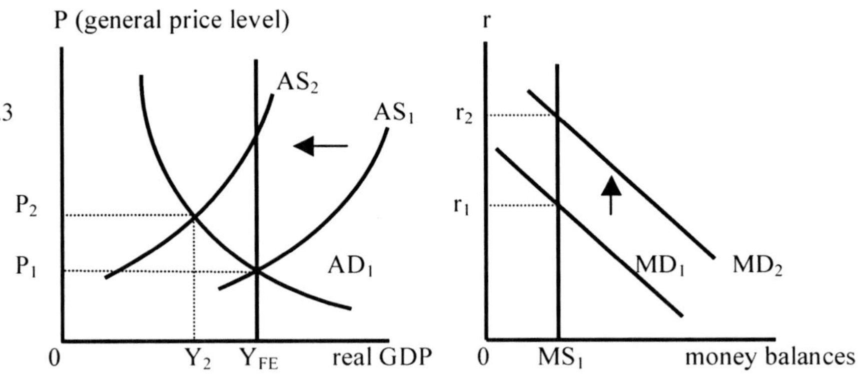

At the original price level, P_1, firms want to produce less than Y_{FE}, because of the increase in production costs.

At price level P_1, aggregate demand is still Y_{FE}.

The result is a disequilibrium with production less than demand.

If demand is greater than production, it means that buyers will bid up prices.

As the general price level rises above P_1, the demand for money increases, causing interest rates to rise, thereby causing the economy to move up AD_1, from the initial equilibrium point P_1, Y_{FE} to the new equilibrium at Y_2, P_2.

Although firms initially wanted to decrease output to less than Y_2 (to the GDP determined by where AS_2 intersects the horizontal line at P_1), because of the increase in production costs, the economy does not actually end up in equilibrium at a GDP less than Y_2. Output does decrease, but not as much as firms originally intended at the original price level, P_1. The reason is that prices are rising.

The equilibrium price level increases from P_1 to P_2.

The equilibrium level of GDP decreases from Y_{FE} to Y_1.

The equilibrium interest rate increases from r_1 to r_2.

The equilibrium level of employment decreases.

Real wages fall, because the price level increases.

And that is a recession with rising prices.

Conclusion.

The increase in production costs affects the general price level, gross domestic product, employment, the real wage, and interest rates. Assuming that the economy began at full-employment (an unnecessary assumption), and that the nominal supply of money and money wages did not change: AS decreases, AD remains the same, the price level is higher; interest rates are higher; total spending is less than it was; real Gross Domestic Product is lower; employment is lower; and real wages are lower.

3. How a negative impact on aggregate demand can cause a recession with falling prices.

The question.

How does a decrease in income, caused by something such as a stock market crash, affect the economy?

(1) The initial equilibrium.

The initial equilibrium is shown in figure 29.4. The equilibrium level of real GDP is assumed to be at the full employment level Y_{FE} and the equilibrium price level is P_1. The money market has normal supply and demand curves.

Figure 29.4

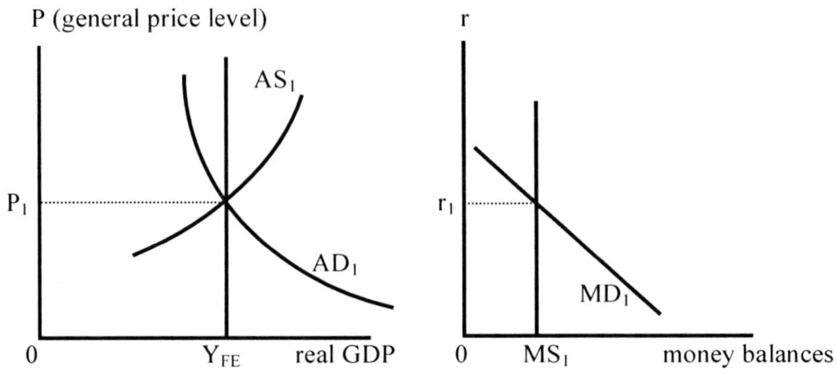

(2) The change.

A stock market crash wipes out a significant percentage of people's income or savings. The result is a change in aggregate demand.

With less wealth, there is less spending at each price level.

In Figure 29.5, the new aggregate demand, AD_2, is to the left of (or below) the initial aggregate demand, AD_1. Aggregate supply does not change.

Aggregate supply does not change, because it is assumed that the decrease in wealth does not affect the cost of production.

Figure 29.5

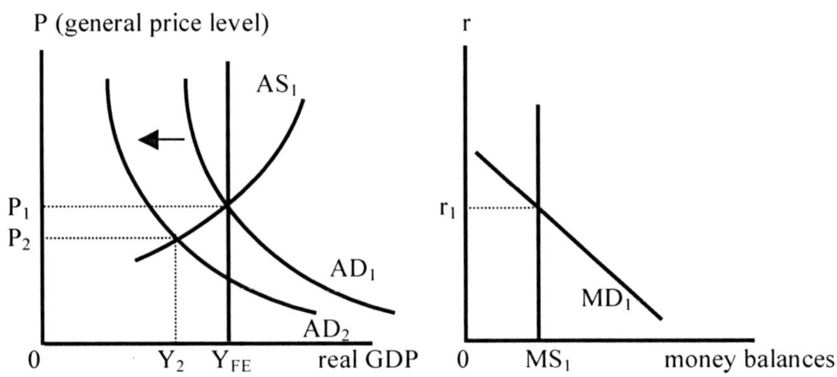

(3) The new equilibrium.

In Figure 29.6, the economy reaches a new equilibrium at output Y_1 and price level P_2, which is where the new aggregate demand (AD_2) is equal to the original aggregate supply (AS_1). In the new equilibrium: real Gross Domestic Product is lower; employment is lower; and the price level is lower. In Figure 29.6, the economy is in equilibrium at less than full employment.

Meanwhile, the falling general price level causes the demand for money to decrease from MD_1 to MD_2 and interest rates to fall from r_1 to r_2. The decrease in interest rates reduces interest-sensitive spending and the economy moves down the new aggregate demand curve to where it intersects AS_1 at Y_2.

Figure 29.6

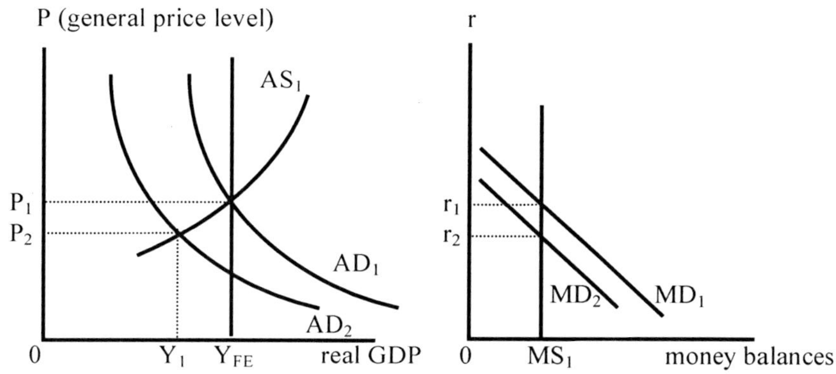

The equilibrium price level decreases from P_1 to P_2.

The equilibrium level of GDP decreases from Y_{FE} to Y_1.

The equilibrium interest rate decreases from r_1 to r_2.

The equilibrium level of employment decreases.

Wages fall, because of unemployment.

And that is a recession with falling prices.

Conclusion.

The decrease in wealth caused by the stock market crash affects the general price level, gross domestic product, employment, the real wage, and interest rates. Assuming that the economy began at full-employment (an unnecessary assumption), and that the nominal supply of money and money wages did not change: AS remains the same, AD decreases, the price level is lower; interest rates are lower; total spending is less than it was; real Gross Domestic Product is lower; employment is lower; and real wages are lower.

4. What if we wait it out?

In the "old days," which, in economic time, means prior to the Great Depression, it was assumed that economies are self-correcting; that if there is an unacceptable level of unemployment, we just have to wait it out.

The idea was that in the long run, markets would clear (meaning wages would fall enough to generate full employment) and everything would be just fine.

It was at that time, during the Great Depression, and in response to such claims, that John Maynard Keynes made the observation, "In the long run, we are all dead."

Keynes' idea was that it was the responsibility of government to manage the economy so that there would be full employment, stable prices, and acceptable growth.

30

The Great Depression

1. The Great Depression was made "great" by bad policies.

The string of stupid things that led to and promoted the Great Depression is not likely to be repeated.

The "roaring twenties" was a time of economic expansion after World War I. But, as in the 1990s, good economic times set the stage for excessive speculation by "investors."

The stock market of the 1920s was fueled by speculative purchases, as was the market of the 1990s. In each case, investors ignored the value of companies, as determined by past, present or predicted future earnings. The difference was that in the 1920's, investors were able to legally purchase stocks on margin, meaning that it was possible to buy a $100 stock by putting up as little as $10. The remaining $90 was borrowed money, from brokerage firms or banks. It was a great opportunity IF prices continued to increase. If the $100 stock increased to $200, the speculator would make a $100 profit on a $10 investment.

However, if the price fell, say to $50, the margin-buyer lost not only his initial investment; he also owed money. He still had to pay back the $90 loan and he received only $50 from selling the stock. So he had to come up with another $40, from somewhere. That is why, when the market collapsed in 1929, people were ruined. They lost not only the money they had invested; they also owed a multiple of that loss to whomever they borrowed from to buy on margin. Many could not pay.

When the stock market crashed in 1929, banks and brokerage firms were also ruined, along with the speculators who could not pay back their loans. From 1930 through 1933, more than 9,000 banks went broke; and as banks closed their doors, people lost their deposits. The Federal Deposit Insurance Corporation, which insures bank deposits, was not created until 1934.

The collapse of banks and the loss of deposits led to a continued contraction of the money supply that pushed the economy deeper and deeper into depression. The Federal Reserve did not protect banks from failure, nor did it protect the money supply.

While the Federal Reserve was allowing the falling money supply to wipe out people's savings and beat the economy into submission, the federal government held to its belief in a balanced budget, adding to the downward pressure of the shrinking money supply. Attempting, although unsuccessfully, to balance the budget during the depression of the 1930s reinforced the downward economic spiral. If tax revenues are shrinking and the government tries to balance its budget by reducing spending, the result is lower incomes, profits, and tax revenues. And if, in response to every additional decrease in tax revenues, the government again cuts spending, thereby lowering incomes and profits and tax revenues again, the government adds to the downward economic spiral.

That is why Keynes argued, in the 1930s, that it was the responsibility of government to make certain that overall demand was high enough to generate full employment. His proposal was that if private demand was not great enough to yield full employment, government spending and the money supply should be increased. The deficit caused by the additional spending was, therefore, not bad, but good. It was an unavoidable part of pulling the economy out of a disaster that the economy could not cure on its own. The deficit was then to be paid off when the depression was over. In other words, Keynes did not believe that the government should run continuous deficits, nor that deficit spending without an increase in the money supply was sufficient.

Keynes did not present his ideas in an economic model. He offered a purely verbal argument with recommendations and conclusions that remain more accurate than the conclusions derived from the "Keynesian models" devised by his followers.

It is sometimes assumed that Keynes convinced the United States government to follow his prescription—if not immediately, at least in time to help with the revival of the U.S. economy. That did not happen. President Roosevelt, after hearing Keynes, continued the attempts to follow a balanced budget program. So did President Truman. It was not until John Kennedy became president that Keynesian ideas were used to intentionally manage the U.S. economy. It may have been a mistake to think, as Kennedy's advisors did, that it is possible to "fine tune" the economy, but it was not a mistake to implement a tax cut financed by money creation.

Although no one should be tricked into thinking that war is good for the economy, it was the massive spending on World War II, along with the huge increase in employment due to the military draft, that brought an end to the Great Depression. Those who like to believe that war is a good way to spend a nation out of a recession should consider alternatives, such as digging huge holes and then filling them in, which is an equally good excuse for buying equipment and employing workers, but without the negative and destructive aspects of war.

2. How to create a Great Depression.

The question.

How can a recession be turned into a Great Depression?

(1) The initial equilibrium.

The initial equilibrium, shown in figure 30.1, is the ending equilibrium from the previous chapter. It is the equilibrium showing a recession with falling prices caused by a stock market crash. As such, we can assume this is what the economy looked like after the stock market crash of 1929.

Figure 30.1

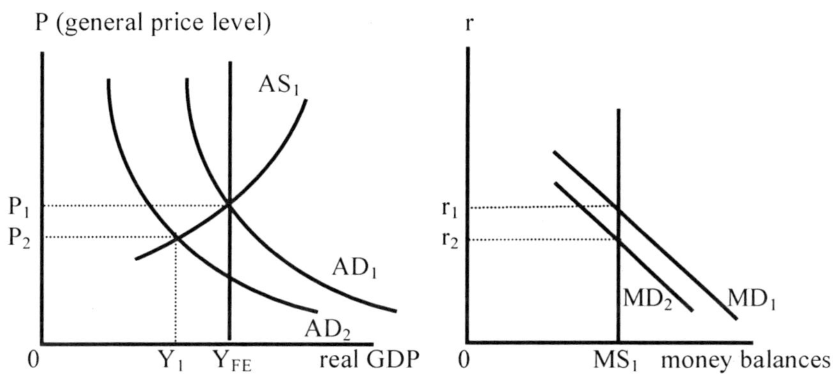

(2) The change.

What can we do to make the recession worse than it is?

One thing that will make it worse is to reduce the money supply. Another is to wipe out more wealth. Another is to reduce government spending.

By not protecting banks and depositors' funds, the Federal Reserve allowed banks to fail, thereby contracting the money supply and letting people's wealth be destroyed.

By trying to balance the federal budget, when tax revenues fell, the government tried to cut spending.

In Figure 30.2: The contraction of the money supply is shown as a change from MS_1 to MS_2. The reduction is wealth is shown as a decrease in aggregate demand from AD2 to AD3. The reduction in government spending is shown as a change in aggregate demand from AD3 to AD4.

Of course, Figure 30.2 shows one-time changes. During the Great Depression, the changes went on and on.

Then, because of a drought, aggregate supply decreased as well, shown as the change from AS_1 to AS_2.

Figure 30.2

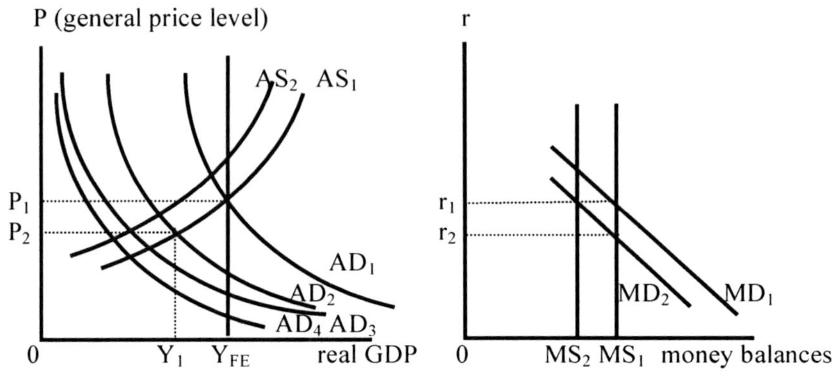

(3) The new equilibrium.

In the incredible messy Figure 30.3, the economy reaches a new equilibrium where AS_2 equals AD_4.

at output Y_1 and price level P_2, which is where the new aggregate demand (AD_2) is equal to the original aggregate supply (AS_1). In the new equilibrium: real Gross Domestic Product is lower; employment is lower; and the price level is lower. In Figure 29.6, the economy is in equilibrium at less than full employment.

Meanwhile, the falling general price level causes the demand for money to decrease from MD_2 to MD_3 and interest rates to fall to r_3. The decrease in interest rates reduces interest-sensitive spending and the economy moves down the new aggregate demand, AD_4, to where it intersects AS_2 at Y_3.

Figure 30.3

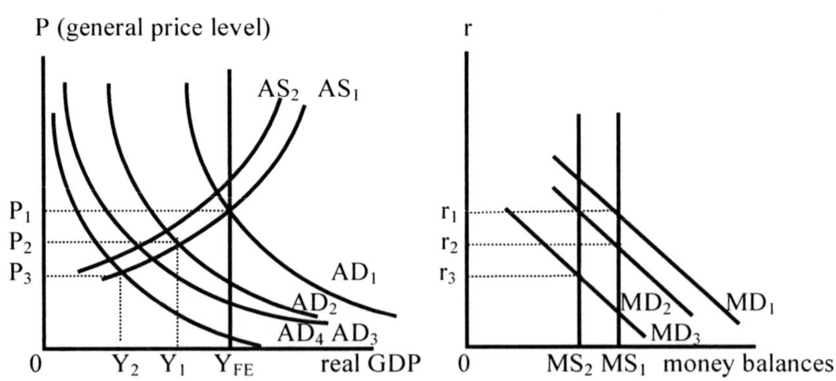

The equilibrium price level decreases to P_3. And will fall lower.

The equilibrium level of GDP decreases to Y_2. And will continue to decrease.

The equilibrium interest rate decreases from r_1 to r_2.

The equilibrium level of employment decreases. And will continue to fall.

Wages fall, because of unemployment.

And that is how to turn a recession into a Great Depression.

Conclusion.

The decrease in wealth caused by the 1929 stock market crash set off a chain of bad decisions. The result was to turn a bad situation into an even worse situation.

It is unlikely that such poor decisions would be made today, because we now have theories and evidence from the 1930s onward to help us make decisions that are likely to help, not hurt, the economy.

As strange as it might sound, the government did not even keep track of economic information until the Great Depression made the need for such knowledge obvious.

31

The "Business Cycle"

1. There are ups and downs in the economy, each of which can be explained.

Economists believe that free-market economies are stable, meaning that the forces of supply and demand turn "greedy" actions by buyers and sellers into pressures that push markets toward equilibrium. Economists also believe that free markets increase a nation's wealth over time. But economists also know that the day-to-day or year-to-year actions of the economy do not always measure up to what is possible. As in other parts of life, reality can fall short of potential.

There is no debate over the fact that economies go through ups and downs. The question is: Why? Not surprisingly, there are many different answers.

Paul Samuelson, in his *Economics* text, discusses a number of business cycle theories. Samuelson separates the theories of business cycles into external and internal explanations. Examples of things external to the economic system that can affect economic performance are "wars, revolutions, and elections...oil prices, gold discoveries, migrations...discoveries of new lands and resources...scientific breakthroughs and technological innovations...sunspots or the weather." Internal theories try to identify things that are part of the economy itself that will automatically lead to bad times following good times, and, hopefully, good times following bad.

Milton Friedman, a key figure in the "monetarist school of economics," argues that the key determinant of economic health is the nation's money supply; that good and bad management of the nation's money supply is the cause of good and bad economic times.

Each of the many business-cycle theories that exists can explain one or some of the past ups and downs of the economy, but not all. Not one theory, by itself, can explain the past or the future cycle of any economy, because there is no single cause for what has happened or will happen.

Overall economic activity is determined not by aggregate demand or aggregate supply alone, but by both. Therefore, changes in either aggregate demand or aggregate supply affect output, employment, and prices.

Even more important is the fact that the economy is also affected, positively and negatively, by government and Federal Reserve actions.

The Great Depression marked the beginning of the end for many old-time economic beliefs, especially the belief that a free-market economy was a self-correcting miracle which, if left alone, will pull itself out of damaging downturns. Lessons learned from the terrible times of the 1930s led to dramatic changes in the government's role in the economy and in the management of the monetary system, although the government's attempt to manage the economy did not truly begin until John Kennedy entered the White House in 1960.

Because of the dramatic changes in fiscal policy and monetary policy ideas that took place as a result of the Depression, including the creation of the Federal Deposit Insurance Corporation that was designed to protect bank deposits, and the first attempts to actually track important economic variables, there is more to be learned by looking at business cycle activity after 1960.

From the early 1960's onward, there have been inflations, recessions, times of solid economic growth, and periods of "stagflation."

After World War II, the U.S. economy entered a "golden age" that lasted through the 1950s. But as the decade drew to a close, John Kennedy campaigned against Richard Nixon partly on the argument that the economy needed help.

The slowdown that Kennedy made into a political issue was turned around by a combination of factors: the Kennedy/Johnson tax cut (it was President Kennedy's idea, from James Tobin and Walter Heller, but it was enacted by President Johnson after Kennedy's death); increases in government spending on the war in Vietnam and on the War on Poverty at home; and, most important, the Federal Reserve's financing of the deficits caused by the tax cut and additional government spending by purchasing bonds and increasing the money supply.

The inflation of the 1970s was the result of politically motivated policies. Politicians did not want to raise taxes to pay for the war in Vietnam or the War on Poverty. Instead, bonds were sold to cover the government deficit. And in order to stop the increased bond sales from causing interest rates to rise, the Federal Reserve bought large quantities of bonds in the open market, thereby increasing the money supply and creating inflation. If taxes had been raised to pay for the two "wars," there would have been no inflation. As the inflation rate increased, putting upward pressure on interest rates, the Federal Reserve increased the money supply even more. The idea was to keep interest rates from climbing by making more money available. The result was a soaring inflation rate.

At the beginning of 1980, Paul Volcker, Chairman of the Federal Reserve Board, announced that The Federal Reserve was switching policies. Rather than continuing with its policy of increasing the money supply to keep interest rates down, which was keeping inflation up instead, he announced that the Federal Reserve would control the growth of the money supply and let interest rates go wherever the market would take them. It was a policy that quickly brought inflation under control. And it was the last time inflation should have been a concern to anyone—unless the Federal Reserve returned to its old ways.

In the meantime, there were "oil shocks" in the 1970s and 1980s. In each case, increases in oil prices led to declines in output and employment.

In 1973, a quadrupling of oil prices accompanied by dramatic weather changes and massive crop failures, brought on the recession of 1975-1975.

The deep recession of 1981-1982 was set off by a combination of factors. One was a tripling of oil prices, blamed on President Carter's decision to impose an embargo against Iran after the 1979 taking of hostages. The other was the Federal Reserve's switch to slow money growth in order to bring a halt to years inflation.

It was in the 1980s, when the recessionary impacts of oil prices and tight money occurred in the middle of an ongoing inflation, that a new term was made up to describe the combination of a stagnant economy and continued inflation--"stagflation."

When the Fed's new plan to carefully control the growth of the money supply was actually put into action, in October of 1980, just before the Carter/Reagan election, the immediate result was skyrocketing interest rates. Aside from helping Ronald Reagan defeat Jimmy Carter, the spike in interest rates helped push the economy into the recession of 1981-1982.

When Reagan took office, he initiated a famous tax cut that was supposed to help the economy by first helping those with higher incomes. The idea was that some of the benefits would then trickle down to those with lower incomes. As many had argued, it mainly helped those who received the tax breaks; there were no "trickle down" benefits to those with lower incomes. Meanwhile, the government deficits climbed. But the huge deficits were not, as is often argued, the result of the Reagan tax cut. The fact is that overall taxes were not really reduced, regardless of the publicity. Lower taxes on individuals were offset by higher taxes on corporations. The deficit was actually caused by large increases in government spending, mainly on defense. Regardless of where it came from, the deficit prevented interest rates from falling as fast as they should have, given the dropping inflation rate, because the government continued to sell bonds to cover its spending.

Although the massive Reagan deficit was a drag on the economy, the declining inflation rate, due to the Federal Reserve's decision to control the money supply, was a positive factor. As inflation disappeared, the economy recovered in time to help Reagan win a second term in office.

On October 19, 1987, the stock market crashed, losing more than 20 percent of its value in what was, at the time, the greatest one-day loss in history. Some believe there was no reason for the crash, but there was. It was caused by the Federal Reserve's decision to raise interest rates to fight what was falsely argued to be a return of inflation. The combination of higher interest rates and a renewed fear of inflation, each of which is bad for stock prices, led to a massive sell-off.

Losses in the stock market, along with the Federal Reserve's continued actions to maintain high interest rates to fight the return of inflation and a doubling of oil prices as Iraq invaded Kuwait, ushered in the recession of 1990-1991.

The economic decline was not bad enough to prevent Reagan's Vice President, George Bush, from winning an election, although his Democratic opponent may not have been the strongest possible choice. And a recovery did occur as the United Stated entered the Gulf War. But the economy did not do as well as hoped, partly because of the leftover Reagan deficit, and President Bush was unable to win a second term in office.

After President Clinton took office, two important economic "actions" occurred. One was the Clinton administration's decision to raise taxes to reduce the deficit in order to allow the economy grow without the burden of high interest rates. The second was that not much else was done.

However, the credit for what turned out to be the longest uninterrupted economic expansion in U.S. history should not go entirely to President Clinton. It must be shared with all the politicians who were so embroiled in partisan politics that no economically damaging policies could be enacted, either by the Clinton administration or by the Republican Congress. The American economy, freed from the large deficits, was allowed to succeed on its own. It could have done even better if the Federal Reserve had not made every effort possible to hold economic growth under control, on the unsupportable premise that fast economic growth leads to inflation.

There was, however, one problem: excessive speculation in the stock market, particularly by "investors" who were happy to pay virtually any price for companies that never had nor ever would earn a profit. That speculation, just as with every similar speculation throughout history, ended badly. It is impossible for "investors" to pay any price for a worthless item and always be able to find another "investor" willing to pay more for it. There is always the day when the market awakes to the realization that a "greater fool" cannot be found. The problem is: No one knows when that day will come, which means there is always the hope that it might be possible to get in and out with a profit before everyone else discovers the truth. The huge decline in stock prices, along with the increase in oil prices, led to the recession that began in 2001.

There are two lessons to be learned from this brief look at history. One is that the reasons for the ups and downs in the U.S. economy are relatively easy to identify. The second is that the reasons are not always the same. That is why there is not one "best" explanation of the business cycle—unless that explanation is that it is necessary to understand how any number of events and policies affect the economy and to be aware of what is happening to all of them.

More important, it is why macroeconomics, since the 1930's, has been concerned with employment, prices, and growth. The Great Depression convinced economists that a free-market economy could slip badly, possibly for a very long time, and the study of macroeconomics became focused on the reasons and cures for unemployment, inflation, and unacceptable levels of economic growth. In order to explain and predict what is happening and, if it is "bad," how it can be changed, economists use models that describe how the interaction of many variables determines the overall working of the economy.

2. There is no "natural" business cycle.

There is no single variable or group of variables that can predict a future business cycle. In fact, there is no cycle at all. There are only ups and downs in the economy, each of which is caused by something that we understand—at least after it happens.

Therefore, the real reason for studying economic ups and downs is to understand how to avoid making the mistakes in the future. And that is a functional use of economic knowledge.

32

"Free Trade"

1. Successful foreign trade policies yield trade surpluses, not deficits.

Free trade is the "sacred cow" of economics, not because there is a good economic theory to support it, but because it is a great way for those who benefit to make a lot of money. Meanwhile, foreign trade deficits have a negative and multiplied impact on the economy.

The economic theory of free trade was developed in three steps in the 1800s. First was the idea that a nation could benefit from trade if it had an absolute advantage over another nation in the production of some product. Then came the comparative advantage argument that showed how each of two nations would benefit from trade if one country could produce one thing using fewer resources than the other and the second country could produce the other thing using fewer resources than the first country. Finally, there was the idea of relative advantage, which "proved" that for two nations and two goods, there would be gains from trade to each country if each had different relative costs of production. Even if one could produce both goods cheaper than the other, each would benefit by specializing in the production of what it was relatively better at producing and trading for the other good.

Each argument is based upon a special case of two countries and two goods. Each ignores the question of whether the idea will work in the real world where thousands and thousands of goods and services, including investments, are bought and sold—not traded—on international markets. Each is absolutely useless in explaining the reality of foreign trade.

What we do know about foreign trade is actually easy to understand.

Specialization adds to wealth.

There is an advantage to a nation if it has a trade surplus with other nations.

There is a disadvantage if it has a trade deficit with other nations.

Imports help some while hurting others.

Exports help virtually everyone in the exporting country.

So it is not surprising for nations to subsidize exports, knowing that doing so will increase production, employment, and profits at home. It may be called "dumping" by producers in nations that cannot compete against subsidized products from abroad, but it was not by chance that Japan's economic miracle occurred while it was running a large foreign-trade surplus. Or that Japan's economic downturn can be traced to the time when its manufacturers began moving production out of Japan and into China, Korea, Indonesia, even the United States. In the 1970s and 1980s it was almost impossible to pick up a quality product that did not say, "Made in Japan." Today it is almost impossible to find any product that is made in Japan; even if it is from a Japanese company.

It is clearly profitable for a corporation in an industrialized nation to move its production to a country with cheap labor and few environmental regulations, and to then ship its output back to the home country, or to other countries, especially if the trade laws allow such importation without heavy duties. But the nation's wealth may not fare as well. The nation may lose while the corporation wins. Do the corporate winnings get spread around the home country? Or trickle down to others? Not according to the historical evidence.

The truth is that when the government interferes in the international market, or when it does not, the winners and losers are easy to predict.

One of the earliest examples of government/no government interference in markets took place in Britain in the 1700s. Tariffs had existed for years on imported grains; the purpose being to protect British landowners from cheap imports. The tariffs worked; they helped support the power of the landed class by keeping food prices high, which helped keep workers on farms while raising the wages industrialists had to pay workers who moved to the factory towns.

As industrialization began to take hold in Britain, the factory owners wanted more and cheaper labor. The tariffs on imported grains prevented both. By protecting the landed aristocracy, the tariffs kept potential factory workers on farms, while also keeping the cost of living high. Because wages were, in large part, based upon what was needed for basic survival, the tariffs kept wages higher than the industrialists wanted.

The political problem facing the New Industrialists was: how to argue for the abolition of tariffs without having to admit the purpose was to gain large profits for themselves. The solution was to claim that Adam Smith said the government should not interfere in free markets. The industrialists were successful. The tariffs were dropped; the resulting decline in agriculture freed workers who had no choice but to come to the cities for work, at poverty-level wages; and industrialists took power from the old landed class.

The argument for the tariff had been that it would "keep Britain strong."

The argument against the tariff was that, according to free-market economics, eliminating the tariff would "keep Britain strong."

The tariffs on grain hurt the people of Britain and the British economy while strengthening the economic and political power of the landowners. Removing the tariffs let the industrialists take economic and political power from the old landed aristocracy and helped promote industrialization. But neither side in the power struggle cared about the people, or the economy itself. Each wanted only to have policies that would benefit its side, which is pretty much how it works today.

Some argue that such concerns are nothing more than self-serving worries over the distribution of income resulting from changes in imports and exports; changes that are good for the overall economy. It may even be possible to find people who are happy to give up their jobs or profits so that others can earn greater profits and incomes.

The more important question, however, goes beyond the issue of individual winners and losers (unless, of course, you are a winner or loser). It is: How does foreign trade affect the wealth of a nation? The answer is clear: The nation's wealth creation, as measured by Gross Domestic Product, is adversely affected by foreign trade deficits and positively affected by surpluses.

In the models economists use to explain the overall economy, the impact on Gross Domestic Product is a multiple of the trade deficit or surplus. (Trade is a not-too-accurate word to use, because nations do not barter or trade stuff for stuff with other nations; goods and services are bought and sold, and the decisions as to who buys or sells what are based upon many factors, including currency exchange rates.)

We know there will be individual winners and losers in a world of international commerce.

We also know we cannot ignore the impact of trade on the nation as a whole.

It is stupid to argue that everyone wins from increased imports, especially when many imports are from domestic corporations choosing to manufacture outside the country in order to increase their profits.

It is not stupid to identify the losers, along with the winners, in order to decide if a policy is good or bad for the country.

In the 1970s, the United States imposed an import tax on motorcycles in an attempt to protect Harley-Davidson, which was on the verge of going under. It was a successful policy, given the recovery and return to profitability of Harley-Davidson.

Taxes and quotas were also imposed on the importation of Japanese automobiles in order to protect the U.S. industry. Those actions not only saved domestic manufacturers, they forced Japanese manufacturers to open plants in the United States.

Would any free-trade proponent want to argue that the United States would be better off today if Harley-Davidson and the United States auto industry had been allowed to vanish in the flood of imported motorcycles and automobiles that better suited consumers at the time? Or that it would have been better if Japanese auto manufacturers had not opened manufacturing plants in the United States?

Foreign trade is a complex issue. Corporations may be willing to sacrifice American jobs in order to increase their profits. But are they willing to sacrifice their own companies in order to let consumers get better and cheaper products from abroad.

On the simplest of all levels, the trade issue is: Do we have a foreign trade deficit or surplus?

2. How an increase in net exports boosts the economy.

The question.

How does an increase in net exports boost the economy?

(1) The initial equilibrium.

The initial equilibrium is shown in figure 32.1. The equilibrium level of real GDP is Y_1 and the equilibrium price level is P_1. Figure 32.1 was drawn with Y_1 less than Y_{FE} in order to show an initial equilibrium with an unacceptable level of unemployment. The money market has normal supply and demand curves.

Figure 32.1

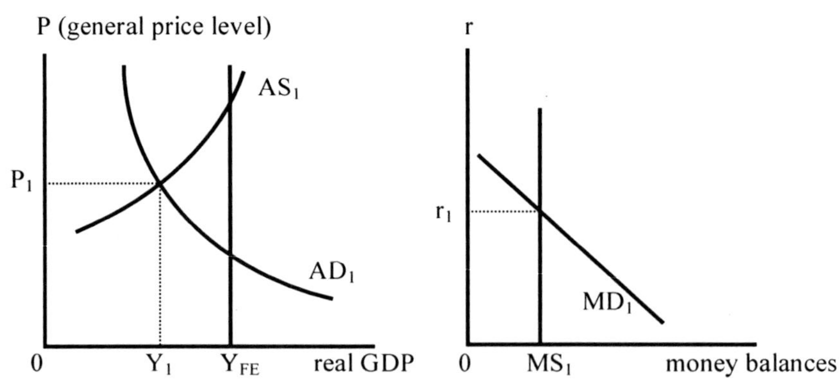

(2) The change.

Aggregate demand represents total spending by government, consumers, and business—including net exports—at each general price level.

Therefore, an increase in net exports increases aggregate demand. At each price level, total spending is now greater. In Figure 32.2, the new aggregate demand, AD_2, is to the right of or above, the initial aggregate demand. Aggregate supply does not change if it is assumed that an increase in net exports does not affect the cost of production.

Figure 32.2

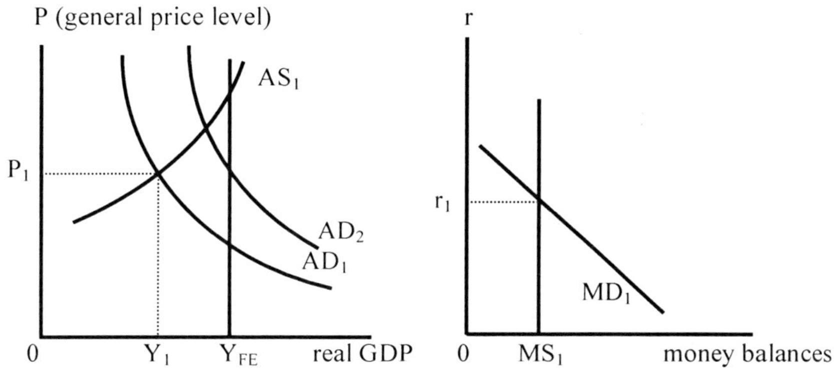

(3) The new equilibrium.

In Figure 32.3, the economy reaches a new equilibrium at output Y_2 and price level P_2, which is where the new aggregate demand, AD_2, is equal to the original aggregate supply, AS_1. In the new equilibrium: real Gross Domestic Product is higher; employment is higher; and the price level is higher. In Figure 32.3, the economy is still in equilibrium at less than full employment.

Figure 32.3

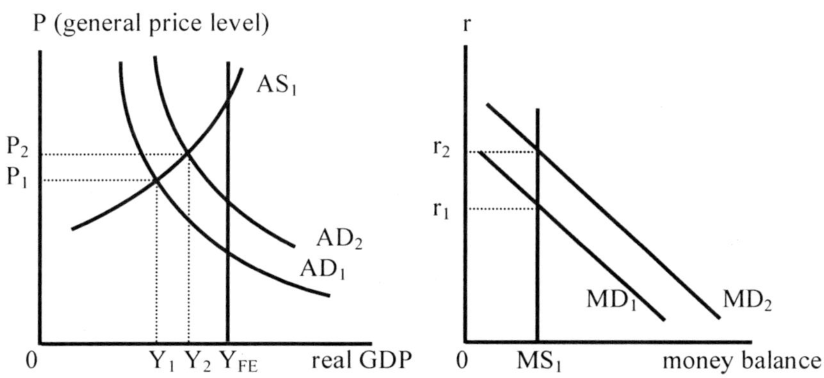

In order to achieve a full employment level of Gross Domestic Product, net exports would have to increase enough to cause aggregate demand to intersect AS_1 at Y_{FE}.

Given the new aggregate demand and the original aggregate supply, there is an excess demand for goods and services at the original price level. In Figure 32.3, the excess demand for goods and services, which is equal to the horizontal difference between the original aggregate supply and the new aggregate demand *at the original price level*, causes prices to increase. As prices rise, the demand for money increases, causing interest rates to rise and interest sensitive spending to decrease, moving the economy to the new equilibrium where AS_1 equals AD_2.

Conclusion.

The economy reaches a new equilibrium where the new aggregate demand is equal to the original aggregate supply. In the new equilibrium: real Gross Domestic Product is higher; employment is higher; and the price level is higher.

However, the increase in the equilibrium value of GDP is less than the increase in aggregate demand—because of the negative effect rising prices have on spending.

The increase in aggregate demand due to the increase in net exports is the horizontal distance between the original aggregate demand and the new aggregate demand, at the original price level.

The increase in equilibrium GDP is the difference between the original GDP, determined by the intersection of original aggregate demand and aggregate supply, and the new equilibrium GDP, determined by the intersection of the *new* aggregate demand and the original aggregate supply.

The change in GDP is less than the change in aggregate demand because, as total spending increases, the rising price level causes some decreases in consumer and business spending.

Total spending is higher than it was before the increase in net exports, but the increase is offset somewhat by the decline in consumer and business spending. Even so, the increase in net exports leads to an increase in GDP and employment.

33

Economic Success in Japan and China

1. Japanese economic success is a textbook case of using what we know.

The Japanese "economic miracle" was based, in part, on the massive decline in world shipping costs that took place during the later half of the twentieth century. It was also due to intentional efforts to increase the quality of goods being produced and to promote exports while limiting imports.

At the end of the twentieth century, Japan achieved success while importing virtually all resources, other than labor and capital, manufacturing high quality goods on Japanese soil, and exporting large quantities of those goods around the world. There was a time when Japanese lumber mills were buying trees in the United States, shipping them to Japan, turning them into plywood, shipping the finished plywood back to the United States, and selling the finished product below U.S. prices.

A few years before that, most products marked, "Made in Japan," were assumed to be of inferior quality. Then, in the 1970s, Japan began its dramatic turnaround. Although some Japanese cameras were already among the best in the world, the incredible increases in the quality of Japanese automobiles and other products seemed to catch the United States' markets by surprise.

Toyotas and Datsuns (Nissans) from the late 1960s were hardly reliable. By the 1970s they had become not only more reliable than many American automobiles, they were a better fit for a market that was looking for smaller, more efficient cars as troubles in the Middle East drove up oil prices.

As Japanese automobiles, and other quality products, poured into the United States, Japanese trade policies restricted imports. It was not by chance that Japan's economic miracle occurred while it was running a large foreign-trade surplus. Or that Japan's economic slowdown can be traced to the time when its trade surplus began to decline as Japanese manufacturers moved production out of Japan and into China, Korea, Indonesia, even the United States.

In the 1970s and 1980s it was almost impossible to pick up a quality product that did not say, "Made in Japan."

But, by the 1990s, it became increasingly difficult to find products that were made in Japan, even if the products were from a Japanese company. Today it is difficult to find any.

The low shipping costs that allowed Japan's economy to surge ahead also led to its slowdown as many Japanese companies began to move production to countries with much cheaper labor and fewer environmental regulations, and to then ship its output back to the home country, or to other countries. As shipping costs became an almost irrelevant part of production costs, it was not even necessary for the "production country" to have any natural resources of its own. Everything could be shipped in and out.

But as the corporations increased their profits, the nation's wealth did not fare as well. The nation lost while the corporations won.

The corporate winnings did not get spread around the home country. Or trickle down to others. Workers who, a few years earlier, had jobs for life were now unemployed.

And, as jobs and wages shrunk, so did corporate profits. The boost to corporate profits from moving production out of Japan was short lived. The resulting recession was not.

Adding to the reversal was the excessive speculation by the Japanese in investment markets and real estate. When the economy turned down, stock prices and real estate values plummeted, wiping out bank loans and individual wealth. Dropping interest rates to zero was not sufficient to pull the economy out of its recession.

Although Japan remains one of the world's wealthiest nation, the economic miracle was relatively short.

The great gains that came from producing and exporting quality products in the midst of falling shipping costs, while also limiting imports, were given up as Japanese production was moved out of Japan.

As the trade surplus, employment, and profits shrunk, stock prices and real estate values collapsed. The collapse, which was an unavoidable conclusion to the speculative run-up in prices, further reduced profits, incomes, and wealth.

Adding to the economic decline was a reduction in exports caused by a growing weakness in world markets.

Aside from the obvious explanation of what happened in Japan is the fact that when the demand for goods and services fell, because production was moved out of the country and international markets dried up, monetary policy was unable to restore the economy's health. Propping up failing banks and reducing interest rates to zero was not enough.

2. The Japanese economic miracle.

The question.

What was behind the spectacular growth of the Japanese economy?

(1) The initial equilibrium.

In the initial equilibrium, shown in figure 33.1, the equilibrium level of real GDP is Y_1, the equilibrium price level is P_1, and the equilibrium rate of interest is r_1.

Figure 33.1

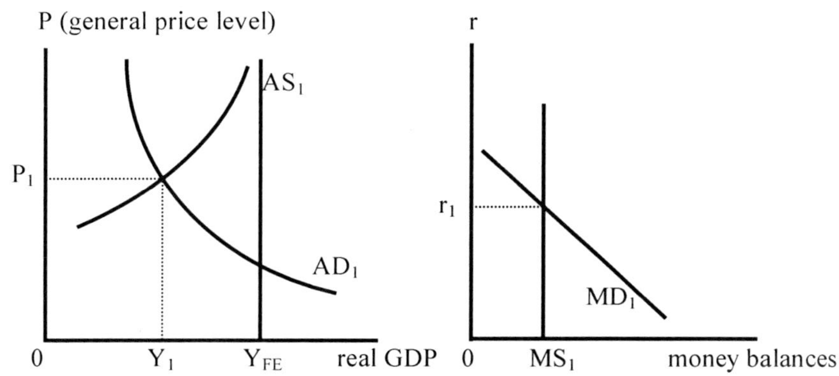

(2) The change.

Many things affect an economy, but two key changes led to Japan's success.

One is that Japan, because imports and exports are a major part of its economy, benefited from falling shipping costs.

The other is that Japan made a decision to intentionally encourage exports while restricting imports.

Falling shipping costs increased aggregate supply from AS_1 to AS_2.

The decision to manage foreign trade led to large trade surpluses that increased aggregate demand from AD_1 to AD_2.

Figure 33.3

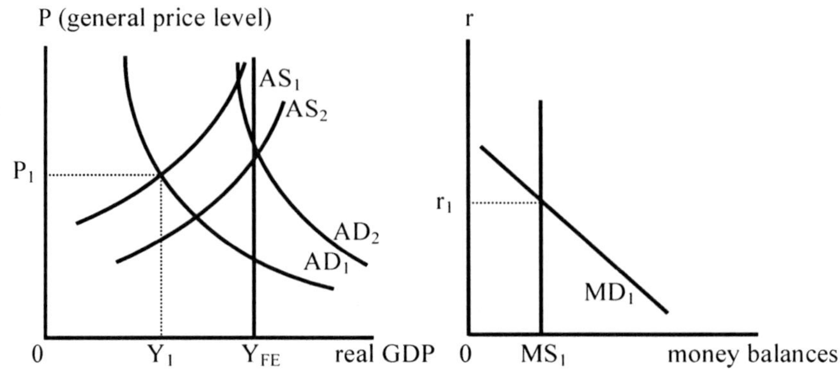

(3) The new equilibrium.

In Figure 33.3, the economy reaches a new equilibrium at output Y_{FE} and price level P_2, where the new aggregate demand (AD_2) is equal to the new aggregate supply (AS_2).

In the new equilibrium: real Gross Domestic Product is higher; employment is higher; and the price level is higher.

Meanwhile, the rising general price level causes the demand for money to increase from MD_1 to MD_2 and interest rates to increase from r_1 to r_2.

Again, the increase in the general price level happened because of how AD_2 and AS_2 were drawn, not because the price level will rise for certain. By now, it should be obvious that when both aggregate demand and aggregate supply increase, the price level can increase, decrease, or remain the same. It is shown to increase in Figure 33.3, because we know that prices did increase in Japan.

Figure 33.3

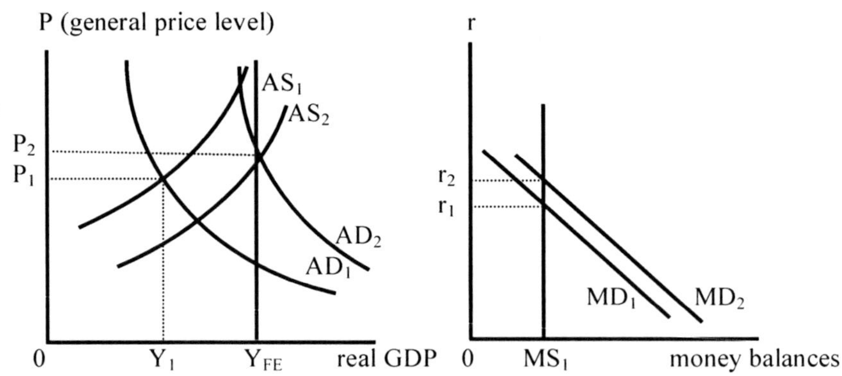

Conclusion.

The lower costs of production, especially for exports, and the managed increase in net exports brought Japan's economy to full employment.

Then, when Japanese producers began moving production out of Japan, net exports fell and aggregate demand decreased, moving to the left of AD_2.

3. Chinese economic growth is an even better example of using what we know.

The Chinese government followed the Japanese model of helping provide capital for production and of promoting exports while limiting imports.

It also benefited from Plato's and Adam Smith's specialization as millions of people were moved from self-sufficient farms into factories.

As such, the Chinese model must account for a tremendous growth in the full employment level of GDP. Therefore, the Chinese model combines Japan's net export policy with the successful implementation of what we know about economic growth.

4. Economic growth in China.

The question.

How can we show China's economic success?

(1) The initial equilibrium.

China's initial equilibrium, with a lot of self-sufficiency, is shown by the normal aggregate supply and aggregate demand curves, AS_1 and AD_1, and the normal money demand and supply curves in Figure 33.4.

The initial equilibrium price level is P_1.

The initial equilibrium level of real GDP is Y_1.

The initial equilibrium interest rate is r_1.

The equilibrium level of GDP is at less than the full-employment level of GDP.

It is assumed throughout this analysis that the economy is at full employment.

Figure 33.4

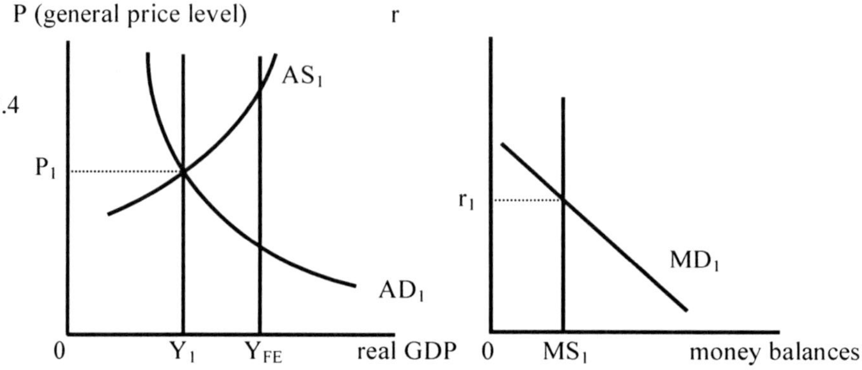

(2) China's change.

In a few years, China made dramatic changes across the board.

Industrial specialization, government financing of factories and infrastructure, the promotion of exports, and restricted imports.

In terms of our model, everything changes.

Aggregate supply increases from AS_1 to AS_2, because each level of total output now costs less to produce than it did.

Aggregate demand increases from AD_1 to AD_2, because of the increase in net exports.

And Y_{FE} increases, because individuals working at specialized jobs in factories financed with government funds can produce a larger GDP for every price level.

Figure 33.5

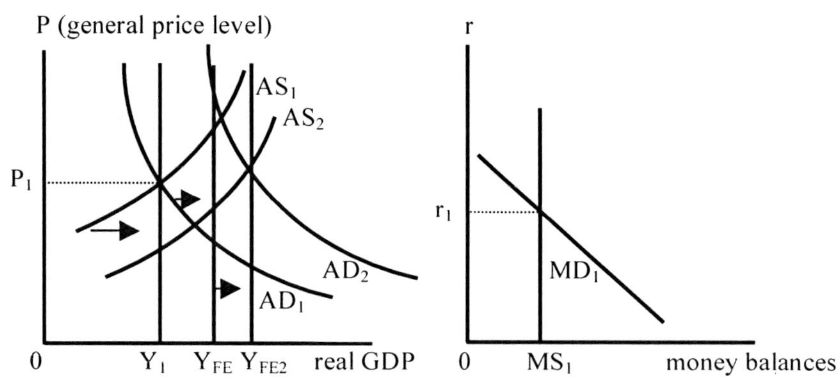

(3) The new equilibrium.

The new equilibrium, determined by the new aggregate supply and the new aggregate demand is shown to be at the new, and higher, full employment level of GDP. (It does not have to be at full employment.)

In the new equilibrium, the price level increases from P_1 to P_2, and the higher price level causes the demand for money to increase from MD_1 to MD_2. The higher demand for money leads to higher interest rates, which cause a decrease in interest sensitive spending. As always, when both aggregate demand and aggregate supply increase, the price level can increase, decrease, or remain the same.

Figure 33.5

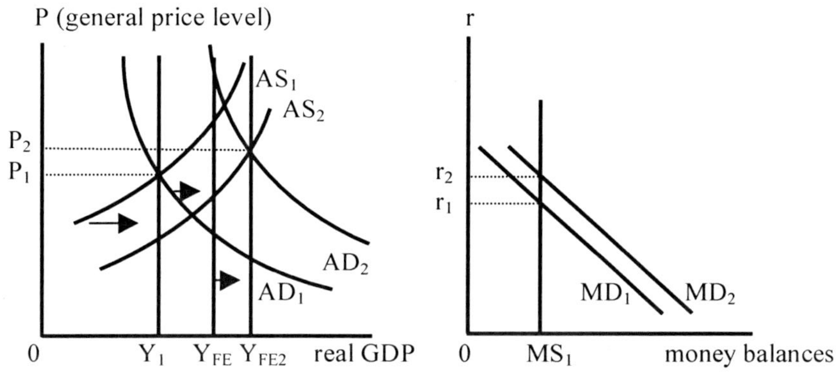

Conclusion.

The Chinese economy is benefiting from increasing specialization, capital availability, and a huge foreign trade surplus.

The result is one of the world's fastest growing economies.

It remains to be seen if China will follow Japan's decision to let production move out of the country. Odds are, it will not, unless it is done very carefully, so that it reaps even more benefits from specialization, which is the only legitimate argument for foreign trade.

34

Foreign Exchange Rates

This is Chapter 16, repeated here because understanding exchange rates is used for both macroeconomic and macroeconomic questions.

1. Buying and selling currencies.

Within a country, a nation's currency gains or loses value, as measured by its purchasing power, as prices change. The higher prices are, the less a dollar will buy. The lower prices are, the more a dollar will buy. That is why people tend to spend money quickly during inflationary times, buying as much as they can before their money loses even more value, and why they want to hold money during recessionary periods, waiting until they can buy even more with their money as prices fall further.

On an international level, a nation's currency gains or loses value against foreign currencies as a result of changes in foreign trade. Each day hundreds of billions of dollar's worth of currencies are bought and sold in currency markets so that importers of foreign goods can pay for what they buy.

Figure 34.1 is an example of a foreign exchange market. It depicts the market for Japanese yen, in terms of dollars. The price axis--dollars per yen--represents how many dollars are needed to buy one yen. The quantity axis represents the quantity of yen bought with dollars during a given time period. A move up the price axis means that more dollars are required to buy one yen; meaning that the price of yen is increasing.

Figure 34.1

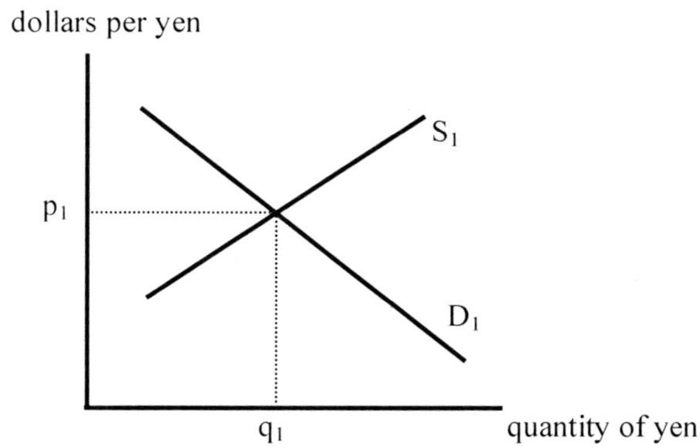

2. The supply of and demand for yen.

The demand for yen in Figure 34.1 comes from Americans who buy Japanese goods and services, or who travel in Japan, or who invest in Japanese assets. Individuals in the United States who buy goods imported from Japan pay for those goods in dollars; but whoever imported those goods had to pay for them in yen. To do so, it was necessary to first buy yen with dollars. Individuals who travel in Japan buy yen with dollars so they can purchase things when they are in Japan. Japanese investments purchased by Americans must also be paid for in yen, which again requires buying yen with dollars.

The demand for yen has a negative slope, because as the price of yen in dollars declines, it means that the prices of Japanese goods and services--in dollars--also decline. If the cost of Japanese goods and services declines, Americans will buy more from Japan. And if Americans buy more from Japan, they will need more yen. Therefore, the lower the price of yen in dollars, the greater the quantity of yen Americans are willing and able to buy. If the price of yen increases, the cost--in dollars--of Japanese goods and services increases, and Americans will buy less from Japan, thereby demanding fewer yen.

Currency exchange rates work two ways: whatever the price of yen is in dollars, the price of dollars in yen is the inverse. If the price of one yen is two dollars, one yen can be purchased for two dollars, and one dollar can be purchased for one-half yen. If the price of yen decreases to one dollar per yen, then it will take one dollar to purchase one yen, and it will take one yen to purchase one dollar.

The supply of yen in Figure 34.1 represents yen used to purchase dollars. It comes from Japanese who buy American goods and services, who travel in the United States, or who invest in United States assets. Although it is called a supply curve, it is also a demand for dollars.

The supply of yen has a positive slope because as the price of yen in dollars increases, it means that each yen buys more dollars and the prices—in yen—of American goods and services decrease. If the prices of American goods and services decrease, the Japanese will buy more from the United States. And if the Japanese buy more from the United States, they will need more dollars. Therefore, the higher the price of yen in dollars, the greater the quantity of yen the Japanese are willing and able to sell to obtain dollars.

But what happens if Americans choose to increase their travel in Japan?

3. Tastes and preferences and the value of currencies.

The question.

What happens to the equilibrium price and quantity of yen in dollars if Americans decide to travel more in Japan?

(1) The initial equilibrium.

The initial equilibrium is shown by the normal supply and demand curves, S_1 and D_1, in Figure 34.2, which is the same as Figure 34.1. The initial equilibrium price is p_1. The initial equilibrium quantity is q_1.

Figure 34.2

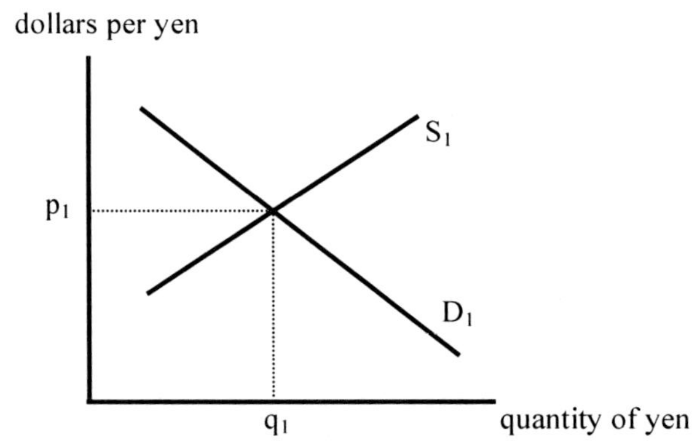

(2) The change.

This is an *exogenous* change. It is a change in a variable that was assumed to be held constant—the desire to travel in Japan. In other words, the change in travel plans is a "change in something that was assumed to be held constant"—tastes in travel. Because it is a change in a "constant," the initial impact is a change in a function. The increase in travel to Japan causes the demand for yen to increase, because Americans now require more yen than previously; the demand curve moves to the right, or upward.

There is no reason to believe that the change in travel will have any impact on the supply of yen. The new demand curve is D_2. The supply curve remains at S_1.

Figure 34.3

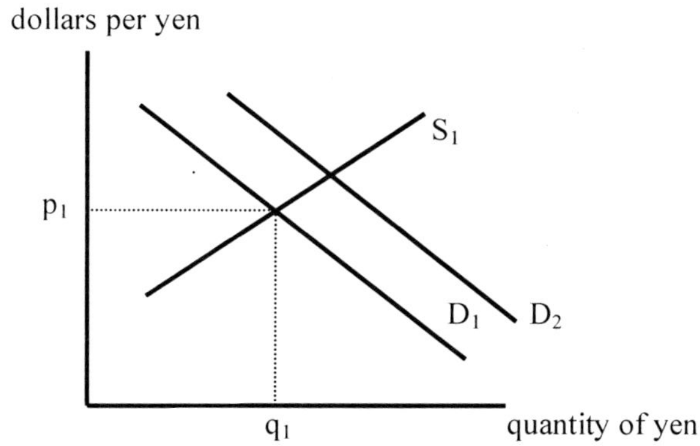

(3) The new equilibrium.

The new equilibrium, determined by the original supply curve, S_1 and the new demand curve, D_2, is at the new equilibrium price of yen, p_2, and the new equilibrium quantity, q_2. The change in demand results in a move along the original supply curve, not a change in supply.

Figure 34.4

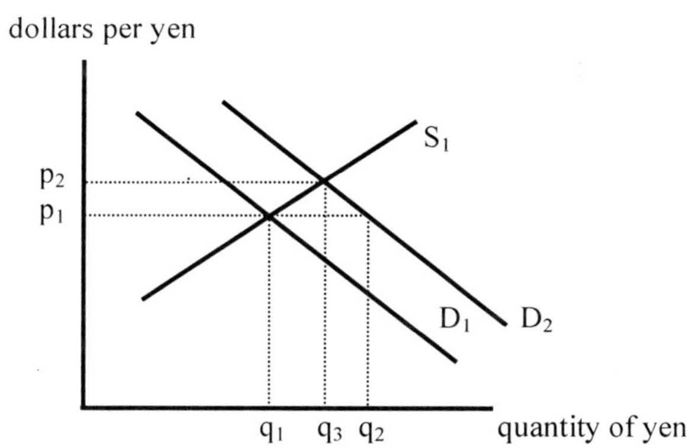

Conclusion.

The equilibrium price of yen increases from p_1 to p_2.

The equilibrium quantity of yen increases from q_1 to q_3.

It can be concluded that increased travel in Japan increases the price of yen in dollars and that the equilibrium quantity of yen traded in the market will increase as well, assuming that all other things remain constant.

It is a change, however, that affects more than international travelers.

If the yen becomes more expensive, increasing in price from p_1 to p_2, Japanese goods become more expensive to Americans and American goods become less expensive to the Japanese. It is a change that may be bad for American consumers but good for American business.

4. It is more than speculation.

Aside from speculating on changing currency values in order to make a personal profit, you may work for a company that is constantly buying and selling currencies, because it is constantly buying or selling goods and services on international markets, which means its profits can also affected by currency values. Being able to explain and predict changing currency values can add to profits, while ignoring such changes can be costly.

35

The Distribution of Income

1. Who needs Robin Hood?

The "proper" distribution of income is a personal issue.

It is also a political issue, because many government programs and policies cause a redistribution of income—from the rich to the poor or from the poor to the rich.

In the 1700s and early 1800s, economists believed that an intentional redistribution of income would disrupt economic efficiency and reduce the nation's wealth.

In the mid 1800s, John Stuart Mill disproved that claim.

Since then, it has been up to each civilization or society to make its own decisions based on its own beliefs and objectives.

What is a "fair" distribution of income?

You have to ask yourself.

36

Final Macroeconomic Notes

1. Single-diagram answers.

Throughout this text, macroeconomic questions are addressed using two diagrams:

One is a general equilibrium diagram with aggregate demand, aggregate supply, and an indicator of potential or full employment gross domestic product. This diagram shows the determination of the equilibrium values of gross domestic product and the general price level.

The second is a diagram of the money market, showing the supply of and demand for money. This diagram shows the determination of the equilibrium interest rate.

By now, it should be clear that the money market diagram is often unnecessary, as long as it is remembered that an increase in the price level increases the demand for money, which, with a constant money supply, increases the equilibrium rate of interest.

As such, most issues can be explained using only the general equilibrium diagram.

The reason is simple.

If something affects either aggregate supply or aggregate demand or both, the general equilibrium diagram shows the expected changes in equilibrium GDP and the general price level. Therefore, once it is understood how a change in the price level changes the demand for money and the rate of interest, and how a change in interest rates leads to a move *along* an aggregate demand curve, but does not change aggregate demand, it is easy to answer all sorts of questions by using the single AS, AD diagram. For each problem, a change in aggregate demand and/or aggregate supply creates an initial disequilibrium at the initial price level. By understanding how that disequilibrium causes prices to increase or decrease and how that change in prices changes the demand for money and interest rates, and how that change in interest rates causes a move up or down the relevant aggregate demand curve, we can better understand the move from the old to the new equilibrium.

So, if we are interested only in the change in equilibrium GDP and the general price level, we can quickly answer most questions, including the change in employment and interest rates, because we know how a change in the price level affects interest rates.

Of course, it is also necessary to remember that the answer is affected by the predicted equilibrium relative to the full employment level of GDP.

2. A few examples.

Figure 36.1

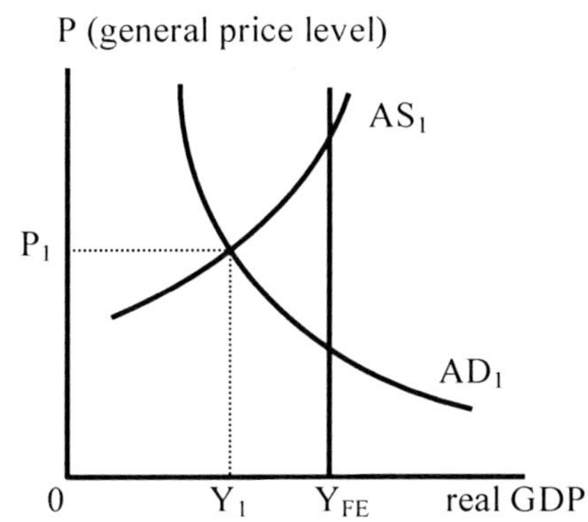

Anything that affects the cost of production changes aggregate supply.
Anything that affects consumer spending, investment spending, government spending, or net exports changes aggregate demand.
A change in equilibrium GDP changes employment.
An equilibrium above GDP_{FE} causes wages to increase and AS to decrease.

A foreign trade agreement increases imports relative to exports:

Aggregate demand decreases. The new equilibrium is at a lower level of GDP and a lower price level.

A reduction in illegal immigrants.

Producers have to pay higher wages, so aggregate supply decreases. The new equilibrium is at a lower level of GDP and a higher price level.

Gains in education.

Workers are more productive, so aggregate supply increases. The new equilibrium is at a higher level of GDP and a lower price level.

3. A final caution.

Throughout this text, we tried to avoid the use of two common "ideas."

One is the idea that a change in something that affects supply or demand, or aggregate supply or aggregate demand, causes a function to "shift." There is no "shift." There are changes that cause changes in supply or demand, or aggregate supply or aggregate demand; or, more precisely, there are changes that create new functions.

The second idea is that an identifiable change causes a "shock" to supply or demand, or aggregate supply or aggregate demand.

The reason for avoiding the "shift" and "shock" ideas is that they tend to replace thinking with the idea that things simply change, without explanation.

In the end, although it is important to understand what happens, it may be even more important to understand why it happens.

Appendix 1

A Logical Explanation of Demand

1. The demand for goods and services by households.

The demand for a good or service comes from decisions made by households on how to spend their money. The quantity of a good a consumer is willing and able to buy during some time period can be determined as a function of the good's price, the price of another good or service, or the consumer's income.

The goal for households is to maximize happiness. It is not necessary to define happiness; only to accept the facts that: households (individuals) make choices aimed at making their lives as good as possible and that maximizing money income is seldom the only goal.

Depending upon the decision being made, the constraints include income or wages, prices, tastes and preferences, time, skills, and education.

Because of time and opportunity cost, there is always a constraint. Even someone with enough money to buy everything they want cannot avoid the reality of time and opportunity cost. No one lives forever. And no one can do everything at the same time. Therefore, even the wealthiest person faces constraints that require choices.

Households make many choices. There are decisions about work and leisure, saving and spending, saving and investing, and how and when to spend money.

When demand is calculated as a function of income, the good is identified as either a **normal good** or an **inferior good**. By definition, normal goods are goods that the consumer buys more of as income increases; inferior goods are goods that the consumer buys less of as income increases.

When the demand for one good is calculated as a function of another good's price, the two goods will be either **substitutes** or **compliments**.

If the two goods are substitutes, an increase in the price of one will cause the consumer to want to buy more of the other--substituting one for the other.

If they are compliments, when the consumer buys less (more) of one they will also buy less (morc) of the other.

In macroeconomics, the aggregate demand function (consumption function) that is the basis for many models is the relationship between total income and total spending.

Because there are few inferior goods, it is a positive relationship: as total income increases, so does total spending.

In microeconomics, the demand for a good is normally calculated as a function of that good's price. The decision-making process by households is straightforward.

The goal is to maximize happiness.

The constraints include income, time, tastes and preferences, all relevant prices, and expectations of future prices. It is assumed that the consumer has no impact on prices.

The choice is how much of the good or service to buy during a given time period.

At given prices, which, it is assumed, the consumer does not affect, the consumer buys various quantities of goods and services during a given time period. The decision as to how much of each to buy is the result of weighing the "happiness" from consuming additional units of each good against the "happiness" lost by not consuming other goods and services that could be purchased instead. The decision-making rule is to buy an additional unit of a good if the benefits (happiness) from the additional unit purchased are equal to or greater than its cost, including opportunity cost.

If the price of a good is increased, *and all other prices remain the same*, the concept of opportunity cost says that the individual will be willing and able to buy less of that good during the same time period. The reason is simple. As the price of the good increases, while the prices of all other goods and services and the individual's income remain constant, more of other goods and services must be given up for each unit of that good purchased. In other words, as the price of a good or service increases, the opportunity cost of purchasing it increases, which means the higher the price, the less of that good the individual will want to buy. The demand curve in Figure A1.1 shows the relationship between the price of a good and the quantity of that good purchased during a given time period, assuming that everything else is held constant. It is a negative relationship, meaning that as the price increases, the quantity purchased decreases.

Figure A1.1

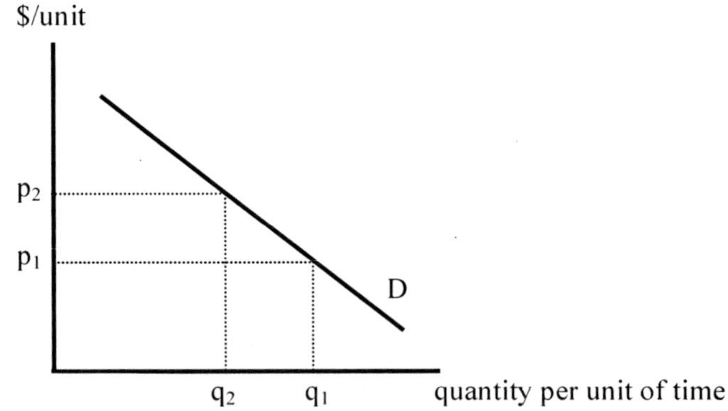

2. The market demand for goods and services.

The above discussion that explains the actions of an individual or household can be extended to derive the market demand for a particular good or service by summing the individual demand curves horizontally. An individual demand curve shows the maximum quantity that a consumer is willing and able to buy at each price. A horizontal summation of the individual demand curves shows the maximum quantity that all consumers are willing and able to buy at each price during a given time period.

3. Happiness is not really maximized.

Although the demand for goods and services can be derived from the decision-making process of households with a goal of maximizing happiness, it is not necessary to assume that happiness is actually maximized. If the analysis rested on the assumption that happiness must be maximized, it would be useless, because that will never happen. The only assumption that is needed is: Given choices, the household (individual) will pick the option that adds the most to, or subtracts the least from, happiness.

4. Demand.

Figure A1.2 shows the demand curve for an individual. Whether utility theory, indifference curve analysis, or opportunity-cost arguments are used, individual demand curves are drawn to have negative slopes.

Figure A1.2

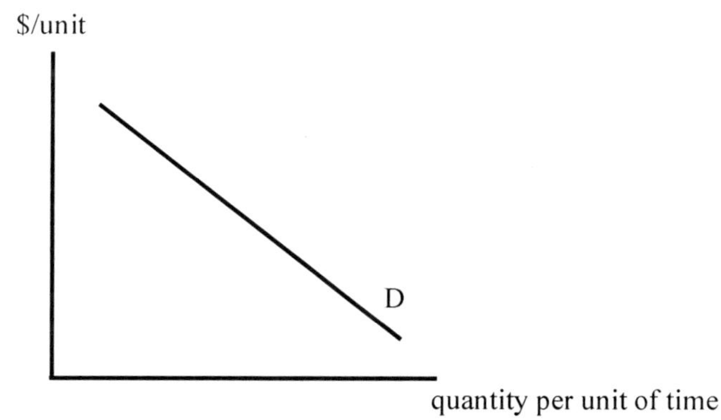

Although no one has yet found an upward sloping demand curve, the historical evidence of demand was taken from market studies, not individual actions. It must be assumed that "irrational" individuals exist--individuals who choose not to act in their own best interest. But there are apparently not enough of them to have affected any known market demand at any time.

Figure A1.3 shows demand curves for a number of rational individuals and the demand curve for the market, which is the horizontal summation of the individual demand curves. The purpose of showing a few individual demand curves in Figure A1.3 is to make the horizontal summation clear. If they were actually added horizontally, the resulting market demand would be a kinked line. In a "real" market, the number of individuals is great enough so that the market demand can be assumed to be a relatively smooth curve.

Figure A1.3

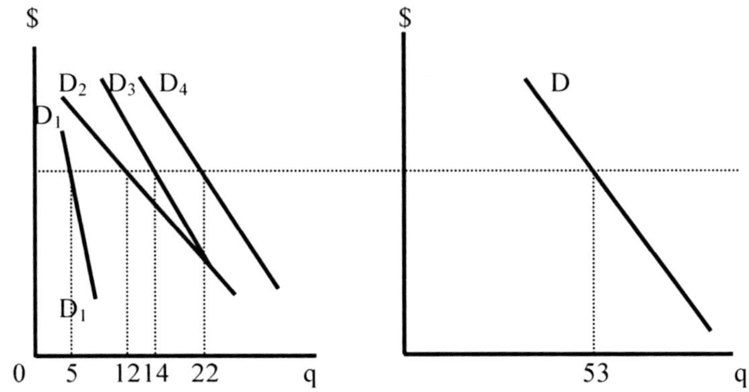

Market demand and market supply determine the market price. But it is a back and forth process. Individuals with no impact on market prices make up the market demand which, together with market supply, determines the price that the individual then takes as given.

Appendix 2

Theory of the Firm

1. The perfectly competitive firm.

Firms, like households, buy and sell things. They buy or hire inputs and resources in order to produce things that they then try to sell.

The goal of the firm is to maximize profits. Unlike "happiness," profit *can* be defined. It is equal to total revenue minus total costs and can be calculated for any level of output. The decision to hire the quantity of a variable input that maximizes its profit yields the firm's demand for a variable input, such as its demand for labor. The firm's decision to produce or sell the level of output that will maximize its profits is what generates the firm's supply curve.

2. The production function.

The basis of the entire argument concerning a firm's costs, as well as the demand for inputs to production, is the **production function**.

Figure A2.1 shows a production function, or total product curve, as it is normally drawn with labor as the variable input. As the number of workers employed increases from 0 to N_1, total output increases at an increasing rate. As the number of workers employed increases from N_1 to N_2, total output still increases, but at a decreasing rate. As the number of workers employed increases past N_2, total output declines.

Figure A2.1

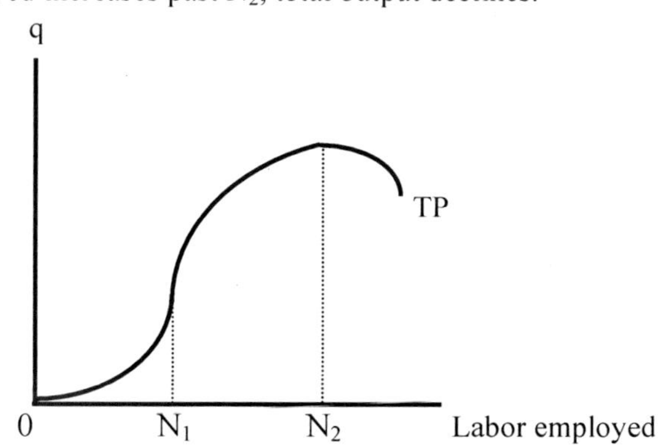

A production function describes the **physical relationship** between inputs (factors of production for the firm) and output (the firm's product). An actual production function includes many inputs. The abstract argument reduces the analysis to one variable factor of production and assumes that all other factors, or inputs, are held at a constant level. The variable factor is commonly assumed to be labor, in which case the total product function shows output as a function of the various quantities of labor employed.

Although it is common to begin the examination of production and costs with a total product function, the argument actually begins with the idea of marginal physical productivity and "the law of diminishing returns," because it is the logic of marginal physical productivity that is responsible for defining the actual shape of the total product function.

If economists had real numbers that could be used to define a "standard" or "general" total product function that could be used for all problems, a logical argument would be unnecessary. But such numbers do not exist. And the numbers that exist for one case, will not necessarily apply to another.

The purpose of the logical argument is to provide a general analysis that is useful in virtually all cases.

The core of the argument is:

The "law of diminishing *marginal* returns" is that as equal increments of labor are added to production, while all other factors of production are held constant, each additional unit of labor adds less to total output than the previous unit did. The marginal physical productivity, meaning the quantity that additional workers add to total output, is diminishing (getting smaller).

What the "law" says is that equal increments of labor add positive, but diminishing amounts to output. And that is the reason the total product curve in Figure A2.1 looks the way it does for units of labor between N_1 and N_2. It is a production function that is increasing at a decreasing rate over part of its range.

However, it is also reasonable to assume that the first units of labor employed may exhibit increasing marginal returns. Gains from specialization and efficiency in production as the first one, two, three, or whatever workers are added to production, while holding all other inputs at the same level, can be assumed to add greater and greater amounts to output. Whether or not this assumption is true, it is logical. And it is the reason the total product function in Figure A2.1 is shown to increase at an increasing rate from 0 to N_1 units of labor.

But the gains from productive efficiency cannot be expected to last forever. The law of diminishing returns eventually takes over at what is called the "point of diminishing returns." The "point of diminishing returns" refers to that unit of labor that adds less, not more, to total output. In Figure A2.1, the point of diminishing returns is at N_1 units of labor.

For the range of labor where marginal physical productivity is increasing, the total product curve has a positive slope and is increasing at an increasing rate. It means that each additional unit of labor is adding (marginal physical productivity) greater and greater amounts to output.

For the range of labor where marginal physical productivity is decreasing, but positive, the total product curve also has a positive slope but is increasing at a decreasing rate. It means that each additional unit of labor is adding (marginal physical productivity) smaller and smaller amounts to output.

Past N_2 in Figure A2.1, marginal returns from labor are negative, which is why the total product function has a negative slope, meaning that adding those units of labor causes output to decline.

Standard examples of the above argument are based upon agricultural situations; partly because such examples seem easy to understand and partly because the examples were first created when agriculture was a more important sector.

Imagine growing corn on one acre of land. The acre of land and all other inputs, with the exception of labor, are fixed. With no workers, the output of corn is 0. With one worker, output is positive. If it is 10 bushels, then the marginal product of the first worker is 10 bushels and average product is 10 bushels. With two workers, it is assumed the workers can specialize or divide up tasks, thereby increasing output to more than twice what one worker could produce. If output with two workers is 25 bushels, the marginal product of the second worker is 15 bushels, (25-10)/1=15, and average product of two workers is 12.5 bushels (25/2=12.5). With three workers, the gains from specialization may still be significant and output might rise to 45 bushels. The marginal product of the third worker is 20 bushels, (45-25)/1=20, and average product is 15 bushels, (45/3)=15.

Eventually, the "point of diminishing returns" is reached and the "law" of diminishing marginal returns sets in. If that happens with the fourth worker, output with four workers might be 62 bushels, meaning that the marginal product of the fourth worker is 17 bushels, (62-45)/1=7, and average product is 15.5 bushels, (62/4)=15.5. For the logic to hold, total output with five workers should be greater than 62 but less than 79 so that the marginal product for the fifth worker will be less than it was for the fourth worker. And so on.

Although such examples are used to support the logic of the argument that defines the shape of the total product curve, the truth is that this example, like all other examples using numbers, cannot be constructed without first knowing the relationship the numbers are intended to have to each other. It is only by choosing numbers carefully that the total product curve can be made to look like it does in Figure A2.5. Therefore, it is the logic behind the function, not a table of numbers, that is most important.

And:

Once the production function is understood, the supply of output and demand for inputs follows easily.

The functions easily derived from a total product function are: Average Product, Marginal Product, Total Variable Cost, Total Fixed Cost, Total Cost, Marginal Cost, Average Variable Cost, and Average Total Cost.

Average Product is not used for anything. Marginal Product, along with the price of the output, yields the demand for an input. Total Variable Cost is the total expenditure on the variable input (such as labor). Total Fixed Costs are total expenditures that do not change with output. Total Cost is Total Variable Cost plus Total Fixed Cost. Total Variable Cost, along with Total Revenue, can be used to determine the profit maximizing output and profit for the firm. Marginal Cost, along with Marginal Revenue, is normally used to determine the profit maximizing output for the firm. Average Variable Cost and Average Total Cost are used to calculate profits once the profit maximizing output is determined. Each is a measure of the cost per unit of output and, when subtracted from the price of the output, gives the profit (or loss) per unit.

Average product is total output divided by the number of workers.

In Figure A2.2, average product for A units of labor is AB/OA, which, by definition, is also the slope of the line OB. Therefore, average product for any quantity of labor is the slope of a line from the origin to the point on the total product curve corresponding to that quantity of labor. As labor increases, the lines first become steeper, meaning that average product is increasing. The line tangent to TP at D is the line with the steepest slope; it identifies the quantity of labor with the highest average product. After that, lines from the origin to the curve become flatter, such as OF. The average product for C units of labor is CD/OC, which is equal to the slope of the line OD.

Marginal product measures the increase in total output due to increases in labor hired.

In Figure A2.2, if labor is increased from A to C, the marginal product of C is the change in output (the vertical distance from B to D) divided by the change in labor (C - A). It is also equal to the slope of the straight line that goes through Points B and D (not shown). As the distance between B and D approaches zero, the two points merge into a single point, which means the marginal product for any quantity of labor is equal to the slope of a line tangent to the function at that point. In Figure A2.2, marginal product at the quantity of labor E is the slope of the line tangent to the total product curve at point F.

Figure A2.2

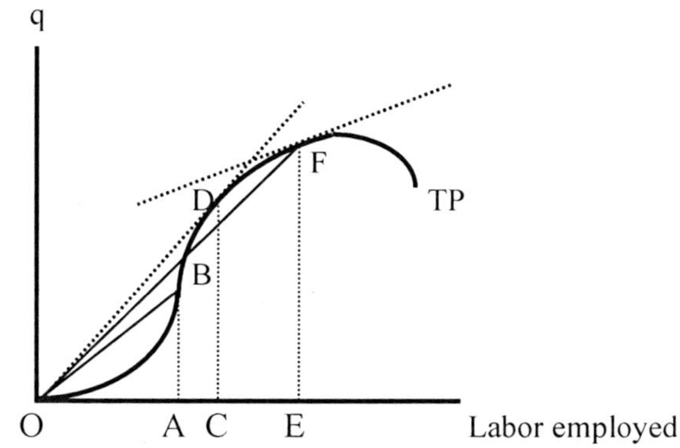

Starting with no labor, lines tangent to the curve become steeper and steeper as labor is increased, up to the point where total product stops increasing at an increasing rate and begins increasing at a decreasing rate. That is the "inflection point" on the curve (represented by point B). It shows the quantity of labor at which marginal product is a maximum. After that, marginal product decreases, as can be seen from the fact that the tangent lines become flatter and flatter. Marginal product is zero at the maximum point on the total product curve. After the maximum point on the total product curve, marginal revenue is negative.

At labor level C, the line from the origin that touches the curve at D is the same line that is tangent to the curve at D. Therefore, average product and marginal product are equal at C units of labor. At less than C units of labor, MP is greater than AP because the slopes of lines tangent to the curve are greater than slopes of lines from the origin to the curve. At more than C units of labor, AP is greater than MP.

To derive the AP and MP curves from a TP curve, only three points must be found:

(1) The point where a line from the origin is tangent to the TP curve shows the quantity of labor where AP is a maximum and where AP=MP. It is at N_2 in Figure A2.3.

(2) The inflection point shows the quantity of labor where MP is a maximum. It is at N_1 in Figure A2.3.

(3) The maximum point on TP shows the quantity of labor where MP is zero. It is at N_3 in Figure A2.3.

Figure A2.3 shows the *exact* relationship between TP, AP, and MP.

Figure A2.3

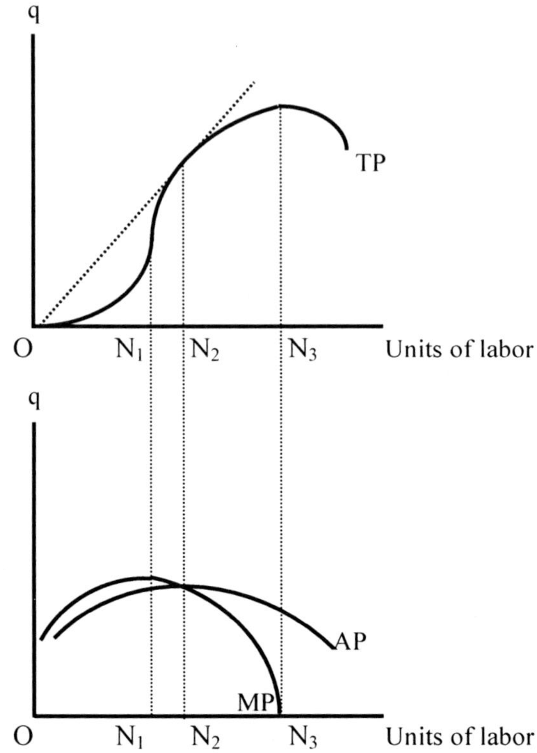

The easiest way to draw the functions is to first draw a line from the origin tangent to TP in the top figure. Come down to the second figure and draw the AP curve--an inverted "U" shaped curve with its maximum at that quantity of labor (N_2). Go back to the TP curve and find the inflection point (at N_1). Come down to the second graph and draw the MP curve--an inverted "U" shaped curve that begins above AP, reaches its maximum at the quantity of labor corresponding to the inflection point on TP (N_1), turns down and intersects AP from above at its maximum point (N_2), then continues down until it reaches zero at the quantity of labor corresponding to the maximum point on the TP curve in the upper graph N_3).

There are two reasons for using geometry to explain economic functions. It is easier to see the relationships by adding geometry to verbal logic. Geometry allows the derivation of relationships without numbers.

3. The cost curves for a competitive firm are derived from the firm's production function.

The goal of a firm is to maximize profits.

The constraints include the production process, the price of the good produced, and the prices of all inputs. For a firm in a competitive industry, it is assumed that no matter how much or little the firm buys and sells, it will not affect the price of the product or the prices of any inputs.

Choices include what to produce, how to produce it, and how much to produce. But because it is assumed that the firm has already chosen its productive process, the production function, which is the physical relationship between inputs and output, is also given.

Therefore, the decision the firm must make is: How much should it produce?

Total Variable Cost is total expenditure on a variable input.

Because the firm takes prices as given, the total variable cost of labor is the quantity of labor times the wage rate. One way to explain the derivation of TVC is to multiply the total product function by the wage rate, w. The TP function shows the output for each quantity of labor hired. Therefore, multiplying each level of labor by the market wage rate gives the total variable cost of each level of output. The resulting TVC curve is shown in Figure A2.4.

Figure A2.4

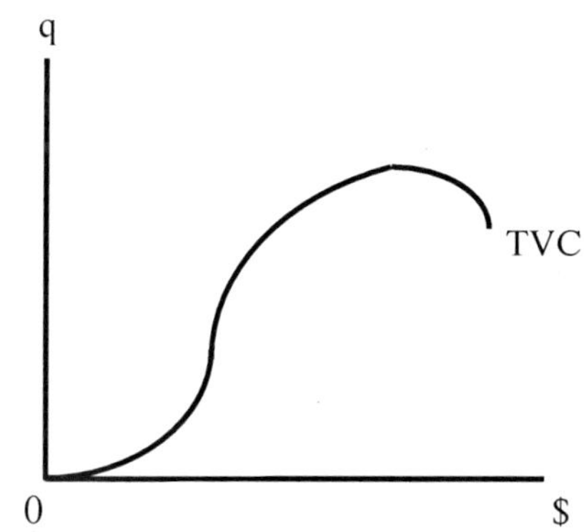

The trouble with Figure A2.4 is that it has dollars on the horizontal axis and total output on the vertical axis. Economists prefer to have quantity on the horizontal axis and dollars on the vertical axis. If the graph in Figure A2.4 is rotated counterclockwise 90 degrees and then flipped over (to the right), it becomes Figure A2.5, which is a standard total variable cost curve, although the backward bending portion is normally dropped because a firm trying to maximize profits would not operate in that range. Any point on the backward bending part of the curve represents the higher of two costs required to produce a given level of output.

Figure A2.5

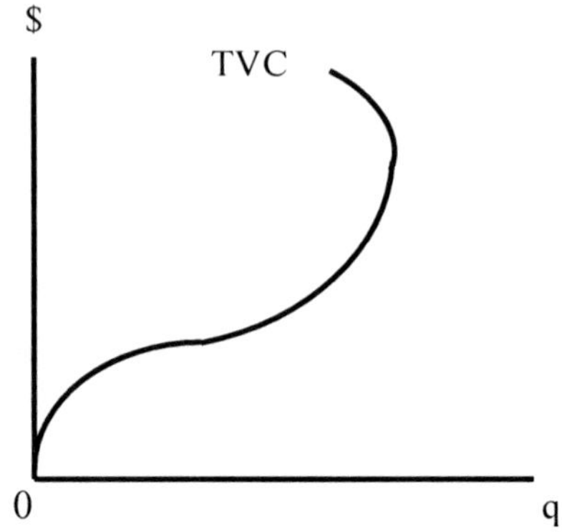

The TVC curve in Figure A2.5 follows the logic behind the TP curve. It increases at a decreasing rate for a while, corresponding to the range on the TP curve with increasing returns. If additional units of labor add greater and greater amounts to output, then it must cost less and less to produce equal increments of output if the wage rate is fixed.

TVC then increases at an increasing rate, corresponding to the range on TP with diminishing returns.

It then turns backward, corresponding to the range on TP where marginal returns are negative.

Because the backward bending portion is not used, Figure A2.6 shows a TVC curve as it is usually presented.

Figure A2.6

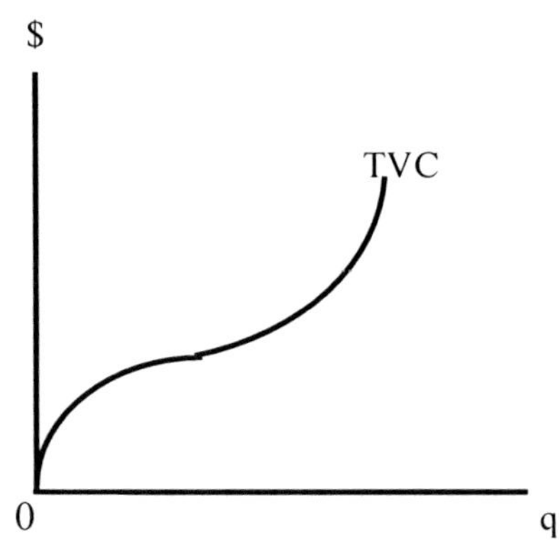

Total Fixed Costs (TFC) are costs that do not vary with output. They are obligations that cannot be avoided even if production is stopped and they do not increase or decrease with output.

Figure A2.7 shows a total fixed cost curve.

It also shows an **Average Fixed Cost** (AFC) curve, which is TFC/q.

Although most texts explain average fixed cost, it is a concept that is seldom used.

Figure A2.7

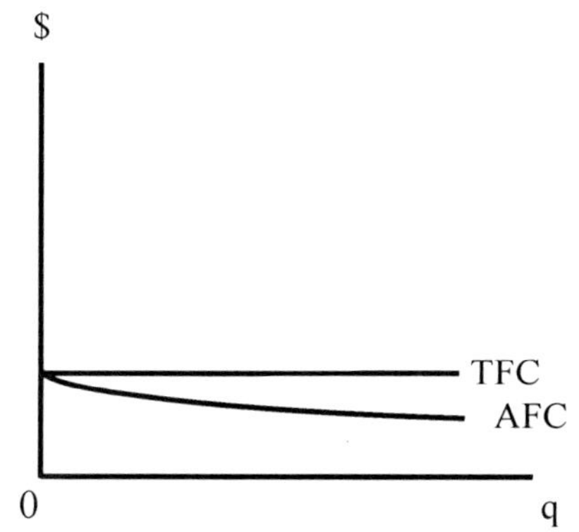

Total Cost is TVC plus TFC. It is shown in Figure A2.8 by adding the TVC curve to the TFC curve. The vertical distance between TVC and TC is equal at all levels of output; it is TFC.

Figure A2.8

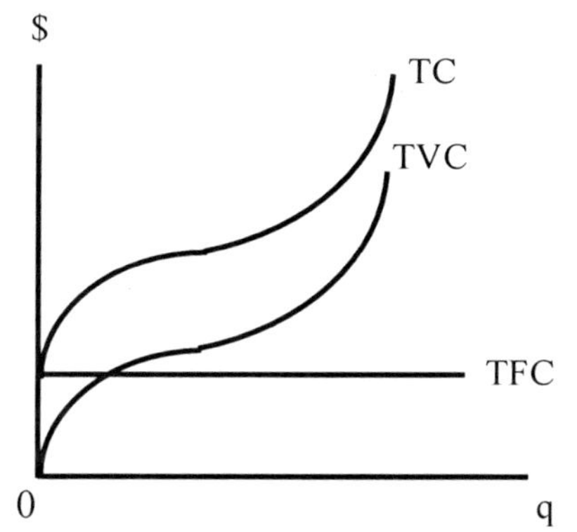

Average Variable Cost is total variable cost divided by quantity.

Given the TVC curve in Figure A2.9 (on the following page), the average variable cost for A units of output is AB/OA (total variable cost divided by quantity), which is also, by definition, the slope of the line OB. For any level of output, average variable cost is the slope of a line from the origin to the point on the total variable cost curve corresponding to that output.

As output increases from 0 to C, the lines become flatter, meaning that average variable cost is decreasing. The line tangent to TVC at D is the line with the flattest slope; it means that C is the output with the lowest average variable cost. After C, lines from the origin to the curve become steeper, such as OF. The average variable cost for C units of labor is CD/OC.

Therefore, AVC is a "U" shaped curve that reaches its minimum at output C. (AVC is not shown in Figure A2.9.)

Figure A2.9

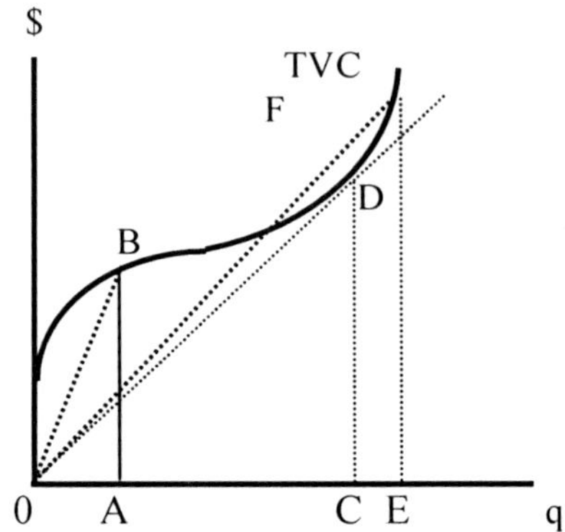

Average Total Cost (often referred to simply as Average Cost) is total cost divided by quantity.

ATC is determined the same as average variable cost. Using the TC curve in Figure A2.10, G is the output with the lowest average total cost. At outputs less than G, ATC is falling. At outputs greater than G, ATC is increasing.

Therefore, ATC, like AVC, is a "U" shaped curve with its minimum at the output where a line from the origin is tangent to the TC curve. But its minimum is at a higher level of output than AVC.

Figure A2.10

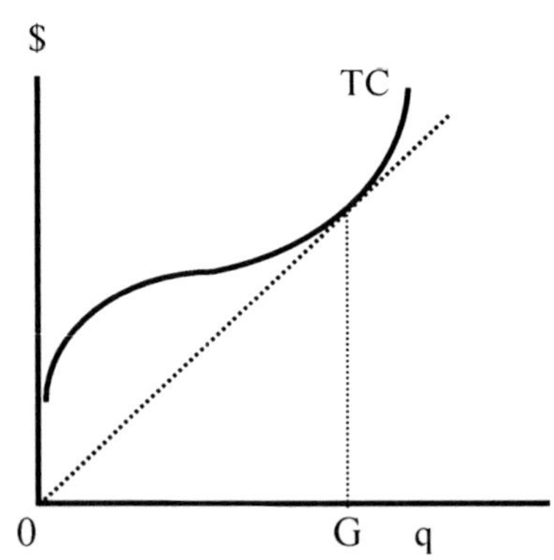

The difference between average variable cost and average total cost is average fixed costs.

If fixed costs exist, TC is greater than TVC and ATC must be above AVC. Therefore, a line from the origin will be tangent to the TC curve at a higher q than a line from the origin that is tangent to the TVC curve.

But because AFC is a declining function, the difference between ATC and AVC becomes smaller as q increases.

Figure A2.11 on the following page shows the *exact* relationship between TVC, TC, AVC, and ATC.

Average total cost is a minimum at q_1.

Average variable cost is a minimum at q_2.

Figure A2.11

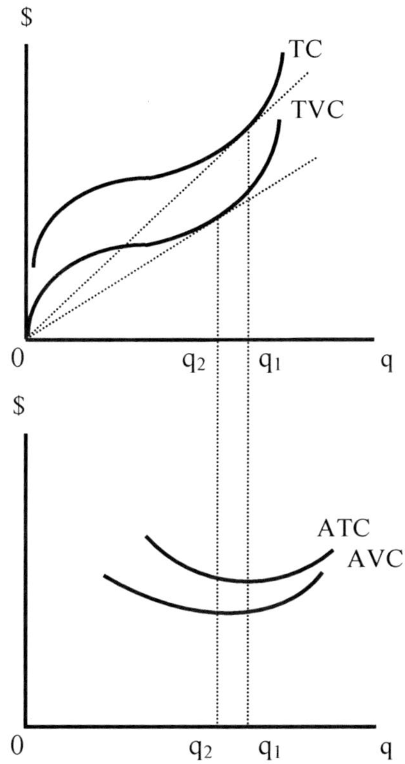

Marginal Cost is the increase in total cost as a result of equal increments in output (often referred to as one unit increases in output).

In Figure A2.12, marginal cost from A to C is the change in total cost (the vertical distance from B to D) divided by the change in output (C - A). It is, therefore, equal to the slope of a straight line that goes through Points B and D.

Figure A2.12

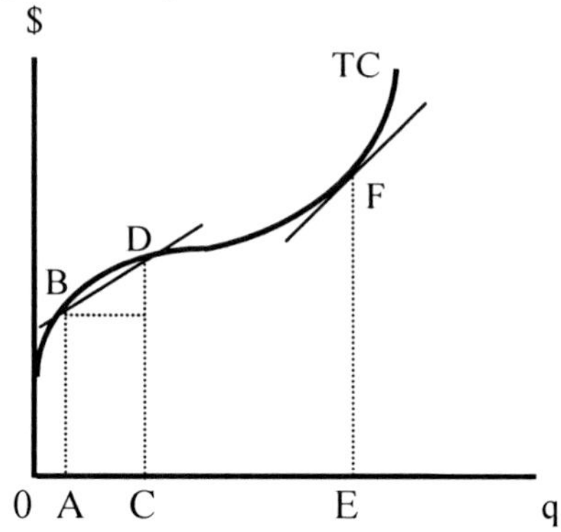

As the distance between B and D approaches zero, the two points merge into a single point, which means the marginal cost for any quantity of output is equal to the slope of a line tangent to the TC function at that level. In Figure A2.12, marginal cost at quantity E is the slope of the line tangent to the total cost curve at F.

Starting with q = 0 in Figure A2.12, lines tangent to the TC curve become flatter and flatter as q increases, up to the point where TC stops increasing at a decreasing rate and begins increasing at an increasing rate. That is the “inflection point” on the TC curve. It shows the quantity at which marginal cost is a minimum. After that, marginal cost rises as output increases; the tangent lines become steeper and steeper.

Therefore, marginal cost is also a “U” shaped function.

Some things to remember:

Marginal cost at any level of output is the same for a total variable cost curve and a total cost curve. Marginal cost is the change in cost resulting from a change in output. Because fixed costs do not change as output changes, the change in TC and the change in TVC are the same.

Marginal cost is equal to average variable cost when AVC is at its minimum. At that output, the line from the origin that touches the TVC curve is the same line that is tangent to the curve.

Marginal cost is equal to average total cost when ATC is at its minimum. At that output, the line from the origin that touches the TC curve is the same line that is tangent to the curve.

Marginal cost reaches its minimum at a lower output than AVC and ATC.

At outputs less than the minimum point on AVC and ATC, MC is below AVC and ATC because the slopes of lines tangent to the curve are flatter than slopes of lines from the origin to the curve.

At outputs greater than the minimum point on AVC and ATC, MC is above AVC and ATC because the slopes of lines tangent to the curve are steeper than slopes of lines from the origin to the curve.

To derive the MC, AVC, and ATC curves for TVC and TC curves, only three points must be found.

(1) The output where a line from the origin is tangent to the TVC curve gives the output where AVC is a minimum and where MC=AVC. (q_1 in Figure A2.13)

(2) The output where a line from the origin is tangent to the TC curve gives the output where ATC is a minimum and where MC=ATC. (q_2 in Figure A2.13)

(3) The inflection point shows the output where MC is a minimum. The inflection points on TC and TVC are at the same output. (q_3 in Figure A2.13)

Figure A2.13 shows the *exact* relationships between TVC, TC, MC, AVC, and ATC.

Figure A2.13

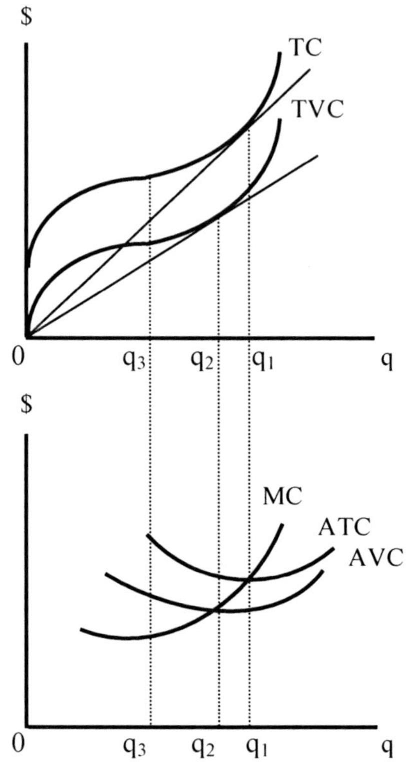

The easiest way to draw the functions, starting with TC and TVC curves, is to first draw a line from the origin tangent to TVC. Come down to the second graph and draw AVC--a "U" shaped curve with its minimum at that output (q_1 in Figure A2.13). Then draw a line from the origin tangent to TC. Come down to the second graph and draw ATC--a "U" shaped curve above AVC with its minimum at that output (q_2 in Figure A2.13). Go back to the TC and TVC curves and find the inflection point. Come down to the second graph and draw the MC curve--a "U" shaped curve that begins below AVC and ATC, reaches its minimum at the output corresponding to the inflection point on TC and TVC (q_3 in Figure A2.13), turns up and intersects AVC and then ATC from below at their minimum points, then continues upward. In order to have a nice looking figure, make certain the MC curve reaches its minimum at a level below the minimum values for AVC and ATC.

As with total product, average product, and marginal product, once the definitions are understood, geometry offers the easiest way to see and use the relationships. Maybe most important, geometry makes it possible to solve many real-world problems without the need for actual numbers.

4. The rule for maximizing profits.

According to the assumptions of perfect competition, a firm can sell all it wants at the existing market price. If it tries to charge a higher price, it cannot sell anything. If it charges a lower price, it can still sell all it wants. Because the goal is to maximize profits, it will not sell for a price less than it can receive.

Figure A2.14 shows price as seen by an individual firm in a competitive industry. To the firm, price is a horizontal line at the market price, p_1. If it is assumed that nothing an individual firm does affects the market price, then the only way p_1 will change is if market supply and/or demand changes--things beyond the control of the firm. Therefore, the demand curve facing an individual firm is the horizontal line at p_1, labeled D=AR=MR. If the firm can sell all it wants at p_1, then p_1 is average revenue and marginal revenue as well as demand.

Figure A2.14

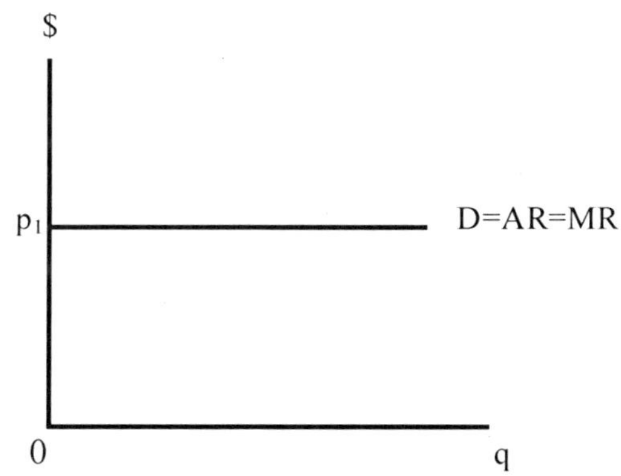

Revenue is what a firm receives (normally money) for selling its product.

Total revenue is price times quantity. The total money a firm receives is equal to the price of the product times the number of items it sells. (TR = p x q)

Average revenue is the price of the product. If all units are sold at the same price, AR is, by definition, equal to TR/q. (AR = TR/q)

Marginal revenue is equal to the change in total revenue resulting from a change in quantity. (MR = the change in TR/the change in q).

By definition, the horizontal price line faced by a firm is the demand the firm faces for its product--the maximum price per unit it can receive for selling any given quantity. It is also the firm's marginal revenue (the addition to total revenue from selling one more unit) and average revenue (the price per unit it receives).

If a firm's goal is to maximize profits, and it can sell as much as it wants at the going price, why not produce as much as physically possible? Because a firm has to pay to produce or sell its output.

If costs were zero, the firm's objective would be to maximize revenue. But because the costs of production are not zero, the firm has to consider the relationship between revenue and cost.

In order to decide how much to produce and sell, the firm compares the addition to revenue (marginal revenue) with the addition to costs (marginal costs) resulting from each additional unit of output.

If marginal revenue is greater than marginal cost for an extra unit, the firm will add that unit to production because doing so will increase profits.

If marginal revenue is less than marginal cost for an extra unit, the firm will not add that unit to production because doing so would reduce profits.

The rule just described is that:

Profits are maximized if the firm produces where marginal revenue is equal to marginal cost.

The rule is nothing more than common sense. To see why it works, assume that marginal cost increases as output increases and that the price of the product remains unchanged. A constant price is one of the assumptions for a firm in a competitive industry.

A price that falls as output increases is the case for (and can be the definition of) a monopolistic firm. A monopolist faces a market demand curve that has a negative slope.

In Figure A2.15, if the price, which is also marginal revenue, is p_1 and the firm produces q_1 units of output, the firm can increase profits if it produces q_2 instead.

Simply by looking at the graph, it can be seen that price (or MR or demand) is above marginal cost (MC) at q_2. Therefore, adding that unit to production adds more to revenue than to costs, which is true for all units up to q_3.

Figure A2.15

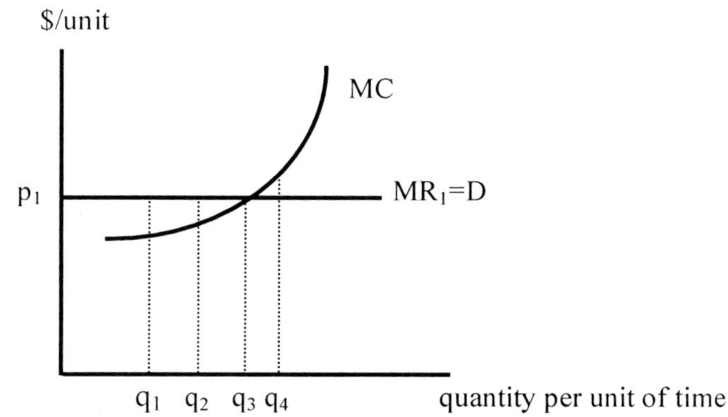

It is also easy to see that if quantity is increased past q_3, to q_4 for example, price, or MR, is less than marginal cost, meaning that each unit added past q_3 adds more to costs than to revenue. Therefore, if profits are smaller when production is less than q_3 or greater than q_3, the firm will maximize profits by producing q_3 units, which is the quantity where marginal revenue equals marginal cost.

What happens to the profit maximizing output of the firm if the price of the product changes?

Figure A2.16 is the same as Figure A2.15, but with a second price shown. Using the above logic, if the price is p_2 instead of p_1, the profit maximizing output increases from q_3 to q_5, because at price p_2, the quantity where marginal revenue is equal to marginal cost is q_5. At any price below p_1, the firm maximizes profits by producing less than q_3 units of output. At any price above p_1, the firm will maximize profits by producing more than q_3 units of output.

Figure A2.16

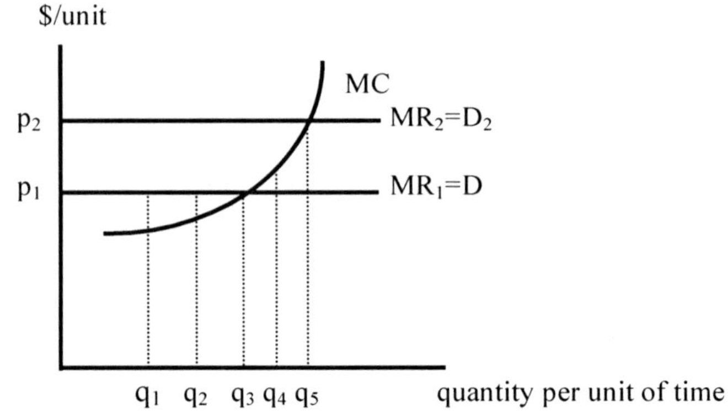

5. Maximizing profits.

The profit maximizing rule is to produce that output where marginal revenue is equal to marginal cost, because any addition to output that adds more to revenue than to costs adds to profit and any addition to output that adds less to revenue than to costs subtracts from profit.

Figure A2.17 is a picture of the competitive firm's decision-making options. It shows D, AR, MR, MC, and ATC.

To maximize profits, the firm produces q_1 units of output, because that is the output where marginal revenue is equal to marginal cost.

Figure A2.17

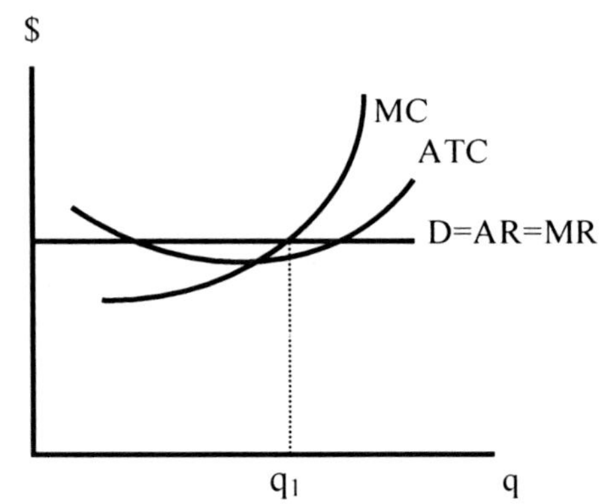

In Figure A2.18, the profit-maximizing output is C.

After determining the profit-maximizing output, profits can be shown two ways:

(1) Profit is equal to the profit per unit times the number of units sold, which is average revenue minus average total cost times quantity.

Profit = (AR-ATC) x q, where average revenue is the price of the product, and average total cost is given by the ATC curve.

(2) Profit can also be calculated as total revenue minus total cost.

Profit = TR-TC, where TR = p x q and TC = ATC x q.

Using the first method above, profits are calculated by first finding the profit per unit, which is DE in Figure A2.18, and then multiplying DE by the profit-maximizing quantity, which is OC. Profit is the **area** ABED.

Using the second method, profits are calculated by finding total revenue and subtracting total cost. In Figure A2.18, total revenue is the **area** OBEC and total cost is the **area** OADC. Subtracting OADC from OBEC leaves the **area** ABED as profits, which is, of course, the same as the first method.

When using graphs, it is important to not confuse distance measures with measures given by areas. In Figure A2.18, the functions shown are AR, MR, D, ATC, and MC. The value of each is given by measuring a distance--the distance from the quantity axis to the curve. Functions not shown are TR and TC. In Figure A1.18, TR and TC would be represented by areas. And although profit per unit is a distance, total profit is an area.

Figure A2.18

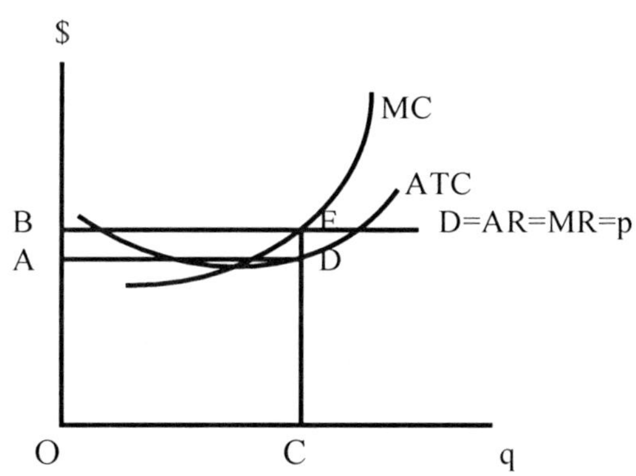

It is also important to know, because it is not easy to see, that Point D is NOT at the minimum point on ATC, except in the case where price, which is equal to AR and MR, is equal to the minimum point on ATC and, therefore, also equal to MC. In that case, profits would be 0.

The easiest way to draw a picture of a competitive firm is:

Draw a "U" shaped ATC curve.

Draw a "U" shaped MC curve that reaches its low point below and to the left of the low point on the ATC curve and that intersects ATC from below at its lowest point.

Draw a price line and label it p=D=MR=AR.

To show a firm earning a positive profit, draw the price line above the intersection of MC and ATC. To show a firm earning a negative profit (loss), draw the price line below the intersection of MC and ATC. To show a firm earning a zero profit, draw the price line at the intersection of MC and ATC.

Draw a vertical line from the intersection of MC and MR to the horizontal axis. The intersection of the line with the horizontal axis gives the profit-maximizing output. Ignore the ATC curve when you do this.

Determine profit or loss in one of two ways.

(1) Find the profit per unit (the vertical distance from AR or price to the ATC curve). Multiply the profit per unit by the profit-maximizing output (the distance from the origin to the vertical line drawn to the horizontal axis). The resulting area is the firm's profit.

(2) Find total revenue (the area defined by price times the profit-maximizing quantity). Find total cost (the area defined by ATC times the profit-maximizing quantity). Subtract the area showing total cost from the area showing total revenue. The area that remains is the firm's profit.

A price between AVC and ATC.

One of the possibilities discussed in textbooks is the case where the price to a competitive firm at its profit-maximizing output is above AVC but below ATC. In such a case, if the firm produces its profit-maximizing output, it does so at a loss, because if ATC is above AR, each unit is produced at a loss. However, if price is above AVC, it means the firm covers at least some of its fixed costs. Therefore, the loss from producing is less than the loss from stopping production altogether.

The conclusion is that the firm's best option is to stay in business, at least for a while, and to maximize profits by minimizing losses. In the long term, unless something changes, the firm will quit. Continuing production under such conditions is a profit-maximizing decision only in the short-term.

6. The competitive firm's supply curve.

Supply is defined as the maximum quantity sellers are willing and able to sell at various prices during a given time period, other things held constant. For an individual firm, the quantity it wants to sell at any given price is the quantity that maximizes its profit at that price. It is the quantity determined by the condition that MR=MC.

But because MC is "U" shaped, there are two different quantities where MR=MC. To maximize profits, the firm chooses the quantity where MC is increasing. The quantity where MR=MC and MC is declining minimizes profits. In Figure A2.19, if output increases from 0 to q_3, with price at p_1, each unit adds more to costs than revenues; not one of those units yields a profit, which is why profits are minimized if output is where marginal revenue equals marginal costs and marginal cost is declining. From q_3 to q_1, each unit adds more to revenue than to costs. After q_1, additional output again adds more to costs than revenue.

As a result, the profit-maximizing rule for the firm is to produce where MR=MC and MC is increasing.

In Figure A2.19, if the price is p_1, the firm maximizes profits by selling q_1 units of output. At p_2, the firm maximizes profits by selling q_2 units. For any given price, the quantity the firm is willing and able to sell is given by the intersection of price, which is marginal revenue, with marginal cost.

For any given price, the quantity the firm is willing and able to sell is determined by where price is equal to marginal cost when marginal cost is increasing.

Therefore, by definition, the upward sloping part of the firm's marginal cost curve is the firm's supply curve.

Figure A2.19

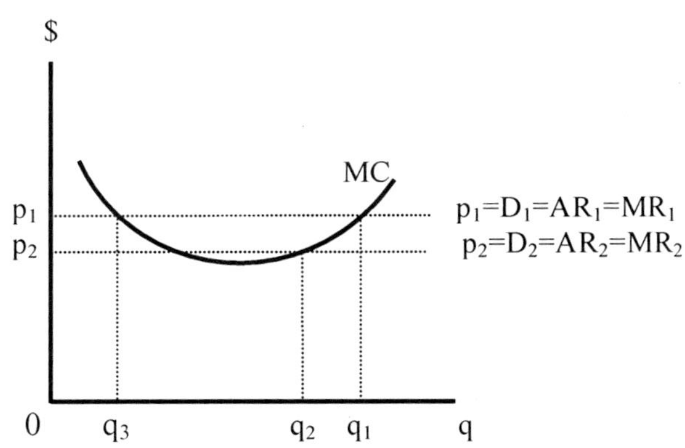

7. Market supply.

Figure A2.20 shows the supply curve for a firm. It is the upward sloping part of the firm's MC curve. It is what a firm's supply curve is assumed to look like without information to the contrary.

Figure A2.20

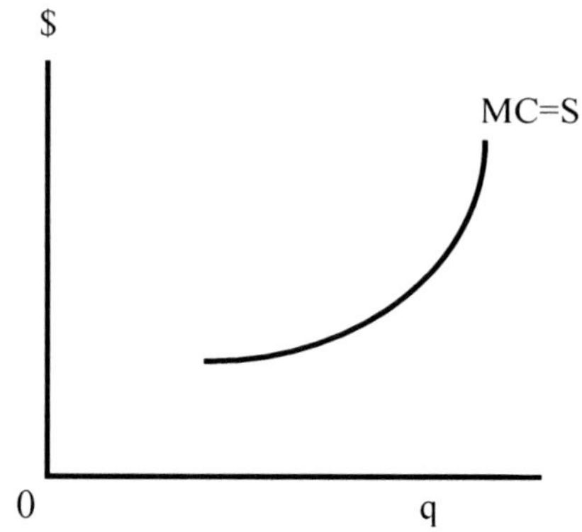

Figure A2.21 shows supply curves for a number of individual firms and the supply curve for the market, which is the horizontal summation of all the individual supply curves. As price increases or decreases, firms will increase or decrease output, some firms will leave the industry and others will enter.

The few individual supply curves shown in Figure A2.21 are simply to make the horizontal summation clear. In a "real" market, the number of firms is assumed to be so large that the market supply can be represented by a relatively smooth curve, often as a straight line.

Without information to the contrary, economic problems begin by assuming a market supply that looks as it does in Figure A2.21.

Figure A2.21

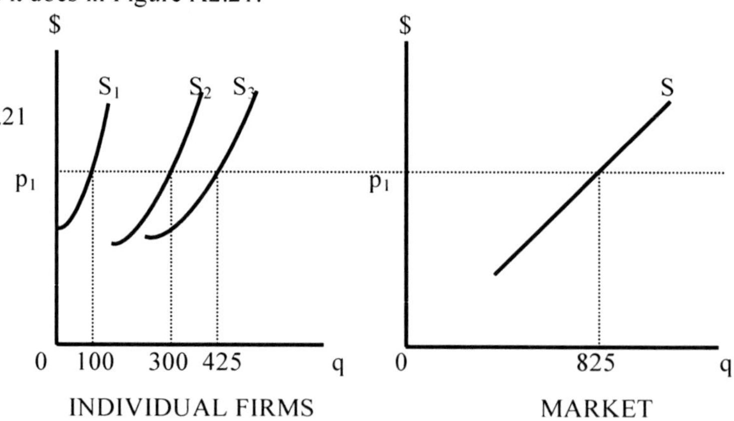

8. Market demand.

Appendix 1 ended with the following figure showing a market demand curve as the horizontal summation of the individual demand curves.

Figure A2.22

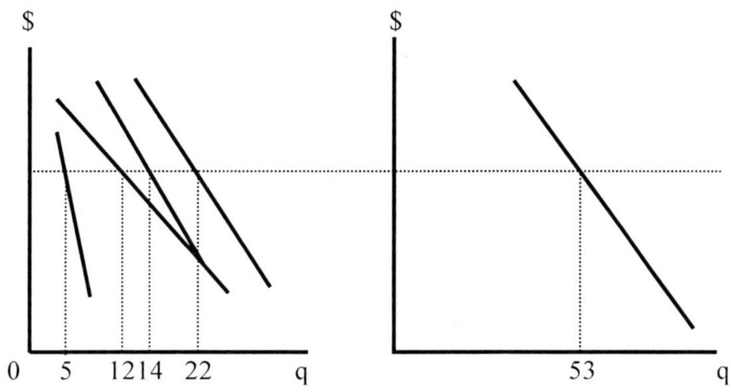

9. The competitive market.

In Appendix 1, Indifference Curve analysis used the decision-making process of the individual consumer to derive individual and market demand curves. The argument was based upon an individual's ability to make comparative valuations of goods and services and to make decisions that maximize satisfaction or wellbeing.

Appendix 2 derived supply functions for the individual firm and the market based upon the firm's ability to make decisions intended to maximize profits. The decisions require valuations of costs and revenues on the margin.

Figure A2.23 is the standard picture of a competitive market. It is the starting point for discussions and problem solving in all cases where there is no reason to believe the functions should look different. It is assumed to be "good," in the sense that the equilibrium price (p_1) and quantity (q_1) represent a situation where the value consumers place upon the product is equal to the cost of providing it.

The market demand curve in Figure A2.23 is from Figure A2.22 and the market supply curve is from Figure A2.21.

Figure A2.23

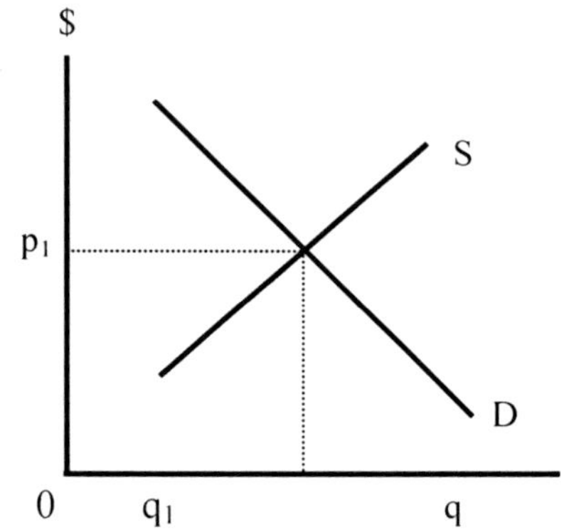

A market equilibrium is determined by market demand and market supply. But it is a back and forth process. Individual firms, with no impact on market prices, make up the market supply, which, together with market demand, determines the price each firm then takes as given.

Depending upon the market price, individual firms may increase or decrease output, and some firms may enter or leave the market.

10. Profit is not really maximized.

Although the supply curve for the firm is derived from the decision-making process of firms with the goal of maximizing profits, it is not necessary to assume that profits are actually maximized.

If the analysis required that profits be maximized in order to derive a supply curve, it would be difficult of impossible to use, because no firm is ever able to actually maximize profits.

The only assumption that is needed is: Given a choice, the firm will increase or decrease production only if doing so adds more to revenue than to costs.

11. An alternative method for showing the profit-maximizing output.

Figure A2.24 shows an alternative way to use total cost and total revenue curves to yield the **profit maximizing output of a competitive firm**. TC was explained above. Total revenue is simply price times quantity (TR = p x q), which is a straight line from the origin with a slope equal to the price of the product. The change in TR for each unit change in q is p. In Figure A2.24, profit is maximized at q_1, where the vertical distance between TR and TC is the greatest, because profit equals TR - TC. It is, of course, also where marginal revenue equals marginal cost, because the slope of the TC curve is MC and the slope of the TR curve is MR, and at point q_1 the slopes of TC and TR must be equal in order for the vertical distance between TR and TC to be maximized. (When using TR and TC curves to determine the profit-maximizing output and profit, profit is a distance, not an area.)

Figure A2.24

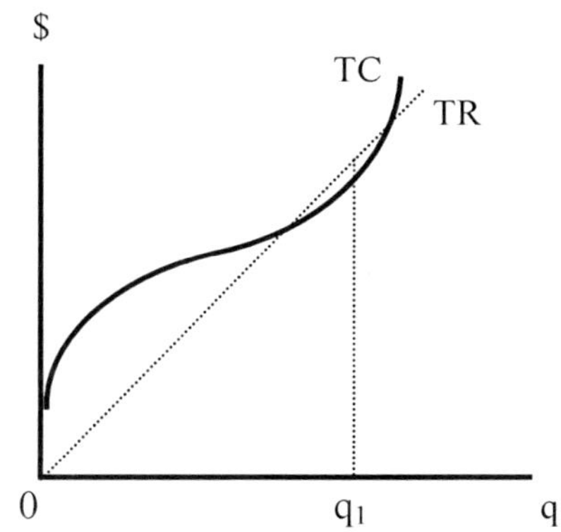

Appendix 3

The Labor Market

1. The competitive firm's demand for labor.

The demand for labor is derived from the competitive firm's decision to hire the quantity of labor that maximizes its profits, meaning that the firm will hire labor as long as its addition to revenue is greater than its addition to costs.

The goal is to maximize profits.

The constraints include the production process, the price of the good produced, and the prices of all inputs. For a firm in a competitive industry, it is assumed that the firm takes all prices as given. No matter how much or little the firm buys and sells, it will not affect the price of the product or the prices of any inputs, including labor. It is also assumed that the firm has already decided what to produce and how to produce it--the production process to be used.

The question is: How much labor should be hired?

Labor's addition to revenue is equal to the price of the product (fixed at the market price) times what labor adds to output (its marginal physical product). Multiplying the marginal physical product times the price of the product gives the value to the firm of each additional unit of labor. It is called the "**value of the marginal product**."

In Figure A3.1, on the following page, the value of the marginal product (VMP) is calculated by multiplying the marginal physical product times the price of the output. Marginal physical product (MPP) is the same as marginal product (MP) explained in Appendix 2. The reason for the different "names" is that marginal product is a general term that applies to any variable input whereas marginal physical product is the specific name given to marginal product when the variable input is labor.

Because the price of output is fixed to the firm, and marginal physical product is an inverted "U" shaped curve, VMP is also an inverted "U" shaped curve; it increases, reaches a maximum, and then decreases. Therefore, the wage rate, which is fixed to the firm at the market price, is the supply of labor as seen by the firm. It is also the average cost and marginal cost of labor to the firm, which means the firm will hire labor up to the point where the marginal revenue from labor (VMP) equals the marginal cost of labor (the wage rate).

But profits are maximized only if the firm chooses to operate in the range where the value of the marginal product is decreasing.

In the range where VMP is increasing, each unit of labor employed adds more to costs than revenues. In the range where VMP is falling each unit of labor adds more to revenue than costs--up to the point where VMP = the wage rate. After that, the addition to costs is greater than the addition to revenues.

Therefore, to maximize profits, the firm hires labor up to the level where VMP = w.

Figure A3.1 shows the VMP and two wage rates, w_1 and w_2. At w_1, the firm will hire N_1 units of labor, not N_2, to maximize its profits. At w_2, it hires N_3.

Figure A3.1

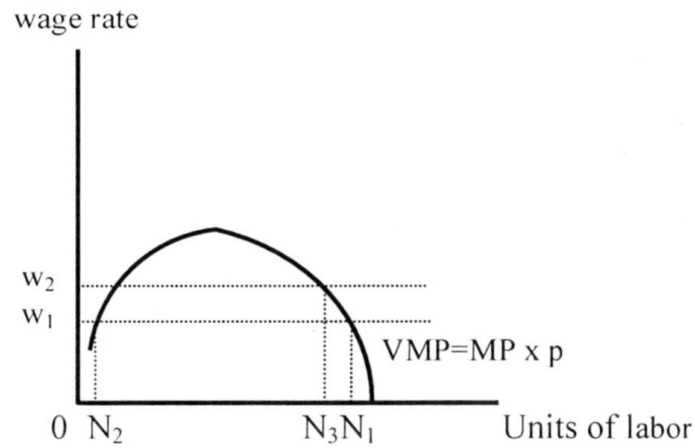

The firm pays labor what labor is worth to the firm--what it adds to revenue. If the wage rate increases, from w_1 to w_2, while the price of the output and everything else is unchanged, the firm will hire less labor; N_3 rather than N_1.

The opportunity cost of not hiring labor is lost revenue (VMP).

Therefore, the firm will continue to hire labor as long as the wage rate is less than the value of the marginal product. If the wage rate is greater than the value of the marginal product, no additional units of labor will be employed.

Figure A3.2 shows the firm's demand for labor. It has a negative slope, because as the wage rate increases, the firm will hire less labor. It should look like the downward sloping part of the VMP curve in Figure A3.1, because that is what it is.

Figure A3.2

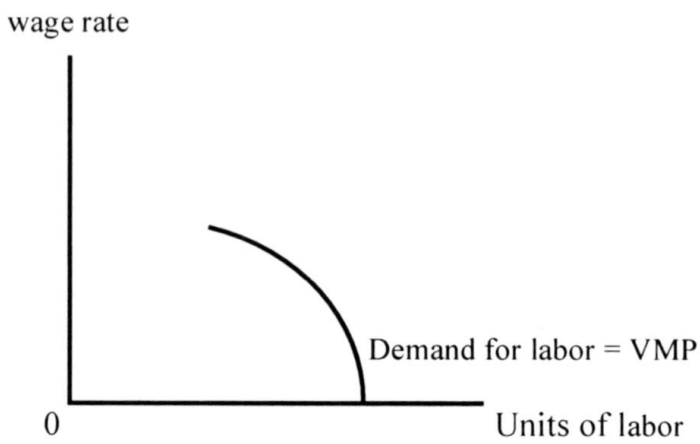

For any given wage rate, the quantity of labor the firm will hire in order to maximize its profits is read off the VMP curve.

2. The market demand for labor.

The above discussion explains how the profit-maximizing decisions of an individual firm yield the firm's demand for labor.

The **market** demand for labor is the horizontal summation of the demand curves for all the individual firms in the market. An individual firm's demand for labor shows the maximum quantity of labor the firm is willing and able to hire at each wage rate. A horizontal summation of the demand curves for all individual firms shows the maximum quantity that all firms in the industry are willing and able to hire at each wage during a given time period.

The market demand for labor will not have the exact shape of any particular individual firm's VMP because each firm has different productive capabilities and because as wages change, the change in the cost of production will cause firms to enter or leave the industry.

Figure A3.3

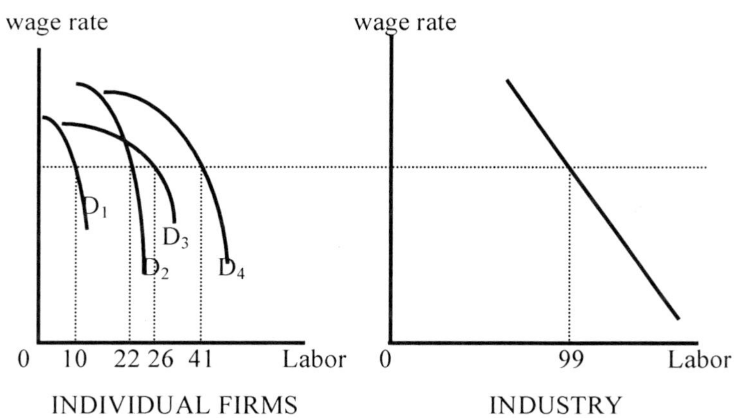

3. The individual's supply of labor.

The decision by households regarding work and leisure yields the supply of labor, which is the relationship between the number of hours labor is willing and able to work during some time period and various wage rates.

Again:

The goal is to maximize happiness.

The constraints include time, tastes and preferences, skills and education, prices, wage rates, and expectations of future wages and prices. It is assumed that the individual has no effect on wages and that all other prices remain constant.

The choice is between hours worked and hours of leisure.

The decision-making process is easy to understand. At a wage rate of zero, most individuals would choose not to work. The decision to not work comes from the fact that if the wage rate is zero, the individual does not give up anything by not working. The opportunity cost of leisure is zero. (The argument does not apply to all the people who work as volunteers.)

If the wage rate rises above zero (to w_1, for example, in Figure A3.4), *while nothing else changes*, the individual will probably want to work some hours per week (h_1, for example). The values w_1 and h_1 are arbitrary. They are not real numbers. They represent one point in a logical argument.

Because the decision regarding work versus leisure weighs the "happiness" from leisure time against the "happiness" from stuff that can be purchased with money earned working, at a wage rate of w_1, the opportunity cost of leisure is not zero. Therefore, it can be assumed an individual will want to give up some happiness from leisure time in return for the happiness gained from being able to buy some things.

At a wage rate higher than w_1 (w_2, for example), the concept of opportunity cost says that the individual will want to work even more hours (h_2, for example).

Why? Because the higher the wage rate, the more stuff the individual has to give up for each hour of leisure, *assuming that no other prices change*. The opportunity cost of each hour of leisure increases as the wage rate increases, which means the higher the wage rate, the more hours the individual will want to work.

Figure A3.4 shows the relationship between wages and hours worked. It is a positive relationship, meaning that as the wage rate increases, so does the number of hours the individual wants to work, assuming that everything else is held constant.

Figure A3.4

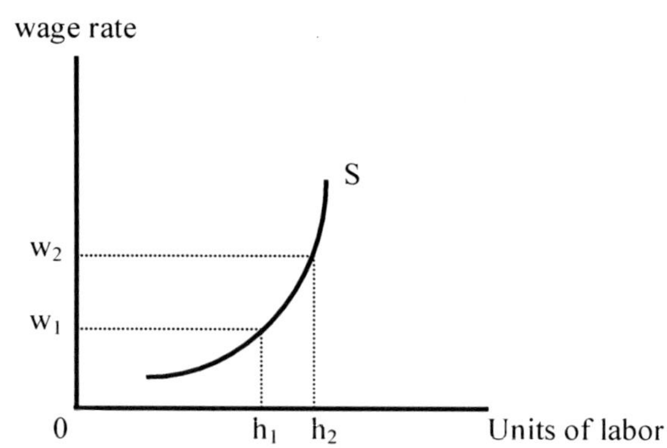

Will the number of hours the individual wants to work always increase as the wage rate increases? Logic says, no.

At some point, the addition to happiness from the additional things that can be bought for another hour of work will be less than the addition to happiness from having another hour of leisure. At that point the opportunity cost of leisure declines, and for each increase in the wage rate after that point, the individual will want to work fewer hours.

Figure A3.5 shows what is called a "backward bending" supply curve for labor.

Figure A3.5

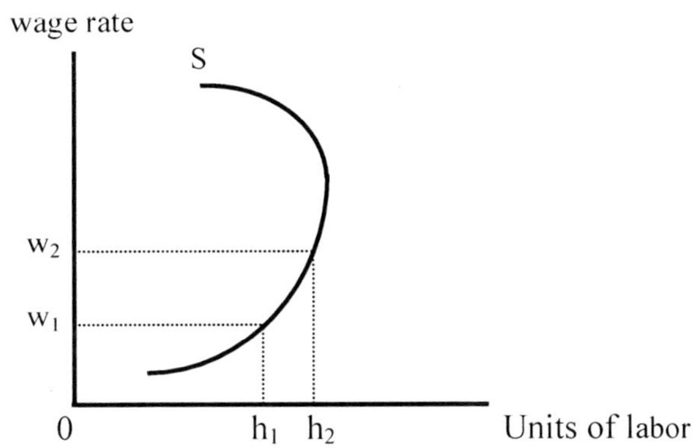

The reason for a backward-bending supply curve of labor is that it explains a situation where the individual has very little leisure time and is already earning a substantial income.

Although the existence of a backward bending supply curve of labor has been supported with data from the real world, it is only used to discuss special cases where it can add useful information.

The typical economic problem assumes a supply curve for labor as shown in Figure A3.4, mainly because wages are almost never high enough to move the supply of labor in an entire market onto the backward bending portion.

4. The market supply of labor.

To derive the supply of labor for a particular market, the relevant individual supply curves are summed horizontally. The relevant individuals are those who are willing and able to work in that particular market.

Summing horizontally shows the total quantity of labor that will be offered at each wage rate.

Figure A3.6

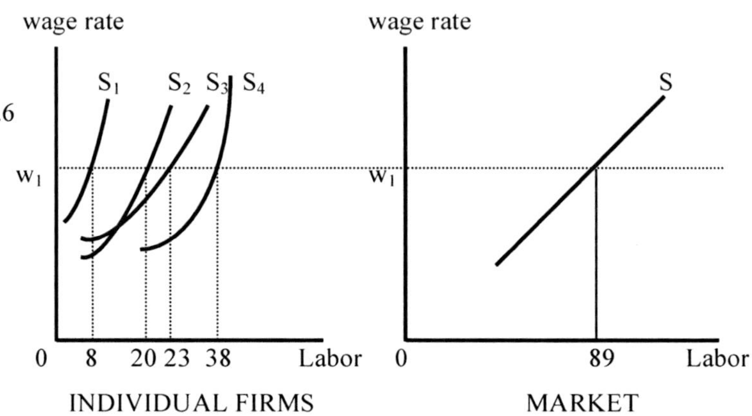

5. The market supply of and demand for labor.

Figure A3.7 shows normal supply and demand curves for labor. The equilibrium wage rate is w_1. The equilibrium quantity of labor is N_1 units.

Figure A3.7

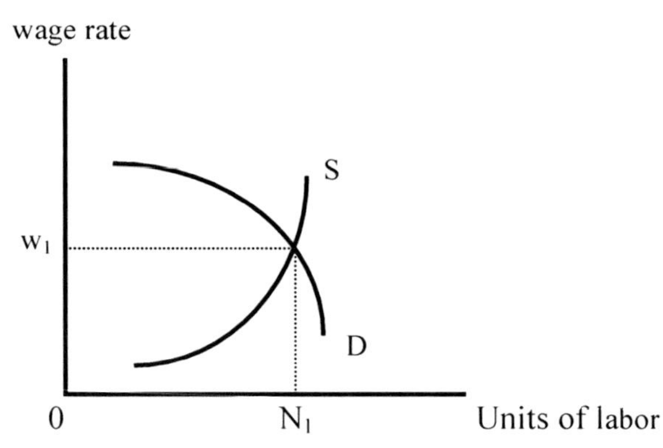

Appendix 4

Elasticity

1. Measuring responsiveness.

Alfred Marshall developed the concept of elasticity in the 1920's to explain the responsiveness of a change in quantity demanded or supplied as a result of a change in a product's price. It is also used to explain the responsiveness of the change in quantity demanded of a good or service due to a change in the price of another product or an individual's income. The need for the concept of elasticity grew out of the recognition that neither the slope of a demand curve (or supply curve) nor the numbers in a demand schedule can easily show such responsiveness.

If a 10-cent increase in the price of corn leads to a 200-bushel decrease in corn purchased, the slope of the demand curve in that range is -10/200 or -1/20. (Slope is equal to the change in y divided by the change in x; in this case the change in y is the change in price and the change in x is the change in quantity demanded.) If the price is measured in dollars instead of cents, the slope of the demand curve is (-1/10)/(200), which is equal to -1/2,000. Both sets of numbers describe the same thing: the change in the quantity of corn purchased due to a change in the price of corn. The only difference is the units used to measure price--cents or dollars. But the difference in the measure of slope is huge: -1/20 versus -1/2,000. In some cases, that difference will not matter; in others it may cause considerable confusion.

A second problem with relying on slope as a determinant of responsiveness is that it does not work when comparing two different markets. A $1.00 drop in the price of corn can lead to a significant change in the quantity of corn purchased per week or month. A $1.00 drop in the price of a television set will have a small, if any, impact on sales. Does that mean corn is more responsive to price changes than television sets? Not necessarily. A $1.00 change in the price of corn is a large change. A $1.00 change in the price of a television set is a very small change.

To deal with such problems, Alfred Marshall defined **elasticity** to be the percentage change in quantity demanded during a defined time period divided by the percentage change in price, if the change is price is small.

If calculated between two points on a demand curve, it is called "arc elasticity." If calculated at a point on a demand curve, "point elasticity."

The major limitation to the use of elasticity is that it can be calculated exactly only if real numbers exist for the demand or supply function under consideration. And if the real numbers are available, calculating elasticity may be an unnecessary step in the process of solving a problem.

2. Arc elasticity.

To calculate the arc elasticity between two points on a demand curve, Points A and B on the demand curve in Figure A4.1, for example, divide the percentage change in quantity by the percentage change in price. Going from Point A to Point B, the arc elasticity of demand is - 2.

(200/1,000)/(-10/100) = (200/1,000) x 100/-10 = (.2) (-10) = - 2.

If price is given in dollars, instead of cents, the percentage change in quantity divided by the percentage change in price is the same:

(200/1,000)/(-.10/1) = (200/1,000) x (-1/.1) = (.2) (-10) = - 2.

Figure A4.1

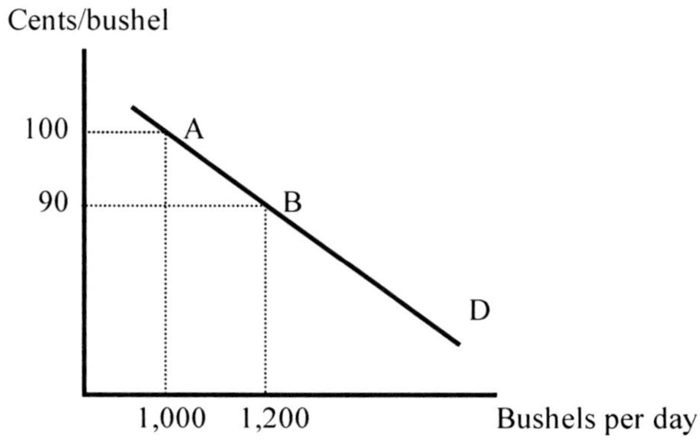

The example shows that the units of measurement do not affect the calculation of elasticity. However, the value of elasticity *is* affected by the order in which the points are used in the calculation.

Going from Point B to Point A, instead of from Point A to point B, the percentage change in quantity divided by the percentage change in price is:

(-200/1,200)/(10/90) = (-200/1,200) x (90/10) = - 1.5.

Therefore, the arc elasticity of demand from Point B to Point A is - 1.5.

Using dollars instead of cents, the arc elasticity from Point B to Point A is still - 1.5.

The problem is: Which number should be used? There is no set answer. In other words, elasticity, which was created to clear up misunderstandings, creates its own confusion.

One solution to the problem of arc elasticity is to calculate "average arc elasticity" between two points. The standard method is to use the actual change in quantity and price, but to use the lower of the two quantities and the lower of the two prices. For the above example, "average arc elasticity" is:

$$(200/1{,}000)/(-10/90) = (200/1{,}000) \times (-90/10) = -1.8.$$

Although elasticity is a negative number, because demand has a negative slope, economists normally write the elasticity of demand as a positive number. In the above example, the average arc elasticity of demand would normally be given as 1.8.

3. Point elasticity.

Point elasticity avoids the measurement problems of arc elasticity by calculating elasticity at a single point on a demand curve.

Technically, point elasticity is arc elasticity with the distance between the two points approaching zero. Using geometry to calculate point elasticity gives results that can be used without requiring actual numbers.

In Figure A4.2, the elasticity of demand at Point B is the percentage change in quantity divided by the percentage change in price:

$$\frac{\Delta q/q}{\Delta p/p}$$

which can be rewritten as:

$$(\Delta q/\Delta p) \times (p/q)$$

Looking at the two terms:

$(\Delta q/\Delta p)$ equals EF/EB in Figure A4.2 and (p/q) equals EB/OE.

Therefore, $(\Delta q/\Delta p) \times (p/q)$ equals (EF/EB) x (EB/OE),

which equals EF/OE.

And the point elasticity of demand at Point B is EF/OE.

If D in Figure A4.2 is a straight-line demand curve, elasticity is also equal to BF/AB.

Figure A4.2

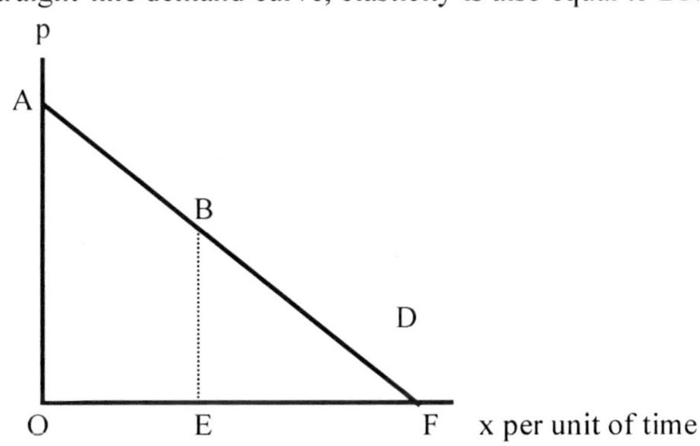

For any point on the demand curve to the right of its midpoint (or to the right of the midpoint of OF on the q axis), BF/AB or EF/OE will be less than 1. (Following convention, the elasticity of demand is written as a positive number.) When elasticity is less than 1, demand is said to be "**inelastic**."

For any point on the demand curve to the left of its midpoint (or to the left of the midpoint of OF on the q axis), BF/AB or EF/OE will be greater than 1. When elasticity is greater than 1, demand is said to be "**elastic**."

At the midpoint on the demand curve (or the midpoint of OF on the q axis), BF/AB or EF/OE will equal 1. When elasticity equals 1, demand is said to have "**unitary elasticity**." At Point A, elasticity is infinite (a positive number divided by zero). Moving down the demand curve from Point A, elasticity declines until it equals 1 at the midpoint on the demand curve. Moving down from the midpoint, elasticity decreases from 1 to 0.

If **demand is non linear**, as in Figure A4.3, elasticity at a point on the curve is determined by first drawing a line tangent to the curve at that point and extending the line to each axis. The elasticity at that point on the non-linear demand curve is calculated by determining the elasticity at that point on the straight line. In Figure A4.3, the elasticity at Point B is EF/OE or BF/AB.

Figure A4.3

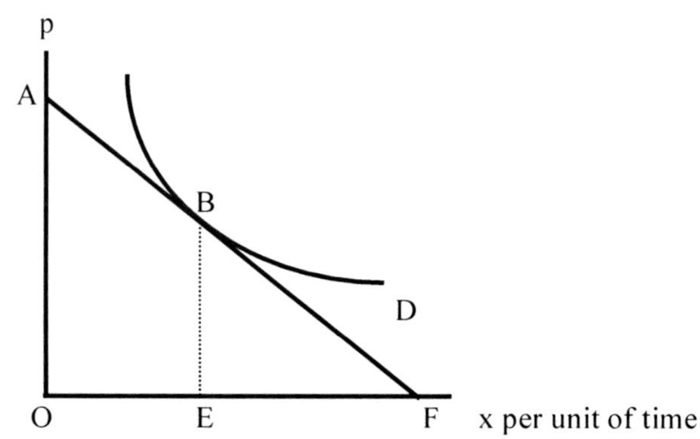

4. Cross elasticity of demand.

Cross elasticity of demand is defined as the percentage change in quantity divided by the percentage change in the price of another good. For example, the cross elasticity of demand for x relative to y is the percentage change in x divided by the percentage change in the price of y.

If cross elasticity is negative, the two goods are called "**complimentary**." Complementary goods are defined as goods where if the purchase of one decreases, the demand for the other decreases as well. A negative cross elasticity of demand means that if the price of y increases, the demand for x decreases. The increase in the price of y, which causes the consumption of y to decrease, also causes the quantity of x demanded to decline. The higher the cross elasticity, the more complementary the goods are.

If cross elasticity is positive, the goods are called "**substitutes.**" Substitute goods are defined as goods where if the price of one increases, consumers will turn to the other as an alternative. A positive cross elasticity of demand means that if the price of y increases, the demand for x increases. The increase in the price of y, which causes the consumption of y to decrease, causes the quantity of substitute goods, such as x, to increase.) The higher the cross elasticity of demand, the greater substitutes the goods are.

5. Income elasticity of demand.

Income elasticity of demand is defined as a percentage change in quantity divided by a percentage change in income. For normal goods, the income elasticity is positive; as income increases, so does the quantity of the good purchased. For inferior goods, the income elasticity is negative; as income increases, the quantity of the good purchased decreases. For many people, beer may be an inferior good, meaning that as their income rises, they buy less of it.

6. Elasticity of supply.

Elasticity of supply is the percentage change in quantity supplied divided by the percentage change in the product's price. It measures the responsiveness of the quantity of the product offered for sale due to a change in its price.

7. Elasticity can help show the relationship between demand and total revenue or total spending.

Total revenue is equal to price times quantity. TR increases as price falls in the elastic part of demand, because the percentage change in q is greater than the percentage change in p. TR decreases when price falls in the inelastic part of demand, because the percentage change in q is less than the percentage change in p. TR is unchanged, and at a maximum, at the point of unitary elasticity if there is an infinitesimally small decrease in price. The relationship is shown in Figure A4.4.

Figure A4.4

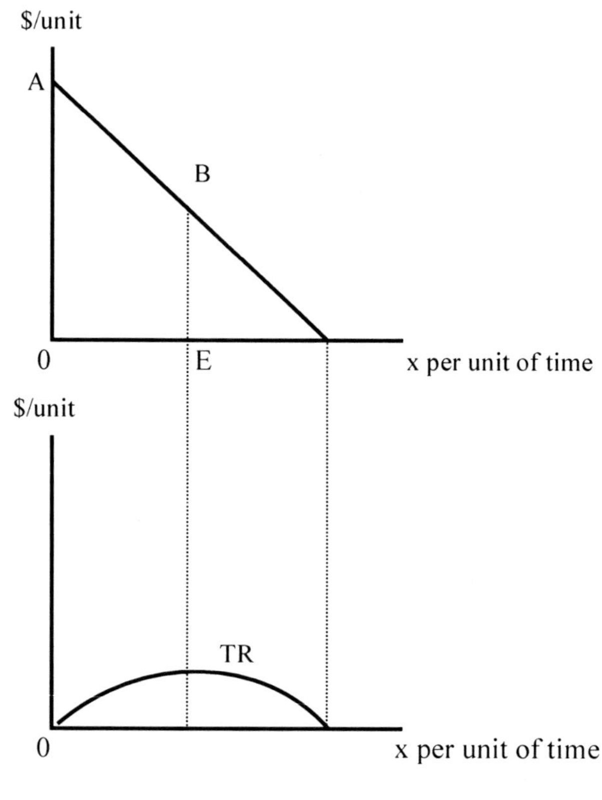

8. The relationship between demand and marginal revenue.

Elasticity can also determine the relationship between demand and marginal revenue. Marginal revenue is defined as the change in total revenue caused by a one-unit increase in output.

Start at Point A in Figure A4.4, on the previous page, and move down the demand curve.

As price falls:

When total revenue is increasing, marginal revenue must be positive. The only way for total revenue to increase is if the additional unit adds a positive amount to revenue. If adding one unit to output increases total revenue from \$100 to \$110, the marginal revenue of that unit is \$10--the amount it added to total revenue.

When total revenue is unchanged, marginal revenue must be 0. The only way for total revenue to remain unchanged is if the additional unit adds nothing to revenue. If adding one unit to output leaves total revenue at \$150, the marginal revenue of that unit is zero--it added 0 to total revenue.

When total revenue is decreasing, marginal revenue must be negative. The only way for total revenue to decrease is if the additional unit adds a negative amount to revenue. If adding one unit to output decreases total revenue from \$200 to \$195, the marginal revenue of that unit is minus \$5, the amount it subtracts from total revenue.

Figure A4.5 shows the marginal revenue curve, MR, corresponding to the demand curve D. It is equal to demand at point A and must cross the quantity axis at the quantity corresponding to unitary elasticity, which is half way between O and F or at B, the midpoint on D. The MR curve shows that MR is negative at outputs past OE.

Figure A4.5

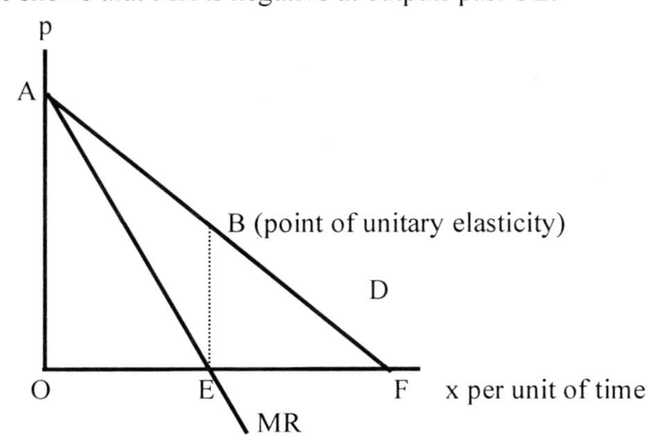

The relationship between market demand and marginal revenue is used to help explain why a monopoly reduces the wealth of the nation.

Appendix 5

An Early Keynesian Tax-Cut Argument

1. An early Keynesian explanation of tax cuts.

The "early" Keynesian models predicted that the change in equilibrium GDP, as a result of a change in taxes, would be equal to the actual change in aggregate demand, which was equal to a multiple of the change in taxes (although less than the multiple of a change in government spending).

The reason for that conclusion is that the early models ignored two issues:

The early models ignored the fact that a decrease in taxes creates deficits that may be financed by selling bonds to the public, thereby raising interest rates and reducing all interest sensitive spending.

The early models also assumed that as long as the economy was operating below its full employment level, increases in GDP would not cause the price level to increase.

In Figure A5.1, the Keynesian assumption that prices are constant until the equilibrium level of GDP exceeds the full employment level of GDP is shown by having an aggregate supply curve that is horizontal until it reaches the full employment level of GDP; and then slopes upward after it crosses the full employment level of GDP.

If aggregate supply were horizontal, up to Y_{FE}, it would then be true that a change in the equilibrium level of GDP would be equal to a change in aggregate demand (which is assumed to be a multiple of a change in taxes). Of course, such changes are also based on the implicit assumption that tax cuts do not create deficits. Ignoring the fact that tax cuts create deficits was used in the first argument above.

Figure A5.1

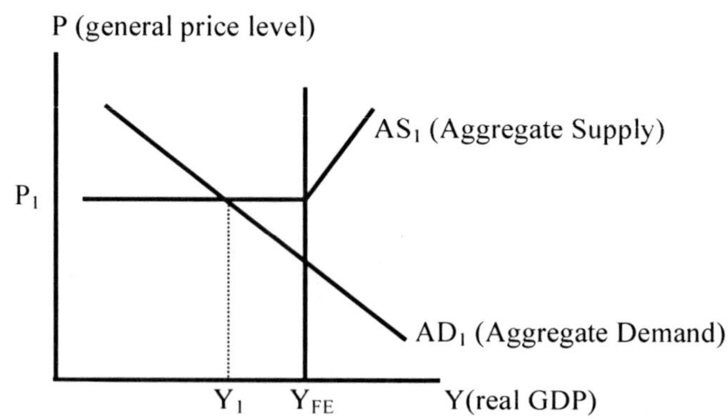

This text consciously ignores outdated theories and theories that economists know to be false. The reason for including a short discussion of the errors in the early Keynesian models is that such models are still used by politicians who want to claim that tax cuts that benefit their friends are good for the economy.

Appendix 6

Using Diagrams

1. Two-dimensional graphs.

Data for two related variables, or an equation with two variables, can be shown on a Cartesian grid.

Two related variables.

A two-dimensional graph has two axes. According to convention, the horizontal axis is the x-axis; the vertical axis is the y-axis. Points on the x-axis to the right of the y-axis are positive x values. Points on the x-axis to the left of the y-axis are negative x values. Points on the y-axis above the x-axis are positive y values. Points on the y-axis below the x-axis are negative y values.

The graph is divided into four quadrants.

Quadrant I is the area where the values of both x and y are positive.

Quadrant II is the area where the value of x is negative and the value of y is positive.

Quadrant III is the area where the values of both x and y are negative.

Quadrant IV is the area where the value of x is positive and the value of y is negative.

Each point on a graph represents two numbers: a value for x and the corresponding value of y.

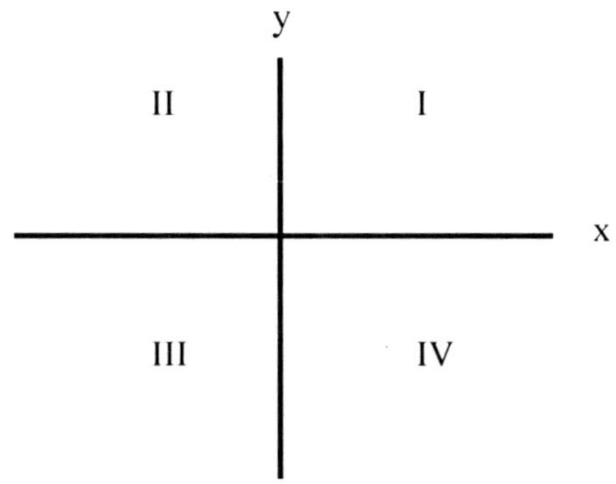

A table can be used to list the corresponding values of two variables. To be meaningful, the two variables should have a common factor, such as time or location.

Table

Point (time or location)	Value of x	Value of y
A	2	3
B	4	-1
C	-2	2
D	-1	-2

The same information can be written as: A (2,3), B (4,-1), C (-2,2), D (-1,-2).

It can also be plotted on a Cartesian grid.

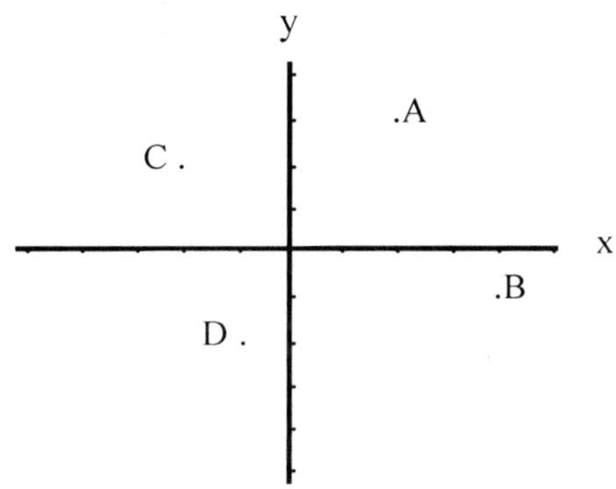

Conversely, given a Cartesian grid, it is possible to determine the corresponding values of x and y. On the grid below, A represents an x value of 1 and a corresponding y value of 3; B represents an x value of 1 and a corresponding y value of -1.

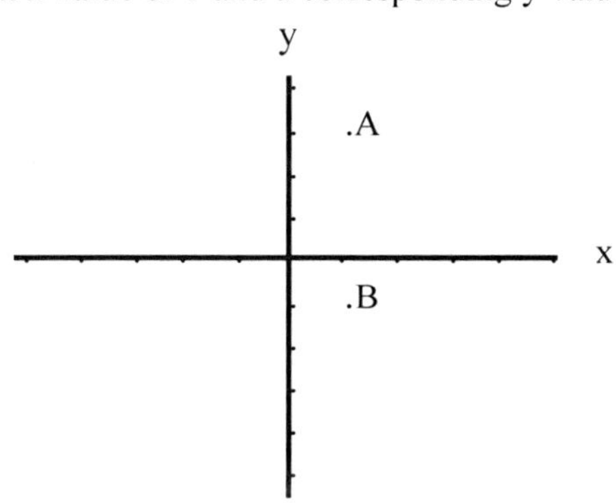

Equations.

The equation for a straight line is: $y = mx + b$.

Given values for m, which is the slope of the line, and b, which is the y-intercept of the line), the equation yields the value of y for any value of x (or the value of x for any value of y).

For example, if the slope of the line is 2 and the line intersects the y-axis at 3, the equation is $y = 2x + 3$. The equation can be used to construct a table.

Table

x	y
0	3
1	5
2	7
.	.
.	.
47	97
.	.

The equation can be drawn on a Cartesian grid, with m as the slope of the line and b is intercept on the y-axis. The slope of a straight line is equal to the change in y divided by the change in x between two points; $(\Delta y)/(\Delta x)$.

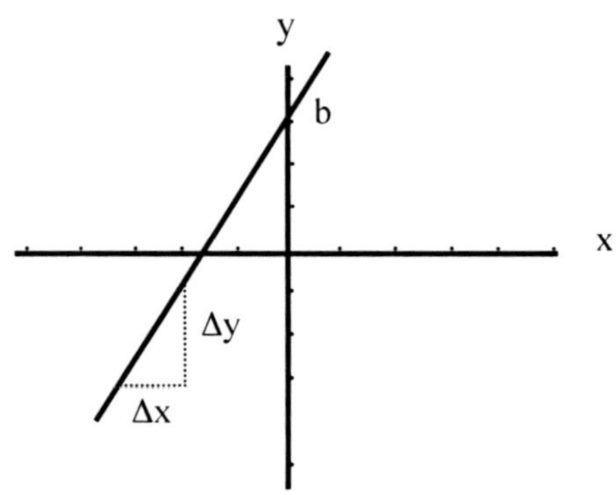

Because two points define a straight line, a line can be drawn on a Cartesian grid by plotting any two points from the equation and drawing a straight line through them.

Changes in m or b cause the line to change. If only b changes (e.g. from 3 to 6 in the above example), the line will move upward, intersecting the y-axis at 6 instead of 3. The new line will be parallel to the original line because the slopes are the same (+2).

If only the slope changes (e.g. from 2 to 3), the line will still intersect the y-axis at 3, but it will be steeper.

Slope of a straight line.

The slope of a straight line is the change in y divided by the change in x between any two points on the line. It is sometimes called "the rise over the run," where the "rise" is the change in y and the "run" is the change in x.

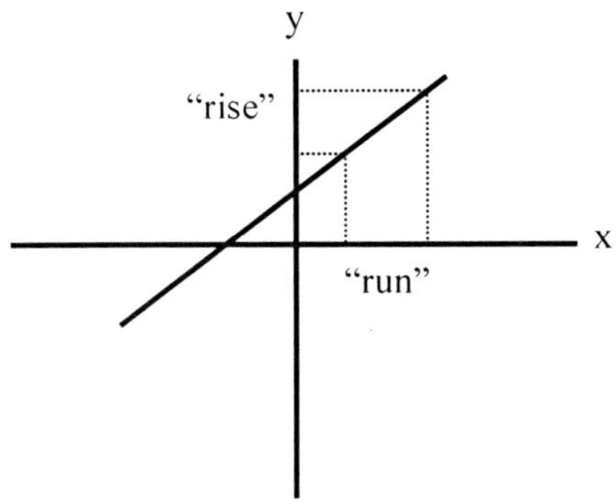

To determine the slope of a straight line, choose any two points, such as A and B, on the line. Then divide the difference between the two y values by the difference between the two x values. From Point A to Point B, the change in the value of y is - 3 (from 4 to 1). The change in the value of x is +5 (from - 2 to 3).

Dividing - 3 by +5 gives the slope of the line, which is - 3/5.

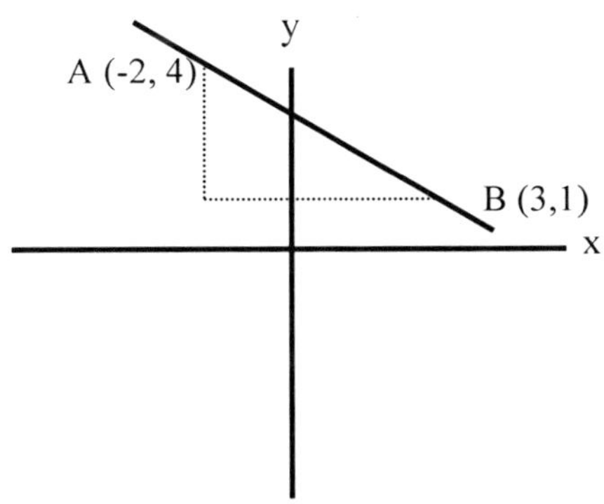

It does not matter if you calculate the differences from Point A to Point B or from Point B to Point A. It is necessary to keep the signs correct. From Point B to Point A, the change in the value of y is +3 (from 1 to 4). The change in the value of x is - 5 (from +3 to - 2). Therefore, the slope is again -3/5. A slope of - 3/5 means that for every 1 unit increase in x, y declines by 3/5 of a unit.

Slope of a curved line.

The slope of a curved line is different at each point on the line. The slope at any point can be calculated by drawing a straight line that is tangent to the curve at that point and then determining the slope of the straight line.

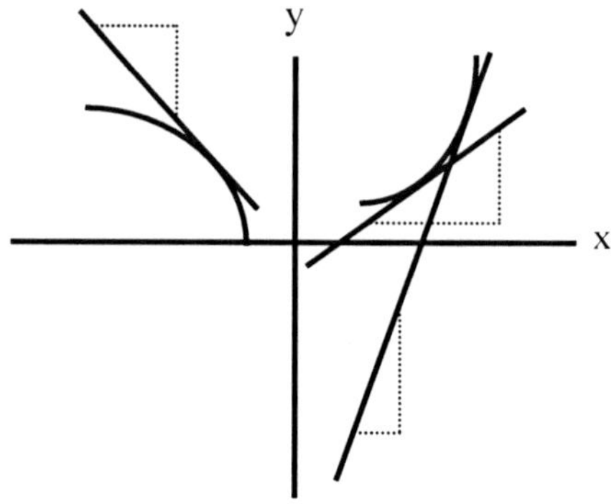

2. Economic graphs.

Economic graphs are commonly drawn to show or represent relationships or functions based upon logic, not actual numbers. Although some economic arguments begin with numbers that are used to make tables and graphs, many problems can be discussed without having real numbers. Because economic variables, with few exceptions, have positive values, economists normally use only Quadrant I on a Cartesian grid. Most economic functions can be described using the following eight possibilities.

1) Variables that are positively related can be described by drawing a line with a positive slope, which shows that when the value of one variable increases, the other increases as well.

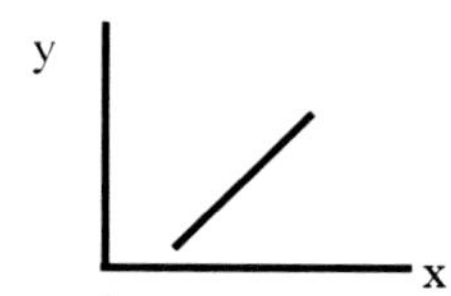

2) Variables that are negatively related can be described by drawing a line with a negative slope, which shows that when the value of one variable increases, the value of the other decreases.

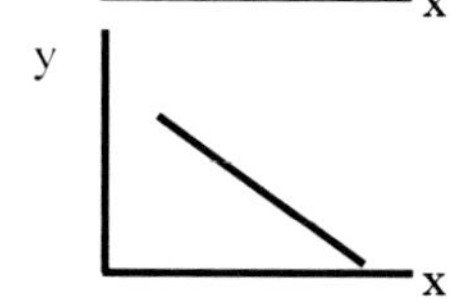

3) A vertical line means the value of x does not change, no matter what happens to the value of y. A vertical line has an "infinite" slope.

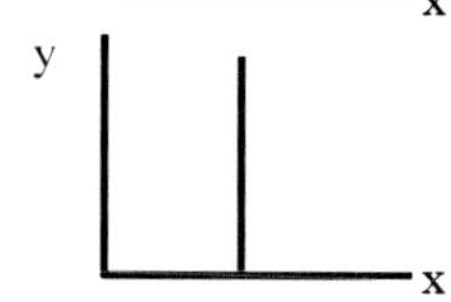

4) A horizontal line means the value of y does not change, no matter what happens to the value of x. A vertical line has a "zero" slope.

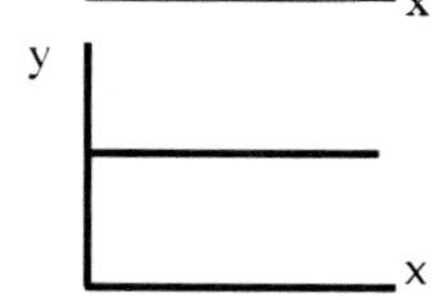

Curved lines describe functions that are:

1) Increasing at an increasing rate. The slope is positive and increases as x increases.

2) Increasing at a decreasing rate. The slope is positive and decreases as x increases.

3) Decreasing at a decreasing rate. The slope is negative and decreases as x increases.

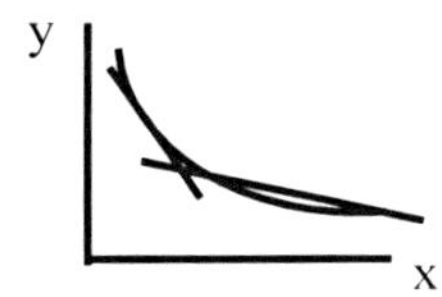

4) Decreasing at an increasing rate. The slope is negative and increases as x increases.

The slopes of straight lines tangent to points on the curved lines, corresponding to different values of x, show each possibility.

Printed in the United States
205710BV00006B/5-6/P